1 Corinthians

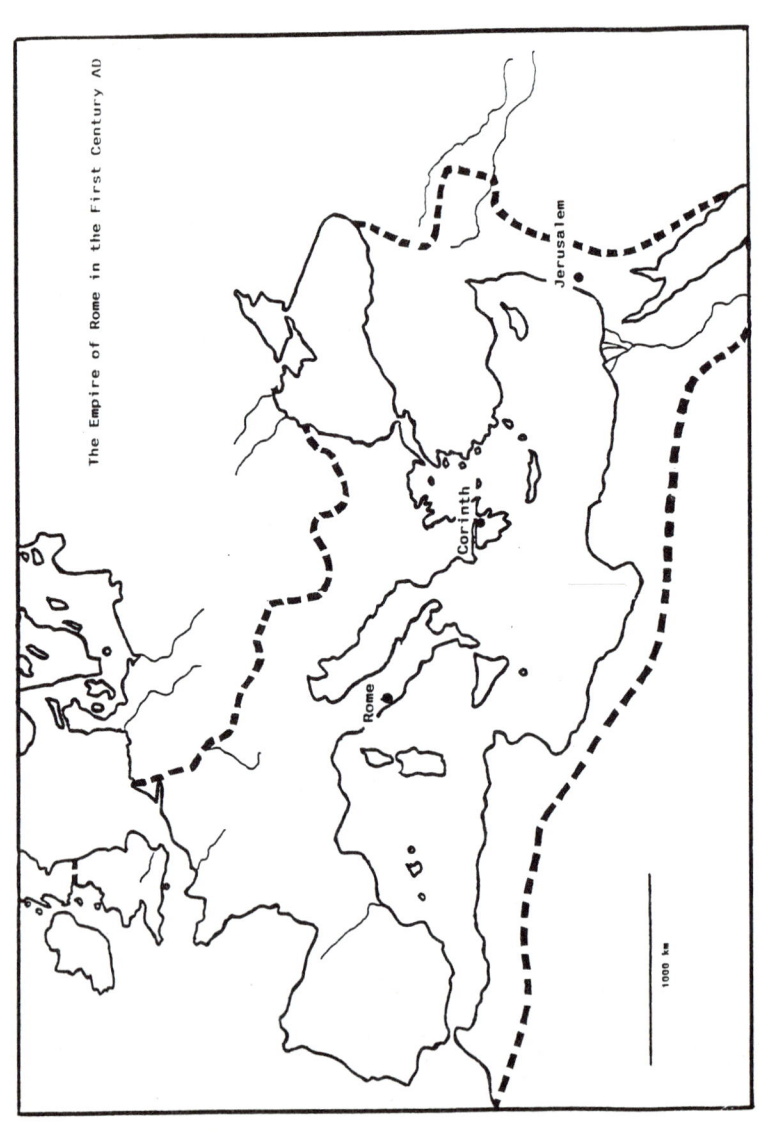

A commentary on

1 Corinthians

Peter Naylor

 ——————— **EVANGELICAL PRESS**

EVANGELICAL PRESS
12 Wooler Street, Darlington, Co. Durham, DL1 1RQ, England

© Evangelical Press 1996
First published 1996

British Library Cataloguing in Publication Data available

ISBN 0 85234 350 7

Unless otherwise indicated, Scripture quotations in this publication are from the New American Standard Bible © Thomas Nelson, 1960, 1977, or are the author's own translation.

Printed and bound in Great Britain by The Bath Press, Somerset

To
Nikos Mpardoutsos
and
the Free Evangelical Church of Corinth

Contents

	Page
Preface	9
The background to 1 Corinthians	11
1. The introduction to the letter (1:1-9)	21
Greetings (1:1-3)	21
Gratitude to God and confidence in God (1:4-9)	24
2. Divisions within the church (1:10 - 4:21)	28
Be of one mind (1:10-17)	30
Wise folly; strong weakness (1:18-31)	35
The realities of ministry (2:1-16)	44
Corinthian favouritism (3:1-23)	63
Stewards (4:1-21)	77
3. Immorality in the church (5:1 - 6:20)	92
There must be discipline (5:1-13)	95
Christians in secular courts (6:1-11)	105
Promiscuity (6:12-20)	114
4. Marriage (7:1-40)	121
Guidance about married life (7:1-7)	122
To the unmarried (7:8-9)	126
Divorce (7:10-11)	127
Christians with unconverted partners (7:12-16)	129
Christian contentment (7:17-24)	139
First and second marriages (7:25-35)	143
When a father might become a father-in-law (7:36-38)	150
The remarriage of widows (7:39-40)	153

		Page
5.	Food offered to idols (8:1 - 11:1)	155
	On eating sacrifices (8:1-13)	159
	An apostle who practises what he preaches (9:1-18)	168
	Paul, slave yet free (9:19-27)	176
	The evil of idolatry (10:1 - 11:1)	184
6.	The covered head (11:2-16)	203
	The principle of headship (11:2-3)	203
	Head-covering, a mark of subordination (11:4-6)	205
	Man, woman and creation (11:7-12)	207
	Sanctified common sense (11:13-16)	210
7.	The Lord's Table (11:17-34)	212
	Abuse (11:17-22)	212
	Institution (11:23-26)	216
	Attitudes (11:27-34)	221
8.	Spiritual gifts (12:1 - 14:40)	227
	The Spirit has come (12:1-3)	228
	One God; different gifts (12:4-11)	230
	The body of Christ (12:12-31a)	237
	Love, the more excellent way (12:31b - 13:13)	251
	Prophecy first; tongues last (14:1-40)	284
9.	The resurrection of the body (15:1-58)	312
	The historic resurrection (15:1-11)	314
	The significance of Christ's resurrection (15:12-34)	322
	Resurrection completed (15:35-58)	342
10.	The conclusion to the letter (16:1-24)	360
	The collection (16:1-9)	360
	Final remarks (16:10-24)	366

Appendix I: 1 Corinthians and the Old Testament	373
Appendix II: Visions and mirrors	376
References	386
Bibliography	399
Subject index	405
Index of persons	409
Index of places	412
Scripture index	414

Preface

This commentary has been a profound challenge. How does one write an easy-to-read exposition of Paul's first letter to the Corinthians, an epistle that for all of us remains far from simple? One can only try.

At the outset an important truth ought to be taken into consideration. Although the letter addresses the Corinthian church and its immediate problems, Paul aimed his words at 'all who in every place call upon the name of our Lord Jesus Christ, theirs and ours' (1:2). Because 'theirs and ours' connects directly with 'in every place' the reference is almost certainly to all the places where believers find themselves.[1]

The apostle needed to remind the Corinthians that they were at best only a part of the universal body of Christ and therefore were in no position to manipulate the faith. That this was a problem he had to address is shown by 14:36: 'Was it from you that the word of God went forth? Or has it come to you only?' Further, he must have been aware that his letter was an inspired document meant for all believers: if he wrote for the Corinthians he wrote for all, without reference to where and when they may live. If we are among the very many who call upon the Saviour, 1 Corinthians was breathed out by the Spirit for us. When we read it we feel that the Lord of glory is speaking to our hearts.

Remember that, like every other letter of Paul in the New Testament, 1 Corinthians begins and ends with encouragements (1:1-9; 16:19-24). Whatever the problems in the church, the Lord had saved his people at Corinth and intended to keep them. Therefore they were not deprived of Paul's support. That particular congregation passed into heaven long ago. The same is true of the apostle himself. But the encouragement and teaching of the epistle live on and are no less real for every succeeding generation of believers.

Furthermore, many of the issues addressed by 1 Corinthians are as modern as this morning: the inspiration of Scripture; marriage, divorce and remarriage; apostolic tradition; the role of women in the churches; the use, abuse and passing away of charismatic gifts; the doctrine of the physical resurrection of the body; and the Christian's duty to give money. We cannot afford to ignore this letter.

In this commentary the New American Standard Bible (NASB) has been adopted as the basic version although I often stray from it. Direct references to 1 Corinthians give chapter and verse numbers only, and endnotes identify the sources of quotations, using the author and short-title system. Full publication details appear in the bibliography.

Peter Naylor

The background to 1 Corinthians

Jerusalem, Corinth and Rome

Look at the sketch-map of the Roman Empire as it was in the first Christian century, a time when the empire was almost at its zenith. You will notice that it wrapped itself around the Mediterranean Sea. This meant that Rome ruled the waves between Spain and Syria and between the Adriatic and Alexandria. Because the 'Roman peace' had swept piracy from the ocean men were able to travel from east to west and from north to south and back again. Nowhere else in the whole world could journeying by sea have been more convenient; storms rather than marauders remained the main threat.

It came about that, in the providence of God, the international politics of the age helped to signpost the way ahead for the first missionaries — westward. Paul even planned to journey from Judea to Spain, and we cannot say that he did not succeed in the enterprise.[1]

The author of this epistle was a remarkable man. Quite apart from his Jewish upbringing in Jerusalem and his origins in a major Greek university city, Tarsus, he was also a Roman citizen. In these respects he was superbly qualified to be 'a teacher of the Gentiles'.[2]

Here is something else: Rome, the fourth beast of Daniel 7:7,19 and the beast from the sea seen by John (Rev. 13:1-2), had given peace, it is true, but at an appalling cost to her enslaved subjects. For many hundreds of years the power of Rome remained like the shadow of an eclipse over much of the known world. It was a Roman who, against the claims of reason and of justice, had authorized the death of Jesus to try to keep the peace as well as his position.[3]

Perhaps it would not be too much to say that the New Testament outlines a conflict between two cities, Jerusalem and Rome. Certainly, the book called 'the Acts of the Apostles' begins in Jerusalem and ends with Paul residing in the imperial city. The apostle had been told on at least two previous occasions that it was essential for him to go there (Acts 23:11; 27:24). This was true of no other apostle and of no other city. Revelation chapters 17-21 portray vividly the downfall of 'Babylon', standing unquestionably for Rome, and the ultimate ascendancy of the city of God, the new Jerusalem.

In any major war many battles have to be fought before final victory comes into sight; if the heart of an empire is to be encircled and penetrated other, less important areas must first be conquered. It was something like this in the early days of the gospel. Paul was a soldier on active service for the noblest of all kings and for the best possible cause. In retrospect he acknowledged that his had been a 'good fight' (2 Tim. 4:7). It was also an intelligent fight. As a warrior in such a magnificent conflict he elaborated his strategy at an early period and kept to it in detail as the years passed. Before he was poised to launch his assault upon Rome by testifying to its emperor, Nero Caesar, he purposed to advance steadily and slowly — sometimes, he must have thought, almost too slowly — preaching Christ in certain key centres. Before he could penetrate Rome the apostle had to be certain that his arms had triumphed in every lesser theatre of war.

Nor was he disappointed. By the grace of God Corinth became the scene of a famous victory; many were converted and a large church was established. Indeed, the epistle to the Romans was written at Corinth and conveyed to the church there by Phoebe, a 'servant' of the fellowship at Cenchrea (Acts 18:10; Rom. 16:1). The letter shows that when he resided at Corinth the apostle contemplated his anticipated visit to Rome in the sure knowledge that the good news could, and did, save Jews and Gentiles alike (Rom. 1:15-16). Further, what the Lord had done so wonderfully in a depraved place like Corinth he would do in the metropolis itself. Of this Paul was assured.

There were, it is true, cities larger than Corinth around the northeast Mediterranean. Ephesus comes to mind immediately. But when Paul sailed from Asia to Europe on his second missionary journey it was not the time for Ephesus and other communities to hear the gospel from his mouth. For the moment Corinth was an essential stepping-stone in the apostle's progress. When a church had been

The background to 1 Corinthians

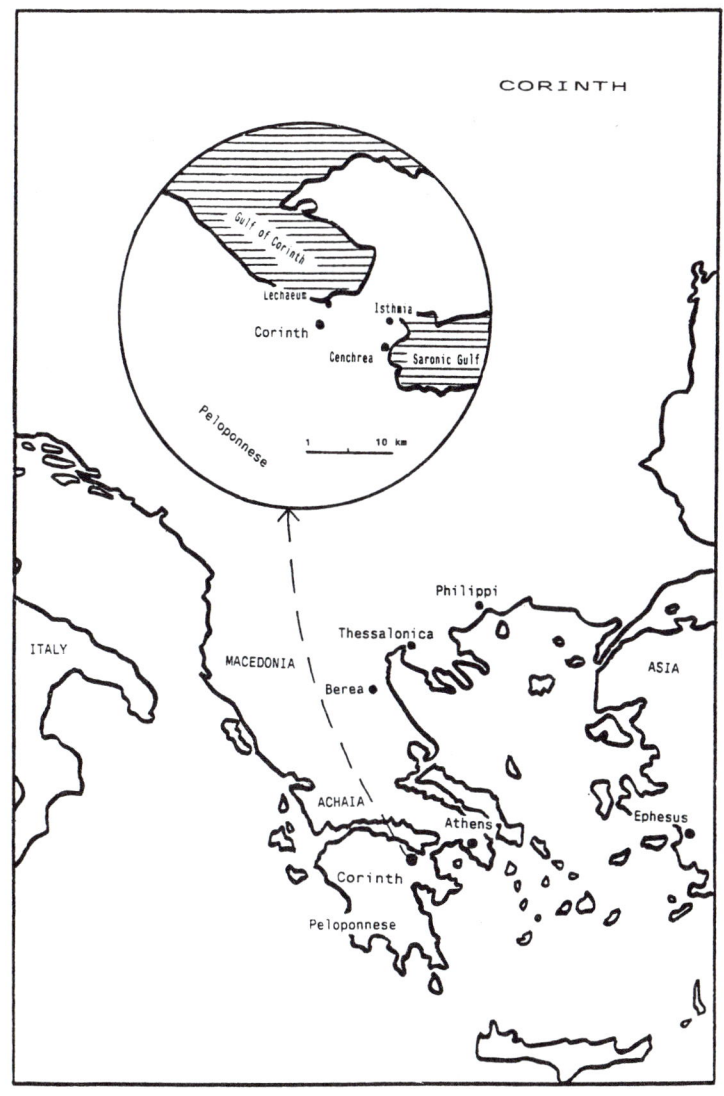

established there, it received letters from him, including the epistle which is the subject of this book.

About the city of Corinth

Take another look at the map of the Roman Empire and consider the northern and eastern shores of the Mediterranean. Paul knew this coastline intimately. You will notice that Corinth lies about halfway along an almost dead straight line, some 2,300 kilometres in length, connecting Rome and Jerusalem.

Now look at the map of Greece. Corinth was situated near the bottleneck connecting the Greek mainland and a large near-island, the Peloponnese. It is not hard to see that in the earliest times the area must have become an important focus for the movement of men and materials between the eastern and western halves of the Mediterranean and also in a north-south direction. Josephus mentions that after failing in their hopeless struggle, young, able-bodied Jewish captives were sent to the 'isthmus' to dig a canal. He assumed that his readers would know that he meant Corinth.[4] This man, a Pharisee, a historian, a patriot who fought against the Romans in the Jewish war of A.D. 66-70 and a natural survivor who lived to tell the tale, will be mentioned again in this commentary, and what he says is always illuminating.

Possibilities for settlement at Corinth became realities at an early date because the site was favoured with an unusually abundant water-supply. A hundred metres or more from the centre of the old city is the celebrated Peirene Fountain. Legend says that it owes its origin to Bellerophon, the winged horse of the hero Pegasus. When the animal's hoof touched the earth water began to gush out. The fame of the spring is perpetuated by the oft-misquoted lines of Alexander Pope (1688-1744):

A little learning is a dangerous thing;
Drink deep, or taste not the Pierian spring:
There shallow draughts intoxicate the brain,
And drinking largely sobers us again.[5]

In other words, study thoroughly before you speak (or write!). Paul would not have disagreed. Sightseers, traders, envoys, passing

The background to 1 Corinthians

travellers and religious pilgrims flocked to the place. There was a saying current in Paul's time that Corinth was the 'prow and stern of Greece'. This meant that the city, a thriving centre of commerce, seemed to be like a merchant vessel plying between the Greek mainland and the Peloponnese.[6]

Rather than attempt the often dangerous voyage around the southern island, merchants and the military often transported their goods, men and hardware (and even their ships) overland. They managed this with the help of a specially constructed slipway, seven kilometres long, stretching from shore to shore across the bottleneck. In peacetime the city of Corinth controlled this lucrative traffic. Dio Chrysostum, a Greek writer born in Bithynia at the time when Paul was beginning his ministry at Antioch (Acts 11:26), mentions that 'Large numbers gathered at Corinth on account of the harbours and the *hetaerae*' because the city was situated, as it were, 'at the cross-roads of Greece'.[7] The *hetaerae* were a wide class of women, ranging from those whose marriages lacked status all the way down to street-walkers.

'It is not every man's lot to get to Corinth' was a Greek proverb that some Romans found amusing.[8] There was also the old story about a certain Xenophon. Five centuries before Paul's time this rash youth apparently vowed that if he won the Olympic crown he would devote one hundred courtesans to the service of the goddess Aphrodite. In victory, the tale goes, he kept his word and sent the specified number of ladies to the shrine situated atop the Acrocorinth, a mini-mountain six hundred metres high and due south of the old city.[9] Whether or not there was any truth to it, the anecdote suggests that, like any other large Mediterranean port, Corinth was thoroughly immoral. Sin abounded when Paul arrived. Perhaps it was no coincidence that it was here that he penned his vivid description of pagan vice (Rom. 1:18-32).

The city was served by two ports, Cenchrea to the east of the Isthmus and Lechaeum to the west. Eleven kilometres apart, these twin havens helped to make Corinth a wide-open boom-town buzzing with people.[10] There might have been about 100,000 people living there in the first Christian century.

When a Roman embassy was sent to Corinth in 147 B.C. the mob hissed at it. This action was unwise because the visitors realized instinctively that the population was hostile and could be dangerous. This sparked off one of the blackest deeds of Roman imperialism.

According to Dio Cassius, a Greek historian of the second century B.C., the Roman commander Mummius 'sold the inhabitants, confiscated the land, and demolished the walls and all the buildings, out of fear that some states might again unite with it as the largest city'.[11] Nothing remained for a century except a ruined heap.

In 44 B.C. Julius Caesar introduced an empire-wide project for the reconstruction of old cities. Corinth was one such. In the interests of Italian prosperity these sites were to be colonized with veteran soldiers and with poor subjects from the great Roman towns. Generally thought to be a step in the right direction, this plan was not prevented from coming into effect even by the assassination of Caesar; Corinth rose from the rubble.[12]

There were many other settlers besides Romans. Philo, a prolific Jewish writer who lived in Alexandria in Egypt during the lifetime of Jesus, claimed that Jerusalem was virtually a mother-city to most of Greece, Corinth included. This was because many Jews settled there. His report is fleshed out by the recent unearthing just off the old city-centre of a broken door-lintel bearing the inscription 'Synagogue of the Hebrews'. It now resides in the site museum.[13]

Greek rather than Latin became the principal language in Corinth. Inevitably, the international character of the city meant that religious cults of all kinds would be introduced. This, plus wealth and commerce, a transient population and an ingrained streak of immorality in what was a revived community with a long memory, meant that the survival of the infant church would be at risk. The New Testament letters to the Corinthians suggest that this was the case.

Paul, the Jews and Gallio

With regard to local politics, during the reign of Claudius Caesar (A.D. 41-54) the direct government of Corinth was transferred from the emperor to the senate. This body had recently sent Gallio as proconsul when Paul arrived late in A.D. 50 (Acts 18:1).

Gallio was a brother of the philosopher Seneca, who regarded him with considerable affection and on one occasion described him as 'my master'. This gives us a glimpse of a man far more amiable than, say, Pontius Pilate. Yet the Corinthian proconsul was by no means a colourless character. Referring to the practice of Roman executioners dragging their dead victims into the Tiber with a hook, Gallio commented that Nero (A.D. 54-68) had raised Claudius, his imperial predecessor, to heaven with just such an instrument. He thought he knew how Claudius had departed this world, and said so. Later, he was put to death by Nero on suspicion of treason, while Paul himself stood before the same emperor at least once.[14] For men who thought for themselves it was a perilous time in which to live.

At Corinth the Jews no doubt hoped that the newly-arrived Roman would be a pawn in their attack upon Paul and the Christians. In the event they were somewhat disappointed. When they bundled the apostle to where they knew Gallio was engrossed in civic matters, the Roman backed away from involvement in what he reckoned was a wrangle about Jewish religious differences ('words and names and the law which you have', Acts 18:15). The Jews made no further attempt to bring Paul formally to trial because Gallio reckoned they had no case. In all probability the initial fuss was a gesture by the local synagogue to disassociate itself from the visitor and thereby to protect its situation in the Roman colony.[15]

Stop reading for a moment, and try to imagine Paul being led to Gallio. As the dishevelled apostle looks up his eyes are met by those of the imposing figure of the proconsul. Irritated by the Jews' ranting and raving, the uninterested Roman is suspicious and rather uncertain about what to do. Paul opens his mouth to speak, but, perhaps for the first time ever, says nothing; with a show of anger Gallio dismisses both accusers and accused.

Behind and to the south of the raised judgement-place looms the towering mass of the Acrocorinth. In the person of the Hebrew from Tarsus the good news of Jesus challenges, and is challenged by, three formidable opponents: Jewish unbelief and self-righteousness; Roman scepticism and worldly-mindedness; and the immorality of city life. It was a confrontation that in its essentials continues to this day.

Paul's experiences before he wrote 1 Corinthians

We need to outline Paul's itinerary before and after his first visit to Corinth but before he wrote 1 Corinthians, and to reflect again about just why the city was deemed to be a strategic centre for the work of the gospel.

During his second missionary journey the apostle was beaten and imprisoned at Philippi. Then he was chased out of Thessalonica by hostile Jews. He went to Berea where he was opposed again by his fellow-countrymen. From Berea, probably travelling alone by sea, Paul went on to Athens (Acts 16:22 - 17:15).

It is possible that his experiences in this prestigious yet pagan city compelled the apostle to think carefully about his tactics. We know that his address on Mars' Hill attracted little more than polite scepticism, and we know, too, that he soon moved on to Corinth, eighty kilometres away (Acts 17:33-34; 18:1). We could draw our own conclusions.

Although a few Athenians were the first converts in Achaia, Paul never regarded them as first-fruits from God, a pledge of a future church. This honour was to fall to a Corinthian family, that of Stephanas (16:15). He never mentions Athens in any of his letters; nor are there any recorded greetings to the believers in that city.

Deeper impressions made upon the apostle following his departure from Athens might be reflected in 2:1-5. You will notice that 'you' and 'your' occur five times in as many verses, Paul obviously revealing how he had planned his mission in what was for him completely new territory: 'And when I came to *you*, brethren, I did not come with superiority of speech or of wisdom, proclaiming to *you* the testimony of God. For I did not determine to know anything among *you* apart from Jesus Christ, and him crucified. And I was with *you* in weakness and in fear and in much trembling ... that *your* faith should not be in the wisdom of men, but in the power of God.'[16]

There is a pronounced emphasis upon 'him crucified' in 2:2. Paul brings to his readers' attention the shame and scandal of an executed Messiah. When the apostle arrived in Corinth he might well have felt it needful to reconsider an old lesson, the truth that the ability of the gospel to win men lies in the message, proclaimed sympathetically and accurately and brought home by the Holy Spirit, rather than in oratorical eloquence. At any rate, it appears that when he set foot in Corinth he was determined to reapply the principle with renewed vigour.

In retaliation for the conduct of the Jews, Sosthenes, the ruler of the synagogue, was beaten (Acts 18:17). His assailants were either anti-Jewish Greeks or Jews who resented the man's failure to secure Paul's indictment. If it is this Sosthenes who is mentioned in 1:1, two Jews, both formerly instrumental in persecuting Christians, co-operated in writing to a church made up largely of Gentiles. These

The background to 1 Corinthians

people would be described in 10:1 as the spiritual descendants of the Israel of the Exodus. Ancient, massive barriers were tumbling in a dramatic fashion.

Notwithstanding the unpleasantness in court Paul was relatively unscathed by Jewish hostility. This meant that he was able to stay in Corinth for as long as he wished, in this case eighteen months, in the home of Priscilla and Aquila. Through no fault of their own they, like other Jews, had been compelled to leave Rome (Acts 18:2-3).

A church was established. When he felt that it was right to depart Paul sailed peacefully from Cenchrea for Syria, stopping on the way at Ephesus. He left Priscilla and Aquila behind him in Asia and journeyed on to his home church at Antioch (Acts 18:18-19). After spending some time there he travelled west by the overland route through Galatia and Phrygia, eventually reaching Ephesus once more (Acts 18:19 - 19:1).

He arrived just in time to miss Apollos. This enthusiastic young Christian from Alexandria in Egypt had stayed for a while at Ephesus where he was helped in his understanding of the faith by Aquila and his wife. Then he journeyed to Achaia, the Greek province in which Corinth was situated (Acts 18:24-28).

It was during his second and considerably longer visit to Ephesus (Acts 20:31) that Paul must have received information from Corinth (1:11; 7:1; 16:17). Much of what he learned would have saddened him. The family of Chloe, possibly a member of the Corinthian church, informed him about serious divisions in the fellowship. It is also likely that he received a delegation from the church in the persons of Stephanas, Fortunatus and Achaicus, whose visit is recorded in 16:17. They may have conveyed a letter from the church — a letter that has not survived.

Stephanas, one of the few at Corinth whom Paul had baptized personally, was an early convert. In all probability he was trusted by both the church and by the apostle — hence his presence in the supposed delegation (1:16).[17] There can be little doubt that the visitors brought more news of divisions.

It was then that Paul wrote to the Corinthians a letter that has not been preserved in the Bible (5:9-11). It probably responded to their uncertainties about sensitive moral issues. Because the church had not, it seems, altogether understood the apostle's previous counsel he developed his teaching in his second letter, our 1 Corinthians, written perhaps in the spring of A.D. 57.[18]

Paul and the Old Testament

Throughout this commentary references will be made to an early Greek translation of the Hebrew Old Testament, a version that Paul knew well. This translation, copies of which in the goodness of God have come down to us, is commonly called the 'Septuagint' (or *LXX*, Latin for 'seventy') because it was said to have been the work of seventy or more scholars. It originated in Egypt about 250 B.C. and is the oldest known influential version of the original Hebrew Bible.

In his letters the apostle's Old Testament allusions and quotations are frequently based upon the Septuagint, although 1:20; 3:19; 13:12; 14:21 and 15:54-55, in this epistle alone, are closer to the Hebrew text that we have. They show that Paul refused to bind himself to the Greek version. This point is important and we shall have cause to refer to it elsewhere in the commentary. Appendix I details the numerous Old Testament quotations and allusions which are present in 1 Corinthians.

1. The introduction to the letter
(1:1-9)

The letter is opened by 1:1-9, 1:1-3 being an initial greeting and 1:4-9 a statement of thankfulness to God for what the Lord had achieved in the lives of the readers. Paul asserts his authority, declaring that he had been called to be an apostle: Christ, not the churches, sent him.

He makes it plain that for their part the Corinthians are separated by the Lord to become holy people together with all believers who call upon him. They are not alone. Their sanctification stems from their renewal by the gracious activity of God in Christ. Furthermore, not only has the good news been confirmed among them, but their **'faithful'** God will confirm them so that in the **'day'** of Christ they will be found blameless (1:8). The apostle is telling his readers that they can never fall from salvation.

Greetings (1:1-3)

Paul begins this epistle in his usual fashion: first, he gives his own name as the writer; second, he identifies the recipients of the letter; third, there are words of greeting.

Although the apostle is the sole author of the letter he associates himself with **'Sosthenes'**, a Christian who would have been known and respected by the Corinthians. Since the latter is mentioned nowhere else in Paul's surviving correspondence, it may be that the apostle wanted the Corinthians to understand before they dived deep into what must have been, even by his standards, a weighty letter, that what he wrote came with the approval of a common friend who had the care of the church on his heart. In other words, Paul shows that he is not some remote personage given to despatching missives from the solitude of an apostolic ivory tower. He softens his approach, not intending his epistle to fall like a thunderbolt upon the heads of the converted, yet somewhat confused and contrary, Corinthians.

He stresses that he was called to the office of apostle **'through'** or 'by means of' the will of God (1:1). The Lord decided the matter beforehand, and it was so. **'Apostle'** means a person who has been sent as a messenger. Epaphroditus, seconded by his church to care for Paul, is a good example. According to Philippians 2:25, he was the church's 'messenger [apostle] and minister to my need'. But in the New Testament the word usually applies to those immediate followers of Christ who were sent by him, whose teaching was inspired and infallible, and who became the founders of the church.[1]

Paul's point in insisting that he was summoned to be an 'apostle' is that there had never been any question of personal ambition or of an appointment set up by the churches. His God had placed him apart for special service. Compare with Galatians 1:1,15 and 2:7, and particularly with Acts 13:2-3. At Antioch Paul and Barnabas had been separated by the Lord for the work of mission, and were conscious that they had been called by him. Even so, they did not begin their labours until the Lord spoke to the church. The fellowship recognized the commission and then dismissed them. Ultimately, of course, it was all of God. As we read 1 Corinthians we understand why Paul felt it necessary to begin with such a claim.

The Corinthians, to whom he writes, as well as all other believers, had been set apart because they were called by God to be **'saints',** or holy people (1:2). There may be a deliberate play on 'in': their new situation was that they were **'in Christ'** even though they remained as residents in Corinth. In the words of Ephesians 2:17, 'He came and preached peace to you who were far away, and peace to those who were near.'

Similarly, although as believers we may live in our own particular localities, we are 'in Christ'. We belong to him and he is more real to us than anything or anybody else. Not even death changes this: 'For if we live, we live for the Lord, or if we die, we die for the Lord; therefore whether we live or die, we are the Lord's' (Rom. 14:8).

The introduction to the letter (1:1-9)

The verse teaches more. When the Lord calls someone to repentance and faith, that person will call upon the Lord. If *you* do not deliberately cry to the Saviour for his help you are almost certainly not a Christian. Test yourself — now!

'Sanctified' (1:2) is dramatic: not only had the Corinthians been set apart, they remained, and would remain, God's special people. When they were united to the Saviour through faith they came into new life. It is exactly like this for all believing Christians. We are 'saints' because God has separated us from the world in order to belong to him eternally. Therefore, if you do not refer to Charles Haddon Spurgeon as 'Saint Charles' ('Mr Spurgeon' might suffice), or even to your own minister as 'Saint ...', why speak about 'Saint Paul' or 'Saint Peter'? That Spurgeon was, and your minister is, a saint is beyond doubt. But you too are a saint, and so is the newest convert who does not know much about prayer and for whom the Bible is at the moment a somewhat strange book.

The Corinthians are said to belong together in a **'church'**. The word 'church' (Greek, *ekklesia*) can signify any local assembly, religious or otherwise. There was the riotous *ekklesia* in the stadium at Ephesus (Acts 19:32,41), and in Deuteronomy 4:10 Moses recollects the time when the children of Israel assembled before the Lord at Horeb. According to the Greek version of the Old Testament the latter were a 'church'. It would almost certainly be a mistake to expound *ekklesia* by means of a doubtful etymology ('called out'), as has sometimes been the fashion.

They who call upon the Lord

The Corinthians **'call upon the name of our Lord Jesus Christ'**. In the Old Testament the people of God are described nearly ninety times as those who called upon the name of Jehovah, or who were required to do so. The first Christians, too, are often portrayed by the New Testament as those who called upon Christ.[2] In addition to implying that the man Jesus is Jehovah incarnate, there can be no doubt that the apostle begins his great letter with every intention of bringing to his readers' notice the direct continuity between the people of God in Old Testament Israel and the believers who make up the Christian churches.

This emphasis is a necessary foundation for the epistle: unlike the hostile Jews in their synagogues, Christian disciples, many of whom were converted Gentiles, are seen as the members of the true Israel of God.[3] Unlike the men of Athens (Acts 17:21), these Christians had not latched on to some new thing that is here today but will be gone tomorrow. Their holy religion was rooted firmly in the remote past in order to endure for ever.

It follows that the Lord's people are, in principle and in practice, one in Christ, whatever their various backgrounds and whoever they may be. This solidarity means that there can be no fundamental separation between Jews and Gentiles, nor between those who knew the Lord before his first coming and those of us around the globe who have been born (and born again) since Christ came. Abraham and the last sinner to be converted belong to each other because they both belong to the Lord Jesus. Indeed, the convert belongs to the seed of Abraham (Gal. 3:29).

Paul insists that the Corinthians and all other saints **'in every place'** are in a blessed relationship with God (1:3). Because Jesus Christ is their Lord, God is their Father. They have received the grace of God, that is, his unmerited favour and all that it brings. Moreover, peace is mutual: God delights in them and their regenerated hearts rejoice in him.

Peace

'Peace', a word with a rich Old Testament background (Hebrew, *shalôm*), implies that the believer possesses every conceivable benefit. This is the case even when he is not sure that it is so. He is truly prosperous because, just like every Christian, he is the direct object of the grace of God. Also, because grace and mercy lead inevitably to peace, it is something all believers possess. The world did not give it and the world cannot steal it (John 14:27). Nor will the Lord remove it.

Gratitude to God and confidence in God (1:4-9)

Paul **'always'** thanks God for all the Christians in Corinth (1:4), describing the Lord as **'my God'**. In trouble and in joy the apostle

The introduction to the letter (1:1-9)

turned to the God who belonged to him just as much as he belonged to God. Bearing in mind the problems that these people caused him (cf. 1:11: 'There are quarrels among you'), this admission to being thankful is truly impressive. An explanation was in order, and Paul knew it.

First, the grace of God had been **'given'** to these Corinthians **'in Christ Jesus'**. Paul's gratitude was not so much for the church as for the transforming work of the Spirit of Christ in their hearts. The apostle knew that there is no other way in which the Lord saves men, or by which they may experience his mercy. Secondly, the people have been made rich **'in everything'**, that is, **'in all speech and in all knowledge'** (1:5).

Notice again that the benefits given to the Corinthians after their conversion were also **'in Christ'**; Paul knew that the Lord Jesus remained the only possible channel for God's gifts — gifts because of which these immature believers might well have been elated. He is telling them in a manner as gentle as it is insistent that they should not congratulate themselves because of their undoubted abilities.

'Speech' (literally, 'word' — Greek, *logos*), might signify 'utterance' or even 'doctrine'. If so, the people had been **'enriched'** by the Spirit in order to confirm either or both of two things: the apostles' **'testimony concerning Christ'**, or the witness to God given by Jesus himself through the apostles (1:6). The second view is probably better: the people's hearts resonated to what Christ said to them through his servants. The sheep responded to the shepherd.

In the event, Paul's ministry had been **'confirmed'** among the young converts in a spectacular fashion, proving beyond a shadow of a doubt that he did not manipulate the people. As he would acknowledge later in 2 Corinthians 2:17, the apostle always spoke 'in Christ in the sight of God'. Note that Paul does not write that the Corinthians were abounding in spiritual benefits; rather, they had been *made* wealthy. Without Christ they had been truly poor; now, they have much. The gifts, although amazing and wonderful, were infinitely less important than salvation.

That God had spoken to these people through Paul's ministry was not, then, a matter for debate. About this message they were convinced because of blessings that were in no way inferior to those experienced by other congregations (1:7).

That was not all: their own conversion experiences, backed up by the gifts of the Spirit, meant that the church at Corinth possessed a radical but true understanding of the future course of world history. The fellowship lived in daily expectation of the ultimate **'revelation of our Lord Jesus Christ'**. This meant that as the days passed they knew that Christ would eventually come back, and were eager that he should. But this does not mean that they believed his appearance to be imminent. Nor did Paul ever indicate as much (cf. 2 Thess. 2:1-12). What he teaches here is that when the Lord Jesus does come he will be seen in his majesty by the church. But it will be no conventional arrival like, say, that of some visiting celebrity whom the people may have seen already. As Cecil Alexander's hymn says,

> And our eyes at last shall see him,
> Through his own redeeming love.

'At last'! The apostle implies that, whatever their conspicuous faults, because they anticipated that day the Corinthians were spiritually alive.

If the witness of Christ had been 'confirmed' among the Corinthians (1:6), the reverse is equally true: Christ **'shall ... confirm'** the Corinthians in their new situation. The Lord will ensure that these people remain **'blameless'**, without accusation **'to the end'** (1:8). They can never fall away from the good news because God will not allow it. We need to remind ourselves that this dual confirmation is the experience of all who have come to know the Lord.

The **'end'** (Greek, *telos*) could mean one of three things: first, death, the end of natural life in this sinful world; second, the Day of the Lord, ushering in the end of the age; third, 'permanently', meaning that the Lord will preserve the church both before and after the final advent. Perhaps the second approach is best in the light of 15:24 ('Then *comes* the end'). If so, the apostle stresses the security of the saints until the day when the Lord is revealed. From then on there will be nothing but glory. To put it another way, when the Lord is revealed he will be seen by the expectant Corinthians as their Friend at dawn rather than as the thief in the night; they will gain everything and lose nothing. There will be no judgement: 'He shall appear a second time' for salvation without *reference* to sin, 'to those who eagerly await him' (Heb. 9:28).

Paul insists that there is a firm basis for this hope: **'God is faithful'** (1:9). In the Greek text 'faithful' *(pistos)* comes first for

The introduction to the letter (1:1-9)

emphasis, rather as in 1 Thessalonians 5:24: 'Faithful is he who calls you.' The apostle recalls Deuteronomy 7:9 and 32:4, where Jehovah is said to have been faithful in choosing and calling Israel and then keeping the people safe in the desert. It must be like this for the Corinthians; they had been summoned to share in the **'fellowship'** (Greek, *koinônia*) of the Son of God, Jesus Christ. The wilderness will not engulf them.

It is possible that **'fellowship'** does not mean simply that each Corinthian had been called to union and communion with Christ, true though this was. As a body of believers they were led by God to share together in Christ. Spiritual fellowship has both vertical and horizontal components, so to speak. If this is Paul's meaning, he would seem to be launching into his condemnation of divisions in the church (1:10 onwards). His logic is that it must be wrong for there to be functional disunity where there is a God-given oneness.

2. Divisions within the church
(1:10 - 4:21)

First (1:10-17), the apostle informs the Corinthians that he had been told about the miserable way in which they divided into cliques. This was particularly sad because the people were clustering irresponsibly around certain illustrious names such as Apollos and Cephas, not to mention Paul himself. To compound the confusion there was also apparently a group that purported sanctimoniously to follow Christ rather than men. Our imaginations run riot when we think what they might have been like.

The apostle condemns this vicious trend, knowing full well that in the circle of those who were elevated (or reduced) to figureheads there were no disagreements; all spoke with one voice (cf. 15:11). It followed that there was no good reason for the Corinthians to enthuse about some servants of the Lord at the expense of others. For his own part, Paul was thankful that the Lord ordered his circumstances in such a way that it was obvious that he had never aspired to be an empire-builder.

Secondly, the apostle acknowledges that his teaching remained apparently weak and foolish, both in content and in manner of presentation, and that the majority of the Corinthians originated from the lower strata of society; in other words, both he and they were ordinary (1:18-31). But Paul had no regrets. On the contrary, the Lord had planned it this way so that the converts might have nothing to be glad about apart from the grace and mercy of God. Let the church turn its gaze away from men and redirect it towards the Saviour.

The third principal section highlights the gap between conventional, worldly wisdom and the astounding and seemingly paradoxical

Divisions within the church (1:10 - 4:21)

wisdom of God (2:1-16). This divine wisdom (Greek, *sophia*), when proclaimed by Paul, had been blessed by the Holy Spirit to the Corinthians (2:1-5). He tells them that it was by no means an apostolic innovation: some years earlier the selfsame wisdom of God had confronted those evil rulers who in their ignorance had killed Jesus, although they could, and should, have known about him (2:6-9). Now God's wise plan of salvation had been set out accurately in words that the Spirit himself gave to the apostle (2:10-13). From this it follows that the Corinthians were sinfully foolish if they elevated or despised Paul or any of his colleagues. Acting in this fashion they brought themselves down to the level of the men of this world who refuse to come to terms with basic spiritual realities.

Paul's words, although not his person, are of the greatest possible significance (2:14-16). Because he and his fellow apostles really did understand and proclaim the wise counsel of God, spiritual people will acknowledge this to be the case. Let the Corinthians take care.

The next section develops the apostolic criticism of the way in which many in the congregation idolized or (which amounts to the same thing) patronized some of the Lord's servants, specifically Apollos and Paul (3:1-23). Because these men stood together as friends and fellow-workers, albeit with differing ministries, no one should attempt to show that one was more worthy than the other (3:1-9).

Paul, but not Apollos, had laid an inspired and authoritative foundation for the churches (3:10-11). For this reason certain unnamed, shallow Corinthians who endeavoured to bask in the reflected light of better men are warned to be cautious how they handle apostolic doctrine. Paul may have had in mind emerging leaders in the church when he tells them that if they should harm the shrine of God they themselves will suffer harm. In any case, they must one day give account for their treatment of what he handed down to them (3:12-17).

Corinthian condescension and superiority exhibited a pathetically immature understanding of the gospel (3:18-23). Their strident concern to applaud certain leaders when bypassing others was simply a ruse designed to enhance their prestige in the church. They took this cul-de-sac route because they were oblivious to the truth that both this age and the one to come, and even death itself, which acts as the connecting link between the two, exist solely for the benefit of the Lord's people. Because of their blindness they failed to realize that their party agitation was pointless. The reality was that Paul and Apollos and their like remained servants of the churches. So why were the Corinthians bent on propping up their helpers as their leaders? It was nauseating and consummate folly.

The fifth and final section of Paul's overall treatment of internal divisions within the church majors upon his own relationship with the people (4:1-21). He shows that because he is ultimately a servant of God, the Corinthians should not judge him too quickly. Even if they do look askance at him, their opinions do not matter much (4:1-5). Paul's own private circumstances as an apostle are revealed in a startling manner (4:6-13), followed up immediately by a summons to the church to learn from him. Because he is their spiritual father they need to imitate his readiness to surrender personal rights. Should they not drop their childish attitude to him, the apostle warns that his next visit to the church might well display unprecedented displeasure (4:14-21).

Be of one mind (1:10-17)

Paul names his sources (1:10-13)

Fundamentally the Corinthians were united because they had been called by God to participate in Christ (1:9). Even though this was the case their oneness had been exceedingly well disguised. This is why Paul brings in the little word 'but' or 'now': **'Now I exhort you, brethren'** (1:10). They needed to be one in practice because they were one in principle.

Sometimes we must tell what we know (1:10-11)

Although these people should have been saying the 'same thing', they were not doing so. The NASB uses the word **'agree'**, which is not incorrect although it tends to water down Paul's emphasis upon the need to give up feuding and fighting. As is sometimes the case in church life, the sad spectacle of internal Corinthian tensions was more significant than its causes. What we do know is that the fellowship had divided into splinter-groups, each circle adopting a name as a sort of slogan for where it thought it stood.

Divisions within the church (1:10 - 4:21)

The church is told to get rid of these divisions. If they obey, the people will be **'made complete'** as a church. The verb that Paul uses conveys the meaning 'to repair', 'to put right' or 'to make good' (Greek, *katartizô*). Some other examples in the New Testament are the mending of fishermen's nets and the help given by the spiritual members of a church to someone who has fallen into sin (Matt. 4:21; Mark 1:19; Gal. 6:1). The sense in 1:10 is that the Corinthians will be in good repair and fit for useful work when, but only when, they think alike and share the same opinions.

Not only were there divisions in the church; 1:11 shows that there were **'quarrels'**. How unlike our Lord! He could, and did, disagree with other men, yet never involved himself in word-battles and never lost his temper (Isa. 42:2; Matt. 12:19). No doubt at Corinth the people were given to shouting at one another, a not unknown phenomenon in badly managed churches. The strife had been disclosed to Paul by **'Chloe's people'**, by which might be meant her family, although we cannot tell and do not need to; it was enough for Paul to let the Corinthians be aware that he knew.

Two applications arise from 1:10-11. First, when there are serious divisions brewing up in a church it is right to inform the elders. This is a matter of loyalty to God's people rather than a question of telling tales or splitting on others. Secondly, like Paul, we must always reveal our sources. In general we should avoid criticizing others on the basis of anonymous information, launching out with a cheap and inflammatory statement such as, 'They are saying...' Going about matters in this way always exposes us to the twin charges of spitefulness and slander. In addition, it is only fair that the person criticized should know the origin of the charge against him or her. One other thing: if what you have to say is negative always check it before you pass it on.

Role models (1:12)

The way in which Paul refers to Corinthian domestic quarrels suggests that he accepted as true just about everything he heard, hence the remark: **'Each one of you is saying...'** Over the sea at Corinth, many kilometres from Ephesus, each person was letting it be known that he or she had a decided preference for some individual Christian leader such as Paul or Apollos or Cephas (Peter); seemingly, the problem was endemic.

The apostle had no time at all for evangelical stereotypes. He must have known that some men are better preachers and teachers than others and that a few might even be excellent. Nor was there — or is there — a problem about this. In the parable of the talents no two men had the same abilities or opportunities (Matt. 25:15). Because 1:12 was intended to be taken to heart not only by the enthusiastic and immature fellowship at Corinth it should be given careful thought now. Never make any minister your ideal or your idol.

It is important to observe that the New Testament does not suggest that the eminent pillars of the church ever disagreed about their beliefs. Peter's celebrated lapse into functional Judaism, as recorded in Galatians 2:11-14, is no disproof of this. From this it follows that the way in which the Corinthians were distinguishing between various men of God had something to do with personality differences, certainly among the ministers and probably among the people, although the latter might not have been so innocent. Was it the case that certain academically-minded Corinthians preferred the quiet deliberations of a Paul (if he was quiet!), while another group opted for the possibly more down-to-earth robustness of a Cephas? Again, we cannot tell.

Anyhow, it was all wrong. Even worse, Corinthian folly seems to have been compounded by some who made out that they belonged to Christ and were no man's men. On the other hand, this surprising revelation might anticipate 2 Corinthians 10:7: 'If any man is confident in himself that he is of Christ, let him consider this again within himself, that just as he is Christ's, so also are we,' a possible allusion to those of Paul's detractors who had heard Jesus during his earthly ministry.[1] Anyway, whatever went on in their effervescent minds, there *was* such a group, equally as pernicious as their possibly less sophisticated competitors.

A call to think things through (1:13)

Questions are next raised in order to expose the deep unspirituality of these Corinthians: **'Has Christ been divided? Paul was not crucified for you, was he? Or, were you baptized in the name of Paul?'**

The apostle demonstrates, first, that because Jesus is the Christ, the divine Messiah, the Lord cannot be different things to different Christians. It follows that no assembly of born-again believers can in principle be divided within itself.

Divisions within the church (1:10 - 4:21)

Secondly, Christ is the Redeemer of his church; he alone shed his blood at Calvary for God's people. For this reason the saints should follow him and do so with humility, rather than bestowing party-allegiances upon his servants, however exalted their status.

Thirdly, maybe the Corinthians had not realized the full significance of baptism, inclining to the fallacy that when they were baptized they entered a society headed, say, by Paul, a personality who appeared out of the blue as its principal teacher. In any event, it does seem that they had lost sight of the truth that the rite signified their union with Christ.

All this means that the divisions at Corinth were unnecessary, unreasonable and sinful.

Where the apostle stands (1:14-17)

In order to highlight the folly of Corinthian divisiveness, the apostle explains something of his own relationship both to the Corinthians and to Christ. He recalls that when he was at Corinth he had baptized only a few people, among whom were Crispus and Gaius (1:14).[2]

This was providential. Had the Lord not overruled, raising up other men as baptizers, many Corinthians would undoubtedly have been exulting in the fact that they were baptized into Paul's name (1:15). Truth to tell, neither then nor ever had the apostle taken any initiative to become the Corinthians' exclusive patron and guardian; the idea had never presented itself to him, and God had preserved him — and them — from it.

In those early days it could be that Paul was not the only man who sensed the peril of being an empire-builder, albeit unwittingly and in innocence. The apostle Peter may have deliberately sidestepped a similar pitfall when he commanded the family of Cornelius to be baptized, presumably by someone else (Acts 10:48). But in 1:15 Paul's cryptic remarks do not tell us if he had been aware of the danger at that time; he does no more than look back and thank the Lord for protecting him.

Before we proceed, let's look at a matter that is often misunderstood. Sometimes we speak about being baptized into the church. Strictly speaking, this is impossible. It is far better to speak about being baptized 'into Christ' (cf. 1:13). The institution is less important. Paul knew this. A minister of the gospel and a servant who knew his station, he was too humble and wise to enthuse about the statistics of the baptistery. Several years had passed and so much had happened since those halcyon days in Corinth. Although he had baptized the members of **'the household of Stephanas'** (1:16; cf. 16:15), he claims not to **'know'** or recollect whether other candidates had passed through his hands. This is the apostle's oblique way of saying that the baptizer is irrelevant as long as the baptism is performed adequately. The intended logic of his words is that what does not come to mind cannot be particularly important. He downgrades triumphalism and flattery, not the ordinance.

The work to which Paul was granted a permanent commission is defined with precision and emphasis in 1:17,: **'For Christ did not send me to go on baptizing, but to continue to proclaim good news (not in wisdom of word, so that the cross of Christ might not be emptied).'** By 'word', or **'speech'** (again, *logos* in Greek) is meant a structured system of belief, in this case a worldly-wise pattern acceptable to unconverted, unspiritual and undiscerning people. Paul will soon contrast this with 'the word of the cross' (1:18), a specific syllabus of doctrine that through no fault of its own is abhorrent to the world.

One temptation against which the apostle must have struggled was that of expounding a spurious gospel that took on board Jewish ritualism as well as Greek ideas about knowledge — a gospel of opposites where all views and practices might be possibilities.[3] It would have been equivalent to today's sterile non-gospels proclaimed by sacramental and liberal churches, systems properly stigmatized by evangelicals with some such epithet as 'works-righteousness' and often bolstered by liturgical sound and colour to give a dramatic and entertaining effect. Tantamount to 'the wisdom of the wise' and 'the wisdom of the world' (1:19-20), such a synthetic gospel would have opposed 'the wisdom of God' (1:21). Had Paul enmeshed himself in this way he would have been seriously compromised, far more than if he had been an evangelical show-off, a minister exhibiting his cleverness while sheltering all the while within the bounds of nominal orthodoxy.

To anticipate our exposition of spiritual gifts, one of the many blessings from the Spirit to the Corinthians was 'the word of wisdom' (12:8). The saving wisdom of God was expressed by some selected believers with God-given words — the exact reverse of what the apostle shuns: 'wisdom of word', conventional human wisdom expressed by men of the world about the world in uninspired language, a message and a medium that save none.

In brief, Paul distanced himself as far as possible from those at Corinth who were scrambling to be his personal disciples. He allowed his readers to imagine the consequences had he educated the church to rely upon him and upon captivating, scintillating speech — of which he was perfectly capable; the apostle was highly talented and had received a brilliant education. In that case the cross would have been emptied of its meaning and saints would have remained sinners, confirmed in their vanity and unbelief.

Wise folly; strong weakness (1:18-31)

The apostle knew that he was under attack: in retrospect, both what he said and his manner of delivery had proved uncongenial to some of the Greeks and offensive to not a few of the Jews in the fellowship, let alone to the world around. But why? Paul realized that the deficiency lay with the hearers: notwithstanding their baptism, many of them showed all the signs of a deep-seated unspirituality, failing to appreciate the genuineness and authority of his God-given ministry. This is shown by 3:1 onwards.

The apostle develops the theme introduced by 1:17. He knew that from the viewpoint of the sophisticated Greeks the gospel message was folly, lacking sense and relevance. It was true, too, that for the self-righteous Jews the call to faith in a crucified Messiah was profoundly insulting.

He senses that his ministry had been generally assessed in terms of the social standing of many of the converts. To the watching world their lowly origins suggested that the good news about Jesus was no more than a weak and trivial thing, fit only for people of no consequence. The perception was that what Paul said had little to do with the busy world of which Corinth remained an important part.

But the glorious reality was that not a few had been saved and had come to an altogether different conviction about the gospel. Paul claims that his message, his manner and those who believed through his ministry remain as a challenge to the world and its false values. The Lord had planned it this way, and for at least three reasons.

First, the intention of God had been that his declared word should never resemble any of the numberless traditions esteemed by evil and ignorant men.

Secondly, it was decreed that the light of the gospel should expose the false values of the world for what they are: helpless and hopeless, unable to save, sanctify and satisfy.

Thirdly, the unique message of the cross was designed to lead the people of God to trust the Saviour whom he had sent. In turning to Christ they discover the power of the Lord and learn to glorify him rather than remaining sinfully self-reliant.

It is not true that the medium and the message are foolish (1:18-21)

Almost a formula, the expression **'the word of the cross'** (1:18) draws attention both to the simple way in which the apostle had preached and to the content of his message. Paul refused to employ fine language in order to flaunt his capacities. Nor did he need to do so; gentle manners and genuine ability are always successful and are never obtrusive. Contrast the apostle's style with the speech of the lawyer Tertullus (Acts 24:2-8). You will see that the latter's flourish of words adds up to nothing.

The high road and the low road (1:18)

Paul's astonishing claim is that those who put their minds to his message divide into two groups: those who **'are perishing'** and those who **'are being saved'**. The apostle was conscious of the discriminating grace of God, a grace that fulfils itself in the separation of those who are being rescued from those who die in unbelief. His dictum is that here and now the gospel message brings to light the irreconcilable gap between the saints and the surrounding world.

A sharp contrast is outlined between the ways in which unbelievers and believers assess the gospel. Both have their standards, considering some things to be wisdom and others to be foolishness. But they remain in complete disagreement about what is wise and what is silly. Paul sees beneath the surface: the unbeliever's supposed wisdom is folly and can never save him; he is perishing. But the believer's wisdom, that of the cross, is nothing less than **'the**

Divisions within the church (1:10 - 4:21) 37

power of God'. The saint is wise because he knows now that his heart has been touched by the living God.

Nothing new under the sun (1:19-21)

The apostle establishes the matter with a probable reference to Isaiah 29:14:

> Therefore behold, I will once again deal marvellously with this people, wondrously marvellous;
> And the wisdom of their wise men shall perish,
> And the discernment of their discerning men shall be concealed.

In context, the prophet denounces the contemporary leaders in Jerusalem, claiming that they were repeating the errors committed in a somewhat earlier crisis. In the troubled times of Ahaz, the house of David paid cash for Assyrian military help when Judah was attacked by Syria, Edom and the Philistines. But because the king and his counsellors did not turn to the Lord for help they brought distress upon themselves.[4] Later, when threatened by Assyria, now an enemy, Jerusalem sought Egyptian assistance, again refusing to trust the God of Israel.

Isaiah insists that because such non-wisdom is sinful folly it must come to nothing. Yet the hand of God was even in this: the divine plan behind the ruination of Judah brings the people to learn by sad experience that they ought to turn to the Lord. Specifically, the prophet insists that the Egyptians remain powerless to ward off Assyria and that only Jehovah saves.

Paul universalizes the principle: nothing in this world can deliver men from the guilt and power of sin and bring them to peace with God. Their every effort must be thrown down by the Lord himself because they refuse to look to him. To back this up further allusions to the Old Testament (probably Isa. 19:11-12; 33:18-19; and possibly Isa. 44:25-26; Job 12:17-18), are introduced by 1:20.

Isaiah 19:11-12 wants to know where the wise leaders of Egypt, 'the princes of Zoan', are now, at a time when Egypt is about to be engulfed. The reader is expected to admit that they have disappeared from the scene. Isaiah 33:18-19 predicts the downfall of the

Assyrian armies occupying Judah. The one who 'counts' (equivalent to Paul's 'scribe') is a foreign official who receives tribute from the humiliated people of God. He vanishes to be seen no more in Israel; alien might is not right and cannot prevail before Jehovah.

For Paul such wisdom is personified by, first, the typical **'wise man'**; second, by the **'scribe'** (the learned, literary man); and, third, by the **'debater'**. By 'debater' (Greek, *suzetetes*) is meant the habitual seeker, the type of person who, in the words of 2 Timothy 3:7, is 'always learning, and never able to come to the knowledge of the truth'.

As in Old Testament times, so in the days of the apostle, clever and materialistic worldly wisdom, whether Jewish or Gentile, falls to the ground and is seen in the light of the gospel to be folly; what does not manifestly succeed in making men holy can neither be right nor of God. Paul challenges the supercilious and shallow Corinthians: 'Is this not the case?' Yes, it is.

In 1:21 the apostle begins with an explanatory phrase, **'For since in the wisdom of God the world through its wisdom did not come to know God...'** The probable meaning is that although men were 'in', or surrounded by, the revealed wisdom of God, both in creation and in the providential ordering of all things, they deemed it wise and prudent not to recognize God;[5] atheism became their own synthetic and preferred wisdom.

Because of this evil non-wisdom, the sovereign Lord has acted in an unexpected manner, taking delight in setting up an apparatus described by the apostle as **'the foolishness of preaching'**. This achieves the otherwise impossible, and, from man's point of view, that which is undesirable: reconciliation between sinners and God.

Accurately paraphrased by the NASB as 'the foolishness of the message preached', Paul means that the presentation of a Saviour who rescues by means of his own crucifixion is undoubtedly an absurdity to the world at large. None the less, the message and its medium are used by God **'to save those who are believing'**. The apostolic present tense lays emphasis upon the necessity for perseverance in faith: only lifelong trust in Christ can bring professing converts to their final salvation.[6]

Although some men never accept the gospel, Paul knows well that others do. He displays his unqualified confidence in the ministry of the Word of God. It goes without saying that we should share that confidence.

It is not true that the message of the cross helps none yet offends all (1:22-25)

In these four verses the leading thought of 1:21 is developed. Because the world goes along its own foolish way, God does as he pleases through his servants, and with immense effect. **'Since Jews ask for signs, and Greeks search for wisdom ... we preach Christ who has been crucified'** (1:22-23).[7] 'Has been crucified' implies plainly that the crucifixion, as an event, has abiding consequences: it reaches out to those for whom Christ died.

Three constituencies are mentioned: 'Jews', 'Greeks' (equivalent to the 'Gentiles', that is, 'the nations') and 'we', the apostles. The last group refuse flatly to identify with any ethnic or social group and preach the cross to all.[8] In doing this they are conscious that although God does bless their message it remains a **'stumbling-block'** to the Jews and **'foolishness'** to others. The expansion from **'Greeks'** to **'Gentiles'** in 1:22-23 shows that it was not only the Greeks who considered the gospel to be absurd.

In stating that his message causes Jews to trip over, the apostle might be recalling Hosea 14:9 and Isaiah 8:14-15, written in the late eighth century B.C. Both passages teach that those who will not put their trust in Jehovah inevitably fall flat on their faces. Paul's application is that if the Lord Jesus is not our Saviour he must be the Judge before whom wretched and guilty sinners collapse.[9] But he knew that some Jews and Greeks had been led to stand apart from their fellows (1:24). Such people are **'the called'**, attracted to Christ by the spoken message of the gospel and by the inner operation of the Holy Spirit.[10] They now recognize two truths.

First, they acknowledge that the Lord must be powerful because through him their lives have been changed dramatically for the better. Secondly, the Saviour is wisdom from God. Searching for wisdom was almost a traditional Greek pastime — witness the biting remark of Luke that the men of Athens were invariably 'telling or hearing something new' (Acts 17:21). 'Possibly' and 'maybe' would have been often on their lips, pompous watchwords for their spurious philosophical meanderings. If they had one, these words might have been incorporated in the motto on their university shield. Certainty escaped them because they desired no fixed body of truth on which to depend. This is how it had been at nearby Corinth. But when they were confronted with God's wisdom the converts there embraced it to the exclusion of all else. Moreover, implies Paul, ancestral racial hatred has been reduced to vanishing-point. Because Christ became exactly the same Saviour to believing Jews and Greeks they found themselves united in him irrespective of background. It was like this everywhere, and Ephesians 2:11-22 makes the truth plain.

Paul rejoices in what he calls **'the foolishness of God'** (1:25), likening the crucified Christ expounded by him to a divine folly: the world would say that if God did send Jesus to die, the Almighty seems to have made a fool of himself. But the apostle insists that the folly remains **'wiser than men'**. Uniquely, it identifies man's basic need, peace with God, and then provides the answer, the way of the cross.

Similarly, this gospel is **'the weakness of God'**. As the world sees things, God acted ineffectively when he sent Christ. Why could he not have done something truly impressive and spectacular, a performance that would move mountains? A classic instance of this spiritual blindness was the apostles' request to Christ just before he ascended to heaven that he might revive the fortunes of Israel. Reluctant to wait in Jerusalem for the promise of the Holy Spirit, they wanted a political paradise instituted without further delay (Acts 1:4-6). Their problem was that they misinterpreted Jesus as a social reformer. Twenty years later Paul, not surprisingly, was wiser than they. He had learned by experience that this weak, insipid thing, the good news of Jesus, is always **'stronger than men'** because it cleanses evil hearts and transforms sinners into saints. The apostle saw the other side to this truth, too, something he had believed since the day he was confronted by the exalted Christ: the world, with its immense acumen and energy, cannot match the evangel. Nor can legislation, not excluding that from Sinai, purge the heart from sin. Christ excels.

It is not true that the people of God are of no account (1:26-31)

Paul has claimed boldly that conventional, human wisdom never achieves anything that is truly good, and has introduced two of the prophets of Israel to reinforce his message.

In the light of this he counsels the Corinthians to take a long look at themselves. As everywhere in the New Testament, with the

Divisions within the church (1:10 - 4:21) 41

probable exception of 7:20, the **'calling'** to which 1:26 refers is not that of secular vocation: the Lord had summoned these people to repentance and faith.

What God does, and why (1:26-29)

Although all sections of society were represented in this expanding community, in the main the Corinthian church was composed of people who were not **'wise'**, not **'mighty'** and not **'well-born'** (1:26). They lacked status; they followed rather than led; what they said about the world and its business did not seem important.

The apostle will reveal why this has been so. Either people of consequence had wisely (in their view) shut their ears to Paul and blocked out his weird message and his God, or the Lord had some strange strategy which required that, in the main, social underdogs rather than the more élite classes of Corinth would respond to the good news. In fact — and Paul glories in this — God had selected **'the foolish things of the world'**, **'the weak things of the world'** and **'the base things of the world, and the despised ... the things that are not'**. He had bypassed many of the wise and influential, abandoning them to their own follies (1:27-28). The Corinthian church was stocked with people from the lower classes because the Lord had deemed this to be in his interests.

There were at least two connected reasons for such an unlikely strategy: first, that God might shame both the wise and the mighty (1:27); secondly, in order to **'nullify the things that are'** (1:28). The apostle's meaning is that all high-and-mighty opposition to the good news is destined to collapse. Again and again David overcomes Goliath with strange weapons not of this world's choosing (1 Sam. 17:39,50).

'To shame', which occurs twice in 1:27, is in the present tense. Paul asserts that, even as he writes, some turn to the Lord because they are being made to feel ashamed of themselves. The predicted overthrow of **'the things that are'** is, then, something that happens here and now, day by day, right around the globe, whenever and wherever the proclamation of the gospel is blessed by the Holy Spirit.

Before we go any further into this letter, let it be said that Paul delights to employ the Greek present continuous tense to stress ongoing activity. Here, in 1:27, is a typical example: God is *always* putting the wise and the strong to shame. The problem for the translator is that a literal rendering, something like 'that he might continue to shame the wise ... and the mighty', is cumbersome. Recognizing this difficulty, the NASB properly employs a simple present tense, but loses something in the translation. The point is that in this passage, as elsewhere, the discriminating reader will try to pick up Paul's present tenses with all their wealth of meaning.

It needs to be said that the triumph of the gospel in the current scheme of things does not exclude a final dénouement. Unquestionably, hell will be the scene in which many self-important people come to regret that they never turned to the God of their poor acquaintances. After his elaborate burial the rich man experienced remorse for the first time when he stared at Lazarus reclining in Abraham's bosom (Luke 16:19-31). But his was not godly sorrow, and it came too late.

Further, **'all flesh'**, mankind in its fallen state, must acknowledge sooner or later the great reality of God. The negative attaches to 'boast' rather than to 'flesh': **'so that all flesh should not boast before God'**, rather than 'that no man should boast'. The point is that whereas all men are unceasing in their arrogant attempts to justify themselves before God, they cannot succeed. Let them look long and hard at those unlikely people whom God has rescued and imitate their faith. Let over-wise Corinthians cease to frown on Paul and his preaching.

The only true cause for rejoicing (1:30-31)

If the Corinthians' standing as Christians does not depend upon what they are in themselves, on what basis does it rest?

In its word-order the assertion, **'But from him are you, in Christ Jesus'**, is emphatic (1:30). 'But from him' sets forth God's gracious initiative that blots out any lingering suspicion of personal virtue; 'are you, in Christ Jesus' stresses the reality of the Corinthians' new situation as believers.[11]

To be **'in Christ Jesus'** probably signifies two things. Principally, these people were enjoying the closest possible relationship with the Lord Jesus. For this reason God the Father was granting them the blessings that Christ had won for his church. In smiling at his beloved Son the Father smiled at them. Secondly, they were in fellowship together as Christian believers. This oneness of heart and

Divisions within the church (1:10 - 4:21)

faith had transcended and eclipsed all the temporary cultural and social distinctions of a fading order.

Paul explains in considerable detail what Christ means to these believers. First, he had become their **'wisdom'**. Because they understand something of the purposes of Almighty God, the philosophies and religious traditions of the surrounding world can safely be discarded as trivial and worthless.

Secondly, Jesus had become their **'righteousness'**. This word carries a legal sense, signifying that the requirements of God's commandments levelled against the Corinthians had been satisfied by Christ. Because their day of judgement was the Friday when Jesus died for them, their time of crisis is past and gone, never to reappear. Deemed by God to be righteous, the Corinthian believers are now under no obligation to keep the law in order to be justified.

Thirdly, Christ became their **'sanctification'**. By means of the gift of the Holy Spirit he transformed them. Now they desire to love and obey God. No longer the condition of their salvation, obedience to his law has become their rule of life.

As if this were not enough, Christ had become **'redemption'** for the Corinthians. Because of the final position of this word in the sequence wisdom-righteousness-sanctification-redemption it almost certainly points us to the end of the world. The apostle's meaning is that at the end believers are to be redeemed once and for all from the effects of original and personal sin.[12]

Jeremiah's broken heart (1:31)

The great purpose to be achieved by God in Christ is summed up in 1:31. Here, as also in 2 Corinthians 10:17, Jeremiah 9:24 is quoted because it presents an important truth. We need to consider the prophet's situation some six centuries before Paul's day in order to appreciate the force of the apostle's reasoning.

Jeremiah was distraught because of the imminent Babylonian invasion of Judah. His sorrows multiplied because he stood almost alone; foolishly, the people did not believe that the land would be attacked (Jer. 9:11-12). The prophetic message was that those who considered themselves to be wise and strong should not be complacent. In particular, their relative affluence was nothing to boast about because it was short-term at the best. He insisted that in his doom-laden situation the only basis for self-congratulation was if a man had come to know the Lord. Here alone was real safety. Whereas the people could not save themselves from judgement and ruin, they had the Lord's promise that he would rescue them were they to turn to him.

The apostle indicates that a principle true for Jeremiah's Jerusalem remains valid for the Corinthians and for all time. The ancient Babylonian scourge stands as a sombre picture of the final, awful reckoning between God and guilty sinners. The only sensible reason for self-congratulation is when a man has come to know Christ as Saviour. All else is worthless.

An important truth should not be overlooked. In the Hebrew Old Testament text Jeremiah 9:24 refers explicitly to 'Jehovah', rendered by the Greek Septuagint as *Kurios*, meaning 'lord'. In citing this verse the apostle applies the Greek translation-word *Kurios* to Jesus because he wants us to make an inference about the person of Christ.

Here is something else. If as Christians we are healthy, wealthy, clever, yet ever mindful of the mercies of God, let us be thankful that he has saved us from conceit. But suppose that we were denied fine education, that our resources remain slender, and that we are not brimming over with fitness. Even so, we should bless God: our situation is fortunate beyond our understanding. Not only are we truly wealthy, we possess insight unattainable by any human discipline, as 1:26-28 shows. The greatest of all teachers has given us free and comprehensive tuition. James 1:9 reminds us that the 'brother of humble circumstances' should 'glory in his high position'.

The realities of ministry (2:1-16)

Paul has sketched the popular, negative perceptions of his message and of the church that, through God's grace, he helped to plant. Now he is positive and expounds the realities of the wisdom and power of the gospel. He reveals that when he arrived for the first time at Corinth he spoke plainly, never at any time attempting to sway his hearers with frothy oratory. Nor did he need such a ploy, for the Spirit spoke through him (2:1-5). As for what he proclaimed, his message was the revealed wisdom of God, beyond the reach of human wit and resource but made known to Paul, again by the Holy Spirit (2:6-12). Further, the Spirit of God gave him the exact words

Divisions within the church (1:10 - 4:21)

with which to tell out the good news; he was blessed with verbal inspiration (2:13).

None the less, the apostle concedes that many continue to spurn his ministry. This is because the **'natural man'**, the unconverted person who neither desires nor finds peace with God, is averse to the truth of the gospel. But this unholy reluctance never upsets the plan of God: those whom he calls always come to recognize and accept his infallible Word delivered to them by his servants (2:14-16).

The authority of the Holy Spirit (2:1-5)

In 1:18-20 Paul took the Corinthians back to Old Testament times in order to learn from the prophets and from the mistakes of the Jews. In 1:26-31 he invited the people to contemplate their own lowly calling. Now, he asks them to recall his first visit to their city (Acts 18:1). The emphatic **'and I'** (2:1) reminds the church of his methods at that time.

One message, one medium (2:1)

Paul concedes that his message might have lacked a superficial **'superiority of speech or of wisdom'**. 'Or' is interesting, suggesting that some of the apostle's hearers hoped that, if his manner was ordinary, perhaps what he had to say might be appealing. In the event, he failed to come up to expectations; when they had heard him out the sceptics concluded that neither his message nor how he put it over were worth a second thought.

In spite of this negative appreciation the apostle's methods were never modified: the message controlled the medium. After all, Paul was in Corinth to announce **'the testimony of God'**, to put on display what the Lord himself had declared rather than setting out his own ideas about the Almighty in words and a style of his own choosing.

Think about how this deliberate self-effacement must have seemed to Corinthian Jews and Gentiles eager to make an impression in their busy world. Even if they were ready to give Paul a few minutes of their time, upon reflection many must have been more than tempted to distance themselves from him as rapidly as possible. 'What,' the Jew thought, 'would the synagogue think?'

'How', contemplated the Greek devotee of Poseidon, the sea-god, 'will belief in this "Christ" affect my family and business ties?' The answer was obvious to each, and each backed off. The apostle had experienced this coolness time and again. In later years the plaintive call of 2 Timothy 1:8, 'Do not be ashamed of the testimony of our Lord, or of me his prisoner,' had been hammered out upon the anvil of long-term frustration and disappointment with men.

Be this as it may, the apostle never attempted to come to the people as a glib word-artist. He never speculated about what might be so as to arouse a little local excitement as lasting as the morning dew.

A double negative (2:2)

During his first journey to Corinth Paul made a conscious judgement both about how he would speak and about what he would and would not say: **'And I did not resolve to know anything among you apart from Jesus Christ, and him crucified.'** What we have here is a striking double negative: 'I did not resolve ... apart from ...', which in effect yields a positive. NASB paraphrases with 'I determined to know nothing ... except Jesus Christ,' tending perhaps to make a flat, two-dimensional thing of the apostle's more solid assertion.

Paul discloses what he did *not* decide. When we read between the lines we can see he allows that he had always been a man for all that, and that he was tempted for a time to reduce the content of his ministry to an emotional, demagogic ventilation of crowd-pulling issues. In the event he held back from such a resolution, committing himself to complete silence unless he could expound the cross of Christ: he resolved upon an emphatic 'no' to apparently exciting methods and material. Would that all preachers would both hesitate yet decide where Paul both hesitated yet decided. Let Christ and all things to do with him be the exclusive theme of a pulpit ministry.

As in 1:23, **'crucified'** bears the sense of an accomplished event (Greek, *estaurômenon*, perfect passive participle). The apostle's ministry had presented at least three related truths: first, that Jesus is the Christ, the Messiah; second, that as the Messiah he had been put to death on the cross; and, third, that his shameful death has abiding consequences.

Divisions within the church (1:10 - 4:21) 47

Fears for the future (2:3)

Paul reveals his thinking after a difficult time in northern Greece and in Athens (Acts 16:19 - 17:34). These and earlier experiences had convinced him that he would never lack formidable opposition. When he arrived at Corinth he trembled for the success of the work in this new sphere: both the human obstacles to be overcome and the superficial foolishness masking his message dissolved any self-confidence that he might have had. Being a Roman, a rabbi and a Greek scholar might not help him now; certainly, these things would guarantee nothing.

When he crossed over from mainland Greece to Corinth, Paul's self-confidence was as low as it could be. To us it is obvious that the man was not a coward; evidence fails to show that he ever feared his fellows. On the contrary, the New Testament insists that he was a leader characterized by enterprise and initiative. Glance at Acts 16:28; 17:22; 27:21 and 28:3 and you will have no lingering doubts about the calibre of this extraordinary servant of God. Yet learning, courage, decisiveness, a clear conscience and a cool head were not enough for a task that demanded more than either he or any other had to offer. Not surprisingly, his knees shook. Therefore he tells his readers that he could not, would not, project himself. Rather, he restricted his ministry to the accurate and affectionate presentation of his Master, one whose presence would not be denied him, one who would say to him about Corinth, 'For I am with you... I have many people in this city' (Acts 18:10).

The message comes before the messenger (2:4-5)

For these reasons both the apostle's message (or, 'word', *logos*) and his preaching (*kerugma*) were designed to persuade, yet achieving this with what Paul calls the **'demonstration [both] of the Spirit and of power'** (2:4). Because he had something to say he told it with authority, although not in an unattractive or domineering manner. The apostle wanted men to see the sense of what he taught and then respond. All the time he trusted in the Lord to give effect to his words. Nor did God let him down.

'Demonstration' (Greek, *apodeixis*, occurring nowhere else in the New Testament) means proof or attestation. Paul was no demagogue, full of fire yet a trickster bent upon winning the admiration of an audience with **'persuasive words of wisdom'**. To repeat, because his message was important, far more than the messenger, his tactic was to appeal to his audiences as reasonable people who would evaluate his message.

Romans 6:17 illustrates this principle: 'But thanks be to God ... you became obedient from the heart to that form of teaching to which you were committed.' This verse assumes that whereas the message is all-important, the identity of the teacher is irrelevant. Moreover, when the Spirit blesses the ministry and moves the heart of a hearer, he does it initially through the man's intellect rather than by appealing initially to his emotions. Then, when the alerted mind appreciates the significance of the truth, the heart is inflamed with godly desire. The sinner converts to Christ.

There were two interlocking reasons for the apostle's procedure. He knew well that only a direct and understandable manner of presentation would ever be blessed by the Spirit. Also the presence of the Spirit was essential because only the Lord is able to move men to such an extent that they repent. Compare this with the Lord's teaching about the work of the Holy Spirit in convicting the world of sin, of righteousness and of judgement (John 16:8-11).

In 2:4 we see the emphasis of understatement. It is true that Paul disdained artificial rhetoric as an aid to speaking, but — and we should be clear about this — his preaching would never have been boring.

It is the same today. The demands and duties of the ministry of the gospel are sufficient to deter the bravest of men, although this is by no means a bad thing because it drives the servants of the Lord to their knees. They who hold their heads high when entering the pulpit often have good cause to let them droop after the benediction. On the other hand, when we despair of ourselves and trust the Lord we might be blessed with a demonstration of the Spirit and of power. Certainly, this can never be the case otherwise. There is no vehicle of evangelism as truly dramatic as Spirit-filled preaching.

Another practical issue arises from 2:4-5. It is possible for a preacher to convince his hearers that what he says is true. Even so, their mental assent does not guarantee that their hearts and affections have been seized. Preachers must think about what they say and how they say it and, having done all, pray that the Lord might break the people's hearts. Tomorrow's church depends upon the calibre of today's ministry. If we fail now, what of the future?

Paul's simple method took the long view (2:5). It was his purpose that after their conversion the Corinthians might rely permanently upon **'the power of God'** rather than upon **'the wisdom of men'**. Were they in later days to addict themselves to novel views touted about by religious enthusiasts, even sustaining themselves with what they could remember of an applause-seeking apostle in yesteryear, they would be in poor shape. Where and what would their church be? Nowhere and nothing.

But if they had been introduced to the faith in the right way they would persevere. This is why 2:4 leads into the next verse. Paul's initial evangelism, when blessed by the Spirit, would yield sound conversions, and sound conversions would give promise of dependable Christian servants.

The gospel: wisdom beyond man's imagination (2:6-16)

This section is almost a parenthesis, inserted to respond to at least three semi-hostile arguments anticipated by Paul. Like an intelligent fighter, his sixth sense told him where the next blow would probably fall. First, he knew that some would ask why worldly wisdom (in the forms of, say, Greek philosophy or Jewish works-righteousness) was deemed by him to be of no account. Are men idiots or blocks of wood unable to think for themselves? Surely not. Secondly, why was it that the Judaean rulers who were alive at the time put Jesus to death? They were men of experience and calibre, by no means devoid of acumen; could they and the majority behind them have been wrong? Could an ancient and sophisticated people really have been in error about the Nazarene? Lastly, bearing in mind that the world cannot and does not appreciate the alleged wisdom of Paul's ministry, why was he determined to continue? He has to explain himself.

The apostle's answers are as follows. Firstly, the conventional wisdom and standards of the world are worthless, and for a profoundly simple reason: they fail to recognize, and do not address, man's fundamental need — salvation from the guilt and power of sin and the attainment of peace with God. The wisdom of God can and does achieve these ends.

Secondly, Christ was put to death by contemporary Jewish and Gentile authorities because they were ignorant about God's programme of salvation. At Calvary they did not know what they were doing.

Finally, Paul and his colleagues had come to understand the wisdom of God solely because the Lord had revealed it to them. Since they could never have worked it out for themselves, the Lord had opened their hearts and minds. For this reason they persevered.

Hidden wisdom (2:6-9)

In 1:18 - 2:5 the apostle referred to specific Old Testament situations, to the opposition shown to his message by Jews and Gentiles alike, to the Corinthians as a congregation and, finally, to his own personal ministry. He has done this in a somewhat negative fashion to show that the message of the cross neither incorporates the stale wisdom of the world nor depends upon traditional but inadequate methods of presentation such as rhetoric and drama.

Now he switches tactics and becomes aggressive: **'Yet ...'** (2:6). His failure to applaud conventional, worldly wisdom does not mean that he lacks understanding. Far from it. He asserts that God always had his own unique wisdom (Greek, *sophia*), reserved for his people, and that his colleagues and he are the channels of communication: **'Yet we do speak wisdom among those who are mature; a wisdom, however, not of this age, nor of the rulers of this age, rulers who are being brought to nothing.'**

In the background Greek text 'wisdom' commences the flow of words in order to give emphasis: 'Wisdom, nevertheless, we are speaking among those who are mature.' The principal matter upon Paul's heart is a divine wisdom that outstrips all competitors.

1. Who were the 'mature'? (2:6)

'Mature', standing for the Greek *teleioi*, occurs in the NASB, although 'perfect' or 'complete' would give the sense equally well, and possibly better. During the last century and well into the 1900s very many books and learned articles struggled to uncover the sources from which Paul may have mined this word. To list even a few notable scholars would clog our endnotes, and therefore the attempt will not be made. Suffice to say that the ideas offered have been as diverse as they have been numerous.

Divisions within the church (1:10 - 4:21)

For example, it was suggested that Paul borrowed from the jargon apparently used in the mystery religions in order to make his message more acceptable to Greek converts, explaining the cross in terms of the culture. Over the years this view has gone out of fashion and is now not much more than a theological museum-piece.

Some, too, have reckoned that in this verse we can detect apostolic irony, even sarcasm. According to this approach, the Corinthians thought that they were mature, perhaps because they possessed an abundance of spiritual gifts ('You are not lacking in any gift', 1:7). So, when Paul says in 2:6 that he and others speak to the 'mature', he really means that he has stooped to addressing people who were grossly immature because they were wise in their own eyes. That many of these clever Corinthians were immature or childish is shown by 3:1: 'And I brethren, could not speak to you as to spiritual men, but as to men of flesh, as to babes in Christ.' The fact that Paul could on occasion be lovingly sarcastic is shown by 4:8: 'You are already filled, you have already become rich, you have become kings without us; and I would indeed that you had become kings.' But the weakness of this approach is that Paul does not say in 2:6 that the Corinthians are 'perfect', whereas he does claim that he addresses other Christians, apparently elsewhere, who are. Irony seems to be absent.

Another interpretation, which has tended to prevail over the years, is that the 'mature' were the more spiritual element in the fellowship, sufficiently wise and experienced to appreciate the apostle's ministry. They were unlike the 'babes in Christ' mentioned in 3:1. To such elevated souls Paul opened his mind and mouth to disclose esoteric truth beyond the capacity of the less discerning believers. The notes on 3:1-3 explain why I think this way of looking at 2:6 is inadequate.

But Paul did not snatch the term *teleioi* out of thin air. It seems likely that he had the Scriptures in mind when he referred to those who were 'complete', or 'perfect', or 'mature'. Men of this calibre, such as Noah and Job, are not infrequently mentioned in the Old Testament. Abraham was told to be perfect, that is, to trust the Lord, after he had made a serious error in his marriage. We read that the Lord is perfect with the man who is perfect. This means that Jehovah in his goodness commits himself to the consecrated and faithful servant.[13]

Looked at from this perspective, the serious saint dedicated to his Lord is ready for life and for death. Because the Lord is his shepherd he lacks no good thing; he is complete and cannot want. What Paul apparently says is that he and others (**'we'**) communicate gospel wisdom, and that it is received gladly by the Lord's true people, the ones who stand in direct succession to the saints of the previous dispensation. In principle the new-covenant Christians lack nothing because they trust in the crucified Messiah. This is the case even if they may be personally immature and somewhat lacking in understanding.

That Paul believed it possible for Christians to be sincere and dedicated yet misguided in some areas of belief is demonstrated without a shadow of doubt by Philippians 3:15: 'Let us therefore, as many as are perfect, have this attitude [stretching forward to Christ and glory]; and if in anything you have a different attitude, God will reveal that also to you.'

This truth applies today, too. If we love the Word of God we are mature, or perfect, even though we are sinful. We have a Saviour and know it. Because we are in Christ and he in us we need nothing more. 'In him you have been made complete' (Col. 2:10).

2. Who were 'the rulers'? (2:6)

The wisdom that Paul and his colleagues proclaim is not **'of this age'**. The same word 'age' (Greek, *aiôn*) appears in 1:20; 2:7-8; 3:18; 8:13 and 10:11, and stands for the world of mankind, with its castles of cards, rather than the universe that God created. The apostle declares that men did not generate the wisdom he proclaims. Nor was it devised by **'the rulers of this age'**. What rulers? They have to be identified, and we need to work out why they are mentioned.

The better view is that the **'rulers'** were men of influence and position in society rather than evil spiritual powers; flesh and blood rather than demons. There are three reasons for this interpretation.

First, in the New Testament the Greek word *archôn*, translated here as 'ruler', normally means a human authority (the statistics are given in the notes).[14] Secondly, Acts 4:26 quotes Psalm 2:2, which tells us that 'The rulers take counsel together against the Lord and against his anointed.' They behave in this way because they are devoid of wisdom (Ps. 2:10). It is likely that Paul has this in mind

Divisions within the church (1:10 - 4:21) 53

in 2:8. Thirdly, the New Testament shows that whereas the satanic powers knew who Jesus was, men were ignorant.[15]

In that they are the rulers **'of this age'** ('this' definitely implying the existence of 'that', or another, better world), powerful leaders have never been able to exercise ultimate control over the kingdom of God; 'that age' remains in command. Nor have these men ever been other than blind to the reality of the gospel truths that Paul now proclaims. Let the Corinthians beware lest they undervalue his ministry among them.

Further, human authorities are even now **'being brought to nothing'**; God does not allow them to endure for ever. Two prominent Old Testament examples among many were the kings of Babylon and Tyre (Isa. 14:3-23; Ezek. 28:1-19). They were brought low by God. What Paul says is that because the world of men, as represented by its greatest and its best, is temporary, it cannot possibly be the well-spring of eternal truth.

In that the 'rulers of this age' are blamed for the death of Jesus, the implication is that Pilate, Herod and the other Jewish leaders represented all who have been, are and ever will be in authority. In other words, the apostle displays a painful awareness that the world maintains an antagonism as inevitable and enduring as it is implacable.

3. God's mysterious wisdom (2:7)

If the wisdom that Paul communicates is not the child of this age, it has to have a different origin, which the apostle proceeds to disclose. This is why the statement of 2:7 opens with a strong word, **'yet'** (or 'but'; Greek, *alla*): **'But we speak God's wisdom.'** The meaning is that because Paul's message could not have been devised by men, it must have come from heaven: 'not of this age ... but God's wisdom'. The apostle describes this divine wisdom *(sophia)* in three ways.

First, it is by definition **'in a mystery'** (Greek, *en musteriô*). This is an adjectival form equivalent to 'mysterious' and as such describes the nature of wisdom. The expression is not adverbial ('mysteriously'); that is, it is not telling us about Paul's manner of speaking, as if he were whispering strange secrets into the ears of a select few behind closed doors. In any case, it was never his practice to confide strange formulae to privileged hearers. The true meaning of 2:7 is that the apostle preached openly, telling out a hitherto mysterious secret no longer concealed, the reason being that God had chosen to publish it. This once jealously guarded secret is now made available to all through the apostolic proclamation of the cross. In the words of Ephesians 3:4-5, 'The mystery of Christ, which in other generations was not made known to the sons of men ... has now been revealed to his holy apostles and prophets in the Spirit.'[16]

It is true, as we know from 2 Corinthians 12:4 and the surrounding context, that some years before he wrote that letter the apostle had been caught up to paradise. There he had heard 'unspeakable' words which he was commanded to keep secret. Nor did he break the charge. But he does let slip (possibly with his tongue in his cheek) that there was an occasion when he had been deposited in a basket in order to escape from Damascus. He recalls this to emphasize that his personal weakness and long-standing humiliation magnify the revealed mystery of Christ. This is why he proclaims it with enthusiasm. His commitment is to candour and to clarity.

In 2:7 the apostle shows his oneness with the writers of the Old Testament. There a mystery never means something permanently concealed from men: it is a truth concerning God's plan for his people that would have remained unknown had Jehovah not disclosed it.[17] From this it follows that the mystery shared with the 'perfect' is *revealed* wisdom. Because the Lord has made it known, men can assimilate it and proclaim it. (Cf. 13:2: 'And if I know all mysteries...'; Matt. 13:11: 'To you it has been granted to know the mysteries of the kingdom of heaven.')

This is why Paul's mysterious wisdom is described as something that *had* been **'hidden'**. True, there was a time when God concealed the plan of salvation. But that era has passed away once and for all. What is more, this wisdom was **'predestined before the ages to our glory'**. 'Predestined' is found also in Romans 8:29-30 and Ephesians 1:5,11 with reference to the ultimate destiny of the people of God. It means to design and to assure the end of a programme before it has been put into motion. Having done this, a supreme intelligence operates and in time achieves the desired end.

God determined that his people should be redeemed, although this is not said explicitly in 2:7. What the apostle does state is that the Lord predestined his secret wisdom to bring about the glorification of the (predestined) church. Christians must be saved because the gospel that carries them to glory is like a perfectly-constructed vehicle incapable of breaking down. Moreover, the final destination both of the pilgrims and of the chariot that bears them was decreed before the world began. Our salvation is certain because the means of transport is secure. All is of the Lord, who is 'the way, and the truth and the life' (John 14:6).

4. 'The Lord of glory' (2:8)

'The rulers of this age', the world of men and those who take a lead in affairs, were first mentioned in 2:6. Now they are reintroduced as personalities who in their day and place failed to recognize the wisdom of God. Unquestionably, the apostle directs our attention to the Jewish and Roman leaders immediately responsible for the death of our Lord. To quote his address in the synagogue at Antioch in Pisidia, 'For those who live in Jerusalem, and their rulers ... found no cause for death ... [and] asked Pilate that he [Jesus] be executed' (Acts 13:27-28).

These people, whom one might reasonably have expected to be aware of the identity of Jesus, suspected nothing of the existence of a divine wisdom centred upon Christ, or how it would function, or what it would achieve. Paul's point is that had they known about its existence they would not have dared to harm the Lord. Tragically, they did not realize that he was **'the Lord of glory'**.

When he penned this statement the apostle might have had in mind the words of Christ: 'They do not know what they do' (Luke 23:34).[18] Be this as it may, the magnificent title 'the Lord of glory' means that Jesus remains the divine Lord, the God of Israel who is all-glorious.[19]

It is true that God cannot die. Nor was he born at Bethlehem. What happened in the city of David was that the divine Son of God became the human Son of God, a single person now with two natures, one eternal and the other assumed. As a man, although not as God, he laid down his life.

The principle brought out in 2:8 is that because Jesus remains one person, not two, the cross is an antinomy, an incomprehensible mystery transcending the imagination of men: 'the Lord of glory', the Majesty from heaven, perished disgracefully as a common criminal. A somewhat similar statement occurs in Acts 20:28 with reference to the church, 'which God purchased through his own blood', and another in Romans 9:5: 'Christ ... who is over all, God blessed for ever'.

5. Unimaginable blessings (2:9)

Notwithstanding their profound ignorance, the appalling blunder committed by the rulers in Jerusalem was by no means accidental, something unplanned that happened inadvertently. Paul insists that he proclaims the fulfilment of what had been anticipated by the Old Testament, 2:8 being almost a parenthesis between 2:7 and 2:9. The sequence of thought is: **'But we speak God's wisdom ... just as it is written, "Things which the eye has not seen..."'** The Old Testament allusion (or, perhaps, quotation) in 2:9 is the remote object of 'we speak' in 2:7.

Neither here nor elsewhere does the New Testament ever suggest that the sovereign action of God in ordaining Calvary cancelled out the guilt of the evil men who devised it. The death of Jesus was their responsibility alone and no one else's.[20] Even so, the cross to which they dispatched the incarnate God was a vital element in working out **'what God has prepared for those who love him'**.

There are two possible interpretations of the **'things'** that God has prepared. First, they could be benefits for the Lord's people here and now, in this world. Secondly, they might be the blessings of the end-time, connected in some way with the place being prepared by the Lord for his own (John 14:3).

Before we come to a decision about these alternatives we need to ask what part, or parts, of the Old Testament Paul is recalling when he claims, 'It is written...' Isaiah 64:4 comes near, as does Jeremiah 3:16, and it is probable that the apostle makes these selections because they reflect the view of the Old Testament as a whole that it is not possible for men to search out the secret things of God.

Isaiah 64:1-3 takes the reader back to the events of Sinai, and 64:4 declares:

> For from of old they have not heard nor perceived by ear,
> Neither has the eye seen a God besides thee,
> Who acts in behalf of the one who waits for him.

In context the prophet prays that God might again work wonderfully for his people, just as he did at the time of the Exodus. Jeremiah 3:16

Divisions within the church (1:10 - 4:21) 57

anticipates the coming of the Messiah when the old dispensation will be eclipsed: 'They shall say no more, "The ark of the covenant of the Lord". And it shall not come to mind, nor shall they remember it, nor shall they miss it, nor shall it be made again.'

Paul would appear to be saying that the final answer to Isaiah's prayer, plus the fulfilment of Jeremiah's prediction, was the *first* coming of the Lord Jesus into the world. If this is the better interpretation, it follows that 'the things which God has prepared' are nothing other than the blessings that we possess now.

Three related assertions are made about the wisdom of God in ordaining the death of Christ.

First, this wise plan of salvation has never been made apparent in and through the created universe: **'Eye has not seen'** the like in nature. Although it is true that the heavens declare the glory of God and that the stars tell out his handiwork, they do not reveal Christ. Only apostolic preaching can do this (Ps. 19:1; Rom. 10:18).

Secondly, **'Ear has not heard'**, or picked up anything about, the programme of redemption from the folklore, myths, religions and cultural traditions handed down from previous generations. This is something that, from time immemorial, fathers were never able to tell their offspring, the reason being that the parents never knew.

Third, the wit and ingenuity of mankind could never have contrived such a plan. Because it remains so unimaginably wonderful, the doctrine of Christ crucified was always beyond the **'heart'** of any of Adam's race.

This triple statement establishes the truth that the sin committed in cold blood by Pilate and the Jews was perpetrated in complete ignorance of their victim's identity.

The Holy Spirit is the sole agent of revelation (2:10-12)

The things that God did through men, although without their knowledge, he has now **'revealed'** (Greek, *apekalupsen*, from which we take our word 'apocalypse'), in order that we might understand (2:10). Although 1:7 taught that Christ is to be revealed at the end-time, this is not the meaning here. Rather, the Holy Spirit has explained to the prophets and apostles of the church (**'to us'**) the significance of what happened at the cross, 'which in other generations was not made known to the sons of men, as it has now been revealed ... in the Spirit' (Eph. 3:5).

This revelation had been granted through the Spirit because he alone **'searches'** that is, explores, understands and interprets **'all things, even the depths of God'**.[21] 'Searches' (Greek, *erauna*) is an example of what is sometimes called by the grammarians a 'timeless present', indicating that the Holy Spirit never goes about, as it were, trying to find out yet more and more truths about God. Always having the measure of everything, he understands all that is to be known.

A simple illustration from everyday experience is provided to show how the Spirit operates (2:11). The apostle reminds us about something we all know to be true, that it is not possible for us to read other people's thoughts: your spirit alone knows the deep and the inscrutable secrets of your own mind and heart. In fun we sometimes say, 'A penny for your thoughts,' because we can often see when someone is thinking hard but are unable to tell what is on his or her mind. By analogy — and this is Paul's point — it is the Spirit of God alone who knows the otherwise unknowable thoughts of God.

The apostle is claiming that his message had led directly to the conversion of the Corinthians. The gospel achieved this because it came from God rather than being the brainchild either of the preacher or of any other Christian. No man, living or dead, could have been sufficiently ingenious and wise to have thought the scheme through, let alone powerful enough to have put it into successful operation. In the event, although it was respectively a scandal and a folly to Jews and Gentiles, God's plan of salvation had been comprehended perfectly and at every stage by the Spirit. Now the same Spirit has revealed it to Paul. All the apostle ever did was to communicate to the Corinthians what he had been taught.

This is the burden of 2:12. Paul, with others, has **'received ... the Spirit who is from God, that we might know the things freely given to us by God'**. What man's reason could not fathom, the Holy Spirit has searched out and explained.

Let's recapitulate before proceeding to the statement of 2:13. What the apostle has said up to now is that he and others had been given certain 'things', by which he means the accumulated blessings of salvation (2:9). Although he, just like all Christians, has received the Holy Spirit (as taught also by 6:11 and 12:13), he and other inspired men had been endowed by the Spirit in a special way so that they might understand and measure these benefits.

Divisions within the church (1:10 - 4:21) 59

But the apostle was aware that to be granted an unprecedented insight into the wisdom of God did not imply that he was personally equipped to unfold it to others. If anything, the reverse must have been the case: how could this converted Pharisee and scholar, a man whose lips were still infected with sin, explain accurately to his fellows a marvel that he never framed nor could have discovered by himself? To be an infallible transmitter of the revealed truth of Jesus Christ Paul required something more if he was to give out what he had taken in. The preaching of the cross demanded original and inspired words from God.

Looking at the issue, if we may, from the viewpoint of heaven, would the unfolding of the intricacies of the gospel have been safe in the hands of Christians who, however eminent, were left to their own devices to explain it? The only possible answer is 'No'. In his time Paul knew that there was a tremendous distinction between revelations to him from the Spirit and his effective communication of those revelations to other men. He understood well that disclosures from God do not guarantee infallible preaching and writing at a later time.

The Spirit gave Paul the words to speak (2:13)

The apostle virtually repeats himself in claiming that he and others had received salvation plus a detailed understanding of the way in which the Lord was redeeming his church. Now a further revelation is given: he had been granted exactly the right words with which to expound Jesus Christ. **'We speak'** occurs in 2:6-7, implicitly in 2:9 and again in 2:13: **'... which things also we speak, not in words taught by human wisdom, but in those taught** [to Paul and other inspired men] **by the Spirit'**. Then appears the qualification that when the apostle unfolds the gospel he does so **'combining spiritual thoughts with spiritual words'**.

A possible alternative translation of 2:13a might be: 'We speak, not in teaching words of human wisdom, but in teaching words of [= from] the Spirit', that is, with instructive and informative words given by the Holy Spirit to equip the apostle for service. But the first approach is better. Although the latter is true it tends to shift the emphasis away from the verbal teaching given *to* Paul by the Spirit towards verbal teaching given *by* Paul in the Spirit, a truth that is not his burden just here. The crux of the issue is what is meant by the Greek word *didaktos* in 2:13a, whether it is active ('teaching') or passive ('taught'). Either way, both approaches show that apostolic statements are the exact word of God.

Didaktos appears in John 6:45: 'And they shall all be taught of God' (citing Isa. 54:13); and also in 1 Thessalonians 4:9: 'You yourselves are taught by God.' These parallels would seem to show that the word has a passive sense. Another typical example might be a remark of Josephus about the colossal Roman war-machine. Soldiers, he writes, were 'trained', or 'taught' *(didakton)*, in peacetime to prepare for war.[22] Similarly, the apostle discloses that the Lord taught him what to say and that he had been obedient to the Spirit, his teacher.

'Combining' means 'explaining' or occasionally 'interpreting'.[23] Paul's meaning is that he explains or expounds spiritual realities by means of Spirit-given words. Some eight hundred years earlier a prophet of Israel expressed exactly the same principle: 'The Lord Jehovah has spoken; who can but prophesy?' (Amos 3:8).[24] When God gives a precise word to a prophet the prophet utters it; he has no choice, nor wants one.

It is true that some commentators take the second occurrence of **'spiritual'** in 2:13 to refer to spiritually-minded people in Corinth and elsewhere. On this understanding, Paul writes that he hands over spiritual truths to spiritual Christians.[25] The grammar would sustain this interpretation. Furthermore, the sentiment is accurate. None the less, it does not seem that this is what is being said. The burden of text and context is the unique selection and peculiar authority of the words which the apostle has employed rather than the calibre of those to whom he speaks.

Paul has taught the doctrine of inspiration (2:12): God has imparted his wisdom to the apostles. Here, we are presented with the related doctrine of inerrancy: in a way that we do not understand the Spirit gave these men specific words with which to teach the churches. Therefore, what the people of God had received via the apostles was flawless in every respect.

A question arises. Could Paul have written 2:13 with a clear conscience unless he genuinely expected that the *whole* of the letter we call '1 Corinthians' would be able to sustain these twin doctrines? Surely not. The apostle realized that on this occasion he was a human author of a part of sacred Scripture. The powerful statement

Divisions within the church (1:10 - 4:21) 61

of 14:37 shows that this must have been the case: 'If anyone thinks he is a prophet or spiritual, let him recognize that the things which I write to you are the Lord's commandment.'

God speaks, and his people hear (2:14-16)

Although, states Paul, the deep truths of God are being explained by the apostles in words given to them by the Spirit of God, the **'natural man'** (Greek, *psuchikos anthrôpos*) does not **'accept'** these **'things'** (2:14). By 'natural man' is meant an unconverted person.[26]

First, the apostle outlines the reason for this rejection: the 'natural man' listens, ponders what he hears and decides that these inspired words and doctrines are **'foolishness to him'**.

Secondly, Paul accepts that this negative evaluation, however regrettable, is inevitable: a person of this calibre **'cannot understand'**. Because the individual is an unrepentant sinner he is unable to **'know'** such things and cannot appreciate the truths of God for what they are.

Thirdly, an explanation is given for this gross inability. The 'natural man' is by no means an innocent prey to some wasting disease of the heart and mind that has debilitated his mental processes. Far from it: the average unbeliever is alert and in full possession of his wits. The man's tragic failure to receive divine truth is because **'They** [the things of the Spirit] **are spiritually appraised'**, which means that they can be evaluated only with the help of the Spirit of God. The logic is that because the 'natural man' has not received the Holy Spirit he remains unable to make a correct estimate of the gospel. From his viewpoint, everything to do with Christ is nonsense.

On the other hand (2:15), **'he who is spiritual'** (Greek, *ho pneumatikos*), that is, the regenerate believer, is in a different position. He can assess **'all things'**, by which is meant that he is able to appreciate spiritual realities and discern the miserable state of men who do not possess the Holy Spirit. Whereas the world does not understand the Christian, who **'is appraised by no man'**, the child of God does recognize what is wrong with the world.

Paul might be preparing the Corinthians for chapter 3, where he attacks the superficiality of many in the church. Because the apostle does possess the Spirit and because some Corinthians give no appearance of being spiritual people (cf. 3:1-3), the latter are in no position to make an intelligent and responsible assessment of his ministry. It follows that their criticisms lack integrity and that they need to come to terms with this failing and be on their guard.

The principles set out in 2:14-15 are expounded quite remarkably in 2:16. This verse alludes to the Greek version of Isaiah 40:13, where the prophet asks, 'Who knew the mind of the Lord ... who counsels him?' Then Paul asserts boldly that **'we'**, that is, other apostles and prophets as well as he, **'have the mind of Christ'**.

The word **'mind'** (Greek, *nous*) is important because it means 'intention', 'plan' or 'purpose', or even 'agenda' or 'programme'. In the apocryphal book of Judith, the Jewish heroine of that name endeavours to persuade the elders of her city not to surrender to the Assyrian enemy. She asks, 'How shall you search out God ... and recognize his mind [*nous*], and comprehend his purpose?' God's 'mind' is understood as his immediate programme for his besieged people.[27]

Paul repeats Isaiah's claim that men are blissfully ignorant of the divine *nous*, the redemptive programme of the Lord. But the apostle does perceive God's great plan of salvation. How can this be? Not because he is inherently superior to his fellows but because the divine counsellor, Christ, has made a disclosure to him: 'We have the mind [*nous*] of Christ.'

This is an attack upon Corinthian smugness and pseudo-spirituality: only those who possess the Spirit (2:6,15) are in a position to assess Paul's teaching, whereas carnal Christians (in this case, many of the Corinthians) are quite unable to evaluate it intelligently. Contrary to what these inflated people might think, the apostle does know what God has done. To repeat, this is because Christ, the favoured counsellor who had always shared his Father's secrets, has chosen to reveal those mysteries to Paul.

We need to appreciate the profound truths of 2:14-16. Unbelievers and worldly-minded Christians are rather like the blind who cannot see the sun and the deaf who do not hear thunder. This being so, do not be surprised or depressed when the world neither understands nor accepts your testimony. It does not because it cannot, even though it should. But by deed and (if possible) by word show that Christ has saved you. Above all, pray that the Lord might use your witness. He used someone else's ministry to bring you, an ignorant sinner, to faith.

Divisions within the church (1:10 - 4:21)

Corinthian favouritism (3:1-23)

Paul has informed the church that he is aware of divisions among them (1:10-17). Now he gives detailed attention to the matter. His remarks, which occupy chapter 3, might be said to fall into three parts.

First, the apostle introduces Apollos and himself as examples of Christian servants who have different gifts but who work together happily (3:1-9). Because such men are perceived to labour in perfect harmony, the Corinthians should not seek to patronize one at the expense of the other.

Secondly, it is not only the congregation that is at fault; there are local leaders who need counsel (3:10-17). It is good that these men are seeking to build upon Paul's foundation. Even so, to be successful they must not stray from apostolic principles in any clever attempt to modify or redefine the faith.

There are two reasons for this limitation. The care of the earthly temple of God has been committed to these unnamed resident leaders, and they should remember that the church is not their property. Furthermore, they are accountable to God for their ministry: he will have the last word. Even so (and Paul is always ready to encourage), whatever their blunders, their final salvation cannot be in doubt.

The third section concentrates upon the vexed issue of cliques in the church: the transformation of certain eminent leaders into figureheads is nothing other than a species of worldly wisdom (3:18-23). This tendency is muddle-headed, sinful, deceptive and unnecessary.

Paul and Apollos stand together (3:1-9)

In 2:1 the apostle revealed his thoughts when he first travelled to Corinth. Now, he tells the church about his impressions after having lived there for a time, possibly recalling his first stay in their city (Acts 18:1-18).

Paul is faced with the trauma that is often the sad experience and always the dread of every minister of the gospel: the presence in the church of those who have professed the faith but who display remarkably little evidence of spiritual growth. In the Corinthian church there were some, perhaps many, who resembled unbelievers rather than born-again Christians. It is to such **'brethren'** (3:1) that Paul addresses his remarks. He recalls earlier contacts when he **'could not speak'** to them as if they were spiritual; his desire to open his mind, heart and mouth had been stifled by a force beyond himself. But it was not the Lord who told him to keep his silence. Rather, the apostle, forced into a corner by the negative attitude of these baptized people, had to address them as **'men of flesh'**, as if they were virtual unbelievers.

Milk or solid food? (3:2-3)

In 2:6 Paul referred to 'perfect' Christians. Although this expression is probably a recall of Old Testament thought, the apostle, ever versatile with words, intends to wound the conceited Corinthians, albeit in love. His meaning here is that although there were mature believers elsewhere, these folk remained **'babes in Christ'**; spiritually retarded, they were not growing up as responsible believers.

1. Mother's milk

Therefore, when he was at Corinth Paul had to speak to them in the most simple terms. He likens his approach to the action of a mother giving milk to her infant, knowing well that it is the only food that the child can accept (3:2).

It needs to be said that there is nothing wrong with teaching Bible doctrines in a digestible manner to Christians young and old. 'Tell me the story simply, as to a little child,' are words sung with feeling by many an aged saint. It stands to reason that it has to be right that the truth, the whole truth and nothing but the truth be taught clearly; nothing should be held back. A comparison of Paul's words in Acts 20:20 and 27 shows that what was profitable to the Ephesians was nothing less than 'the whole counsel of God': the apostle had taught the church a comprehensive syllabus without limitation. Teaching is a skill, and ministers have to estimate the capacity of the people and then give them God's word as they are able to hear it. This was the method Jesus employed (Mark 4:33). Careful feeding can do wonders.

The apostle's principal worry about the Corinthians was that some of them were not like healthy babies whose appetites and

Divisions within the church (1:10 - 4:21)

bodies were certain to develop. As time went by he perceived that it would be almost impossible to give the Corinthians expanded teaching, teaching which he likens to **'solid food'**. **'Indeed,'** Paul remarks bitingly, **'even now you are not yet able.'** This criticism might be placed alongside Hebrews 5:12, where the writer states that his readers 'have come to need milk and not solid food'. Apparently, dullness was not a monopoly of the Corinthians.

But Paul knew that there was nothing wrong either with the 'milk' that he had administered or with the 'solid food' that he had ready. The basic problem was that these children in the Lord were spiritually unhealthy and unready for the apostle's developed syllabus.

2. Primary and secondary levels (etc.) of teaching?

Over the years much has been written by New Testament scholars about the apparent distinction drawn by the apostle between liquid and solid nourishment. One thing is certain: Paul cannot have had one teaching-programme for young converts, retaining higher, reserved truths to impart at some later stage to more advanced believers who made the grade, and perhaps even more mysterious matters to share with ultra-spiritual saints. He had one gospel, and one gospel only, to give to all the people.

This letter disproves the notion of anything resembling a twin-track programme. If, as an exercise, we were to catalogue all the great doctrines that appear in 1 Corinthians we should finish with something like an index to a comprehensive tome of systematic theology. All that the apostle means by the contrast between milk and solid food is that basic principles, simply expressed, should in time be given detailed explanation, as and when believers are ready and willing to hear. Church is like school: if capable and motivated infants learn their alphabet they are ready for spelling-tests and grammar and, later on, the joys of reading. One thing leads to another and another.

Pastoral experience suggests that this must have been the case. In an average evangelical congregation some believers burn to know more about the faith. They read, they listen, they ask and they probe. Pastors find it more easy to share with them in the things of God than with those who attend the Lord's day services spasmodically, who probably do not attend the prayer meeting, and who look blank when the preacher brings out discoveries that thrill his soul.

The man in the pulpit is, after all, a converted scribe who puts on display what he has extracted from God's treasure chest (Matt. 13:52), even if some of his people don't realize it. But because they are the Lord's babies they must have their milk.

3. Youthful maturity

Nor does Christian maturity depend necessarily upon, say, our age, upon how long we have been Christians or upon our knowledge of the Bible. If we are committed to the Lord we are mature, perfect or complete (Col. 2:10). Although the fellowships with which Paul dealt were young, this did not mean that the people were spiritual infants. Their inadequate growth resulted from other factors. Nor did the apostle abandon these squabbling, jealous Corinthians in disgust; he continued to give them what their sickly frames could digest, no doubt praying that one day they could be weaned.

According to 3:3 this inability to come to grips with more detailed teaching was reflected by **'jealousy and strife** [or, 'arguments'] **among you'** (cf. 1:11). Because the people were staring and glaring at one another they could not look at the things of God.

Although 'jealousy' is not always an evil, it was definitely so in this situation: the people remained 'fleshly' (Greek, *sarkikoi*).[28] Paul employs 'fleshly' twice for emphasis, calling upon the church to agree that they were people of this stamp, 'walking' or behaving like unconverted men unable to appreciate spiritual truths. Each one of them resembled the unconverted 'natural man' of 2:14.

An embarrassing question (3:4)

The apostle is shamelessly but lovingly bold. He takes upon himself a role akin to that of a prosecuting counsel in court who subjects a reluctant witness to a hostile cross-examination. The Corinthians must answer. Is it not the case that they give every appearance of being **'men'**, unconverted sinners lacking the power and fellowship of the Spirit? Is this not so when, for example, one will say that he is **'of Paul'**, a second retorting that he is **'of Apollos'**?

Paul and Apollos, workers together (3:5-9)

In reality, not only is such blind discipleship wrong, it is altogether illogical and unnecessary. After all, **'What** [not 'who'] **is**

Apollos?'; **'What is Paul?'** (3:5). They are instruments rather than men who matter. The apostle compels the church to admit that it is virtually impossible for him to discern the work of the Spirit in their lives.

Then he squashes the notion that either man had ever projected himself as an empire-builder. Perish the thought! Such a perception originated among elements within the church, but not with two friends who were no more than **'servants'** through whom these Corinthians believed in Jesus. Moreover, the Lord in his sovereignty **'gave'** conversions both to Apollos and to Paul: the men knew their place and readily acknowledged that they personally had not turned the Corinthians to Christ.

Paul now refers to his friend and to himself in some detail. First, he allows that Apollos and he differ remarkably in their gifts; he has, as it were, **'planted'** and the Alexandrian has **'watered'** (3:6).

The issue is depersonalized. It is true that the two men, the apostle and Apollos, have complemented each other, even as the hired planter and the employee who comes along with a water-hose are both needful in a garden, particularly if the church at Corinth (the garden) is exposed to the day-and-night heat of a sinful society. Although Paul's plants must have water, and although Apollos's watering is a waste of time without apostolic green fingers, the fact remains that God **'was causing the growth'**; during and after the activities of both men the Lord brought about germination in his field.

It follows that neither the man who plants nor his colleague who waters **'is anything'**; neither can bestow life (3:7). Paul repeats himself for emphasis: only God **'causes the growth'**. Therefore, God alone is indispensable. Although the Lord needs no particular individual to be his planter or to irrigate (others could be used), no individual labourer can succeed without God. The Corinthians should have adored the Father, Son and Spirit rather than idolizing dispensable servants. Paul and Apollos **'are one'** because they serve together in the cause of the same Lord even though they do not perform exactly the same work (3:8).

This being so, it is an abuse of emotional energy for the Corinthians to follow the apostle at the expense of Apollos, or vice versa. Both these servants will be rewarded by their Lord on the basis of their individual **'labour'**, their hard, grinding toil (Greek, *kopos*), and not because they have certain gifts. The Corinthians are in error in showing too much interest in personality rather than in perspiration. Faithfulness and hard work are much more important than some rare capacity, or an attractive character. Paul teaches that the relative worth of men who have different gifts but who work equally hard should never be contrasted.

Apollos and he were not simply colleagues; they were **'fellow workers'** (3:9). This means that they stood shoulder to shoulder with their Lord in the same cause. Paul emphasizes that the people to whom they ministered the Word were the property of God rather than of his servants: **'You are God's field, God's building.'**

Found nowhere else in the New Testament, the Greek word *georgion*, translated in 3:9 as 'field', means cultivated land rather than a field left to grass. The principle is that in God's territory something of value is being grown, something not owned by the cultivators. Then the metaphor changes abruptly. The church is like a building that God, and none other, sets up. The Corinthians were wrong when they implied that differing loyalties should be offered to mere servants. They ought not to have reckoned that they belonged either to Paul or to Apollos.

We can take considerable comfort from this. When we work for the Lord we work with the Lord. He is always present to help when, for example, we set up church meetings, bury the dead, work out the financial accounts, bake cakes for the fellowship supper, take the children to Sunday School, operate a crèche or give a lift to a Christian who needs transport.

Notice that 3:9 draws a sharp distinction between the church in general, **'You are God's field, God's building'**, and those who are called to minister the gospel, **'We are God's fellow workers.'** In saying that they belonged variously to Paul or to Apollos, what the Corinthians meant was that Paul and Apollos belonged to them. They were treating God's colleagues as if they were their own ecclesiastical property and therefore the proper objects of praise or blame, reward or forfeit. Corinthian servility was disguised condescension and probably the expression of a desire to control the fellowship. The apostle senses this and reacts by taking ministers out of their grasp. Standing apart from the church as a whole, these two brethren had been given a special status. Let the people, then, respect them.

Divisions within the church (1:10 - 4:21)

Local leaders need counsel (3:10-17)

Paul insists that the Corinthians need to regard their ministers as men whose task it was to expound apostolic teaching, and apostolic teaching only. The ministers need to remember this, too.

No new foundations (3:10-11)

If the church is God's building, Paul possesses the rank of a **'wise master builder'** (3:10), and is a man quietly confident about his calling. The NASB translation 'master builder' comes from the Greek *architektos* (whence 'architect'), a word that in those days signified someone with the status of a senior director of works. Josephus, referring to his direction of the Jewish defence of Tiberias against the Romans in the war of A.D. 66-70, writes that he instructed the 'architects' to put in hand the construction of the town walls.[29]

Similarly, although Paul had worked hard and wisely for the churches, he was never their proprietor. Nor had he elevated himself to his position of subordinate responsibility. Always a man exercising authority because he was under authority, he remained what he was and did what he did because of **'the grace of God which was given to me'**: the Lord could quite easily have chosen someone else.

When the apostle came to Corinth there was no Christian church there; when he departed there was such a community. Nor was it tiny. By any standard it was large. The promise of Acts 18:10, 'I have many people in this city,' had not fallen flat. When Paul wrote 1 Corinthians he was aware that he had already **'laid a foundation'**. But he was aware, too, that others would continue after he had vanished from the scene and that they would be required by the Lord to build on the apostle's infallible teaching and practice. In 3:10 he gives his approval to succession because he knew that it would be both right and inevitable.

Although in context all believers might have been in his mind, Paul appears to target his shafts particularly to Christian workers. This is suggested by the caution, **'Let each person see how he is building upon it'** (the foundation). Notice the emphasis upon continuous review: the servant should always be looking at his work, asking himself if it fits neatly upon the apostolic platform.

The 'foundation' is defined carefully as **'the one that is laid, which is Jesus Christ'** (3:11). Christ had been set in place by Paul as the only possible basis for the churches. Moreover, the Lord, considered as the foundation, is lying permanently in position, never to be dislodged.[30]

But Paul says much more than this. Not only should there be no alternative basis for the church; there can be none. Not only will God not modify or replace the foundation; any attempted re-establishment of the true church of God by other men on a different basis would be a feat quite beyond their power: **'No man can lay a foundation other than the one which is laid.'** This is effectively a dire apostolic warning: because all other hypothetical or actual foundations are sand, anything resting on them must eventually collapse.

The intended meaning behind **'Jesus Christ'** is crucial, no less so today than when the letter was written. Paul's intended meaning is plain: his unique exposition of the gospel *is* Christ, beyond which there is no salvation; as such it remains the only possible foundation for the church.

Consider Romans 2:16, where Paul (writing from Corinth) states that one day 'God will judge the secrets of men through Christ Jesus', doing so 'according to my gospel'. There is a similar claim in Romans 16:25: 'Now to him who is able to establish you according to my gospel and the preaching of Jesus Christ.' 2 Timothy 2:8 comes to mind as well. The apostle was always profoundly conscious of the fact that Christ had permitted himself to be expounded solely through the ministry of such as he. Because of this burning awareness, and not because of a non-existent egoism, he was never reluctant to insist that his teaching was inspired and definitive. If anything, Ephesians 2:20 brings this out even more plainly: the churches had been 'built upon the foundation of the apostles and prophets, Christ Jesus himself being the corner stone'.

It is for this reason that the Corinthians must keep strictly to Paul's teaching and principles. If they were to try to build upon an alternative foundation their own designs would sooner or later crumble. What, in those days, might such an alternative platform have been?

It would not have been an open rejection of Christ; blatant apostasy was not in Paul's mind. Unquestionably, he was thinking in terms of some sort of modification or revision of apostolic

Divisions within the church (1:10 - 4:21)

doctrine: unreliable and unsent teachers introducing their scissors and paste to add to or take from his teaching. In effect, a warning is being addressed to those who, even then, wished to refashion the God-breathed truths being deposited with the churches.

There is a principle here that cannot safely be ignored. The hard fact is that doctrine decides the day, and we ought to be thankful for it. In time, a church without adequate doctrinal foundations must lose God's people. Let's illustrate the matter from church history. In 1524, at the age of twenty-eight, the Dutchman Menno Simons was ordained a priest of the Roman obedience. During his years at the altar he searched the New Testament to obtain confirmation of his beliefs. In one essential respect, at least, the effort was a complete failure (or success, depending on how you look at it): he could not discover where the Bible teaches the sacrifice of the mass. Courageously, he concluded that it did not.

This precipitated a crisis of confidence in Rome leading to Menno's voluntary departure from his comfortable presbytery and pulpit. He committed himself to the service of Christ among the non-revolutionary, orthodox Anabaptists. In his own words, his desire was to 'preach his [Christ's] exalted and adorable name and Holy Word unadulterated and make manifest his truth to his praise'.[31] During the twenty-five years that remained to him Menno wrote many books and tracts. Each was prefaced with 1 Corinthians 3:11: 'For other foundation can no man lay than that is laid, which is Jesus Christ.'

Menno Simons' problem was that he found himself in a church that professed Christ, but not the apostolic Christ. He realized that because the Roman foundations were wrong nothing good could be built upon them. Casting himself upon the Lord, he quit.

Ministers, take care how you build (3:12-15)

The apostle knows that he has laid a sure foundation upon which all subsequent church-builders should proceed. But in spite of his holy boldness he remains sensitive to the fact that not all who reckon themselves to be pioneers will necessarily be competent, or even honest. In plain terms, he anticipates that inadequate or downright false doctrines would be put about at Corinth, as elsewhere, even though their proponents might formally acknowledge Paul's authority.

This explains the illustration of 3:12-15. Men would build upon this unique foundation with diverse materials such as **'gold, silver, precious stones, wood, hay, straw'** (3:12). The clue to the meaning of the metaphor lies in the considerable difference between these substances: some are elegant, valuable and durable; others are conspicuous because of their proven utility; and yet others are virtually useless or, at best, fit only for crude, temporary shelter. 'Precious stones' would doubtless be granite and varicoloured marbles, as in the palace of King Ahasuerus (Esth. 1:6).

It might be that Paul takes us intentionally beyond our real world, asking us to imagine houses built completely, say, of gold or of silver. Be that as it may, the metaphor is of a cluster of buildings standing side-by-side, each put up by a particular man (**'each man's work'**, 3:13). The constructions range from the palatial to the expensive, going down to the ordinary and then to the mediocre, finishing with shacks and shanties. The picture would have been familiar because in Paul's world, as now in many parts of the world, luxury and squalor were close neighbours.

Notwithstanding this diversity, each structure is assumed to rest on a solid foundation, Paul's infallible and definitive exposition of Christ. It follows that the buildings stand for practical applications, whether good, bad or indifferent, of the apostle's original gospel.

Men have always employed wood and fibres as well as stone for their buildings. Remember the straw that the Hebrews gathered to make bricks (Exod. 5:12). But sanctuaries were, and usually are, constructed with hewn stones so that they will endure, and adorned with gold and silver in order to impress all who see them. The Parthenon at Athens was ancient in Paul's day and still stands; even after all these years it is a lovely thing to look at.

Furthermore (and Paul stresses this), a stone building does not easily burn down. Should there be a fire, the flames might damage it, but not like something made from timber or other combustible material. And such a hazard is to be expected. The apostle predicts that one day the labours of every Christian servant, performed either with sincerity or in pretence, must be tested: **'Each man's work will become evident; for the day will show it, because it is to be revealed with fire'** (3:13). This is a remarkable statement.

Earlier in the letter Paul referred to the ultimate revelation, or uncovering, of Christ (1:7). Now he maintains that the work of the

Divisions within the church (1:10 - 4:21) 73

Christian will also be revealed or uncovered. Further, the two revelations are connected: Christ, when revealed, will reveal the quality or poverty of what had been performed in his name, and will do it **'with fire'**. Here, 'fire' stands for judgement because flame separates precious metal from dross, the genuine from what is false. The Bible often pictures the anger of God in this way.[32]

If a servant of God has taken the trouble to select and employ the proper materials (that is, healthy teaching and practice), and has built something worthwhile for the Lord, he is to receive a **'reward'** (3:14). In the words of 2 John 8, 'Watch yourselves, that you might not lose what you have accomplished, but that you may receive a full reward.'[33] Conversely, if a worker's doctrines and conduct have been grossly inadequate, his work must be burned and he will **'suffer loss'** (3:15); he will witness all, or much, of that for which he had striven disowned and reduced to ash.

We have here what might be termed the doctrine of secondary judgement. Although all our sins are forgiven for Christ's sake and our salvation is sure, as Christians we are still accountable.[34] In glory the saints will enjoy varying degrees of blessedness, depending upon our stewardship in *this* world.

Now is the time to get ready for heaven. It is impossible for us as believers to ponder our eternal state too much. Not only are we to enter the gates of the Celestial City; our situation in glory depends upon our faithfulness here and now, where we are. We make plans, of course, for our welfare in this brief world. But, as Christians, are we making arrangements for our situation after we are dead?

Notice that in 3:12-18 Paul directs his comments repeatedly to **'any man'** or (3:13) to **'each man'**: God is no respecter of persons; there are no exceptions. What of someone who has been supplied with a good apostolic foundation but who erects a poor building? **'He himself shall be saved, yet so as through fire'** (3:15).[35] This means that the man will enter heaven lacking a good reputation; in the presence of the angels the King will decline to issue an enthusiastic 'Well done'.[36]

This teaching has nothing to do with the Roman Catholic belief in purgatory.[37] The fire anticipated by Paul is to break out at the terminal day of reckoning, a day when only glory lies ahead for believers. Destructive only in that the flames will expose ministerial folly, they are in no sense a preparatory purification. Nor can the fire be literal, any more than Paul intends us to think about his sure foundation or other men's building materials in literal terms. The reference is to the approval or disapproval of Christ.

Let's be clear about another matter as well. If 3:11 condemns any dramatic redefinition of the Christian faith, 3:12-15 is no less scathing about men who claim to be more or less evangelical, but who implicitly reserve the right to criticize or modify Paul's teaching. In these verses the apostle assumes, first, that his doctrine is perfectly understandable, and insists, secondly, that it is not to be altered in any way. It is non-negotiable.

A solemn warning (3:16-17)

The question in 3:16 is the apostle's way of compelling his readers to admit, perhaps reluctantly, the truth of what he writes: **'Do you not know that you are a temple of God, and that the Spirit of God dwells in you?'** Yes, they do know it.

'Temple' (Greek, *naos*) signifies a shrine, the inner, central sanctuary of a temple rather than the surrounding complex. Because Paul's Greek does not demand the English indefinite article ('a') in front of 'temple', as supplied in our translation, the definite article ('the') can safely be assumed. The meaning, then, is that the Christian churches are uniquely *the* sacred dwelling of the Holy Spirit: God is within them, and within them only, to the exclusion of all other faiths and religious devotees. Surely, the people must realize how exclusive and sacred their status is. It follows that **'If any man'** — again, it does not matter who — **'destroys'**, or damages this shrine, **'God will destroy'**, or damage, **'him'** (3:17).

In Old Testament times a person who defiled the sanctuary exposed himself to the extreme penalty (Lev. 15:31; Num. 19:20). In 3:17 we learn that God is no less concerned for the assembly of the saints: **'For the temple of God is holy, and that is what you are.'**

Paul has shown that Christ's ministers, of whom Apollos and he are typical, are nothing. Therefore it was wrong for the Corinthians to reckon these servants as their leaders. Should they persist in this folly they must harm their fellowship, a local shrine of God. If this happened, they would be in grave danger. But a lesson taught is not always a lesson learned, for which reason the people needed to think long and hard about their attitudes.

Divisions within the church (1:10 - 4:21)

Worldliness in worship: self-examination, please (3:18-23)

Back to the Old Testament (3:18-20)

The Corinthians are warned not to continue their tedious self-deception (3:18). If **'any man'** considers that he is wise **'in this age'**, perhaps after the pattern of those who are 'wise according to the flesh' (1:26), he needs to become foolish in order to become wise. The meaning is that the wisdom of the world and the wisdom of God are mutually hostile and lack common ground. Therefore the truly wise man rejects the standards of this age. It matters little to him that he stands before the world as a fool.

The rationale for this exchange of wisdoms is stated in 3:19-20. **'Before God'** this world's wisdom is **'foolishness'** because, as God sees it, nothing of lasting good is achieved. Such wisdom is simultaneously evil in design, in action and in effect because it leaves God out. But the Lord refuses to be ignored, as a result of which this supreme folly brings disaster upon those who enthuse over it. Job 5:13 and Psalm 94:11 are recalled by the apostle to give weight to his teaching.

1. Eliphaz and Job (Job 5:13)

Eliphaz the Temanite informs Job that (in Paul's adaptation) God **'catches the wise in their craftiness'**. In this, at least, it seems that Eliphaz was right enough, although later the Lord was angry with him because the man was wise in his own conceits (Job 42:7).

The application for the Corinthians is that, in God's providence, wise and powerful people tie themselves up with the cords with which they hope to entangle others. Scripture abounds with such examples, two notable specimens being Ahithophel, David's renegade counsellor, and Judas Iscariot (2 Sam.15:12; 17:23; Acts 1:18-20). Both committed suicide.

2. Psalm 94:11

Jehovah knows well that the **'reasonings'** or evil machinations of the enemies of God's people are entirely **'useless'**: historically, these opponents have never been survivors. The apostle applies the truth. Should the Corinthians persist in their devaluation of Paul's ministry they identify with earlier, worldly-wise enemies of both God and the saints. They, too, must bring themselves down.

The situation of the Christian (3:21-23)

The prescribed apostolic therapy is that **'no one'** should **'boast in men'** (3:21). No longer should the people at Corinth congratulate themselves because they succeed somehow in associating with favoured evangelical celebrities. But Paul goes further. The truth is that these exciting men of the moment are there to serve all the Corinthians; the former belong to everybody because they belong to nobody.

Since **'all things belong'** to the church, the practice of applauding Paul or Apollos is a symptom rather than a sickness, revealing a flawed understanding of the way in which these devoted men think and work. What Paul is really saying, albeit in carefully guarded terms, is that sycophants are parasites; as such they neither assist their reluctant victims nor, if they think about it, can they do themselves any good.

Compare 3:21-23 with Romans 8:28, which tells us that 'all things' serve the interests of the people of God, finally ushering in our inheritance. Here, in the Corinthian letter, we find that 'all things' include the apostles and their colleagues.

No great stretch of the imagination is required to see the Corinthians swelling up with pride because they pretended to be the valued and perhaps indispensable supporters of certain well-known ministers. Sadly, the same sort of thing is always happening. Respect other men but be no man's man, unless that man be Christ. Then, grow as well as glow.

'Whether' is repeated eight times in 3:22-23 for extreme emphasis: it does not matter who or what is the object of consideration, whether servants of Christ, or the present world-system, whether life or death, whether things that occur now, or things that are to take place — 'all things belong' to the people of God.

There is a grand reason for this. Paul's loving logic is devastating because he knows that what he says defies contradiction: Christians belong to Christ and to none other, and Christ belongs to God and to none other. God, it is assumed, is omnipotent and controls all things through Christ in the interest of the church.[38]

Divisions within the church (1:10 - 4:21)

Because believers are one with the exalted and omnipotent Saviour and therefore belong in a special way to the Father of the Lord Jesus (cf. John 20:17), nothing can be hostile or even indifferent to their situation. Everything serves them. They are uniquely the masters of the universe and the slaves of none. It follows that to allow themselves to be led about by men, whoever they might be, is nothing less than a practical denial of the principle. Compare this with what 7:23 says about Christians who consider selling themselves off as slaves in order to resolve their financial problems: 'You were bought with a price; do not become slaves of men.'

Although Paul is concerned about followers and men-pleasers, what he says is not inappropriate for would-be party-leaders. Those who yearn to take charge of their fellows might in time discover that they have become the tools of their factions. In this way they oppose the principle of Christian liberty.

Stewards (4:1-21)

Paul unburdens another great concern. Not only should ministers of the gospel see themselves for what they are, stewards who serve the Lord; they should be recognized as such by others.

The apostle applies the principles laid down in the previous chapter. First (4:1-5), the people ought to regard Paul and his colleagues as servants of Christ rather than as leaders behind whom they should group. As a steward aware that he has always been faithful to his master, Paul refuses to be depressed by the opinions about him touted around by some Corinthians.

Even though his conscience does not trouble him, the apostle declines flatly to try to assess his usefulness. The reasoning is that if *he* cannot and will not indulge in such a vainglorious exercise, it must be wrong for the high-handed Corinthians to measure his value as a minister of the gospel. The Lord alone is competent to issue an evaluation and will do it at the right time.

Secondly (4:6-7), to expend precious energy either in criticizing or clustering around various servants of the Lord is contrary to the spirit of nothing less than the Old Testament. The sober fact is that the conceited Corinthians possessed nothing that had not been given them. In short, they ought not to reckon themselves to be Paul's peers, qualified to weigh him up.

In truth, the outward circumstances of the apostles were wretched, lacking the affluence of some Corinthians (4:8-13). The latter despised Paul and his fellow-workers as men who had let themselves drift downwards. Despite appearances, the apostle insists that his economic problems were not due to any personal folly: this is how God had planned his life.

Finally (4:14-21), Paul reminds the church about the unique relationship, that of children to their father, which exists between the Corinthians and him. For this reason he chides them and warns that unless they mend their ways his next visit will show that he can be severe.

The apostles are servants, not leaders (4:1-5)

The immediate context is concerned with ongoing attitudes. As is often the case elsewhere in the letter, this is why observations, commands and prohibitions are couched in the present tense: **'Let a man regard us in this manner, as servants of Christ ... it is required of stewards that one be found trustworthy ... it is a very small thing that I should be examined... I do not even examine myself ... the one who examines me is the Lord. Therefore do not go on passing judgement.'**

Stewards and servants (4:1-3)

Paul has described himself already as an 'apostle', as a 'servant' and as a 'master builder' (1:1; 3:5,10); now he introduces two new words to identify his position: 'assistants' and 'stewards'. **'A man'**, that is, each and every person in the church, must reckon Apollos and him as **'assistants'** ('servants', NASB) of Christ and **'stewards of the mysteries of God'** (4:1).

To recapitulate, a 'mystery' is a specific revelation from God about the otherwise unknowable way of salvation (see comments on 2:7). Apollos and Paul were not more, but certainly not less, than reliable transmitters of what the Lord had made known.

In the world in which these men moved an **'assistant'** (Greek, *uperetes*) was a lowly underling who rendered humble and hard service. In picturing himself in this way the apostle might have been thinking about his conversion experience when the risen Lord revealed to him that he would be just such a person (Acts 26:16). A

Divisions within the church (1:10 - 4:21)

'steward' (Greek, *oikonomos*) was a dignified senior servant, an administrator managing the affairs of his master. Erastus, a member of the Corinthian church, was a highly-placed steward in his city (Rom. 16:23), and it is unlikely that the parallel would have escaped the notice of the first readers of 1 Corinthians. Paul was a master of subtlety. The point which he makes forcibly is that he and others like him were answerable to Christ, rather than preachers at the beck and call of the churches, and should be considered as such.

Unlike Apollos, Paul was an apostle. But despite this difference the two men were both assistants and stewards. From this it can be inferred that the apostle presents his friend and himself as typical ministers of the gospel. The implication, which Paul no doubt intended, is that every elder finds himself in precisely the situation of these servants: not only is he given managerial status, he is supposed to work hard.[39]

This truth needs to be remembered in the ups and downs of church life where ministers should feel exposed if they receive too much applause. Suppose that you, an 'average' church member (if there is such a creature), are foolish enough to virtually idolize a minister of the gospel known to you. Paradoxically, you show that you do not really appreciate the man for what he is. If he is discerning he will not take too much notice; if he loves the limelight he will be damaged.

'Here' is placed strategically at the beginning of 4:2 to emphasize the importance of loyal service for Christ. 'Here', in a church situation, it is required that the individual manager be found trustworthy. In modern terms the picture might be that of a mid-level executive always under the critical scrutiny of his senior director. The apostle is aware that, even as he writes, he continues to be assessed by a master who knows all the facts and who never misunderstands or misinterprets.

In the Bible there is a close connection between personal trust in God and personal trustworthiness in the Lord's service, between faith in the Lord and faithfulness. Abraham, according to Nehemiah 9:8, was just such a person: 'And thou didst find his heart faithful before thee.' Those who rely upon the Lord are concerned for his business. Paul sees himself as a servant who must work at the matter twenty-four hours a day and seven days a week. Therefore, as a manager accountable to his superior, he declines to worry overmuch about what others think of him (4:3).

Other people's opinions (4:4-5)

It is probable that since apostolic times no believer has had a conscience as innocent as that of the author of 1 Corinthians. When we make mistakes we need to accept constructive criticism from others if it is offered. In particular, a congregation has the right to review its minister's teaching and conduct in the light of Scripture. Should he fail seriously and habitually the people must act. 'Observe those who cause dissensions and hindrances contrary to the teaching which you learned, and turn away from them' (Rom. 16:17).

On the other hand, although he is painfully aware that he is not perfect, the minister should not allow himself to be upset by irresponsible sniping if he does his work to the best of his ability. Paul's comment needs consideration. Even so, the opinions that other people might have about us *do* matter, and in his day the apostle was never entirely oblivious to the fact that others passed remarks about his ministry. The claim here is that he had a good conscience (4:4), by which is meant that malicious criticisms did not distress him unduly. He served one who listened but did not overreact when contradicted by unworthy people (Heb. 12:3).

The theme of assessment has occurred already in 2:14-15. In 4:4-5 the apostle continues to personalize the matter, having just written that it is 'a very small thing', effectively nothing to him, that his work should be evaluated by the Corinthians. In literal Greek his expression is **'by human day'** (4:3), meaning these present times in which men express their usually derogatory views. Paul's point is that if he is to be dragged, so to speak, to a court to spend a day there being judged by his fellows, what they say is of no consequence.

Although he was always painfully aware of his human imperfections (read Rom. 7:24-25), the apostle could not recall any way in which he had erred in his dual capacity as an assistant and manager for the Lord: **'I am conscious of nothing against myself'** (4:4). A striking parallel to this statement is found in Job 27:6 in the Greek version of the Old Testament, a text which Paul might have had in his mind. Job protested his personal righteousness and made out that his conscience was unblemished. Because this was how it stood the suffering patriarch paid no attention to argumentative critics who reckoned they had summed up his situation better than he. Paul was similarly placed.

Divisions within the church (1:10 - 4:21)

Never other than a faithful and laborious servant, he did not conclude that introspection hallmarked with a quiet conscience showed that God reckoned his work to have come up to the mark. Here is one way of rendering the middle and last parts of 4:4: **'But in this I have not been justified. It is the Lord who is assessing me.'** The NASB gives 'acquitted' for 'justified', but the latter is probably better. The main truth presented here is that the apostle's healthy conscience was not infallible. That is, while he was in the process of composing this epistle Paul knew that the Lord was even then measuring his servant against his own absolute standards.

This principle needs to be understood. Because we are fallen sinners who have not yet been glorified we dare not suppose that our consciences cannot let us down. They have done so and will do so again — frequently. Sincerity and wisdom do not always go hand in hand. Perhaps they are rarely seen together. Jesus predicted that some of his followers would be killed by men who believed that they were serving God (John 16:2). Paul himself was a persecutor, but what he did was perpetrated in ignorant sincerity (1 Tim. 1:13). Because the heart is notoriously deceitful and because emotions can fail we should never rely too much on them. Let the objective truth of the Bible be our light and our lamp.

One outstanding example of the proper submission of the heart to the revealed will of God was the confession of Martin Luther (1483-1546), the great Reformer, before the leaders of his nation. Early in 1521 he was excommunicated by Pope Leo X because of alleged heresy. Some weeks later Luther was brought before the German Parliament and the Emperor Charles V to answer for his writings. He told the assembly that 'My conscience is captive to the Word of God. Therefore I cannot and will not recant, since it is difficult, unprofitable and dangerous indeed to do anything against one's conscience. God help me. Amen.'[40] In the last resort Luther wisely allowed his judgement of what was right and what was wrong to be determined by Scripture.

Paul's remarks about the subjection of the heart to the known will of God come to a conclusion in 4:5. He accepts that the Lord does have a current assessment of him, his servant. But it remains confidential, to be revealed only when Christ comes; not even Paul himself has an insight into what the Lord proposes to declare about him. Therefore the Corinthians must not make a habit of judging their apostle. One day they may (perhaps) do so, when Christ shall 'bring to light the hidden things of darkness'. As it is, their uninformed censoriousness usurps the lordship of Christ and renders grave injustice to his appointed servants.

In time the Lord will bring to public gaze the inscrutable desires that lie behind every man's activity, and will disclose **'the motives of men's hearts'**. Then, and only then, will each man receive praise from God. Unlike 3:8,14-15, where wages and forfeits are in his mind, Paul refers to the commendation to be given to faithful servants, the quality of whose work is undoubted.

The apostle knew that God alone is the Judge of men, yet claims here that Christ has been appointed to assess our deeds and the forces which impel us. Paul makes, not for the first time, an intentional implication about the person of our Saviour, and requires his readers to come to a conclusion about who Jesus is.[41]

Keeping in step with the Old Testament saints (4:6-7)

These principles (**'things'**) are said to be **'figuratively applied'** to Apollos and to Paul (4:6). Because they are servants working harmoniously together (3:4-6), the two men should not be played off the one against the other, and the Corinthians should not travel beyond **'what is written'**. Paul's presupposition is that the body of Old Testament teaching remains on the record specifically for Christian attention. What the Lord has written remains written.

Because no particular book, chapter or verse from the Old Testament seems to be in the apostle's mind, his remark would appear to embrace the totality of the Scriptures. These teach everywhere, albeit in different ways, the need for humility, a virtue noticeable for its rarity at Corinth. Once more the Corinthians are reckoned to be the spiritual children of old-dispensation Israel.

As in chapter 3, Paul and Apollos are presented as typical ministers. This is because the apostle is convinced that personal examples speak more effectively than abstract teaching. Since what applies to these two good friends is true for all, the Corinthians should not be inflated disciples of their favoured elders, vying against others who, no less foolishly, enthuse **'on behalf of one against the other'**.

Now appear some more queries (4:7), to which there are obvious answers. This is why the questions are posed: the bubble of

Divisions within the church (1:10 - 4:21)

Corinthian pride needs to be well and truly burst. First, who is it who makes the Corinthians out to be different, that is, special or **'superior'**? By implication, no one. The unvarnished reality is that they are ordinary Christians.

Second, what do they possess that they have not received? The question is rhetorical: all that these believers have, whether spiritual or material, has been given to them.

Third, if they are receivers rather than acquirers, a proposition against which they can hardly object, why do they 'boast'? Why do they pride themselves as the patrons of up-and-coming preachers whom they neither called nor equipped? They are silly, immature people.

Paul tries to break hard hearts (4:8-13)

Having criticized the conceit of the Corinthians, the apostle now employs unconcealed irony. Because Paul cares for these people and because they know that he would never want to make them appear ridiculous, he can employ such a bitter and precarious weapon. We who are of lesser calibre should seldom, perhaps never, express ourselves in this way. If we take it upon ourselves to do so, we must first be sure that those whom we address are convinced that we love them and accept that we are genuinely concerned for their interests.

Complacent Christianity (4:8)

The Corinthians remained **'filled'** or satisfied. Not only so, they had become 'rich'. Furthermore, they were now **'kings'**. And, to cap it all, they achieved their exalted status apart from Paul (**'without us'**), a man whom some at least neither wanted with them nor felt they needed.

Plainly, many in the church were complacent. They reckoned that they had attained a level of Christian spirituality superior to anything that Paul had to show. Undoubtedly they felt that they were men to whom others should give attention, peacocks rather than sparrows. Perhaps it was in those days as it can be now: affluent, well-heeled evangelicals sometimes tend to pass their poorer brethren by on the other side of the road.

Superficially, Paul's words might seem strange, bearing in mind that the church had sent a three-men delegation to him to seek counsel on a number of issues (7:1; 12:1; 16:17). But the community was large and divisive. Perhaps Paul declines to name names because he knows that the targets for his shafts will be recognized.

Heavy irony continues in order to press home the truth that misplaced Corinthian self-importance should be replaced with sober humility: **'I would indeed that you had become kings so that we might also reign with you.'**

There are two possible interpretations of these words. First, the apostle could be giving expression to his yearning for the final revelation of the kingdom of God when Paul and the Corinthians will be seen as kings (compare with 1:7; 3:14; 4:5).

Or the meaning might be that the Corinthians were desperately shallow, never having come to terms with the triumphs and tensions of everyday Christian living. On this interpretation they were paupers rather than the monarchs they should have been, and in some sense were. The truth was that 'all things belong' to them (3:22). Writing not long afterwards when he was residing at Corinth, Paul informed the Roman Christians that all who receive the 'gift of righteousness' will 'reign in life' (Rom. 5:17). Christians are, in truth, kings.

The second approach is preferable: Paul's desire is that the Corinthians might reign *now* with the apostles, not vice versa; the emphasis seems to be upon present growth rather than upon future glory.

It is for this reason that the Corinthians have much ground still to occupy. If and when they do take possession of it they will meet Paul. His insinuation is that in terms of practical Christian discipleship he remains far, far ahead of them.

We live in a time when much emphasis is placed upon Spirit-given experiences. Not all that we hear is good. It seems that the Corinthians had fallen into the same trap. Don't forget that the ultimate experience of the Holy Spirit is to occur when he raises our bodies from the dust (Rom. 8:11). To date none of us has travelled this far.

Refuse (4:9-13)

The apostle longs for these things because he supposes that God has **'exhibited us, the apostles'** as **'last of all men'** (4:9). The remarkable

Divisions within the church (1:10 - 4:21)

display of which he has become a part is rather like a gladiatorial circus to which the Lord had dispatched him to fight for his life.

Words could not be more dramatic, and this is not the last occasion in the Corinthian correspondence where the spectacle of the arena is employed. Paul was always keen to use illustrations from the real world in which his readers lived and moved in order to expound the great truths of the Christian life. In 2 Corinthians 4:9 he likens himself to a gladiator who has been overthrown in the ring but whose opponent is refused permission by the presiding dignitary to administer the deathblow: the servant of the Lord is 'struck down, but not destroyed'.

Here, in 4:9, Paul and others with him have been set in an arena as men having no prospect other than death. They are a spectacle to the **'world, both to angels and to men'**, that is, to all rational creatures other than evil angels. Had the devil and his servants been included a qualification would almost certainly have been given. As it is, the ministering angels who marvel at salvation (1 Peter 1:12) witness the apostolic architects of the church appointed by their God as an entertainment for the world and even for those Christians who do not think too hard about matters.

Therefore the apostles are **'fools because of Christ'** (4:10). This is deep irony: at the same time as the Lord is causing his obedient servant a great deal of trouble and personal loss, the Corinthians are **'prudent in Christ'**. Confident in exact proportion to their ignorance, they have avoided adroitly any form of Christian commitment that could menace their creature comforts.

The apostles are **'weak'** (or, 'sick') and without honour whereas the Corinthians are supposedly **'strong'** and **'distinguished'**. Perhaps these darts were being hurled against certain would-be leaders in Corinth. We may infer this because in 1:26-31 it is said that not too many of the people were of rank, from which it follows that the majority would hardly have been so boastful about their real-life situations. Some — yes; but not all.

Notice that Paul makes no attempt to justify himself. Perhaps in anticipation of his elaborate display of 'a little foolishness' in 2 Corinthians 11:1 - 12:10, all he gives here is a stark, black-and-white contrast between the tensions and pathos of his own situation and the pleasant shallowness of the converts.

Irony fades rapidly because it must not be overdone. The usual lifestyle of the apostles is outlined in 4:11-13. Even while Paul writes this letter he and others with him remain hungry, thirsty and poorly clothed (literally, **'naked'**, 4:11). Their deprivation was severe. Further, they were unsettled, lacking any permanent home, and knew what it was to be knocked about physically. The apostle must have been aware that his Master was on one occasion struck in the face (Matt. 26:67).

There was also manual labour: **'We toil, working with our own hands'** (4:12). What, the Corinthians might have asked, is wrong with hard work? Nothing. But the apostle, never ashamed to roll up his sleeves, knew that he should have been maintained financially. It was true that sometimes money changed hands, but this was not always the case. Moreover, such were the occasions for critical backlash that Paul realized it to be in his own and in the general interest for him to be seen to work.[42]

Pathos continues. Paul is **'reviled'**, yet will **'bless'** those who insult him. He is **'persecuted'**, or chased, probably by malevolent Jews, who were always a problem. But because he is motivated he will **'endure'**. The brief catalogue of misfortune climaxes in 4:13. A prime object of slander and always a target for malicious gossip, the apostle along with others **'encourages'**; abuse is countered with kind words instead of hot anger. The NASB gives 'try to conciliate'. A rather harsh paraphrase, this makes Paul out to be some sort of negotiator, which he was not. He goes on to add that he and others have become the **'scum of the world, the dregs of all things, even until now'**.

The Greek word behind **'scum'** *(perikatharmata)* originally stood for an accumulation, or surround, of dirt. As time passed the expression took on additional meaning, 'scum' now being filth that had to be removed by some sort of cleansing agent. From this emerged the idea of purification by means of sacrifice. The word occurs in this sense in the Greek Old Testament in Proverbs 21:18, where we read that 'The wicked is a *ransom* for the righteous.' The second word, **'dregs'** (Greek, *peripsema*), is much the same, in this case meaning the elimination of dirt by wiping something, perhaps a dish, all the way around. Again, the idea of cleansing gave rise to that of sacrifice, as in the apocryphal Tobit 5:19: 'Be not greedy to add money to money: but let it be as *refuse* in respect of our child.' In the context, a mother, Anna, reminds her somewhat avaricious husband that Tobias, their boy, is more important than money, and that the father should sacrifice his ambition to be rich.

Divisions within the church (1:10 - 4:21) 87

The apostle introduces these words because he was sensitive to the fact that the world regarded him and his colleagues as an obscenity to be cleansed away if it were ever to be whole. Nor was this attitude totally foreign to some of the Corinthians. In consequence, they took precautions, tending to walk away from Paul **'even until now'**, that is, when these words were being written.

The apostles were not the last to be regarded as garbage. If we love the Lord we will identify with a universally despised faith and with those who profess it. Read Matthew 25:31-46 and Hebrews 13:3, yet recall the courage of, and consolation given to, Ebed-melech (Jer. 38:1-13; 39:16-18).

The concern of a true father in the Lord (4:14-21)

To summarize, the preceding irony was not egocentric, intended to make the Corinthians ashamed of themselves so that in due course they would tender their apologies to an aggrieved apostle. Rather, he regarded these people as his own children, yearning that the Corinthians might imitate him and appreciate the bond which really did link them.

Fathers and tutors (4:14-16)

Paul was determined to convince the church that he lived to serve the Lord's people. But some were malignant and required considerable persuasion. Therefore a letter was insufficient; a valued helper and friend had to be sent to them. Paul knew well that there are times when face-to-face contact is vital and that just such an occasion had presented itself.

Timothy was the obvious man for the task. He would prepare the way for Paul, travelling to Achaia to remind the congregation about what the apostle taught and about his situation. Although Paul was ready to criticize them to their faces for their unspirituality, he was loath to do so. He hoped that Timothy's visit would make this unnecessary. If so, the apostle's planned meeting with them would turn out to be profitable for all concerned.

In more detail, these unstable Corinthians remained Paul's own **'beloved children'**, in that the Lord had employed him to bring them to faith (4:14). Compare with 9:2: 'You are the seal of my apostleship in the Lord.' Although he has no intention of scoring points in an argument, the apostle asserts his unique relationship with them **'in Christ'**. Let them imagine, then, that they have **'ten thousand tutors'**. Even if this were the case it would remain that they do not have **'many fathers'** (4:15). As in 14:19, 'ten thousand' means a very large number.

The apostle had **'begotten'** them as their unique spiritual father, albeit **'in Christ Jesus'** and **'through the gospel'**. The NASB's 'became your father' possibly over-emphasizes Paul's relationship to them rather than the really important point, that the Corinthians became Christians through his ministry.

The Greek word for **'tutor'** is *paidagôgos*, meaning someone who leads a child. More than a teacher but considerably less than a foster-parent, the pedagogue was usually a slave given the task of supervising the education of the youngster placed in his care. Josephus, who has already been quoted on more than one occasion, retained such a person as a tutor for one of his children.[43] In general, as time passed and when the youth in question grew up the services of the instructor were obviously no longer needed. This is why Galatians 3:24-25 teaches that Moses' law was a temporary 'tutor', or pedagogue, charged to lead the people of God to the maturity of faith in Christ.

In 4:15 Paul's meaning is that because his relationship to the Corinthians remained uniquely and permanently that of a loving parent, they should show him due respect. As far as they are concerned, *he* was no pedagogue. Therefore he pleads with the people to be his imitators (4:16). That Paul strove to be a pattern for his converts comes across again and again in his letters.[44] **'Imitators'** is significant. A lesser figure than the apostle might have established a following, much like Diotrephes or the evil men who would emerge in the church at Ephesus (3 John 9; Acts 20:30).

Timothy was on the way to Corinth (4:17)

So that the Corinthians could be informed about Paul he had already sent Timothy to them from Ephesus, possibly on the slow overland route, to be met at Corinth by the anonymous sea-travelling bearer of this letter. Acts 19:22 may refer to this journey: 'Having sent into Macedonia ... Timothy and Erastus, he [Paul] himself stayed in Asia for a while.'

Divisions within the church (1:10 - 4:21)

The younger man had been charged to tell the people about the apostle's **'ways ... in Christ'**, that is, the circumstances of his ministry. Timothy is said here to possess two qualifications for such a task. First, he was Paul's **'beloved child'**; second, he was **'faithful in the Lord'**. Or, as the NASB has it, the words could mean 'my beloved and faithful child in the Lord', which amounts to the same thing. Like many of the Corinthians, Timothy had come to faith through the ministry of Paul (Acts 16:1; 1 Tim. 1:2). In fact, until the end of his life's work the bond was precious to the apostle. Unlike many of the Corinthians, this young man could be trusted.

The apostle intended to follow Timothy (4:18-21)

Paul was sensitive that there were some at Corinth ready and eager to call in question his personal integrity. This was always a favourite ploy of his detractors.[45] He also knew that it was important for his opponents to be made aware that he had always behaved as an apostle should, and that there was no hidden, darker side to his character; wherever he went he was always the same man with the same message.

To illustrate, an evangelical bishop once told me that, notwithstanding the enormous shift in doctrinal innuendo, he elected to wear different robes when visiting different types of congregation in his diocese: black-and-white in 'low', relatively evangelical churches, and multi-coloured vestments in 'high' churches celebrating the mass. Had Paul worn clerical garb, which he did not, he would have had just one type of outfit, never changing his hue or his theological stance.

Some of the Corinthians were **'puffed up'** (from the Greek, *phusiô*; NASB, 'arrogant'). The word suggests inflation. These glorious believers were like mini hot-air balloons floating high in the sky to display their colours to all who would raise their eyes to behold the fascinating sight. That they were like this is demonstrated by Paul's repeated use of the expression (4:6; 5:2; 8:1; 13:4). Their arrogance had been fuelled by the expressed hope that Paul would never dare to show his face in the church. How convenient! With him away they could rule. Imagine the hurt felt by this gentle man across the sea at Ephesus.

But he remained steadfast. Neither Corinth nor anywhere else was a no-go area for the apostle. In principle he had decided to visit the church **'soon'**, but only **'if the Lord wills'** (4:19). These last words, abbreviated in Christian jargon as 'D.V.' (from the Latin, *Deo volente*), show that Paul anticipated that the Lord might have other arrangements. If the apostle did not arrive at Corinth it would not be because he was scared.

Acts 16:6-8 and Romans 1:10 show that Paul never took travel plans lightly, and never assumed that his planned itinerary would always be put in motion by the Lord. On some occasions providence made the way smooth; on others, the apostle was delayed, sometimes seriously. Either way, the ever-travelling servant of Jesus knew that his journeyings remained safely in the Lord's capable hands.

If and when he finally reached Corinth he would **'find out'** (literally, 'know') the **'power'**, the true capacity, of those who retained an exaggerated opinion of themselves. Were they aware of the presence of the Spirit in their own hearts, or did they rest content with an outward veneer of godliness, failing abysmally to walk with the Lord? The apostle sensed that the latter was probably the case. Should a confrontation come about it would only lead to a display of the people's gross shortcomings.

'The kingdom of God' is the church (4:20). As we shall see when we come to look at 15:24, God's 'kingdom' can stand for the authority that the Lord exercises in the world at large. But here the meaning is that the churches do not depend ultimately upon human talent and resources; they are maintained by their God, the King with his own special domain.

It is likely that this reference to the 'kingdom' finds its roots in 4:8, where the Corinthians are said to have 'become kings'. Perhaps their perception of the kingdom of God was that it was like some sort of earthly empire in which men vie against one another. If so, how mistaken these Christians were! The apostle indicates that if they do not come to their senses before he arrives he will make them see both themselves and him in a true light. The warning is sombre: in the presence of their father-in-God the superficiality and pompousness of these beloved, yet wretched, folk would be unmasked.

It was for them to decide. If they retained their conceit he would exercise his authority and use a **'rod'** (4:21); he would tell them the truth about themselves, and it would hurt. If they reformed he would meet them **'with love and a spirit of gentleness'**; there would be no

Divisions within the church (1:10 - 4:21)

recrimination, no reminder of past follies, no hurt feelings. Which, he asks, is it to be?

'Spirit' in 4:21 probably means the Holy Spirit rather than Paul's human spirit. Analogous expressions might be 'the Spirit of adoption' and 'the Spirit of truth' (Rom. 8:15; 1 John 4:6). If so, the meaning is that, should the people prove sufficiently humble to acknowledge the truth of what he writes, 'the Spirit of gentleness' would help Paul to respond to them in just the right fashion.

In effect the apostle admits that he was no more than a man and that he, too, had powerful emotions. He, just like anyone else, must have the aid of the Spirit of God if he was not to overreact in tense situations.

The end of the beginning

The first part of this great letter is now at an end. It is perhaps a foundation and, paradoxically, almost an apologia for what is to appear in the next twelve chapters. Paul has asserted his office, his authority, his determination and his love. Now, he will particularize about great issues that convulse the Corinthian church, issues that deserve, demand and are addressed by the revealed Word of God through his servant.

3. Immorality in the church
(5:1 - 6:20)

Scandal and the blind eye

We come now to Paul's response to the church's mishandling of an internal scandal. Sadly, someone in the Corinthian fellowship was incestuous. Even worse, his activity did not shock or disgust the church — at least, not too much. Nor was the guilty person overwhelmed with remorse; both the church and he were complacent about the man living in sin yet still identifying with the saints. In effect, the verdict of the Corinthians was that his action was not altogether wrong.

But it was evil. So, too, was the indulgence offered by the church. Paul's accusation is that standards had slipped to a level conspicuously lower than that of the degenerate, unblushing society in which the Corinthians found themselves.

The apostle wrote in the awareness that this case represented only the tip of the iceberg. Looking across the Aegean Sea from Ephesus towards Corinth, he knew that the atmosphere within the fellowship was being systematically poisoned by continual arguments. These quarrels fragmented the people and, as an evil by-product, cut away all resolve to discipline their offending brother. The latter's continuing presence in the church was symptomatic of a deeper, more widespread malaise.

Court action

Although Paul must have had some detailed knowledge of the strife within the church, confidences and names are not betrayed. Nor did they need to be. Almost as a matter of course the people refused to settle their arguments about material possessions in an amicable fashion. Instead, they went the way of the world, resorting to the apparatus of the Corinthian courts to coerce and even to fleece one another.

Sin abounding

There was more. Paul was well aware that not a few of the Corinthians were prone to gross sexual misconduct. In short, sin abounded in this large, clamorous, squabbling, Spirit-endowed community of believers.

Greater magnification

Because these three issues were (and are) so important we look at them in a little more detail before proceeding to chapter and verse.

Ill-discipline

First, there was the church's failure to react to incest (5:1-13). Paul concedes that Christians cannot avoid meeting immoral people in the world. But he insists that it is both possible and necessary for believers to sever such contacts when those who live like this emerge within the church.

Furthermore, banishment is remedial and in no way some sort of punishment exacted by a horrified congregation. The hope is that the offending Christian might repent and eventually be readmitted to the fellowship.

Paul makes the profoundly important point that sexual sin is dangerous because it is highly addictive. When tolerated in a church it is rather like leaven in dough: spreading easily, it rapidly affects the whole lump. The apostle shows that even as the Israelites removed all the leaven from their dwellings during the Passover feast, the church can only rejoice in Christ, its unique sacrifice, when it makes every effort to be pure.

Dissension

The second section addresses the scandal of Christians taking one another to court (6:1-11). The fellowship is reminded of the astounding truth that the saints, the redeemed people of God, have been designated by the Lord as the judges of other men and of angels. It must be wrong, then, for the Corinthians to appeal for justice to those whom they must eventually judge.

The apostle allows that serious personal disagreements had arisen within the Corinthian church. His counsel is that those concerned should seek out trustworthy Christians to act as unbiased and disinterested arbitrators. Should this course fail, it would be better for believers to suffer loss rather than to go to the courts for redress of grievance.

Paul shows that there is reason for this. Although it was bad enough for the world to witness the sorry spectacle of believers at war among themselves, there was the ever-present risk of a greater evil: Christians in court might well strive to take material advantage of their brethren even when they knew that they, the accusers, were in the wrong. The apostle realized that the virus of greed is always present in Christian hearts.

The readers of the letter are reminded that deliberate and persistent sinners can never enter the kingdom of God. It follows that the Corinthians needed to beware. Even so, the apostle gives encouragement. Whatever their problems, these people were the Lord's: they had been washed and justified by Christ and by the Holy Spirit.

Personal immorality

The third section deals with private sexual misbehaviour (6:12-20).

It is conceded that the Christian believer enjoys a considerable degree of liberty in his private conduct. But this does not mean that it is right for him to be sexually promiscuous.

Paul introduces what was probably a sensitive issue. His teaching is that because the stomach and food were made for each other by God, the believer is not governed by any dietary restrictions and is free to eat anything he chooses. But it is not like this with God-given sexual instincts: the Christian's body was not fashioned by the Lord with a view to extra-marital intimacies. A free table does not imply free love. Rather, the body was designed to belong to the Lord. It follows that if a Christian fornicates Jesus becomes involved indirectly in immoral conduct, something that should never happen. The only way to pre-empt such an appalling situation is to run away from temptation.

Immorality in the church (5:1 - 6:20)

There is another remarkable truth bound up in Paul's analysis of sexual immorality. In its way the latter stands by itself in that there is no other sin quite like it. This is because in this area of misconduct the body exploits its own energies to do wrong. Whereas other sins injure the temple by exploiting materials brought in from outside, sexual impurity desecrates the shrine of God from within.

Furthermore, because the believer has been bought by Christ he is not free to act in a way contrary to the will of his purchaser.

There must be discipline (5:1-13)

Paul turns to the Corinthians' failure to deal adequately with scandal among themselves. He outlines his own decision about the matter and then clarifies what he wrote in an earlier letter on the subject of sexual misconduct.

The decision has been taken (5:1-8)

The apostle was aware that Corinth was a thoroughly immoral place. But he knew that the Christians there were now 'saints', or holy people; the Lord had purged their hearts. We recall that this letter began with a definition of believers as 'those ... who have been sanctified in Christ Jesus' (1:2). Even so, Paul was acutely conscious that it must have been no light matter for some, perhaps a sizeable minority, to break completely with the customs and behaviour of those among whom they lived. He understood well that the body can 'burn' (7:9).

Even the world would have blushed (5:1)

One believer, tactfully unnamed by Paul although certainly known to him and to the whole church, had disgraced himself. The problem was aggravated because the fellowship turned a blind eye to what he had done, steadfastly refusing to remove him from their communion.

Dismay and shock were felt by many Christians elsewhere when this sad news reached them: **'It is actually reported that there is immorality among you.'** The Greek word *holôs* behind 'actually' means 'everywhere' or 'generally' (as in our 'holistic'); the story had been spreading through the churches like wildfire.

Moreover, what had happened was unusually repulsive. Paul observes that the offence was rare among the **'Gentiles'**. The apostle is realistic, rebuking the church because in this respect they had fallen beneath the shockingly low standards of society. A man in the church had taken a woman who previously was his father's wife, and had committed this sin after being converted and baptized. He had infringed the law of nature and that of Christ.

The world in which Corinth found itself was broadminded, although not usually to this extent, about what the New Testament terms 'fornication'. Cicero, a Roman lawyer who lived a century before Paul, wrote disparagingly about Sassia, mother of one of his clients and a lady who had married a son-in-law. The lawyer declares with righteous indignation, 'Oh! to think of the woman's sin, unbelievable, unheard of ... in all experience, save for this single instance!' Perhaps he exaggerated because there is, after all, nothing new under the sun. Such incest was perpetrated by Reuben, was prohibited by Moses' law, and became a device by which Absalom sought to discredit his father.[1] The Corinthians had managed to excel themselves by acquiescing in this folly.

In stating that the church could be, and perhaps was, the object of 'Gentile' comment, Paul implies deliberately, and not for the first time, that the non-Jewish Christians there were no longer Gentiles; rather, they had come to belong to the Messianic Israel. This principle is vitally important. As we travel through 1 Corinthians we shall find again and again that Paul builds upon the truth that the churches are the counterpart to the Israel that left Egypt under the guidance of Moses.

This sordid relationship between a man and his father's wife is seen by Paul as a marriage rather than an affair. This is indicated by the delicate allusion to the fact that the transgressor **'has'** the woman.[2] It follows that the illicit partner, **'his father's wife'**, must have been the man's stepmother. Had she been his natural parent Paul would undoubtedly have mentioned the fact.

To appreciate the sensitivity of the situation we need to take into account 2 Corinthians 7:12: 'So although I wrote to you it was not for the sake of the offender, nor for the sake of the one offended, but that your earnestness on our behalf might be made known to you in the sight of God.' Almost certainly the reference here is to both the offending incestuous man and his outraged natural father.[3] From this

Immorality in the church (5:1 - 6:20)

it would appear that the latter was still living, thus aggravating an extraordinarily serious post-baptismal sin.

Cowardice and conceit (5:2)

The church as a whole remained **'arrogant'**, or 'inflated'. These self-assured Corinthians refused flatly to react to one of their own who had entered into a form of marriage with his stepmother. It is likely that their hesitation was reinforced by their own perverse logic rather than by a naïve ignorance of just what they ought to do. Not only were these people slippery, too scared to grapple with the matter; they may have felt themselves pushed into a corner. Were they to do something about this particular offence they could have been embarrassed by an accusation rather like that of Romans 2:22: 'You who say that one should not commit adultery, do you commit adultery?' If one cupboard were opened, how many more skeletons might be seen lurking behind other doors when they came to be unlocked?

Paul was able to speak candidly about such matters because his pure conscience did not trouble him about sex. The whole fellowship (**'you'**, plural) should have **'mourned'** this appalling act. 'Mourn' might suggest that the man in question had contrived to sever himself from the body of Christ as if by dying. But the church had failed to see this and had not come to terms with its sad loss. Had they been ready to lament, the person **'who had done this deed'** (with some emphasis upon 'this') would have been removed from **'your midst'**, from the heart of the fellowship. We can picture the scene. Possibly accompanied by his consort, this man remained in the centre of a not disapproving community.

Paul steps in (5:3-5)

Although the Corinthians did nothing, Paul exercises his authority to excommunicate, as indicated by the words, **'in the name of our Lord Jesus'**. This was no new formula. A few years earlier the apostle had instructed the Thessalonians: '... in the name of our Lord Jesus Christ, that you keep aloof from every brother who leads an unruly life and not according to the tradition which you received from us'.[4]

Paul knew that although Christians are not condemned by the law of God, they are obliged to obey everything he commands. He knew also that the Christian code of conduct was even then being handed over to the churches.

Although the apostle's not infrequent longer sentences can sometimes be split up in translation to make for easier reading, the exercise runs the risk of over-simplification. It is like this with 5:3-5. Let's write these verses down as a single sentence and then try to work out the meaning:

> **For I, indeed, being absent in body but being present in spirit, have (as one who is present) in the name of our Lord Jesus already judged the person who has accomplished this in such a way: when you and my spirit are assembled, together with the power of our Lord Jesus, to deliver such a person to Satan for the destruction of the flesh, so that the spirit may be saved in the day of the Lord.**

The NASB and Lenski attach **'in the name of our Lord Jesus'** to the following phrase, **'when you and my spirit are assembled'**, conveying the thought that the church, as Christ's executor in this matter, would act in his name. This may be the intended meaning although it might be better to attach these words to 5:3, as Hodge does. On this interpretation they give necessary weight to the apostle's authority in a stressful situation: 'I ... have ... in the name of the Lord Jesus already judged the person.'[5]

Writing from Ephesus, the apostle asks his readers to imagine that he is in a sense present with them at Corinth. Without Paul the church could, and should, have expelled the offender, but did not. Now the apostle is unprepared to take the burden from their shoulders: they must face up to their responsibility and show their revulsion and repentance by exercising discipline as if he were there in person chairing their meeting. Compare this requirement with the way in which, centuries earlier, Israel had to isolate and then deal with Achan. The Lord told Joshua that someone had offended but left Israel to see to the matter.[6]

Paul reveals his verdict, given in the name of Christ, and explains exactly how it is to be put into effect. The church must assemble. Although he is absent physically, his apostolic authority remains with the people: they are to abide by the instructions that he now delivers to them. Further, his authority is accompanied by the **'power of our Lord Jesus'**: the risen Christ will ensure that the gathered

Immorality in the church (5:1 - 6:20)

church obeys Paul's judgement, that the man who has accomplished this atrocious act be handed over, as a prisoner to his guard, to Satan.

Occurring twenty times in Paul's letters but only twice elsewhere in the New Testament, **'accomplished'** (5:3; Greek, *katergazomai*) conveys the idea of a sense of achievement: Paul suspects that the guilty person, together with his cronies, reckoned the deed as an innovative and triumphant challenge to established standards.

In the New Testament deliverance to the prince of darkness is mentioned elsewhere only in 1 Timothy 1:20, where Paul writes that Hymenaeus and Alexander had been 'delivered to Satan, so that they may be taught not to blaspheme'. The sense is much the same although the meaning may not lie on the surface.

A possible interpretation of 5:5 could be that the Corinthian offender, cast out by the church and left in a world dominated by Satan, will find himself in a prodigal-son type of situation (Luke 15:11-32). All restraints are removed and he gives himself up to unbridled sin. But in spite of everything he remains a believer in whom the still, small voice of conscience makes itself heard. For this reason his numerous excesses finally disgust and exhaust him. He repents and turns back to the Lord, resolving to terminate the marriage with his stepmother.

This is plausible, but there might be a better approach: the deliverance of the man to Satan precipitates the providential infliction of some severe physical evil, namely, the **'destruction'** of the **'flesh'** abused by the offender. In other words, Paul anticipates that the married man's health is to be brought to ruin. Grievously ill, or even dying, he seeks the Lord. Eventually he departs this world and goes to be with Christ, ultimately to be saved **'in the day of the Lord Jesus'**, that is, at the end of the world when the Lord shall appear. This dovetails with what Paul has written already about Christians being confirmed permanently in the faith, and vice versa, and about ministerial failures who will do no better than scrape into heaven (1:8; 3:15).

That grievous sickness and even death *were* inflicted upon some Corinthians because of their carnality is shown by 11:30: 'For this reason many among you are weak and sick, and a number sleep.' There are other considerations as well that give weight to the second interpretation of the judgement of the offender. Satan was the divinely-appointed agent of Job's sufferings. Paul was afflicted acutely by the evil one, as was a certain 'daughter of Abraham'.[7]

Even though these people were not living in sin, such parallels might reinforce the suggestion that deliverance to Satan meant illness, leading ultimately to the decease of the incestuous believer.

Leavened and unleavened bread (5:6-8)

When he wrote these instructions the apostle was acutely aware that the Corinthians would probably remain truculent. He knew also that they were **'boasting'** about the manner in which they played fast and loose with established standards, an assertiveness that was **'not good'** (5:6). We can imagine him sighing in sorrow as he deliberately understated the issue.

Now comes a question to which the answer is affirmative: do the people not realize that a tiny amount of leaven can affect a large quantity of dough? But what leaven and what dough? In Galatians 5:9, as in Matthew 16:6-12, Mark 8:15 and Luke 12:1, leaven is either a combination of bad doctrine and malpractice or a profession of faith not backed up by holy living. The latter was the case at Corinth, where gross misconduct followed baptism. We could compare with 15:33, 'Do not be deceived, "Bad company corrupts good morals,"' and this might throw some light upon the problems addressed in chapters 5 and 6. The dough stands for the church because it had placed itself at risk through an indifferent attitude to sin.

In a deliberate recall of Moses' regulations for Passover, Paul instructs the people to cleanse away the **'old leaven'**[8] old because the incestuous man represents the unregenerate world to which the Corinthians no longer belong. Because their hearts are **'unleavened'** they need to present themselves as a **'new lump'**, making every effort to resemble bread baked without yeast (5:7).

Connected with this is a second reason for the church's separation from this sinful man: Christ had **'been sacrificed'** as the Corinthians' **'Passover'**.[9]

According to Exodus 12:39, at the time of the original Passover the people of Israel left Egypt so rapidly that there was no time remaining for the bread for that day to be leavened. Had they prepared their loaves with yeast they would have delayed themselves, and a delay would have implied a desire to stay where they were and share the sins of Egypt. As Moses reminded the people forty years later, they came out of Egypt 'in haste' because they knew that this was their only sensible option (Deut. 16:3). The angel

Immorality in the church (5:1 - 6:20)

of death was abroad and they could not afford to waste a single minute. It was so, too, with Lot and his family. Because his wife's affections remained in Sodom, so did her body (Gen. 19:26; Luke 17:32).

Paul's application of the Passover procedure is that if Christians do not hasten to remove the leaven of sin from their private lives and from the church they are saying something. They declare that they want to remain in the evil and perishing world from which their Passover Lamb, Christ, redeemed them by his death. They contradict their baptismal vows and dishonour their God. They bring rapid judgement upon their defenceless heads.

An encouragement is supplied: **'You are in fact unleavened.'** Compare with Romans 6:7: 'For he who has died is freed from sin'; or with John 13:10: 'He who has bathed needs only to wash his feet, but is completely clean.' The apostle is saying that the Corinthians *are* dead to the world and that they *have* been cleansed: they are truly converted people who remain the objects of God's powerful grace rather than unregenerate sinners controlled by evil desires. This glorious state to which they have been brought means that any residual leaven, or sin, in their lives would be a gross contradiction. Therefore, let them do something about the incestuous man.

The application is developed in 5:8. **'The feast'** is neither the Jewish Passover meal nor the Lord's Supper. Wonderfully, it is the whole of a Christian's earthly existence. Because every day is part of our lifelong festival, **'Let us therefore celebrate** ['continue celebrating', present tense] **the feast.'**

In Israel the feasts were times separated for the worship of the Lord (read, for example, Exod. 12:14 and Lev. 23:2). Paul indicates that a new system has been introduced to the churches, fellowships that in the aggregate are nothing other than the Messianic Israel anticipated by the Old Testament. In this final situation there are no set festivals. Right around the clock and right through the calendar the disciple is to shun the **'old leaven'**, described further as that of **'malice and wickedness'**.

Perhaps an observation might be made about Jewish Christians, those of the natural family of Abraham to whom God has given saving faith like that of the patriarch (Rom. 4:12). There is no absolute necessity for the Hebrew believer to keep the Passover, an outdated yearly anticipation of Messianic reality. His whole life is in principle a Passover feast because the Anointed One is his Passover Lamb.

In 5:8 **'malice'** (Greek, *kakia*), a stronger word than **'wickedness'** (Greek, *poneria*), implies a heart that feeds on wrongdoing. The believer is not to eat up, and be eaten up by, hatred. His sole diet for the lifelong festival is to be **'unleavened loaves of sincerity and truth'**.

Clearing up deliberate misunderstanding (5:9-13)

Apparently, some of the Corinthians did not understand, or had chosen not to understand, earlier counsel from Paul on the subject of Christian morality. This is why the apostle refers to the contents of a previous letter to the church, a letter that has not survived (5:9).[10]

Making matters plain (5:9-11)

Paul reminds his readers that he had instructed them not to associate with **'fornicators'**. The NASB gives 'immoral people'. This weakens the sense because not all immorality is necessarily sexual, whereas a fornicator is, by definition, someone who is sexually active beyond the bounds of marriage. To put it another way, fornication can be committed by unmarried people. Then it is a sin other than that of adultery. Or it can be committed by those who are married, but not to each other, in which case it is also adultery.

The problem of mingling habitually with sexually promiscuous people is addressed. Although these evil associations must stop there is one obvious situation where the principle of avoidance does not hold good (5:10). When the saints meet, as is inevitable, with unconverted folk, they cannot escape contact with sexually impure, covetous, extortionate and idolatrous men **'of this world'**. To do so the Corinthians would **'have to go out of the world'**. Quitting the street or the building which they share, perhaps, with unbelievers, they would need to rocket away from the planet to a different habitat in order to relax in sanitized seclusion. Paul is eager to show that this counsel of despair is unnecessary: there is a tactic more efficient and less complicated than extra-terrestrial monasticism.

The earlier communication was unambiguous. Even so, because the people seem to have misunderstood his words the apostle explains the matter again. A very patient teacher dealing with disciples who have to unlearn, he spells out his requirements in no uncertain terms.

Immorality in the church (5:1 - 6:20)

The Corinthians (5:11) should not mingle with any **'so-called brother'**, that is, a professing Christian, who is a known fornicator or who is perceived to be an **'idolater'** or **'reviler'** (slanderer) or **'drunkard'** or **'swindler'**. They should not even eat with **'such a one'**. Because the latter is a renegade whose notorious conduct is unacceptable he must be quarantined by the church.

By **'idolater'** could be meant the saint who eats heathen sacrifices in the company of unbelievers, maybe in order to cement social or business ties. Paul will enlarge upon this ultra-sensitive issue in 10:14-22. The practice, apparently not unknown at Corinth, is roundly condemned by 5:11. Then as now, Christian principles apparently were in danger of collapse before the pressures of family and business life.

The apostle decrees that in the event of immorality being detected the church's response must be something more drastic than the removal of the guilty persons from the privileges and formalities of church life. Even so, church action is to be less than handing over to Satan: at most, offenders are to be avoided socially by the fellowship. Although Christians inevitably meet people of this stamp in everyday life, they must shun a baptized person who disgraces himself.

Paul, the church and the outside world (5:12-13)

The apostle knows that his authority extends only to Christians: **'For what have I to do with judging outsiders?'** (5:12). The words 'What have I to do with?' are peculiarly Jewish.[11] The meaning here is that it is not Paul's responsibility to sit in judgement upon those who remain outside the kingdom of God; they are not his problem and he will have nothing to do with adjudicating their complaints. His attitude is reminiscent (perhaps deliberately so) of the way in which our Lord handled an aggrieved brother who wanted Jesus to sort out an inheritance (Luke 12:13-15). The principle is that, if it was not Paul's calling to get involved in this way, the Corinthians should not be similarly entangled. They were to imitate him, be anxious for their own church, assess Christians who lapsed into grievous sin — and avoid probing the sins of others.

An explanation is given for the limitation: God **'judges'** those who are **'outside'**, those who had not been received into church fellowship (5:13). The verb 'judges' might be 'will judge', depending upon the Greek accentuation (*krinei*, present; *krineî*, future), although this does not change the sense. Because of what the Lord does, or will do, the Corinthians are to commit the world and its sins to God. The misdeeds of others are not their responsibility.

An apparent problem looms: it looks as if Paul is in the process of contradicting the rhetorical question of 6:2, 'Do you not know that the saints will judge the world?', and the accompanying flat statement that 'The world is judged by you.' The difficulty is that in 5:12 he says that the saints ought not to judge the world and in 6:2 claims that the saints are judging it. In the event, as we might expect from an inspired writer, and as we shall see when we come to look at 6:2, there is no clash.

The apostle redirects his attention to the professing Christian who married his stepmother: **'Remove the wicked man from among yourselves.'** This instruction is an unmistakable recall of the law of Moses (Deut. 17:7; 19:19; 22:21,24; 24:7). Idolaters, slanderers and sexually impure people were to be removed from Israel once and for all by death. Once again, it is implied that the Corinthians are the counterparts of Israel at Sinai.

The apostle has already delivered the man to Satan. Therefore the church must exclude him from their company. Up to the time of writing of 1 Corinthians they had singularly failed to do this.

Excommunication

Before we pass to chapter 6 and to an issue which was (and is) red-hot, we ought to apply the teaching of chapter 5 about church discipline.

Basically, removal from a local church is the prerogative neither of any association of churches, nor of the minister or elders within a wounded fellowship, even though in this type of situation the leadership must give a lead. It is a decision for the gathered congregation only. With regard to the incestuous man at Corinth, Paul showed what had to be done because the church was the executive authority. It should be like this today: the Bible legislates and the people act.

Nor is excommunication optional. A church *must* respond in this way when the situation warrants it, both in its own interests and in those of the offender. If action is not taken the communion of saints will soon become the communion of sinners.

There is more. Christian churches have no warrant to go beyond avoidance when they discipline their people. In the Israel of the Old

Immorality in the church (5:1 - 6:20) 105

Testament offenders were removed by death. In the Israel of the New Testament they are to be shut out from the fellowship. This is all.

The relevance of 1 Corinthians 5 for today

At the present time the question of homosexuality is a live issue in some Christian communions. It would appear that this vice is increasingly acknowledged as somehow being a legitimate expression of sexuality. Admittedly, 1 Corinthians 5 is concerned with heterosexual rather than homosexual sin, even though the latter was not unknown (6:9). Even so, and this is the abiding significance of the chapter, churches which decline to remove known sinners (and sodomy *is* a sin) from office find themselves in precisely the same impossible situation as that of the Corinthians with their incestuous brother: because they tolerate evil the world looks on and the faith is laughed to scorn.

Christians in secular courts (6:1-11)

The letter passes without a break to another scandal, that of Christians taking fellow-believers to court. Paul claims that the practice is altogether wrong. His doctrine is that difficulties among Christians should not arise, but if and when they do they ought to be resolved within the congregation. The secular tribunals to which appeals were being made were inappropriate because they represented a world alienated from Christ and from all who belong to him. It follows that the Corinthians demeaned themselves by such malpractice.

Sanctified common sense, please (6:1-4)

An appeal is addressed to the people's sense of reason (6:1): **'Does any one of you, having a matter with another person, dare to be judged by the unrighteous, and not before the saints?'**

The verb **'dare'** is in the present tense, indicating that litigation had become a settled habit among the Corinthians; this is how they were accustomed to settle their differences. In Paul's day **'having a matter'** (Greek, *pragma echôn*) was virtually a technical expression for being involved in a lawsuit. Josephus uses the same turn of phrase, remarking that wealthy folk often hired those who administered 'matters' to go to court on their behalf.[12]

The world and the church (6:1)

By **'unrighteous'** Paul means unbelievers, described in this way because they do not submit to what God reveals to them about himself. They prefer to remain in the wrong about the most important issue of life, man's duty to love and serve his Maker. 'Even though they knew God, they did not honour him as God, or give thanks' (Rom. 1:21).

It follows that **'saints'**, the holy people of God, have no business to appeal to tribunals belonging to the wicked world. Why not? Let's be sure about what Paul says. His argument is not pragmatic, based on the notion that nothing succeeds like success and that what could turn out to be a costly failure is wrong for the believer. He does not warn the Corinthians away from the courts because Christian plaintiffs would do better to settle their own affairs among themselves rather than receive rough justice from the magistrates. Although prudence might favour the private arbitration of their quarrels, this is not his meaning.

The author of this letter, we know, appealed to Nero Caesar on one memorable occasion (Acts 25:11). We have come across this monster already.[13] Suetonius, a Roman historian, records that the emperor planned to drown (or crush) his mother Agrippina in a collapsible boat. When the scheme failed he sent someone to assassinate her. Many Christians, said by another writer, Tacitus, to have been 'detested for their abominable crimes', were cruelly put to death by Nero to satisfy his blood-lust. Even so, Paul had no scruples about submitting what was in effect part of the Lord's business to such an evil man.[14]

In a courtroom scene the apostle told one of his assessors, King Herod Agrippa II, that the latter was 'knowledgeable in all customs and questions among the Jews' (Acts 26:3). True though this may have been, the monarch was also notoriously immoral, a petty princeling and a client of Rome who lacked stature. We recall that the apostle was prepared to answer for himself before Gallio at Corinth, a man who could not have cared less about Jewish religion or perhaps any religion (Acts 18:14-15). Apparently, when it suited

Immorality in the church (5:1 - 6:20)

him Paul did not practise what he preached. An explanation is required.

Bear in mind that when he was hailed involuntarily before judges the apostle's disputes were never with other Christians. What he teaches here is that when believers find themselves at loggerheads with their brethren in the Lord about personal relationships, as might happen, they should work through their problems with the help of the church, the Christian family. Their difficulties ought to be considered essentially as in-house tensions, remaining hidden from unbelievers who, because they are in their sins, would not be able to give effective counsel.

The church, the world, and angels (6:2-3)

Elsewhere Paul sometimes confronts his readers with the challenge, 'Do you not know...?' in order to impress important truths upon their minds.[15] This is how it is in 6:2: **'Or do you not know that the saints will judge the world?'** The underlying Greek word for 'world' is *kosmos*, by which is meant the ordered realm that God created. The verse teaches that there will be a time when Christian people will sit in judgement over their fellows and also over the angelic host, that company of blessed non-human messengers sent from God. That the church will participate in the judgement of the world is a truth taught by the Bible, and Paul must have been aware that he was not introducing some novel, hitherto unknown doctrine.[16]

Then follows a statement that is even more astonishing: **'By you the world is judged.'** The present tense (Greek, *krinetai*), which could be rendered 'is being judged', is dramatic. When Paul was writing these words he must have visualized the process of judgement, that of the world, but presumably not of the angels, already in operation. His meaning is that both the judges and the accused have taken their places in court and that the assessment procedure operates here and now, although obviously not by church intervention in political and social issues.

Even though the apostle is not hard to understand, his claim is so subtle that its inner meaning almost eludes us. What is said here has its foundation in the preceding verse, 6:1, with its flat statement that unbelievers are 'unrighteous' and that believers are 'saints'. The sense is that sheep and goats, wheat and tares and saints and sinners are being separated out from one another in this present world. The implication is that saints stare at sinners with a glare so intense that it amounts to a sentence of condemnation.

At first sight this is baffling. How can this be if, according to Paul's express declaration, Christians cannot 'go out of the world'? (5:10). Like the psalmist, they lack the wings of a dove with which to escape (Ps. 55:6). How can there be a court procedure? How can the Lord's people be sitting in judgement on their fellows when they live alongside them, breathe the same air, drink the same water, buy from the same shops and eventually find themselves buried in the same earth as those who are without God and hope in this world? But, claims Paul, they *do* judge their unbelieving friends and neighbours, and they are doing it all the time.

The meaning is that there is always a spontaneous tension when Christians and non-Christians come into personal contact. Because their values and allegiances are diametrically opposed, the church being in the right about God and unbelievers in the wrong, even the quiet, unassuming presence of a saintly believer is a rebuff to the unconverted person. The latter senses that here is someone who is strangely different, and he feels uncomfortable. Perhaps, like some whose partners are Christians, or like the Philippian jailer, he will be converted; perhaps not (7:16; 1 Peter 3:1-2; Acts 16:29-30). What is definite is that the tension is felt on both sides: the Christian sorrows because the other does not at the moment receive the truth, and the unbeliever is resentful because his godless status quo is being quietly challenged.

Consider solitary Christians in their families, colleges or places of work, or isolated evangelical churches in towns or villages, say in France or Malaysia, or in any one of a thousand other places around the globe. The truth is that neither those believers nor those churches remain unnoticed by others. It is impossible. The families, institutions, work-colleagues or neighbours where there are born-again Christians *know* that they are being condemned by the presence of some among them who love the Lord and who loathe unbelief.

This is exactly how it was in the Corinth of Paul's time. Those in the licentious crossroads city who had washed themselves (6:11), but who had no prospect other than that of staying in the place, were a permanent rebuke to their fellows. It was in *this* respect that the Corinthians were judging others, and it is in this respect that every

Immorality in the church (5:1 - 6:20)

godly believer who lives for the Lord condemns his society. He alone is light and salt; everywhere else there is degradation and darkness (Matt. 5:13-14).

The apostle continues. If the whole world is being, and will be, judged by the church, are believers **'unworthy'** of the **'smallest tribunals'**? (6:2). He pleads for a negative answer. 'Smallest' could be rendered 'least significant', and 'tribunals' as 'lawsuits'.[17] The NASB gives 'not competent' instead of 'unworthy'. But Corinthian loss of face, rather than incompetence, was the primary issue.

The insignificant tribunals or lawsuits were not arguments thrashed out in the courts. Rather, they were heated discussions bubbling up among Christians, men who broke bread together. Paul asks if it is beneath the dignity of non-involved Christians to concern themselves with relatively insignificant issues that occur among their own people. Certainly not. This is because even apparently serious disputes in a fellowship are almost as nothing in contrast to the gravity of the scene in which the saints will exercise a judicial function. If the church is inextricably involved in the greater, it ought not to ignore the lesser.

'Do you not know that we shall judge angels? How much more, matters of this life?' (6:3). Paul's argument expands: the Corinthians' future involvement with mighty angels demands that they must look to their own business now, attending with care to the relatively trivial dissensions that sometimes exasperate their own people in this world.[18]

Because **'angels'** are mentioned without qualification (cf. 4:9: 'We have become a spectacle ... to angels'), the reference would be to the holy angels rather than to the devil and his messengers. In what sense are believers to judge these servants of the Lord who never fall into sin? The answer might be that judging is equivalent to governing, as in Matthew 19:28, when Jesus says that the twelve apostles are to be seated on twelve thrones, judging or administering the twelve tribes of Israel. The meaning would be that the glorified church is to be given a status superior to that of the angelic host.

People who worship idols are despicable (6:4)

The tragedy of legal battles in which some Corinthians engage is now mentioned. The verse is probably a question: **'Therefore, if you have tribunals of this life, do you appoint them, those who**

have been despised by the church?' The NASB paraphrases well by describing 'them' as 'judges'. The reference is not to an element in the church more contemptible than other believers, but to the despicable world which the Corinthians, in their selfish folly, have introduced to arbitrate in their quarrels.

According to 1:28, the majority of the Corinthians were despised by the world. Here the apostle acknowledges that the feeling is mutual. Paul's language is strong, reflecting the opinion held by the Corinthians, and by him, about unconverted idolaters: people who commit this disgusting sin are themselves worthy of disgust. It is a shocking thing, then, if the services of contemptible idolaters are obtained, possibly with money, to settle disputes among the believers. Because the former are natural men who cannot 'understand ... the things of the Spirit of God' (2:14) there is no chance that they would be able to apply godly wisdom and a loving spirit in reconciling Christians at war with one another. Their common sense and experience in handling the law would not count.

Paul intends to make the Corinthians feel ashamed and can do so because he is not involved personally in their unnecessary disputes (6:5). We should compare with 4:14: 'I do not write these things [about myself] to shame you, but to admonish you'; the apostle would never, ever, embarrass the people in order to justify or gratify himself.

The church should put its own house in order (6:5-7)

Paul wants to know if **'there is no man among you who is not wise?'** He uses a double negative which implies that yes, of course, there must be someone competent to **'decide'**, that is, to arbitrate or adjudicate, for his brother (6:5). The idea of arbitration comes to the fore because the believers who might be brought in to advise are not judges whose word is law.

'Brother' in the singular rather than the plural 'brothers' is found in the underlying Greek text of 6:5, contrary to the NASB reading. Paul's probable meaning is that one brother could be concerned with one difficulty and another brother with a different quarrel. No one man in the church should be appointed as the instituted conciliator for all the people.

Many of the Corinthians were at fault in at least two respects (6:6). First, there were some who sought judgement at law rather

Immorality in the church (5:1 - 6:20)

than settling for private arbitration. Second, they sought such judicial satisfaction **'before unbelievers'**. This folly was almost beyond belief. On the other hand, given the shallowness and selfishness of many of the Corinthians, perhaps some of them did not care overmuch about principles. Putting this to one side, the apostle wants to know how they can be confident that worldly courts will give them the satisfaction they crave. He knows that there can be no such certainty.

Apart from the sad fact that the Corinthians took their complaints to court, the impulse to look for judgement was already a **'defeat** [or, 'loss'] **for you'** (6:7), irrespective of what might or might not be the outcome. The word 'defeat' (Greek, *ettema*) occurs in Romans 11:12, which teaches that Israel had forfeited much by its rejection of Christ; blessings that the people could have had passed them by. Similarly, the Corinthians have lost both personal dignity and spiritual blessing by defending themselves and accusing other believers in the local courts.

Paul tells them what to do: why not **'be wronged'**? Why not **'be defrauded'**? Note the present tense in both cases: the people should be big enough to go on absorbing injuries and insults without hitting back. In other words, the Corinthians would help themselves by not fighting in court. Quite apart from the fact that litigation would presumably be far from cheap, a squandering of money which Paul does not even mention here, the desire to take such action must degrade all concerned. From a purely practical view non-retaliation is much more effective.

How low could they get? (6:8-10)

The apostle has more to say about this misconduct: some Corinthians were being exploited deliberately by other Christians. He is explicit: **'On the contrary, you yourselves wrong and defraud, and that your brethren'** (6:8).

Apparently, some of these saints were going to court, not to protect themselves, albeit in a misguided fashion, but in cold blood to seize the assets of other believers. Paul shudders. How despicable could they be? He asks the church seriously if it does not realize that habitually **'unrighteous'** people can never **'inherit the kingdom of God'** (6:9-10); some of them were perilously near disaster even though they had been baptized.

In 4:20 'the kingdom of God' means the church of God now, in this world. But here the expression indicates the blessed state to be ushered in when Christ appears again. This ties up with 15:50: 'Flesh and blood cannot inherit the kingdom of God.' The long-term security of some professing believers was on the line.

In 6:1 unbelievers are characterized as 'unrighteous'. Here, exactly the same word is applied to those Corinthians who were busily defrauding their brethren. The epithet is brought in because they behaved like unregenerate men who live in their sins; if there was a difference it was well disguised. Perhaps there is an anticipation here of 2 Corinthians 13:5, which challenges the people to 'test' themselves to see if they were 'in the faith'.

Be this as it may, what we read in 6:9 is an astonishingly objective analysis of the church's low spiritual condition. The Corinthians basked in considerable self-esteem, reckoning themselves to be prudent and strong (4:10). In reality they remained ignorant of one of the first principles of true religion, that a tree is known by its fruit and a man by what he does (Matt. 7:16,20; 12:33; Luke 6:43-44). They seemed to be oblivious of the fact that someone who sins habitually must have an unclean heart and can be no child of God. Because such a person has no wealthy Father whom he loves and who loves him there can be nothing of value for him to inherit. The church, then, should not **'be deceived'**, or (better), 'be led astray'. These words imply that it is remarkably easy for men to live in sin all the while supposing that they will eventually go to heaven. By no means, writes Paul.

A representative list is given of those who must be excluded from the kingdom of God should they not repent. Adulterers are married people who break their marriage vows; the effeminate are those who are soft or tender, that is, voluptuous; while homosexuals are, in terms of the background Greek word, 'those who go to bed with men'. Idolaters might be included in this catalogue of vice because idol worship was invariably unclean.[19]

'Love believes all things' (6:11)

The church's spiritual father does not despair. Paul cannot, and will not, jettison the conviction that although the Corinthians do tend to deceive themselves they are not flagrant sinners at heart. He

Immorality in the church (5:1 - 6:20) 113

anticipates 13:7 and echoes the thought of Hebrews 6:9: 'We are convinced of better things concerning you, and things that accompany salvation, though we are speaking in this way.' Although some in the fellowship had been evil, the Lord had intervened.

The interjection **'but'** is employed three times, no less, to emphasize the tremendous threefold change in the lives of these people. Let's modify the NASB reading slightly to try to bring out the emphasis: '**... *but* you have had yourselves washed, *but* you were sanctified, *but* you were justified in the name of the Lord Jesus Christ, and in the Spirit of our God'**.

The meaning behind **'washed'** is as clear as could be: the Corinthians had taken steps to make themselves clean. Although the reference might not be solely, or even primarily to water-baptism, this should not be ruled out entirely. After all, the ordinance is part of the complex experience in which a sinner cleanses himself, identifies with Christ and is received into the church. We could compare with 10:2, where the apostle writes that by following Moses the children of Israel had sought baptism in the cloud and in the sea. In Acts 22:16, too, he records that he had been instructed to get himself baptized and washed.[20]

The burden of 6:11 is that the formerly sinful Corinthians had taken an eager step towards spiritual and moral cleanliness. Further, their determination had been acknowledged by God: they were set apart by him and considered as righteous. Perhaps it would be useful to parallel this statement with Ephesians 5:26, which connects baptism and holiness: 'that he [Christ] might sanctify her, having cleansed her [the church] by the washing of water with the word'. This makes at least two related assertions: the separation of the church is undertaken by the Saviour in person, and the process by which he does this includes the ordinance of water-baptism.

The qualification of 6:11 that the Corinthians had been justified and sanctified '**in the name of the Lord Jesus Christ, and in the Spirit of our God**' is essentially trinitarian, with reference being made to the Father ('**our God**'), to the Son and to the Spirit. It is for this reason that the verse cannot teach baptismal regeneration, the false but common notion that a person becomes a child of God when he or she is baptized. The meaning is that the Corinthians' desire to be clean plus their spiritual sanctification and justification flowed from inward and outward experience: the bringing of the name and truth of Christ to them by gospel preaching had been accompanied by the inner prompting of the Spirit of God. Water-baptism was their public and unashamed response to the work of God in their hearts.

The reference to **'our God'** shows that some of the Corinthians were grieving their heavenly Father, the God who had given them so much and who had reconciled himself to them. How could they behave as they were doing?

Promiscuity (6:12-20)

Sexual licence was endemic in Corinth. It stained and degraded almost everything and everybody. An addiction as much as any other controlling habit, it was no easy matter for the Corinthians to give it up. Paul asserts that they must. Furthermore, they could; practical holiness was not beyond their grasp.

At this stage in his exposition of sexual holiness the apostle is aware that a reformation of heart and manners has to be shown to be desirable as well as within reach. Merely to tell the people what to do and what not to do would be inadequate; the Corinthians needed to know in detail exactly why impurity is wrong and how it can be overcome. His doctrine is that the dynamic, as well as the incentive, for self-cleansing springs from the relationship between the believer and his Lord.

The teaching of 6:12-20 is that the Christian's body in its entirety should be dedicated to Jesus because it has become a shrine in which the Holy Spirit resides. Not even death and decay are able to cancel this: because God raised Jesus he will raise us from death and then we shall remain in relationship with the Lord (6:14). Now, having established this doctrinal foundation, the apostle interrogates his readers about three issues, each time leading with the provocative challenge: 'Do you not know?' (6:15,16,19). This is a pre-emptive strike intended to disable any opposition: because they are not ignorant the saints must react to reality.

Looking to the future (6:12-14)

Fornication is as short-sighted as it is evil. Attaching undue importance to a sinful activity that is for this world only, it is grossly inconsistent with the eternal destiny of the Christian. Paul, as ever,

Immorality in the church (5:1 - 6:20)

takes the long-term view. Why be dominated by desires that are not only wrong but which are strictly temporary, destined to vanish in a few years?

Self-control (6:12)

For the apostle **'All things are lawful'**. Although what Christians may or may not do is opened up in more general terms in 10:23 and context, here, in chapter 6, the discussion is limited to the matter of sexual purity.

Paul reasons that although he personally has complete freedom to do just as he pleases, provided always that he does not break the commandments of God, it cannot be to his advantage to abandon self-control: not everything that is right in itself will necessarily serve his interests. Therefore he will not be **'mastered by anything'**; there is nothing, either good or bad, with which he intends to over-indulge himself. Planned self-discipline of this type helps him to avoid becoming an addict.

The unfolding of his more intimate feelings is intentional. As in 4:16, the apostle presents himself as an example to the Corinthians. There are two reasons for this. First, he does not wish them to be gripped by anyone or anything other than Christ. Secondly, perhaps some of these devious people had become attached to the erroneous notion that they could give free reign to their baser instincts. Compare his biting question in Romans 6:1: 'Are we to continue in sin that grace may abound?' Paul knew that professing Christians can wriggle and squirm when truth is hard to accept.[21]

In those days, as is certainly the case now, extra-marital sex seems to have been reckoned by some believers as not entirely wrong. It appears that an element in the church concluded that if they were at liberty to exercise themselves below the belt in one respect, that is, in eating and drinking, why should they not let themselves go sexually?

It might be added that if some did think like this, their concept of sexuality was grossly inadequate, typical of how the world understands 'love'. This is somewhat speculative because the apostle does not go into details. Nor was there a need to do so because his argument as it stands remains perfectly understandable: liberty in the exercise of a certain natural function in the abdominal region does not mean that we possess unrestricted freedom in that area.

Food, yes; fornication, no (6:13)

'Food is [meant] **for the stomach, and the stomach is for food.'** This is Paul's way of saying that no Old Testament dietary restrictions remain for the believer.[22]

1. Nothing is taboo

We ought to apply this principle because as Christians we can get ourselves into a muddle in such areas. Some believers shun alcohol like the plague whereas others are not too fussy about spending far too much money at the drinks-counter. The truth is that what we eat and drink has no moral or spiritual significance. Therefore it cannot be wrong in principle to consume alcohol, albeit in strict moderation. Even so, there is a qualification: because drunkenness is sinful it might be wisdom for believers to renounce alcohol if it is a standing temptation to others or to them.

2. Preparing for marriage

The apostle looks forward to the time when God will do away with **'both of them'**, that is, the stomach and food; neither will they exist, nor need each other. But for the moment eating and drinking are as right as they are necessary. Not so promiscuous sex. This is another matter because our bodies are temples that will never cease to exist, a truth to be unfolded in chapter 15.[23] God has decreed that in body and soul Christians are the property of the Lord Jesus.

Because the Saviour and the saved belong to one another, the way believers use or abuse their bodies is important. The church is like a bride betrothed to Jesus (as taught, for example, by 2 Corinthians 11:2-3; Ephesians 5:27 and Revelation 21:2,9). How can a betrothed woman entertain a sexual relationship? She should not and, if she is loyal to her beloved, she will not. Therefore, while we await the Great Day, physical immorality should be out of the question. Christians are to keep themselves to themselves because they are reserved for Jesus.

Why waste time and energy? (6:14)

The union between regenerate sinners and their Lord will be perfected at the glorification of the church: the God who raised up

Immorality in the church (5:1 - 6:20) 117

the body of Jesus **'will also raise us up through his power'**.[24] Paul's point is that, given the prospect of the resurrection of the body, there is nothing to be gained by dissipating ourselves in this sinful world.

Christ, the Spirit, the believer — and an affair (6:15-20)

Again comes a question with an obvious answer (6:15a). Do the Corinthians not realize that their bodies are **'members** [or, 'parts'] **of Christ'**? Amplifying 3:16 and anticipating 6:19, the verse teaches that the relationship between Christ and all believers is of such an intensity that even our bodies are in some sense in union with him.[25] Because they are constituent members of the Lord they should not be made available to others in sexual relationships outside marriage.

The believer who falls into sin (6:15b-17)

The second part of 6:15 is daring, yet understandably so, given the attitude of the Corinthians to sexuality and the need to be candid with them. To emphasize the shocking nature of sex outside marriage, Paul contemplates what it would mean for him were he personally to engage in such activity.

'Then' (or, 'therefore'), in the light of the truth that all the elements of Paul's body are **'members of Christ'**, would it be right for him to make them physically the **'members of a harlot'**? To act in this way would bring Jesus into an illicit union with someone who hires out her own body. How should one react to such an unthinkably awful act? Quite simply, **'May it never be!'**

Don't forget that again Paul brings himself forward as an example, intending at this point to show that the sorry principle of union between Jesus (via a Christian man) and an unclean woman would hold good for every saint who fails in this way.

A further question, to which the reply is obvious, is put to the congregation (6:16). Do they not realize that the man who **'joins himself** [sexually] **to a harlot'** becomes **'one body with her'**? Perhaps Paul employs the present tense because he was aware that some Corinthians were indulging the habit.

The apostle's argument needs careful consideration. He takes it for granted that when a woman sells herself to a client the two become temporary partners, although partners driven by opposite and irreconcilable impulses: he seeks gratification; she, money. Because this is the case the whole operation is a degradation of God's gift of love to a man and woman; sexual union was never meant to be like this.

Paul reinforces his teaching with the introduction of Moses' observation in Genesis 2:24 about a man leaving his parents. For the apostle, as for Jesus, they remain words from God: 'For this cause a man shall leave his father and his mother, and shall cleave to his wife; and they shall become one flesh.'[26]

Here we have a binding principle. Notice that when a man joins himself sexually to 'his wife' (literally, 'his woman') they become **'one flesh'**; they belong to each other. Even so, and this is the sombre truth that the apostle brings into the open, when the woman concerned is *not* the man's wife their sexual union means that the two find themselves in a marital relationship. Their fleeting cohabitation is an impossible *de facto* marriage union rather than what they probably imagine to be a furtive adventure for him, or just another money-making exercise for her: the two are now 'one flesh'. They have fulfilled the terms of Genesis 2:23-24, albeit unwittingly and with no intention of staying together.

Possibly recalling the command of Deuteronomy 10:20 for Israel to be joined to Jehovah, Paul insists that the believer **'who joins himself to the Lord is one spirit with him'** (6:17). He has entered into an intimate relationship with the Lord Jesus, and the Spirit of Christ dwells in him. In the words of Romans 8:9-10, 'You are not in the flesh, but in the Spirit... Christ is in you.' How, then, does this tie up with improper sex? It does not because it cannot.

Run for your life (6:18)

For these reasons, all of which have to do with the Christian's experience of salvation, the Corinthians are to **'flee from fornication'**; holiness of body is to be an ongoing attitude. It is striking that the apostle does not appeal to the commandment prohibiting adultery (Exod. 20:14; Deut. 5:18); in his theology commitment to Christ replaces the demands of Sinai.

Notice that vulnerability to sexual sin can be so strong that there is only one way in which we ought to react: run for our lives. Joseph did exactly this when solicited by Potiphar's wife (Gen. 39:15). In his masculine weakness he was wise.

Immorality in the church (5:1 - 6:20)

Paul elaborates on the awfulness of sexual immorality, although we can assume that he did not believe that this sin is necessarily worse than other faults. Perhaps we need to remember that our Lord denounced the hypocritical Pharisees far more emphatically than he condemned the harlots and tax collectors (Luke 7:36-50; John 8:7). In these sensitive matters a sense of proportion is vital.

The apostle indicates that there is something uniquely repulsive about fornication. Every other sin that a man might commit **'is outside the body'**. Sins like drunkenness and drug-taking depend upon materials brought in from elsewhere, whereas sexual immorality is different, an activity in which the body unleashes its internal desires in such a way as to injure itself: the fornicator **'sins against** 'fails'] **his body'**. No other evil can be quite like this.

Keeping the temple clean (6:19-20)

Another rhetorical question appears. Do the people not realize that the body of the individual Christian is a **'shrine'**, the inner sanctum of a temple? (6:19). Compare with 3:16, which states that the church collectively is a 'shrine'. Paul knows that the Corinthians understand.

It follows that should the believer besmirch his body in this way he offends the Spirit sent from God. Conversely, because the Holy Spirit dwells within him the Christian is not at liberty to fornicate.

There is more: **'For you have been bought with a price'** (6:20).[27] This dramatic statement occurs again in 7:23, although in a rather different context. The assertion is significant. Nowhere else in the New Testament does the verb 'bought' attract 'with a price' as a qualifier. The combination is as emphatic as words will permit: Paul intends his readers to realize that Christ purchased the church with nothing less than the sacrifice of his own life.

The irresistible logic is that because Christ's freehold acquisition is that of the whole man, Christians must glorify God with their bodies, shrines intended for holy purposes only and for inhabitation by the Lord. Therefore we should have nothing to do with leasing or subletting these bodies temporarily to other people.

Observe that Paul believes in the Trinity. God the Father is to be glorified by Christians who are one with his Son and who are the dwelling-place of the Holy Spirit. The principle being emphasized is that our experience of the Trinity is the springboard for holiness.

In conclusion

Before we give thought to chapter 7 and Paul's comprehensive teaching about marriage, let's apply the lessons of 6:12-20.

It is essential to bear in mind that the case levelled against impurity relates to the saints only. This is because the physical bodies of non-Christians do not belong to the Lord. Undoubtedly, for unbelievers fornication must be wrong and damaging, and may well be seen to be so. But it cannot possibly be as evil as it is for believers.

To put it another way, it is true that being clean in body and mind often appeals to the consciences of worldly men and women. Added benefits are that chastity avoids sexually transmitted diseases, illegitimate children, broken relationships, divorce courts and material hardship. But the Bible looks at the matter in a very different way: sexual purity is considered strictly within the framework of the relationship that Christians have with their Lord. The two approaches have nothing in common.

Here is a down-to-earth question: is it possible to draw a distinction between someone having an affair with an acquaintance and a man who engages a prostitute? If a Christian plays fast and loose, but not with a lady of the streets, is his sin any the less offensive?

The truth is that there is no difference. The underlying Greek word for a female 'prostitute' *(porne)* is no more than the feminine variation of the masculine word 'fornicator' *(pornos,* 5:9-11; 6:9; whence 'pornography'). One does not have to pay a professional to be a sinner of this type.

Further, the reference to union with a harlot is probably an extreme example which Paul brings in to show what is always involved in extra-marital sex (6:16). It follows that when married or single Christians have affairs they offend against the truths made plain by 6:15-16.

Although the apostle does not emphasize the matter because it is not germane to his flow of thought, this sin is aggravated immensely when the transgressor is married. In indulging a liaison the Christian husband gives himself in wedlock, albeit temporarily, to the woman concerned. This means that he is effectively bigamous, damaging his own integrity, his marriage, his church and, worst of all, the honour of his Lord.

4. Marriage
(7:1-40)

We know that the apostle had written at an earlier time to the Corinthians about their contacts with immoral people ('I wrote you in my letter', 5:9). It might be that this previous epistle was itself an answer to a request from the church for counsel about sensitive issues. Alternatively, Paul's letter might have generated discussion at Corinth, stimulating the people to write to the apostle. Either way, he now gives written replies to written queries.

To judge from the reappearance of **'concerning'** elsewhere in 1 Corinthians, the people had problems not only about marriage (7:1), but also about eating meat sacrificed to idols (8:1), about spiritual gifts (12:1), and about what to do concerning financial help for poor Christians in Judea (16:1). All these matters were immensely important.

The apostle launches into a detailed discussion of matrimony in a chapter that can be divided into eight sections.

First, 7:1-7 gives guidance about married life. Then 7:8-9 is directed to unmarried Christians and also to those who have been bereaved. The delicate issue of divorce is raised in 7:10-11, and the situation of Christians whose partners have not yet come to know the Lord is given attention in 7:12-16. The related but much wider question of Christian contentment is addressed in 7:17-24. This theme is developed in 7:25-35, but with particular reference to those who have not married and to those who contemplate divorce or a further marriage after divorce. The Christian father pondering the situation of his single daughter is considered in 7:36-38. The final two verses, 7:39-40, concern the remarriage of widows.

Guidance about married life (7:1-7)

In 7:1 **'good'** means 'better' and **'to touch'** probably signifies marriage.[1] Note that, unlike 7:8,11,32 and 34, 'unmarried' and 'married' do not occur, possibly because the discussion focuses upon the intimacies of married life; 'touch' is an appropriate euphemism. In context, the apostle indicates that it is better to remain single.

As the following verses show, matrimony is not reckoned by Paul as an evil. In later years he castigated those in the churches who instructed Christians not to marry (1 Tim. 4:3), and would have said so here had ascetics or libertines reared their heads in Corinth. His concern at this point is to show that the single state is preferable.

Why is the single state better? (7:1)

In downgrading marriage did Paul write as a misogynist, someone who hated women, or were his words impelled by good and proper principles? Over the centuries there have been many interpretations (and misinterpretations) of the apostle. We shall consider two approaches: first, what could be termed the 'pragmatic' view; second, the 'ideological'.

The pragmatic approach

According to Charles Hodge in his excellent commentary on 1 and 2 Corinthians, Paul considered the church to be like an army poised for battle. For the believers in a hostile city it was no time to take husbands and wives. This commentator holds that any other approach to chapter 7 would show that the apostle estimated marriage as something like a union of animals. Paul, Hodge reckons, would never have depreciated the matrimonial knot unless the circumstances were peculiarly inappropriate. Therefore, and consistently with Genesis 2:18, 'It is not good for the man to be alone,' Paul directed his counsel solely to the fraught situation in which the Corinthian church found itself.

Lenski has taken a similar view: 'In Eden God spoke for the human race. Paul writes to Corinth, to the Christians only, and such as were living in the worst pagan surroundings.'[2]

Marriage (7:1-40)

The ideological approach

With due respect to these expositors, I beg leave to disagree. Did Paul really mean that because most people are actively or potentially opposed to the Christian faith the saints *must* repudiate marriage?

We know that Peter, the other apostles and the brothers of Jesus were married, as were Priscilla and Aquila, Paul's close friends and helpers.[3] There is, of course, the possibility that they married before they became disciples and for this reason were in no position to match up to what we may term the 'pragmatic' interpretation of chapter 7. Simon Peter, it is true, certainly had a wife before the Lord called him.

According to the Hodge-Lenski reconstruction Paul might seem to imply that it would have been better had these pillars of the faith never married. Given their circumstances, he accepted that there was not a lot that they could do about it. The apostle saw his task as that of guiding singles away from matrimony.

Let's be clear. This is in no way a straw man set up to be knocked down. A scenario like this *is* implied by Hodge and Lenski. Even so, it does not seem to add up. Priscilla and Aquila, not to mention the big fisherman and his lady, would not have taken kindly to such semi-concealed aspersions on their unions. To take up the picture, does this mean that Peter, the brothers of the Lord and also Aquila, followed by their respective wives, to some extent stood apart from an army about to enter an unequal conflict in enemy territory? No.

In short, it does not appear that Paul's evaluation of the single and married states is pragmatic, defined by the sort of world in which many of the Lord's people then found, and now find, themselves. This does not mean, let it be said, that outward circumstances are unimportant when marriage is contemplated, as 7:26 shows: 'In view of the present distress ... it is good for a man to remain as he is [that is, single].'

The view adopted here would be that the issue is not discussed solely, or even primarily, by Paul at this practical level. It seems that the apostle's words apply to all Christians everywhere: *unless* a person's situation suggests that remaining single is impossibly difficult, which may well be the case, the believer should never make marriage his ambition; to this principle there are no exceptions.

The real world (7:2)

Paul was not made of wood. He knew that Christian people do have natural desires. Further, they live in a sinful world. Because of past or potential **'immoralities'**, that is, repetitive sexual misconduct, everybody should be contemplating marriage as an option (**'each man ... each woman'**). There is more. In keeping with the original institution of marriage, monogamy remains the only allowable standard. In positively approving marriage, 7:2 does not contradict 7:1, as will be demonstrated by 7:7 and 7:32-35.

There can be little doubt that this counsel was targeted at the first readers of the letter. But it would be a mistake to limit Paul's teaching to one congregation only, that at Corinth all those years ago. Remember, the epistle is addressed specifically to all believers (1:2). Corinth and its filthy world are ever with us.

Libertines and ascetics (7:3-7)

Reading between the lines, 7:3 might be a response to some at Corinth who believed that married people should not have sexual intercourse (7:5). If so, the church could have included both libertines (cf. 15:32) and ascetics, a strange but by no means impossible meeting of extremes. Paul insists that a man and his wife each have an ongoing debt to the other, the reason being that neither partner retains **'authority'** over his or her body (7:4).

Marital harmony (7:3-6)

'Authority' has occurred already in 6:12, where Paul declares that he will not be mastered by any external influence. Now he teaches that the married person must be controlled to some extent by his or her partner. Further, even though the husband is admittedly the 'head' of his wife (11:3), in this matter he can exercise no more than an equal right.

Therefore, man and wife must **'stop depriving one another'** (7:5). 'Deprive', or 'defraud', implies that there is something dishonest about imposed celibacy within marriage.[4] Further, the prohibition suggests that some Corinthians had arbitrarily severed relations with their partners. Tactfully, Paul does not go into details, but clearly he does not approve.

Marriage (7:1-40)

His instruction is not absolute. A married couple should deny each other temporarily, strictly by mutual agreement and for one specific reason: that each can be **'undisturbed in prayer'**. To illustrate, 'undisturbed' occurs in Matthew 12:44 and Luke 11:25 in connection with an unoccupied house where there is no activity. Because peaceful prayer is more important than marital relations the latter should be suspended from time to time.

But only for a time. Otherwise, Satan will **'tempt'** the couple to contemplate, or indulge in, some form of sexual sin and thereby destabilize their marriage. Notice that Paul, a bachelor, knows that even God's good gifts can become unwitting instruments to bring down a man and his wife, and this because the adversary is utterly unscrupulous. Selecting his words exactly and with the greatest possible delicacy, he indicates that where there is no physical satisfaction immorality becomes a possibility. The reason is that even the most mature believers are prone to a want of self-control. Otherwise expressed, a balanced marriage avoids sin.

The **'concession'** (or 'permission') of 7:6 concerns 7:1-5 as a whole rather than the immediately preceding verse. Paul does not mean that he has been permitted by the Lord to teach these things. Rather, as an accredited apostle he permits marriage as a possibility but refuses to **'command'** it as a Christian duty.

A charisma (7:7)

The sentiment of 7:1, **'It is good for a man not to touch a woman,'** is developed by the introduction of a personal reference. Paul wishes all Christian men to be as he is in one particular respect: that they remain single with no desire to marry. **'As I myself'** is emphatic, and the apostle might be applying the earlier teaching of Christ, as reflected by Matthew 19:11. There the Lord responds to the pessimistic conclusion of the disciples in the preceding verse that 'It is better not to marry': 'But he said to them, "Not all men can accept this statement, but only those to whom it has been given."' The ability to enter into and honour a husband-wife relationship over the years is special, a gift from God not necessarily granted to all men.

Paul warns against entering into matrimony lightly and unadvisedly rather than thoughtfully and reverently, and teaches that marriages are (or ought to be) made in heaven: ultimately it is God who moves us to think decisively about the matter or overrules our hearts so that we elect to remain single: **'Each man has his own

gift [*charisma*] **from God.'** A *charisma* is a gift bestowed graciously and not because the recipient deserves it.[5] Marriage *and* the single state are unmerited blessings.

To the unmarried (7:8-9)

The apostle accepts gladly that if marriage is not everybody's destiny, nor is being alone. Perhaps he enlarges upon 7:2. As we have seen, this prescribes matrimony as an antidote to sin.

We might compare this passage with 14:5, where Paul declares that he would like everybody to speak in tongues but accepts that this will never happen. There is also the apostle's moving courtroom statement in Acts 26:29: 'I would to God, that ... all who hear me ... might become such as I am, except for these chains.' These passages illustrate well the meaning here: Paul would prefer the Corinthians not to marry, but realizes that God in his grace bestows the need for marriage upon some when to others he gives a willingness and an ability to remain single.

The point is that if we are happily single we should thank God for granting us such a considerable blessing, and that if we are married we should equally be thankful to God for his leading. This applies to each and every Christian.

Before we pass to the next section let's not overlook the delicate and pure manner in which the apostle treats the question of Christian marital relations. Here, too, his conscience allows him to present himself as an example.

The doctrine of 7:1 that the single state is preferable is applied directly to believers who either have never married or who are widows. For emphasis, 7:8 repeats the personal reference in 7:7, which is that it would be **'good'** for such people to be like the letter-writer; their present happiness would be enhanced were they to remain single.

Those women who had been bereaved are given particular mention, perhaps because opportunities for second husbands might not have been remote. This could be implied by 7:40: **'She** [the Christian widow] **is happier if she remains as she is.'** Lonely and impatient singles needed and got a quiet word in the ear.

A wise man, the apostle was not ignorant of human nature. The burden of 7:2 is amplified by 7:9, which admits that there are times

Marriage (7:1-40)

when unmarried people do not control themselves. Paul is concerned with what Christians can be in the heat of that awkward moment when passion overrides commitment and principle. He assumes that only a fool or an extraordinarily self-disciplined man ever imagines that his self-control would be on immediate stand-by in fraught situations.

Therefore, **'Let them marry; for it is better to marry than to burn.'** The grammar behind **'to burn'** yields the sense 'to go on burning oneself' (Greek, *purousthai*, middle voice). If marriage is the only way by which an otherwise spreading fire can be put out, so be it.

Divorce (7:10-11)

Attention is now given to all in the church who **'have married'** (7:10). If you will forgive yet another language lesson, please bear with the comment that 'have married' is a Greek perfect participle *(gegamekosin)*. This is significant because the Greek perfect tense normally indicates that an action, now complete, history rather than news, has a consequence that lasts indefinitely. In this case Paul implies quite deliberately that the Corinthians' marriage commitments gave rise to lifelong relationships. Once married, always married.

The apostle commands (7:10)

Contrary to 7:6, Paul does not inform these believers about what they are permitted to do; he **'commands'** them. 'Commands' is better than the NASB's 'gives instructions', which implies inaccurately that we are about to be given a set of rules.

The requirement is that the woman should not **'be separated'** from the man. Because the sad possibility of an absolute termination of marriage is in the apostle's mind he addresses himself to the problem of a woman abandoning her husband once and for all to begin a new life. She considers this step even though he has not cheated on her by committing adultery.

The sands of time

To illustrate what the context means when it refers to 'separation', a Greek-language marriage contract, dated to about A.D. 66 (a decade after 1 Corinthians was written) was uncovered from the sands of Egypt. The papyrus tells that Chaeremon, a young husband-to-be, worked out with his prospective father-in-law, Sisois, who should receive what in the event of Sisois's daughter, Thaisarion, and he eventually 'separating' and then proceeding to a legal divorce. The parties concerned felt that they could not be too careful. Separation was understood as the irrevocable end of the proposed union rather than a makeshift, temporary alienation.[6] It is exactly like this in 7:10. 'Separated' is passive (Greek, *chôristhenai*), suggesting, perhaps, a married woman who allows herself to be put away.

Paul, the accredited ambassador

There can be no doubt that the apostle issues his directive as a command from Christ. Compare with 14:37: 'Let him recognize that the things which I write to you are the Lord's commandment.' There and in this passage Paul knew that he was an inspired penman revealing the mind of the Lord of the church, and doing so in precise terms.

There is something more. During his earthly ministry the Lord Jesus spoke about marriage and divorce (Matt. 5:32; 19:3-9; Mark 10:11-12; Luke 16:18). Undoubtedly what he said was not hidden away by those who heard him, from which it follows that we cannot claim that his teaching was unknown to the Corinthians. We might make a comparison with Paul's statement in Acts 20:35: 'Remember the words of the Lord Jesus, that he himself said, "It is more blessed to give than to receive."' At Miletus the apostle assumed that the Ephesian elders were aware of a saying of Christ that has not come down to us in the Gospels. Both 7:10 and 13:2 ('so as to remove mountains', cf. Matt. 17:20; 21:21; Mark 11:23) suggest that when it was appropriate and possible Paul was eager to recall the known words of Jesus. But the process of transmission was probably unlike 11:23-34 regarding the Lord's Table, and 15:3-4 concerning matters 'of first importance', where Paul refers to words and doctrine communicated *directly* to him by Christ. In 7:10, the apostle would seem to restate what Jesus had said a number of years before.

Marriage (7:1-40)

Harsh realities (7:11)

Paul accommodates to the realities of life, realizing that in the churches there will be some wives who desire divorce. What is a woman in this difficult situation to do? His directive is that if reconciliation to her husband proves impossible and if the marriage must end, she should remain unmarried and not contract a new union.

Turning his attention to the menfolk, the apostle instructs a Christian husband never to **'send his wife away'**. That is, he must not allow his partner to drift from him, eventually to join another man. He is to exert himself to the utmost to maintain the present marriage.

In practical terms, 7:10-11 warn husbands and wives to be careful if and when their marriages grow weary. Sadly, the people of the world are not unknown to change their partners in order to bring excitement into their lives. Josephus sent away his first wife, the mother of his first three children, because in some way or other she did not please him. Then he married an allegedly superior woman who presented him with two sons.[7] Believers are not allowed to do things like this.

Christians with unconverted partners (7:12-16)

Christians whose partners are unbelievers come under the spotlight. These brethren and sisters are described as **'the rest'** (or, 'the remainder', 7:12) because they are the only married people in the church whose situations have not so far been reviewed. For the apostle the subject of Christians and marriage was so important that no potential or actual problem area could be ignored.

Paul's modest yet firm authority (7:12-13)

In the light of the optimistic questions of 7:16, **'For how do you know, O wife, if you will save your husband? Or how do you know, O husband, if you will save your wife?'**, it would appear almost certain that 'the rest' had been brought to know the Lord *after* they married. Unfortunately, their partners had not yet come to share their faith.

It is easy to imagine the intolerable tensions that must have arisen. Reading between the lines we gain the distinct impression that some of the unbelieving partners considered breaking away from their chaste Christian husbands or wives. If the worst came to the worst, what action should the latter take?

Paul seems to have been aware that during his earthly ministry Jesus said nothing about this issue, an observation supported (but not proved) by the silence of the four Gospels on the matter. Undoubtedly, the apostle was also aware that Christ proposed to continue and perfect his teaching ministry after his ascension. The Lord promised that the Spirit would guide the disciples into 'all the truth' (John 16:13), and Acts 1:1 states categorically that Luke's Gospel recounted 'all that Jesus began to do and to teach'. Unquestionably, Christ intended that his teaching should be amplified and committed to writing. In 1 Corinthians 7 as elsewhere, the apostle is quietly conscious that as he wields the pen he reflects the mind of his Master.

Why marriage should be maintained (7:14)

The apostolic judgement is that if the unbelieving partner is willing to honour the marriage the Christian husband or wife must reciprocate; in no circumstances should he or she separate.

The holy estate of matrimony

Perhaps there were some in the church who believed naïvely that the married person who became a Christian ought to strive to sever the union with the unbelieving partner. The apostle shows that there are convincing reasons for the Christian remaining with the unconverted spouse who is happy to stay: **'For the unbelieving husband has been sanctified by the wife, and the unbelieving wife has been sanctified by the brother; for otherwise your children are unclean, but now they are holy.'**

By any standard this is a weighty saying. The *Textus Receptus* reads 'husband' instead of 'brother', but the weight of evidence seems to favour the latter even though the sense is the same. According to the NASB, the unbelieving husband or wife 'is sanctified', a translation that is not wrong although it might fail to

Marriage (7:1-40)

do justice to Paul's statement that the marriage agreements gave rise to an enduring state of holiness. The Greek verb behind **'has been sanctified'** is *hegiastai*, perfect passive from *hagiazô*, 'to separate' or 'to consecrate'. The meaning is that the unbelieving partner had been made holy once and for all and remains set apart for the believing spouse.

Therefore, the ground rule for Christians who weigh up whether or not to maintain their unions is that their unregenerate partners are sanctified persons. Further, the instruments of their sanctification were their (now) believing partners. These are two most important points. It is upon this *de facto* state of affairs that Paul's argument hangs.

The word **'otherwise'** (Greek, *epei ara*) is significant. It occurs also in 5:10: 'For then [or, 'otherwise'] you would have to go out of the world.' As we have observed, a hypothetical situation is suggested: to avoid all contact with immoral people the Corinthians would need to abandon the planet. In 7:14 the apostle contemplates another equally impossible situation. Were the union between the two partners, one unbelieving and the other now a Christian, not holy, their children would be unclean. But this is not the case, nor can it be. Paul insists that the offspring of such marriages *are* holy. Therefore, arguing backwards, the union must be holy. It follows that if at all possible the relationship should be preserved.

What is 'holiness'?

Many Bible-loving Christians hold that 7:14 assumes the children of Christian parents to have been set apart *spiritually* by God for a special purpose. It is believed that this is why they possess a status not given to the children of unbelievers. It is usually conceded that the principle operates even in what are occasionally termed 'mixed marriages', where one partner only is the Lord's.

Negatively, it is almost always maintained that the children's holiness does not derive from spiritual rebirth: the little ones are in some sense spiritually holy even though they have not yet been born again. Furthermore, this approach to 7:14 and its context is sometimes held to be compatible with the practice of infant baptism.[8]

Equally, there are those of the Lord's people who do not accept that 7:14 has anything to do with the *spiritual* status of the children of Christians. They find it hard to see that the unconverted offspring of believers possess any innate spiritual privileges. Formed in the image of God, yet defiled both by inherited and personal sin, these infants are in these respects just like other babies.

It is neither the task nor the intention of this commentary to detail the arguments either way. Library shelves have been filled with learned works on the pros and cons for both sides, and they can always be consulted. But not to sketch an interpretation might be unsatisfying for the reader.

Sanctified unbelievers

First, we remind ourselves that the unbelieving partner had been 'sanctified'. Paul has used precisely the same word with exactly the same grammatical construction in 1:2 when outlining the blessed status of Christians: they are 'sanctified in Christ Jesus' and 'call upon the name of the Lord'. But in 7:14, although the expression is identical, the apostle must have something else in mind.

Whatever else sanctified unbelievers might be, Paul knew that they are certainly not saints who call upon the Lord; by definition they are in their sins because they do not rely upon Christ for their salvation. Nor does the apostle suggest that they possess unwittingly any special spiritual benefits conferred by their believing partners.

Second, there is no reason to suppose that the sanctification ascribed to the children is anything other than the admitted holiness of their unbelieving mothers and fathers. To imagine a fundamental shift in the frame of reference is far too much for one verse and would lead to intolerable confusion. It seems obvious that this equivalence of holiness between unbelieving parent and child, if it may be so expressed, is almost certainly the crux of the whole issue.

It follows that the children are not spiritually pure. Considered as individuals they find themselves in precisely the situation outlined by the penitent David in Psalm 51:5: 'Behold, I was brought forth in iniquity, and in sin my mother conceived me.' David knew that he was a legitimate son of Jesse. He does not deny this. Nor does he cast aspersions upon his mother's pre-marital chastity, even less blaming her because he, now an adult, had recently sinned with Bathsheba. His affirmation in the psalm is that because he is a child of Adam he belongs to a sinful stock. Here is the ultimate reason for his error.

Marriage (7:1-40)

This is how it is for all children prior to conversion, irrespective of their parentage. Before they are regenerated by the Spirit through hearing the gospel neither are they saved, nor can they be presumed to be among the elect. It goes without saying that some enjoy the blessing of being loved by parents concerned for their spiritual welfare, as was the case with Timothy (Acts 16:1; 2 Tim. 1:5; 3:15), but this is not the question addressed by Paul.

Nor can his meaning be that these little ones are morally clean. He must have known well enough that the sun does not always shine out of the eyes of children of Christian mothers and fathers, hence his remarks in Ephesians 6:1-3 and Colossians 3:20. But the stubborn fact remains that, exactly like their unbelieving parents lawfully married to Christians, these children are now in some sense 'holy'. Otherwise expressed, they are uncontaminated and lack impurity. To repeat, this situation arises because the individual child is the offspring of his married mother and father, one à Christian and the other confessedly an unbeliever.

Marriage is sanctification

To understand the apostle's teaching it is necessary to bear in mind that the meaning of 'sanctification' is to set apart or to be set apart for some special purpose. Take, for example, the reference in 1 Timothy 4:4-5 to daily food: 'For everything created by God is good, and nothing is to be rejected, if it is received with gratitude; for it is sanctified by means of the word of God and prayer.'

Clearly, the bread on Christian tables does not possess a mystical spiritual sanctification that leads ultimately to its salvation. Although some men and angels are elect, this cannot be said about loaves set apart by thankful prayer even though the bread is sanctified. It is obvious that there is a shift in the frame of reference, and if this must be the case in 1 Timothy 4:4-5, why not in 7:14?

By an inescapable process of elimination it appears that 7:14 refers to what has been termed 'legal holiness', by which is meant the dignity and integrity of these children's family backgrounds. That is, the way in which they were brought into the world remains beyond reproach. This would seem to be what the passage is all about. Essentially, Paul is giving assurance to Christians who are united to unbelievers. Because they are not living in sin there is no need for them to end their marriages.

First, the unbelieving husband was sanctified on the occasion of his marriage, not later on when his partner was converted. At his wedding he separated himself and was separated from all others to belong uniquely to his own wife. Happily, the conversion of the woman of his choice has not led him to contemplate ending the relationship.

Now consider the union from the situation of the married Christian woman. It is with her, let it be observed, that Paul begins. At marriage she set herself apart for her new husband: he took her and she took him. It is true that since their wedding-day she (though not he) has come to know the Lord. It is implied that this does not in any way destabilize the sanctity of the original contract. Further, because adultery has not occurred the Christian wife has no reason to terminate the marriage. That her partner might be an idolater is irrelevant and does not count.

Secondly, the children are holy. When they exchanged their vows the parents-to-be set themselves apart exclusively for each other. This was before babies were conceived. It follows that these little ones, born within the purity of wedlock, remain legitimate. They are not the product of sexual uncleanness.

1 Thessalonians 4:3-7 provides powerful confirmation for this approach. 'Sanctification' (Greek, *hagiasmos*, related to the verb *hagiazô*) is mentioned twice for emphasis and means Christian purity in a world characterized by open sin. Here are 4:3 and 7 from that letter: 'For this is the will of God, your sanctification, that is, that you abstain from sexual immorality... For God has not called us for the purpose of impurity, but in sanctification.'

It would seem that 7:14 falls within exactly the same reference. To repeat, Paul reminds the 'rest' (7:12) that the married believer who is now a co-parent with an unbeliever is *not* living sinfully. Therefore the wife has no reason to be alarmed either about her own marital status or about the legitimacy of the children.

Abraham's example

Perhaps Paul's teaching might be illustrated by Malachi 2:15, which contrasts the status of Isaac and Ishmael, both sons of Abraham yet by different women: 'And what did that one [Abraham] do while he was seeking a godly offspring?' Here, the Hebrew behind 'godly offspring' means literally 'seed of God', in this case Isaac, a child

Marriage (7:1-40)

given by God to Abraham. He was brought into the world in the Lord's ordained way through Sarah, Abraham's true wife.

Malachi's probable meaning is that after Sarah disowned Hagar, Abraham abandoned the notion of Ishmael, his boy by the slave-girl, ever becoming a son within the line of the Messianic promise. Pondering his dilemma, he reverted to his wife in the renewed confidence that in time she would bear him a true heir. Read Genesis 16 and 21:2,10-12 and compare with Galatians 4:30.

Part (but only part) of the prophet's application is that Abraham's descendants ought to imitate the patriarch. They should honour their marriage vows by rejecting divorce and extra-marital associations. They, too, should live by what they know to be right. He implies that children born out of wedlock are unclean. In this respect his message anticipates the teaching of Paul in 7:14, although the apostle does not refer to either Abraham or Malachi.

Paul's Jewish background

We need to take into account that the principle of what I have called 'legal holiness' was common in the Jewish world into which the apostle was born. The Mishnah, a codification of rabbinic traditions compiled not later than about A.D. 500, preserves long-standing beliefs about marriage. On occasion 'holiness' stands for betrothal and 'cleanness' means legitimacy of birth.[9]

Although Paul did not draw directly upon rabbinic tradition, it would be unsafe to overlook the likelihood that in this respect the Mishnah's teaching and the apostle's thought derived ultimately from a common conceptual background, that of the Old Testament and centuries-old Jewish culture. If so, the apostle's words could best be interpreted in terms of what Jews thought about marital sanctification and sexual permissiveness. In the light of this teaching that children are holy when born within lawful marriages, it is not hard to imagine that this was the only way in which the verse would have been understood by a church containing a considerable Jewish element (Acts 18:8). Nor would these words have been a mystery to converted Greeks.

It ought to be said that not a few able commentators reject this approach. Lenski holds that the unbelieving partner had been sanctified because he was 'party to a Christian marriage' and that the children were holy because they were born in 'Christian wedlock'.

But the assumption cannot be proved and the commentator does not try.[10]

No loopholes

To go back to 7:14, what is true for the unbelieving husband and his Christian wife applies if the situation is reversed: the unbelieving wife has also been 'sanctified'. Paul will not cloud what he intends to be an exact statement.

Intolerable tensions (7:15)

The apostle continues in the knowledge that domestic bliss is seldom uncomplicated. He visualizes a situation in which the unbelieving husband or wife becomes disgruntled because the partner is a Christian. In Paul's mind's eye the unbeliever **'separates'**. By this is meant a permanent break or a preliminary separation leading up to it. Either way, the deserted Christian partner is left with a considerable problem.

Acceptance of the inevitable

The apostle declares his mind. If the non-Christian spouse goes away the believer must acquiesce: **'Let him leave'**; let the unbeliever be gone for ever if this is his final decision; let the abandoned Christian abandon the struggle to retrieve the irretrievable. The union has been destroyed, albeit sinfully by someone who does not know the Lord.

A bond which has become bondage

The deserted believer must not reckon that he **'has been enslaved'**. The Greek is *dedoulôtai*, a perfect passive form which means being introduced once and for all to a permanent state of bondage. If he were to consider himself tied for the rest of his life to the vanished partner the fictional marriage bond would be an intolerably crushing burden for the Christian, nothing less than a species of servitude. The non-existent marriage would be an endless tunnel without light and hope.

Marriage (7:1-40)

The apostle's good cheer is that this is not how things are. Relief is brought to the anxious and abandoned brother or sister: such people need not reckon that they have been enslaved for ever to their departed partners. This is because the marriage bond has been effectively severed by desertion and doubtless by adultery.

To repeat, in this context separation means the final termination of a marriage rather than a couple living apart for a time with a view to possibly getting together again at some later stage. Furthermore, as in the Gospels, there is no reference to court action. This is a most important point in view of the prevalence of divorce in our society and the sad fact that many Christians are no strangers to the trauma.

Another observation is essential in order to avoid a misunderstanding of the apostle's teaching. Although the two English words 'bond' and 'bondage' sound much the same, if you think about it you will agree that they have different meanings: while a 'bond' implies a voluntary union, 'bondage' means slavery. The truth is that neither Paul nor the Bible generally teaches that the marriage bond as such is a form of bondage. In 7:15 the apostle's single contention is that a bond existing only in name *has* become a form of bondage, something it was never intended to be. For this reason the intolerable tie should be cut.

Legal proceedings

What about court action? As we have noted in our consideration of 6:1-8, there were a few occasions, it is true, when Paul did go to court even though he taught that there can be situations when this would be altogether wrong for believers. Here, in 7:15, the apostle is concerned solely with a marriage terminated by desertion and presumed infidelity. For him, the legal ratification of divorce by, say, a magistrate would be no more than a sequel, a seal, a public recognition of what had happened already to the union.

This is not to say that Paul would necessarily have discounted proceedings by an abandoned believer in order to tie up loose ends and thus make a fresh start. His sole point in context is that because permanent desertion *is* tantamount to divorce, the non-offending Christian is left with no marital obligations. Unburdened and untied, he or she is in theory now free to marry again, notwithstanding the preferred course outlined by 7:11.

Be at peace

The end of 7:15 makes explicit what has been implied already: God has called Christians to remain in peace. Should the unbeliever wish to stay the Christian must honour the marriage. But if the unbeliever departs, effectively divorcing the believing partner, the latter does not need to trouble himself any longer about a *fait accompli*. Because the tie has been broken he is not now a slave to the impossible and undesirable. He knows that a further marriage could be contracted with honour. In the wake of all the misery and trauma of desertion the Lord has now given him peace of mind, heart and conscience.

Divorcees — and churches — be careful

In this commentary the view is taken that Matthew 5:32 and 19:9 permit rather than encourage divorce, and do so on the single ground of adultery. This means, first, that an abandoned and presumably aggrieved partner may marry again, and, secondly, that 7:10-15 does not contradict the express teaching of Christ. This point will be borne out by the exposition of 7:27-28.

Notwithstanding this, experience suggests that divorce on the ground of adultery is not essential; the aggrieved partner is under no legal or scriptural compulsion to depart and settle matters in court. Repentance and reconciliation are not impossible. Perhaps it should be said that neither a divorced nor a divorcing person ought to think too quickly about a new marriage. The 'rebound' syndrome is an error into which many believers fall. When it is impossible to put the clock back they rue the day they rushed into a second union.

Furthermore, a church and its minister should be extraordinarily careful when invited to host the marriage service of a divorced Christian. This is not to say that the matter is impossible. Prayerful, confidential and frank sharing, plus a great deal of time, are essential when a fellowship is involved. The elders must keep control and not be manoeuvred.

It goes without saying (or does it?) that a minister and his church premises should be involved neither in the wedding of an unbelieving couple, nor of a Christian who plans to marry a non-Christian. The latter arrangement must be, in terms of 2 Corinthians 6:14-16, an unequal yoke.

Hopefulness (7:16)

An added incentive is given for working hard at marriage with an unbeliever. If the two continue together the Christian might become the means of the unbelieving partner's conversion. **'For how do you know?'** is a positive expression of hope.[11] Nothing is too hard for the Lord even if the Christian partner cannot know how or when it might happen.

Christian contentment (7:17-24)

Turning from the subject of marriage, Paul addresses a much wider issue, that of Christian contentment. He teaches that the single and married states are not the only situations in which the people of God should consider remaining as they are; it ought to be so for believers in whatever walk of life they find themselves.

Remain as you are (7:17-18)

He begins with unexpected abruptness in 7:17: **'Only ...'** (or, 'except', as in 7:5 and 8:4). Even as Christians possess freedom to marry or not to marry, yet are advised not to be too hasty to alter the status quo, equally they are under a certain obligation not to strive to change their position in society.

We say sometimes that the grass looks greener in the next field, yet experience suggests that it is not always so. Paul's thought is not dissimilar: if God is in control of our lives (and we must believe this), let us be content with his providential mercies even if our situation does not appear to be as favourable as those of other men. As the apostle told the Athenians, it is God who has determined when and where we live so that we should seek him (Acts 17:26-27).

This principle of contentment might appear strange. After all, many of us live in democracies that on the surface do not threaten evangelical Christianity and in which men are in law perfectly free, even encouraged, to seek self-advancement. But perhaps we should remember that in Paul's day (as ever since in many places) Christians were vulnerable to the charge of sedition. The apostle was sensitive to the perils of being over-keen for a quantum change in personal circumstances. Further, he knew that wealth corrupts.[12] Being upwardly mobile was not, for him, necessarily beneficial.

'**The Lord has assigned**' (literally, 'divided') to each one his role in society. Therefore he must walk in the way in which God called him and in which he remains. This means that the call of God, previously issued and received, still holds good (as indicated by the Greek perfect tense, *kekleken*, 'he has called'). This call is either the summons to faith in Christ, as in 1:2, or, to judge by 7:20 ('Let each man remain in that condition in which he was called'), the call to the real-life situation in which believers find themselves. Perhaps one overarching summons, that of loving and serving God in the places where he sets his people, is meant.

Paul informs the Corinthians that '**I ordain**' this rule '**in all the churches**'. 'Ordain', a verb in the Greek middle voice and therefore signifying a personal interest, is strong (*diatassomai*): the apostle intends to display the authority given to him by Christ.[13] He, ex officio and with an eye to upholding the dignity of his apostolic office, can and does teach Christians both what to believe and how they should behave.

He continues. Because believers ought to be content with their lot, a circumcised and now converted Jew should not seek the surgical removal of the sign of circumcision (7:18). That this surprising and abominable practice was not unknown is proved by 1 Maccabees 1:15 in the collection of books usually called the Apocrypha: time was when young Jews who wanted to be on a par socially with their Gentile friends sought the removal of the sign of the covenant. Josephus also mentions it.[14]

Equally, if an uncircumcised man was called by the Lord he should not seek circumcision. There were, we know, converted Pharisees in the churches who sought to convince baptized Gentiles to do precisely this. They were wrong, and in acting in this way they added to Paul's problems.[15]

'One thing is needful' (7:19)

In short, converted Jews and Gentiles should remain Jews and Gentiles, the fundamental reason being that neither circumcision nor uncircumcision is a matter of any importance; both are '**nothing**', matters of indifference because both lack the status of divine law. What *is* essential is '**the keeping of the commandments of God**'.

Marriage (7:1-40)

For Paul, the ancient command to Abraham and to his natural children to be circumcised was not understood as a requirement for those who belong to Jesus by faith and who are therefore the spiritual children of the patriarch. We may recall that the apostle makes this as plain as could be in Galatians 3:29 and 5:1-15.

It follows that if Christians seek either circumcision or uncircumcision they make something out of nothing and embroil themselves in all manner of racial and doctrinal tensions. Paul implies that this must not be.

In the first century A.D. there was an almost insurmountable barrier of mutual hatred between Gentiles and Jews. The former were held in odium as unclean, and Jews were perceived as obnoxious folk who held themselves aloof but who did not always live in the way that their law demanded (Rom. 1:18-32; 2:17-24); neither side knew much about the restraint that the fear of the Lord brings. Here the apostle indicates that for Christians traditional Jewish-Gentile tension together with Old Testament ritualism are in principle dead and buried, and ought to be considered so in practice.

Two callings (7:20-24)

Paul often comes across as a versatile word-artist, and nowhere more so than here. He rests two meanings upon **'calling'** and **'call'**, a noun and verb which together appear no less than six times.

The Lord gives us our vocation (7:20)

'Let each man' remain **'in the calling** [or 'that condition', NASB] **in which he was called'** by God. Although 'call' and 'calling' elsewhere refer normally to that sovereign act of the Spirit by which he draws men to faith (1:2; Eph. 1:18; 4:1,4; 2 Tim. 1:9; 2 Peter 1:10), it might be better to interpret 'calling' here as 'vocation'. The other sense would give the superfluous idea that Christians should remain Christians.

He calls us to believe in Christ (7:21)

Unlike 7:20, the call mentioned in this verse is almost certainly the call to faith: **'Were you called while a slave?'** This question accepts that even being a slave is an example of divine vocation, and teaches positively that God has been known to call slaves to faith in Christ. It follows that the born-again slave is not to despair about his lowly station in the world. On the other hand, if it becomes possible for him to obtain his freedom, he is to grasp the opportunity because there is no law which says that he must remain in bondage. But if his condition does not alter he is not to **'worry about it'**, or plan to abscond. Paul sent the runaway but converted Onesimus back to his master (Philem. 12).

Let rich and poor rejoice (7:22)

There is a reason for acquiescence. The man who was a slave when he was **'called in the Lord'** is now **'the Lord's freedman'**.

The teaching here is that the believer who might still pass his days as somebody's slave has been released by Jesus from a far more terrible bondage, subjection to the guilt and power of sin.[16] **'Called in the Lord'** is unusually emphatic: Paul stresses the new-found dignity of the believing slave, a man despised by the world and at the bottom of the social heap. Equally, the person who is free in the world in which he lives and who has come to know the Saviour is now **'Christ's slave'**; his new-found relationship with the Lord is to lead to obedient service.[17]

In short, what we are, where we are and who we are in this world are of no lasting significance; that we are Christians is all-important. In the words of James 1:9-10, 'But let the brother of humble circumstances glory in his high position; and let the rich man glory in his humiliation, because like flowering grass he will pass away.'

'A ransom for many' (7:23)

The powerful claim of 6:20 is repeated: **'You were bought with a price.'** Although the slave who is a Christian should welcome freedom if it is available, the free man, now a purchased slave of Jesus, must struggle against becoming the property of any other person. Because he has been bought by the Lord he is in no position to sell himself.

This instruction was given to the whole church. Although Corinthian statistics are obviously not available, it might be reasonable to assume that many were freeborn or emancipated, unless their descriptions as 'foolish', 'weak', 'base', 'despised' and 'things that are not' indicate otherwise (1:27-28). Because poverty was always a threat maybe Paul knew that the temptation to put themselves on the slave-market must have been a not unattractive option for some.

Christians ought to ponder 7:23. In our high-pressure society believers sometimes find themselves in jobs that pay well but make them feel that even their free time is not their own. If and when they get into what seems like a cul-de-sac, God's people need to think hard.

Summing up (7:24)

The threads are drawn together. The situation in which, or to which, the Lord called the Christian should not be changed, however irksome it might be. Paul's explanation for this makes the heart dance: the believer is never alone: **'Let each man remain with God in that condition in which he was called.'** 'With God' means 'by God's side' and is a tremendous qualification: the Corinthians remain permanently close to their heavenly Father.[18] Nothing could be more safe. It is like this for us too.

First and second marriages (7:25-35)

'Now' (or 'but', 7:25) connects with the flow of thought of 7:8-16, concerning single people (7:8-9), divorce (7:10-11) and believers with unconverted partners (7:12-16). An intentional digression about the call of God to contentment appeared in 7:17-24.

Paul, a man upon whom the Lord relies (7:25)

'Concerning virgins' suggests that Paul responds to a Corinthian query about marriage. The Greek text gives the definite article, 'the', before 'virgins' (*peri ... tôn parthenôn*; compare 7:28,36), implying that the younger women at Corinth might be the subjects of the immediate discussion. A literal rendering could be: 'But concerning the virgins I do not have a command of the Lord.'

The meaning is that the apostle had received no specific instruction from Christ about the matter. Also, he appears to acknowledge that during the Lord's earthly ministry Jesus did not address this particular real-life situation. We should compare with 7:10, where the apostle refers back to what the Lord did teach about marriage, and with 7:12, where it is implied that Jesus had said nothing about 'mixed marriages'.

The apostle had received mercy in order to be trustworthy. In the event, as the New Testament relates, he was never other than faithful. Because of this personal qualification he can give his **'opinion'**, conscious that Christ communicates via the apostolic hand and pen, and that he, Paul, records accurately the mind of his Lord. This is neither the first nor the last time in the letter when the apostle virtually presents what evangelicals have come to understand as the twin doctrines of inspiration and inerrancy (cf. 2:16; 7:40; 14:37).

Why does he offer an opinion, and not an authoritative statement about the matter? It may be that tactful Paul wished to deflect the arrogance of some who were intent on raking up any little bit of circumstantial evidence to show that he always wanted his own way in the church. Anticipating the pitfall, he employs gentle irony to appeal to the people to keep to what he believes; after all, the Lord had not found him unreliable. The apostolic iron fist is covered with the velvet glove of compassion and of concern for his antagonists.

'The present distress' (7:26)

'Then' (or 'therefore'), in view of his status, Paul thinks that **'This is good ... that it is good for a man to remain as he is.'** 'Good', which means 'better', carries over from 7:8 and is repeated for emphasis: the apostle stresses that his advice would be to the advantage of the Corinthians. Just for the moment he floats before the church the benefit of remaining single. **'Man'** stands for 'person', whether male or female; all are targeted by Paul's counsel.

'Distress' (or 'necessity', or 'compulsion') refers either to the actual situation of the Corinthians or possibly to impending difficulties. Either way, a further consideration in favour of the single state is that matrimony might well be hazardous, given the perils facing the church. Would it really be wise for a Christian to take on a responsibility of this magnitude? Probably not.

From 7:26 alone it is not possible to be certain what the 'distress' would have been. Perhaps Paul realized that the spread of the gospel

Marriage (7:1-40)

must lead inevitably to persecution, of which he had firsthand experience.

A first marriage, and marriage after divorce (7:27-28)

He insists that if a man happens to be married he should not try to alter the status quo: **'Have you been bound to a wife? Stop seeking release'** (7:27). Because the marriage union is intended to be permanent, lasting until death parts the partners, disconsolate spouses should abandon their efforts to end their marriages. It is as if the apostle says, 'Don't even think about it.'

He continues: **'Are you released from a wife? Stop seeking a wife.'** That is, if someone has contrived successfully to terminate his marriage he ought to remain single. 'Stop seeking a wife' means that any ongoing search to find a new partner should grind to an abrupt halt: 'I know that some of you are thinking about it. Don't.'

'Release', 'released' (7:27)

The Greek noun *lusis* and verb *lelusai* in **'Do not seek release'** and **'Are you released from a wife?'** mean the severance of a connection, the cutting of a bond. A good example of the usage would be the untying of the donkey requisitioned by our Lord: effectively the creature and its owner parted company (Matt. 21:2; Mark 11:2; Luke 19:30). Paul's assumption is that if and when there is a dissolution of the marital bond it is not by death: the two partners have left each other in order to work out their separate lives.

Nowhere in the Bible does 'released' ever mean the conclusion of a marriage through the decease of a husband or his wife. The reason is that bereavement is not understood in such a superficial fashion. When the Lord took away Ezekiel's wife from him, 'the desire of his eyes', the prophet was not released from her (Ezek. 24:16-18). Lenski comments helpfully that 'bound' and 'released' concern 'present conditions as the result of a past act'.[19] Just so. Death is not an act.

Therefore 'Do not seek release,' and 'Are you released?' in 7:27 refer respectively to the contemplation of divorce and to an accomplished divorce. To repeat, Paul's considered opinion is that both married and divorced Christians should stay as they are.

Remarriage is not wrong (7:28)

The statement, **'If you should marry, you have not sinned,'** is important. Note that the apostle does not contradict himself by directing that a divorced man must marry again. Writing specifically to the Christian whose marriage to an adulterous partner has been terminated, he gives his reluctant permission for a further union: were it to come to pass it would not be wrong. Apparently, the apostle says this with the awareness that during his earthly ministry the Lord never referred explicitly to such a situation. He knows that he, the faithful servant of the Lord, has been commissioned as a scribe by God the Holy Spirit.

Further, **'If a virgin should marry, she has not sinned.'** This is an extraordinary assertion. No doubt we would say that it must always be preferable for a maiden to marry rather than to remain a permanent spinster. But not Paul. Even in a situation with no marital complications the apostle is less than enthusiastic about a prospective union.

The reason is that should both the divorced person and the maiden contract marriages, **'such'** people must accumulate **'trouble'** for **'the flesh'**. By 'flesh' is meant human nature rather than just the body: the apostle is convinced that any and every marriage must generate all manner of stress. Because he wishes to **'spare'** the people such difficulties Paul discourages matrimony.

The fleeting years (7:29-31)

The apostle develops his thesis against marriage by introducing a revelation: **'But this I say, brethren, the time has been shortened'** (7:29). The Greek word (*sunstellô*) behind 'shortened' occurs in Acts 5:6, where the body of Ananias is said to have been wrapped or packed up prior to removal. The meaning is rather the same here: the 'time', a set season, is on the verge of being removed.

Troubled times

It is not easy to understand what is meant. Perhaps Paul had in mind a situation something like that faced by the prophet Jeremiah. The latter was instructed by the Lord not to marry and raise a family

Marriage (7:1-40)

because time was short; the place where he lived would soon be subject to invasion and associated disasters (Jer. 16:1-4).[20]

Because a 'time' can hardly be an event it is likely that Paul's reference is neither to death nor to the coming of Christ. The better interpretation would be that the apostle considers the vexed seasons through which the churches travel in this temporary, passing world. This would tie in with 'the present distress' mentioned in 7:26. Since, in the words of Henry Lyte's hymn, 'Swift to its close ebbs out life's little day,' the Corinthians should not exaggerate the importance of getting married. Compare this with the teaching of our Lord in Matthew 24:38 and Luke 17:27 about a world that disregards eternity and for which marriage is usually a number-one priority.

Heaven is near

More applications of the necessity of looking a long way ahead continue through to 7:31.

First, these verses do not claim that married men should ignore their wives (7:29); nor that both tears and joy should be suppressed; nor that those who acquire goods should discard their new possessions (7:30); nor that Christians should refrain from making proper use of what the world has to offer (7:31).

The meaning is that time must eventually run out. When it does there can be no further opportunities for marriage, sadness, happiness and profit-making. Therefore Christians should not be engrossed with matters that are to vanish for ever as soon as eternity dawns.

This explains the exhortation of 7:31: **'and they who are using the world** [be] **as those who do not use it too much'**. The Greek verb *katachraomai*, rendered here by 'use too much', occurs also in 9:18, where Paul indicates that he never over-asserts his rights as an apostle. In both places the idea is that preoccupation with possessions or status, or the status which possessions are sometimes deemed to give, is unwise and even dangerous.

The reason for such detachment has been proposed in 7:29; here it is repeated unambiguously: **'For the form** [or, 'scheme'; Greek, *schema*] **of this world is passing away'** (cf. 1 John 2:8,17). 'Form' means the appearance of a thing as it really is. Philippians 2:7 states that our Lord was found in the 'form' of a man, the reason being that he had become a man. The sense in 7:31 is that this godless world in substance and in appearance is currently passing from view. Because one day it will be gone for ever there is nothing to be gained in being overenthusiastic about joys that take their leave. Nor is anything to be gained by nursing a heart broken by vanishing sadnesses.

A further reason for staying single (7:32-35)

Now appears a fifth reason for not marrying (7:32). Before we consider it, let's recapitulate what Paul has said thus far in favour of the single state. First, it can be a *charisma* that ought not to be disdained (7:7). Secondly, it is appropriate to the impending, or even imminent, distress (7:26). Thirdly, marriage can bring trouble for the flesh (7:28). Fourthly, matrimony is essentially a temporary matter (7:31).

Married people are preoccupied people (7:32-34a)

Paul desires the Corinthians **'to be free from concern'**, to live without the worries attendant upon married life. Positively, the single Christian is in a position to be **'concerned about the things of the Lord, how he may please the Lord'** (7:32).

The problem for the married man is that he loads himself at one stroke with the duty of looking after his wife. He knows that he has an enduring responsibility to the lady he brings to his house and that she must not be ignored (7:33). Because this is how it is, **'He has been divided'** (7:34a) and is in no position to give undisturbed attention to the Lord's work. This construction is preferable to linking 'divided' with **'unmarried woman'** and **'virgin'** in the same verse; the latter have no such distractions. To this extent the NASB translation is helpful. However, in giving, 'His interests are divided', the NASB masks the subtle emphasis, which is that the married man, rather than his responsibilities, is fragmented.[21] A possible translation of 7:33-34a could be: 'But the married man is concerned about the things of the world, how he might please his wife — and he remains divided.'

The last part of the statement is laconic, as if bachelor Paul says, 'This, men and brethren, is how it is when you get married. You travel in two ways at once and can never be entirely comfortable.'

Marriage (7:1-40)

Notice that both a husband and his wife are supposed to **'please'** each other. Their mutual responsibility is considerably more than a question of living and surviving for a number of years under the same roof, she getting meals on time and cleaning up, he being the principal bread-winner, and both bringing up the children, if any, decently.

Single women (7:34b)

In 7:32 reference was made to the single man. Now attention is directed to the **'woman who is unmarried'** (that is, a widow or a divorced woman) and to the **'virgin'**. It is acknowledged that in each case the lady will be **'concerned about the things of the Lord, that she may be holy both in body and spirit'**. Note incidentally Paul's acceptance that a saint who has been through the trauma of divorce might well work effectively in his church; without domestic distractions he is now in a position to separate himself for loyal and valuable service. It would be unwise for us to put this truth to one side.

A superficial reading of **'that she may be holy both in body and spirit'** suggests that marriage brings with it physical and spiritual impurity, and that, *ipso facto*, the single person is holy and pure. But this cannot be the true interpretation. Recall that the basic meaning of 'holy' is separation or consecration, as in 7:14. There, a man and his wife who committed themselves to each other on their wedding day are said to remain in a 'holy' state.

Let's put this into focus. Total, undivided attention in 'body and spirit' to the work of the Lord is being discussed. It is strictly within this frame of reference that the unmarried believer is said to be better qualified than her married counterpart. Because the former has nothing else to think about she is in this respect (and in this respect alone) 'holy' or separated. If it happens that she is morally more pure than her married sister in the Lord it is not because she is single and the other is not. This explains the last part of the verse: **'... but the married woman is concerned about the things of the world, how she may please her husband.'**

Wise guidance (7:35)

Although the apostle's words are designed to **'benefit'** the Corinthians, he advises rather than commands. Nor does he write in order to throw a noose around them. **'Noose'**, translated by the NASB as 'restraint', is the proper meaning (Greek, *brochos*).[22] Paul refuses to lassoo his readers to make them go exactly where he wants. They remain free; they do not have to be single. The apostle's sole purpose is to outline a way for Christian service that will be **'seemly'**, **'established'** (or 'constant') and **'without distraction'**.

As a matter of interest, we might contrast the believer who serves without being sidetracked with 'distracted' Martha, a woman who was, as far as we know, unmarried (Luke 10:40). Concerned about many things, this busy spinster made insufficient time for the one matter that really was important in her life, listening to Jesus. It might appear that there is no guaranteed, primrose path to serenity in the Lord's work. Even so, the truth held out by 7:32-34 is that for the conscientious believer remaining a bachelor or a spinster has its distinct merits. Think about this if you are contemplating marriage.

It is perfectly true that many unbelievers opt for the single state, although never for biblical reasons. There is an infinite gap between the outlook of the world and that of the saints in this, one of the most important issues of life.

What, it might be asked, of ministers and elders who do not marry? In practice it cannot always be easy for a single man to succeed in the eldership role. But it is not impossible, particularly if he works with fellow-elders and if there are godly women in his church who can cope with feminine problems.

When a father might become a father-in-law (7:36-38)

Each of these three verses addresses a Christian father who has **'his virgin daughter'** (7:36). The parent discovers that the young lady desires to marry. Presumably under some filial pressure, he now faces up to giving away a daughter and gaining a son-in-law.

Father and daughter (7:36)

The apostle insists that the father must not allow the suitor to relieve him of his daughter just because the couple seek marriage. Because the parent is still responsible for the girl's future welfare even at this

Marriage (7:1-40)

relatively advanced date, he possesses the right of veto. This is to be exercised if he concludes that the marriage would be unwise.

'His virgin'

The emotive expression **'his virgin'** in 7:36 and the more dramatic **'his own virgin'** twice in 7:37-38 are introduced to highlight the preciousness of the bond that ought to exist between father and daughter. 'Daughter' does not occur in the Greek text, deliberate emphasis being placed upon the maiden state and the vulnerability of the young lady.

The strength of the words 'his own virgin [daughter]' might be gauged by the contents of an old Egyptian papyrus letter. Sent off by an aggrieved householder, Orsenouphis, to his local police chief, Serapion, about A.D. 29, the former complained that when he was away at work a local jobbing builder came to his home to knock down a wall. While doing this the workman unearthed a jewellery box. Allegedly, the builder handed the contents to 'his own virgin daughter' to take away to his own house. Because of the theft, aggravated by the parental perversion of the hitherto innocent girl, Orsenouphis demands that the police chief bring the thieving builder to justice.[23]

The apostle employs a similar expression to remind the Corinthian father that he is responsible for his daughter and that he must do what is right for her.

Losing a daughter; gaining a son

Notice that the girl is assumed to be a maiden and that her father might be **'acting unbecomingly'** were he to withhold consent. That is, in some circumstances refusal would be positively shocking and shameful. Perhaps the girl might be goaded by her truculent father to do something wrong because he arbitrarily obstructed a union obviously so right.

It follows that if the young lady has arrived at **'full age'**, when her natural attractions and personal desires are not to be denied, permission to marry ought to be forthcoming: **'If it should be so ... let them marry.'** The father would not sin if he assumes the mantle of a prospective father-in-law.

'No!' (7:37)

But the girl's father might perceive that a union would be unsafe. Therefore he refuses, but only after he has pondered the matter carefully.

Thinking things through

First, he must **'stand firm in his heart'**. Convinced that a negative response must be to his daughter's ultimate advantage, he will not be moved. Her pleas avail nothing, nor those of the young man and his family, should they be sufficiently undignified to remonstrate.

Second, there must be no external **'constraint'** or necessity thrust upon the parent. Paul considers the situation of the father who is aware that there is no compelling reason for his girl to marry. If he is under no such compulsion, let him deny permission. In practical terms, what might bring him to say 'no' is left to the imagination of the reader. Perhaps the father senses that she is infatuated rather than a woman in love, and that in her immaturity she is not yet able to tell the difference.

Father's word should be final

The principle is also expressed in the opposite way: the father **'has authority over his own will'**. This means that the final decision is the prerogative of the parent, and of the parent alone, and that he is perfectly free to act according to his own conviction, should he have one. Therefore, if he **'has decided this in his own heart, to keep his own virgin daughter, he will do well'**. An apostolic compliment is in effect paid to the father who, after weighing up all the factors, has made an affectionate, settled and possibly expensive decision to maintain his daughter permanently rather than deliver her to another man's care.

This is important. Paul implies that a father may block his daughter's marriage, but only if he is prepared to assume responsibility for her future welfare. A man may leave his parents, but if a daughter remains at home her father must support her to the best of his ability.

Marriage (7:1-40)

The better decision (7:38)

The matter is summed up. Although the father who **'gives his own virgin daughter in marriage does well'**, if he refrains he **'will do better'**. In short, it is preferable for him to put a stop to the romance, taking this apparently drastic step for each and all of the reasons stated in the preceding verses. The fathers of young Corinthian ladies are expected to read, mark and inwardly digest. Can we doubt that the apostle had many other fathers in mind, too? His teaching is timeless.

It is clear that Paul assumes that if a father does not wish his daughter to marry she would be willing to obey him. We may ask if this pattern of filial obedience is true to life nowadays. It ought to be. But bear in mind the apostle's overall insistence that the hesitant parent has to take every consideration into account before he turns down the suitor. He must be disinterested, seeking her benefit, not his. Paul must have known that this could be a problem because then as now daughters were sometimes considered a liability, offspring to be married off as soon as possible. The apostle shows that young women are a long-term responsibility, whether for fathers or for husbands.

The remarriage of widows (7:39-40)

Thought has been given to everybody within the Corinthian fellowship. But Paul has a little more to say. Developing his comment in 7:8, he gives further consideration to the situation of Christian widows. His doctrine is strictly in line with the teaching of the Gospels about marriage.[24]

'Until death do us part' (7:39)

A wife is **'bound'** to her husband. Having been tied to him on their wedding-day, she remains attached for as long as he and she are alive. This is taken for granted. As Romans 7:2 states tersely, 'The married woman is bound by law to her husband while he is living.' But if the husband **'has fallen asleep'** the widow is free to marry any one provided he (or, possibly, the marriage) is **'in the Lord'**.

'Falling asleep' and 'soul-sleep'

We should not overlook the truth that when the Bible speaks about death as 'falling asleep' it does so with exclusive reference to the passing away of Christians. Unbelievers are never in mind; they are said to die rather than slumber.[25] Here it is assumed that the widow's first husband was a believer.

When Christians 'fall asleep' their bodies revert to dust and their souls enter the immediate presence of the Lord where they enjoy full consciousness. The case of the dying thief is an obvious example (Luke 23:43). This point needs to be made because there have always been Bible-loving Christians who hold that at death the spirit remains asleep until the resurrection morning. With the greatest possible respect, not so.

'In the Lord' — only

Observe, too, the description of the contemplated union between the widow and another man: it must be **'in the Lord'**. If Christ does not surround and contain, as it were, the husband as well as the wife-to-be, the lady must not present herself to him for matrimony.

The benefits of widowhood (7:40)

The widow will be happier if she remains as she is. Although the apostle asserts that this is his **'opinion'** he adds that **'I think that I also have the Spirit of God.'**

Paul's courteous modesty overwhelms. As in 7:25, concerning single people, and in 2 Corinthians 8:10, where he gives his views about planned and disciplined giving to the Lord's people, the apostle deploys the emphasis of understatement. He does this to show his humble awareness that what he believes and says is from the Lord. Let the Corinthians, then, read his words carefully. The word 'also' — 'I *also* have the Spirit' — might be ironic: he protests that he, the apostle, no less than certain gifted Corinthians, does know the will of God in such sensitive issues.

5. Food offered to idols
(8:1 - 11:1)

Not a few of the Corinthians were uncertain about how they should relate to unbelievers in their city, most of whom must have been practising idolaters. It would have been virtually impossible for the congregation not to have been confronted with, and tempted by, the traditional paganism that it now renounced. Were such contacts a serious problem which could disable the saints? Some felt keenly about the matter and winced, and others made light of it.

'Strong' Christians

Those who had few qualms of conscience about eating sacrificed food reckoned themselves strong enough to shrug off the fascinations of the surrounding world. The other, less pleasing side of the coin was that they tended to show scant concern for the hesitations of their not-so-confident brothers in Christ. Why, they let it be known, should the rest not think through a matter that was transparent for them, the more sophisticated element in the fellowship? Why should others have a problem about an issue that for them was strictly a non-issue?

The question of associations with idolaters was felt by the church as a whole to have been a burning and formidable difficulty, which is why they presented it to the apostle for his counsel. **'Concerning'** in 8:1 suggests strongly that Paul writes in response to the fellowship's request for guidance.

A complex problem

There must have been several side-issues tangled up together. Was it right for Christians to eat out with idolaters in a temple? Was it acceptable for them to buy and then consume in their own homes meat which they were aware had been sacrificed previously to the gods? Could a Corinthian believer accept without demur the hospitality of an unbeliever whose table would offer such food? What about the involvement of Christians in the ongoing commercial and social life of the city, a city never other than intensely religious? What of family associations with loved ones who had not come to know the Lord?

A double response

The fact that three chapters, 8, 9 and 10, are dedicated to the matter indicates its importance for Paul as well as for the church. Two principal replies are given. Looking at the same problem from somewhat different points of view, both responses insist that the believer ought never to eat within the precincts of a pagan place of worship, and that at no time and in no situation must he accept food which he knows has been offered to the gods.

Are the gods real?

First (ch. 8), the apostle shows his awareness that although the Gentile Christians in the church had renounced belief in the existence of the gods, many were still influenced by inherited superstition. The problem was that their new-found faith in the living God, being relatively naïve, sometimes wilted when confronted by the ancient polytheism. Because they suspected in their weaker moments that perhaps the Olympian gods were not entirely unreal, they developed a defence mechanism, shunning anything even remotely connected with these beings. Inevitably, their black-and-white approach made them suspicious and even intensely critical of those believers who did not see eye to eye with them about this.

Paul acknowledges that not everybody would be prone to such suspicions. But he realizes that even the relative maturity of the stronger element within the church was generating its own problems:

Food offered to idols (8:1 - 11:1)

the head-knowledge of some would not necessarily heal the heart-sickness of others. He teaches that the Christian who now ridicules the gods must take into account the reservations of less aware people in the fellowship.

Suppose, the apostle writes, that the more mature saint eats food previously sacrificed to one or more of the gods of the Greek pantheon. How might his action be interpreted by other brethren when they hear about it? Would not rash, arrogant and unthinking participation by an overconfident Christian encourage the less sophisticated believer to imitate him, but in his case as an act of deliberate homage, perhaps to Poseidon or Athena or Aphrodite? Would not such an apostasy turn out to be spiritually and morally disastrous?

Bear in mind that the centre of Corinth was dominated by a centuries-old temple dedicated to Apollo and was replete with other shrines, all hardly less obvious. Consider that it was impossible for Paul or anyone else to go out of his front door without being exposed almost immediately to the affront and challenge of idolatry, an idolatry manifested blatantly in every avenue, in every plaza and on every hill. It was not easy for any believer to dismiss these abominations as unreal. After all, too many Greeks believed in them, as had generations of their forefathers. Could time-honoured traditions and the consensus of Greek opinion really be in error? Paul did not underestimate inherited superstition.

Demons

The second response is given in chapter 10. Although the apostle accepts that the gods are fantasies, he teaches unambiguously that demons and evil spirits do exist. Further, they are always present in temple worship. It follows that any sacrifice to non-existent gods is effectively, although perhaps not intentionally, an offering to demonic powers. This is a pitfall that Christians must avoid at all costs. The sad precedent of Israel in the wilderness is introduced to establish the matter.

The Lord first, others second and oneself last

Chapter 9 bridges the flow of thought from chapters 8 to 10 by bringing in details about Paul's own lifestyle. This is to show that the hesitations of others, rather than one's own opportunities, are of paramount importance. The apostle offers himself as a model of practical courtesy and consideration for the Corinthians to mull over.

The Council of Jerusalem (Acts 15)

Interestingly, no reference is made in these chapters to the Council of Jerusalem, described in detail in Acts 15. A few years before the gospel ever came to Corinth the council, with Paul present, decreed that Gentile converts should as a matter of policy refuse food previously dedicated to heathen worship (Acts 15:20,28-29).[1]

We need to ask why it was that the apostle studiously ignored what had been decided by the apostles, the elders and ultimately the Holy Spirit. The only possible answer is that he knew the complexity of the matter demanded that it be discussed on its own merits. This is why Paul invites the Corinthians to think the issue through with him.

Converted Jews never had problems in this area. For them, saying no to idol-food was an open-and-shut issue. Just like Daniel, Shadrach, Meshach and Abed-nego centuries earlier in Babylon, or like the apostle Peter at Joppa in more recent times, nothing prohibited by Moses or offered upon a heathen altar would ever pass their lips (Dan. 1:8,16; Acts 10:14).

It was otherwise for converted Greeks. They sprang from a culture that since time immemorial remained devoted to Olympus. It followed that much of the food available to them in the markets was polluted by pagan rites. But for the saints the perspective had changed. Whereas the Greek Christians had previously enjoyed this meat, now they belonged to Jesus. Therefore, the old routine should alter. Or should it? If so, how?

Were these believers supposed to abandon their eating habits? Were they to shun occasions when their families, friends and associates feasted in honour of the gods? Must believers pick and choose between commodities on display for fear that the food might be spiritually contaminated? Conversely, if Christians rightfully chose to eat anything they desired, why should they be stigmatized as libertines? Might not such boldness be a much-needed lesson in true Christian freedom for less confident brothers? Because the

Food offered to idols (8:1 - 11:1) 159

Jerusalem Council did not touch on such sensitive matters Paul grapples with them in detail.

On eating sacrifices (8:1-13)

First, the church is reminded that there is, after all, only one God and only one Saviour (8:1-6). Second, the people are taught in no uncertain terms that those who are not sure about this are vulnerable to temptation and can easily be led into sin (8:7-13).

One God; one Saviour (8:1-6)

Not for the first time, Paul responds to queries put to him by the congregation.

The Corinthians were clever

The apostle opens by countering local claims to superior know-how in these controversial matters, asserting aggressively that **'We know that we all have knowledge'** (8:1). Although there were some in the church who rejoiced in their sophistication, they must not imagine that they had a monopoly of insight; Paul and many with him appreciated that there is one God and that the ethnic deities are nothing.

'We' could refer to believers generally who by definition have professed Christ and have renounced old allegiances even though some might not have allowed the conviction to work itself out in practice. If so, the audacious Corinthians should not reckon that they had superior enlightenment; they were just the same as the rest. Alternatively, 'we' might refer to more mature Christians like Paul who did bring doctrine to bear upon what they did or did not do. The first view is preferable because the apostle was not in the habit of stratifying believers even though he did recognize that some have a deeper relationship with the Lord than others (Gal. 6:1, 'you, the spiritual').

The apostle says that there is a rather unpleasant problem about saints who know that they know and who perceive slyly that others do not: their knowledge **'inflates'**. Neither for the first nor the last time, this rather harsh word is employed because Paul knows something else: that self-conceit is damaging the church. **'But,'** he insists, **'love edifies'**; it builds up a congregation.

Not-so-clever Corinthians

Some Corinthians smirked because they were sufficiently strong to apply their beliefs in tricky situations, although solely for their own advantage and with scant concern for other believers. The trouble was not with what these splendid people knew, but that they did not use their sterile knowledge in the right way. Therefore their comprehension was an insult to genuine knowledge, bearing no resemblance to the incandescent, loving wisdom that yearns to meet the needs of the people of God. The clever but indifferent Christian **'has not yet known as he ought to know'** (8:2). These words, selected with the greatest care, must have caused some of the Corinthians to writhe.

'The fruit of the Spirit is love' (8:3)

The reference to being **'known'** by God falls within a logical sequence of thought. The Christian who does know the truth of God knows God. This is another way of saying that he loves God. Knowing and loving God in a vital way, he will recognize and love his fellow saints for what they are. If this is the case it is because **'He has been known by him'** (God). The man's loving nature springs from the amazing fact that originally he had been chosen and now has been renewed by the Lord.[2]

If this is the meaning, and it probably is, it is not hard to see that a fundamental challenge is being thrown down by the apostle: it is only God's true people who love the church. If the Corinthians did not love with overflowing hearts they needed to ask themselves if they were really in the faith. Their undoubtedly vigorous monotheism was no guarantee.

'The Lord our God is one Lord' (8:4)

The sensitive issue of eating idol-sacrifices is addressed. Principally, both the Corinthians and Paul were instinctively aware of two related truths. First, **'There is no such thing as an idol in the world'**; second, **'There is no God except one.'**

Food offered to idols (8:1 - 11:1)

By 'idol' is meant the deity which the image represents. Like the prophets of the Old Testament, Paul asserts that popular objects of worship are powerless, and that there is just the one true God.[3]

The gods of this world (8:5)

The apostle acknowledges that every society gives lip-service to **'so-called gods'** that allegedly exist **'in heaven'** or **'on earth'**. But he goes further. Again taking the Old Testament as his platform,[4] Paul asserts that although the traditional deities are fabulous, the constructions of sinful imaginations, behind them lurk spiritual personalities: **'There are many gods and many lords.'**

Although such beings cannot be gods and lords in an absolute sense, it is insisted that they are the principals behind the idols and fictitious gods served by vast numbers of deluded people. In terms of Ephesians 6:12, these invisible powers are nothing less than 'the world forces of this darkness ... spiritual forces of wickedness in the heavenly places'. Although Paul will elaborate on this sombre truth in 10:19-20, for the moment he shows that there are so-called gods which do not exist and malignant spiritual powers which, although not divine, do operate in the real world of Corinth and elsewhere.

People who dwell alone (8:6)

Turning away from the error of popular belief, the apostle is positive: **'For us there is but one God.'**

First of all, this God is **'the Father'**. Paul assumes that God is Father uniquely and essentially in his relationship with Christ, the Second Person of the Trinity, and that for this reason he is the Father of those who are united to Christ. Neither is he the Father of all men in general, nor are all his children.

Secondly, **'from whom'**, that is, from the Father, **'are all things'**. This means that the one God is the sole Creator of the universe, beyond which there is nothing.

Thirdly, **'We exist for him'** (NASB), or, more literally (and certainly more vividly), 'and we — for him'. 'We', by which are meant believers, are under solemn obligation to worship and to serve the Father alone to the exclusion of all other beings, whether imagined or real.

Let's pause. The statement that only Christians are in a position to live for the Father does not mean that unbelievers are not duty-bound to turn to Christ and worship the one God. After all, before writing this letter the apostle had proclaimed boldly at Athens, an ancient centre of clever paganism, that 'God now commands all men everywhere to repent' (Acts 17:30). The meaning of 8:6 is that because born-again Christians do have a heavenly Father they can respond to him and should avail themselves of their privileged status.

Fourthly, there is **'one Lord, Jesus Christ'**. That Jesus is the personal Lord of every believer is gloriously true, although the principle is not brought to the fore here. The apostle's teaching is that ultimate authority in heaven and earth has been delegated by God the Father to God the Son. Jesus is in control of all men, angels and events; there is no other lord of the universe.[5]

Fifthly, the Lord Jesus is said to have been the sole agent of creation: **'by whom are all things'**.[6] We need to consider this statement carefully. The reality is that when he created the world the eternal Son of God was *not* the man Jesus from Nazareth, and that the cosmos was *not* brought into being by the incarnate Saviour. It was afterwards, many years later, that the eternal Word of God became the human Son of God, the real man that he never was before.

This means that since the birth at Bethlehem God the Father remains Father to his Son in two modes. First, within the eternal divine Father/divine Son relationship; second, as the divine Father of a human son, a relationship that began two thousand years ago when God fathered a human baby mothered by the virgin Mary (Luke 1:35).

Coming back to 8:6, Christ is seen by Paul as one person, albeit with two natures, the one truly human and the other truly divine. For this reason the apostle felt free to expound the man Jesus conceived in the womb of Mary as the Creator. And he was right. If the Saviour were some sort of hybrid, two persons sharing a body, Paul would have been in grievous error. But, consistently with the rest of the Bible, 8:6 insists that the God-man is essentially one person: it was *this* Jesus, the Saviour of his people, who brought 'all things' into being.

Although in his letters and recorded sermons the apostle never refers to the circumstances of the birth of Jesus, his reticence is no

Food offered to idols (8:1 - 11:1)

proof that he was ignorant of what happened. When Galatians 4:4 states that the pre-existing 'Son of God' was 'born of a woman', and when Romans 1:3 expounds Jesus as born 'of the seed of David', Paul signals that he knew and believed all the data that we have in the Gospels.

Sixthly, it is Christ alone who has brought us to salvation: **'And we exist through him.'** This is an elaboration of 1:4, that the grace of God has been given to his people 'in Christ Jesus'.

The thrust of these six statements is deliberate. If it is true that the Corinthians owe everything to God in Christ, it has to be the case that they owe nothing at all to any spiritual being, either imagined or real. It follows that every appearance of idol-worship must be abandoned.

Ruining fellow-believers (8:7-13)

Unhappily, among some of the Corinthians such convictions were lacking (8:7a). A literal rendering might be: **'But not in all is knowledge.'** Paul displays pastoral discretion and names no names. Some believers **'until now'** were **'accustomed'** to the view that the temple food that they ate had been **'sacrificed to an idol'**, offered to the personality represented by its nauseating image. They persist in gross immaturity. Earlier traditions and imaginations still flickered in spite of the fact that when they were baptized these Christians had acknowledged the living God.

Reeds shaken with the wind (8:7b)

The immediate effect was that **'Their conscience being weak is defiled'**, or stained. Because they were not sure if what they did was right or wrong they felt unclean and possibly regretted what they had done. Pricked in their hearts, they might well have asked themselves what action, if any, they should adopt. Paul was aware that they usually took the easy way out, stifling their whimpering consciences and carrying on regardless. He knew that it would have been difficult to resist the pressures put upon them by fellow-Christians, let alone the world.

But bruised reeds should not be broken (8:8-9)

1. The pre-eminence of love

The apostle realized that when the weaker saint is smitten with pangs of conscience the more knowledgeable Christian might well ponder what counsel to offer. He might conclude that he should instruct his straying brother to brush away unnecessary scruples and enjoy the food of the non-existent gods. Paul takes issue with such an implied plan of action (8:8): it is love that conquers, not argument.

Let's apply this. Compare, for a moment, 8:1 and 8:7. All believers have knowledge, yet none has much knowledge. One of the realities of church life is that we Christians can be exceedingly shallow in our faith. The average congregation is a fragile thing. Because this is so elders, like Paul, should be gentle. When 8:1 states that 'Love builds up', the meaning is that victory in argument can be tantamount to defeat: when an opponent is shown to be in the wrong he might be antagonized to the extent that in his acute embarrassment he refuses to come over to your position and regards you as his opponent. The guiding principle is that we should never reckon those with whom we disagree to be targets for our clever wit and wisdom. Although consideration for other people's feelings might not in the short term boost the ego, church-building cannot get far without it.

2. Principles

Christians ought to have principles. But we need to be sure that they are biblical: if they do not come from Scripture we can tie ourselves up in knots. With regard to food sacrificed to idols, some Corinthians were sincere in their views, yet were sincerely wrong. Explosions were imminent and Paul had to defuse the situation. Similarly, it is possible for us to be mistaken in our opinions, yet genuine enough when we act consistently with them. If we rebel against our misguided convictions we offend (remarkably) against God. 'Whatever is not from faith is sin' (Rom. 14:23). One saint's meat can be another saint's poison.

Food offered to idols (8:1 - 11:1) 165

3. The joy of capitulation

'But food will not commend us to God' (8:8). Whether or not the future tense indicates that the ultimate Day of Judgement is under consideration, the apostle's logic is that in this present world believers are not better Christians if they eat, and are none the worse in the sight of God if they refrain from eating. It follows that should mature Corinthians decline what is for them harmless temple food they cannot damage themselves. But they might well help someone for whom participation is by no means an innocent act. How much better it would be to give up the practice! The example of personal renunciation might work wonders.

It is true that the believer has been given complete **'authority'** (NASB, 'liberty') to eat anything (8:9). Even so, he must **'see'** (NASB, 'take care') that this freedom does not become **'a stumbling block to the weak'**. Perhaps some of the complacent Corinthians, blithely aware that they did not have a problem with temple food, were acting with no thought for the less mature; quite simply, they did not care that their well-publicized behaviour might devastate the spiritual lives of other Christians. They were happy to remain oblivious to the principle of Romans 14:13: 'Let us not judge one another any more, but rather determine this — not to put an obstacle or a stumbling block in a brother's way.'

The wandering believer, because of whom Christ died (8:10-12)

1. The wanton destruction of an immature believer

The effect of such crude zeal is outlined in 8:10. Paul addresses a hypothetical individual (**'you'**, singular) to bring home the awfulness of what is happening.

'You' need to think carefully about an immature Christian who suspects that the gods do exist. Perhaps he watches you with interest, you, a knowledgeable brother in the Lord, **'reclining in an idol's temple'**, a public place open to all. He observes that you take your ease with idolaters in enjoying the food of the gods.

As a result of what his eyes show him he dismisses any lingering scruples. He is **'edified'**, strengthened in his delusion to the extent that he persuades himself that it is safe and even advantageous to follow your example. You also vainly imagine that this personal *de facto* demolition of another Christian is nothing short of a building-up process for him. After all, you are where you are both to see and to be seen, and if a less convinced brother follows your example, you are pleased with what you, with your advanced knowledge, are doing for him. How wrong you are!

That it cannot be right to acknowledge the Olympian gods or any other gods does not in the excitement of the occasion occur to the Christian with an unsteady conscience. If he has any qualms he does not let them trouble him too much. He eats. He sets his seal upon someone else's sacrifice and confesses someone else's god. In doing this he denies Christ. What he does is inconceivably awful.

That Paul was not indulging in idle theological speculation might be illustrated by the martyrdom of Polycarp, Bishop of Smyrna. He perished at the stake in about A.D. 160 because of his refusal to sacrifice to 'Lord Caesar'. The aged elder confessed that such an offering would be blasphemy against Christ, his 'King' for eighty-six years. That he could save his life by sacrifice did not count. He was afraid to present to Caesar worship due to Christ alone.[7]

The direct consequence of the mature Corinthian's involvement is that **'through your knowledge'** the weak person **'is ruined'** or (better) 'is being destroyed' (8:11).

2. What is meant by 'being destroyed'?

Charles Hodge considers that Paul has in mind a foolish and naïve church member who never knew the Lord and who honours the gods by eating such food. Because his apostasy is deliberate his eternal destruction has become certain.[8] This line of interpretation is doubtful.

It needs to be borne in mind that the death of Christ is presented in 8:11 as having occurred **'because of'** the Corinthian **'brother'**. NASB gives 'the brother for whose sake Christ died'. Although this is not incorrect it tends to mask the starkness and intentional abruptness of Paul's expression. If you will allow a further mini-lesson in grammar, the Greek terms behind 'because of' (*dia* + the accusative) can mean nothing other than cause and effect. In fact, 8:11 is the only place in the New Testament where it is said explicitly that Christ died 'because of' an individual, although Romans 4:25 and 1 Peter 1:20 come near.

Food offered to idols (8:1 - 11:1)

As Hodge sees it, this has to mean that the Lord suffered to secure benefits other than, but not including, the poor man's certain redemption. Because he had never been brought to know the grace of God he could not fall from it. Because he is provoked by an unwise church member he filters back to the sinful world that he always loved.

This approach is unnecessarily complicated. Paul does not choose to identify the man under consideration as an apostate. Otherwise expressed, he sees the erring brother as someone who has come to know the Saviour because Christ's sufferings procured his faith.

Furthermore, the apostle cannot have believed that in the church there was a contingent of baptized but unconverted and practising idolaters of whom this man was a specimen, and that as 'brothers' they were to be cosseted and encouraged to stay in active fellowship. Paul would surely have advocated their removal. His silence on this point does not help Hodge's interpretation. Our options narrow.

The obvious view is far better. To repeat, Christ died 'because of' this particular 'brother' in order to save and to sanctify him. It follows that the apparent idolater was a redeemed saint, an elect child of God and no apostate, one who would never lose his salvation.[9]

3. A life wasted

Undoubtedly, the apostle agonized over the wretched situations to which some naïve Corinthians had already come. Perhaps the brother who foolishly followed another's arrogant but no less foolish example was filled with remorse; perhaps not. We are not told.

What seems certain is that the weak believer has become confused about reality. He is now in peril of surrendering his confession of faith and of sliding back, albeit unwittingly, to the world from which he came and to which in heart he does not belong. If so, his usefulness would be at an end. An unhappy man, emotionally alienated from his church and a probable absentee, he would entertain long-term, grievous doubts about the claims of the gospel.

An acute student of human nature, the apostle knew that Christians can and do astonish themselves with their sins. Identifying with the man, Paul's white-hot indignation is cast into the face of the person responsible for the calamity: his unwary conduct has led to someone else's gross misconduct.

As if this were not sufficiently shocking, the saint at risk remains 'the brother because of whom Christ died'. The believer armed with much more theoretical knowledge than love has damaged someone who was the reason for the death of Jesus. This means that because the clever Corinthians are **'sinning against the brethren and wounding their conscience when it is weak, you** [plural] **sin against Christ'** (8:12). Although their action may not be wrong in itself, it strikes out at others, provoking them to sin against their Lord. In doing this the Corinthians offend Christ.

Paul learned long before that to harm the church is to wound the Lord. He personally had attempted to compel disciples to renounce Christ, hence the terrible question from the Saviour: 'Why are you persecuting me?' (Acts 9:4; 22:7; 26:11,14).[10] It is not difficult to see that the apostle felt acutely for the weak Christians. Nor was he without a concern for those who were wise in their own conceits, in just the same way that Stephen might have included the arrogant Saul in his dying prayer (Acts 7:60).

Paul and vegetarianism (8:13)

The apostle reveals what he would do if he suspected that what he ate or planned to eat would cause a Christian to stumble. Note the delicate but decisive manner in which he expresses himself. He fears that he might trip up someone with whom he has a valued relationship (**'my brother'**), leading the man to do what the latter incorrectly believes to be wrong. It must not be. Were the possibility to arise, the apostle would never eat **'meat'**, sacrificed animal flesh; he would be a vegetarian until his dying day in order to prevent offence.

An apostle who practises what he preaches (9:1-18)

Paul continues to project himself as a pattern of Christian meekness. He opens his heart to his readers, and we can only be deeply moved when he remarks on his right to take a wife, to be paid regularly, about his view of the ministry of the gospel, and, perhaps most controversially of all, about the law of Moses and the Christian's ultimate code of behaviour.

Food offered to idols (8:1 - 11:1)

The Lord's steward has promised already that if needful he would surrender his right to eat meat. The Corinthians should be equally prepared to give up the consumption of sacrificed flesh.

Paul is an apostle (9:1-2)

He reminds the fellowship that he possesses all the freedoms that they enjoy as Christians, and that as an apostle he has additional privileges.

'Am I not free?' Does Paul not have liberty to act according to his own enlightened conscience? (9:1). Certainly. **'Am I not an apostle?'** Of course. His credentials cannot be faulted. Had he not **'seen Jesus our Lord'** after his resurrection? Yes.[11]

Although others might be reluctant to consider him an apostle, the Corinthians could not deny Paul's claim. He was the spiritual father of the church (4:15) and they were his **'work in the Lord'**, the living **'seal'** or proof of his office (9:2).

We need to evaluate this. Admittedly, a ministry which brings men to Christ does not make the preacher an apostle. But it would be difficult for that man to lie to his converts about his situation or for them to refuse him their attention. In exactly the same way Paul cannot be other than truthful when he reminds his own children in the Lord that they are the living evidence of his status. Conversely, because they know him for what he is, what he is about to say carries all the more weight.

An exposition and defence of apostolic meekness (9:3-18)

Having established that he is truly an apostle, Paul proceeds to catalogue his own rights and discusses the right that he has to dispense with these rights if he decides (9:3-11). Each freedom and privilege has been sacrificed in the wider interests of the gospel (9:12-18). Let inflated Corinthians take this as an example.

Paul's rights (9:3-11)

There are some who made it their business to **'examine'** Paul (9:3). Remember that in 4:3-4 he has alluded already to these hurtful

Christians. Again he refuses to name names. This man knew the value of tact.

1. The apostle's self-defence (9:3-6)

Paul indicates that **'this'**, what he is about to write, will be a sufficient **'defence'** against his critics. It needs to be said that not all commentators agree with this interpretation. Hodge argues keenly that 'this' is retrospective, pointing back to 9:1-2, where Paul allegedly defends his claim to be an apostle. But he has made no such apologia. Verses 1 and 2 are no more than a reminder to the people of what he had become.[12]

Although elsewhere the apostle often refers to his defence of the gospel, 9:3 is the only occasion in his letters where he justifies his personal actions. The rationale is that what he chooses to do in his private life is so unusual that he must explain himself to the critical and the inquisitive.[13]

Paul asserts himself: **'Do we not have a right to eat and drink?'** (9:4). Yes. He, with other apostles, deserved creature comforts equal to those enjoyed by the Corinthians. Similarly, did he not have **'authority to lead about a sister, a wife'**? (9:5). The meaning is that the lady of his choice, were there such, would have accompanied Paul on his journeys and that her expenses, too, would have been the responsibility of the churches. She would, of course, have been a 'sister', a Christian.

It is added that **'the rest of the apostles, and the brothers of the Lord'** (the natural children of Mary and Joseph) and, significantly, **'Cephas'** were married.[14] To judge from 1:12 and 3:22, it would appear that Simon Peter was held in considerable esteem by some at least of the Corinthians. The argument is that if Peter's wife was supported by the churches, Paul's partner, should he marry, would have an equal right. He would have no intention of leading a wife into probable penury with the specious excuse that because she was called to live by faith she need not be given an adequate income. No other woman would be expected, or would expect, to live like this.

In declaring that he could marry a Christian woman, should he wish, the apostle implies that he must not wed an unbeliever. Remember that in this matter the apostle offers himself as an example to his readers. We can draw our own conclusion.

Were Paul and Barnabas the only apostles who did **'not have a right to refrain from working'**? (9:6). That Paul did work hard at

Corinth is certain, as Acts 18:3 reveals. But selling his time and labour is not the issue here. Rather, if all the other apostles had been supported to the extent that they had no need to generate their own funds, was it reasonable for Paul and Barnabas to be singled out as the only exceptions, denied the right to give up work? If the Corinthians were ready to maintain others, why shouldn't they keep Paul and Barnabas in reasonable comfort? The question is fair.

As an aside, Acts 15:39 shows that there was an occasion when these two good men separated in hot anger. It might be that the reference in 9:6 to Barnabas suggests that they had now been reconciled. In Christ divisions can be healed; it is not impossible for old friendships to survive knocks.

2. Paul's salary (9:7-11)

Although Paul did not claim necessary expenses, as 9:12 shows, in theory he held himself ready to exercise this right whenever he thought fit. Nor did he allow the churches to forget their obligation to him. Three different real-life situations, those of the soldier, the landowner and the hired shepherd, are introduced to reinforce the principle (9:7).

First, what soldier is told to provide for himself when he goes to war? Paul's picture is by no means inappropriate. Armed men denied their necessities by a commander would be a menace to society. John the Baptist had faced a problem like this with some soldiers who asked for baptism (Luke 3:14).The apostle knows that Christ never intended his apostles to be a band of thieving villains.

Secondly, who plants a vineyard without enjoying its produce? Paul might have in mind Deuteronomy 20:6: 'Who is the man who planted a vineyard and has not begun to use its fruit?' Plainly, no one in his right mind.

Thirdly, who is hired to care for a flock of sheep and is not permitted to enjoy milk and cheese? It is unheard of. By implication, Paul the soldier, Paul the planter and Paul the shepherd (or 'pastor') deserves and can expect remuneration. Further, he shows that there is nothing strange about this; payment for services rendered is not just a principle that makes the world go round: **'I am not speaking these things according to human judgement, am I?'**, or, more literally, 'Do I really speak after the manner of men?' (9:8).[15] He spells out the fact that the Bible, too, has something to say about work and payment: **'Or does not the Law also say these things?'**

Deuteronomy 25:4 is recalled in 9:9. Moses prohibits muzzling an ox when it drags the threshing instrument over the corn. The apostolic meaning is that if an animal's routine work feeds it, it is inconceivable that the Lord's busy people should be worse off than beasts of burden.

A principle of Old Testament interpretation is introduced alongside the observation that God's concern for domesticated animals proves that human workers deserve their pay: **'Or is he speaking altogether because of us? For it was written because of us'** (9:10). A truth is brought out vividly: when the Lord inspired Moses to write Deuteronomy 25:4 he had Christian churches and their leaders ('us'), in mind. Perhaps Moses had the same long-term view. Notice that God is said to be **'speaking'** through this Old Testament passage rather than having spoken; Paul believes Scripture to be the never-silent word of the Lord.

He continues. The command about the ox was written because **'The ploughman ought to plough in hope, and the thresher to thresh in hope of sharing the crops'**: men who look after animals, whether in turning the soil or several months later in grinding the grain, deserve to eat just as much as their beasts. Maybe the double reference to ploughman and thresher is intended to show that every workman for the Lord, be he apostle or not, is to be paid. The principle was not new. Compare the words of Jesus in John 4:36: 'That he who sows and he who reaps may rejoice together.'

Paul applies the truth to the Corinthians, to himself and to his colleagues (9:11). Perhaps the apostle is ironic: is it any **'great thing'** if, having **'sowed spiritual things'** for the Corinthians, the workers should **'reap'** the Corinthians' inferior but necessary **'material'** benefits? It isn't asking the earth, is it? The point is that Paul and others plough human soil and plant the gospel seed in hope of spiritual blessing *and also* in anticipation of reaping a personal material reward. God gives the first, and the people should ensure the second.

Why these rights are suspended (9:12-18)

1. A polite protest (9:12)

Here there might just be a veiled criticism of the Corinthians because of their inclination to favouritism. Other, unnamed, ministers

Food offered to idols (8:1 - 11:1)

do **'share the right over you'**. These men, who did not establish the Corinthian church, look for support and get it. Harbouring no grudge, Paul asks politely, yet firmly, if this should not be the case for him and his colleagues.

Let's be careful. The apostle does not suggest that assorted church treasurers had failed to give him his due; there is absolutely no hint of sharp or sloppy practice, either at Corinth or elsewhere. The principle being laid down with typical understatement is that if others had indulged their undoubted right to payment, how much **'more'** should this be the case for Paul and his associates?

Now comes a dramatic and quite magnificent anti-climax. The self-evident principle of a fair day's pay for a fair day's work was unquestionably scriptural and had been accepted (no doubt with relief) by some apostles and ministers. Nor did the world sneer at it. Moreover, it was acknowledged by the Corinthians. Paul, too, sets his seal on it. Even so, he had put it decisively to one side: **'We did not use this right.'**

The statement is extraordinary. A reason must be given, and the apostle will not disappoint: **'But we endure all things, that we may cause no hindrance to the gospel of Christ.'** The word 'hindrance', found only here in the New Testament, has the sense of cutting, or severing (Greek, *egkope*). Were Paul to demand payment for services rendered he would be cutting back the advance of the good news.

This explanation for his practice is, if anything, more astonishing than the practice itself. A reader might reasonably ask if it could have been in the interests of the gospel for Paul to put to one side a proper condition of service. Further, it might not have been clear to some that he had the right to do this. Sensitive to a host of probable queries, he prepares to clarify his policy statement.

2. Other people's pay (9:13-14)

But before he explains himself Paul raises the temperature to fever pitch with some well-chosen remarks about the rewards that others were known to receive.

Were the Corinthians not aware that the priests and Levites who laboured in the temple of God at Jerusalem and at its altar ate from the sacrifices that they prepared and offered (9:13)?[16] Yes, they appreciated this.

Nor were they unaware that the rule determined for the priests of the earlier dispensation had been transferred by Christ to his ministers: **'So also the Lord directed those who proclaim the gospel to live from the gospel'** (9:14; Matt. 10:10; Luke 10:7; cf. 1 Tim. 5:18).

3. Renunciation (9:15-16)

The picture is now complete: all things cry 'Amen' to the principle of payment. Were Paul to demand a proper material reward no man could accuse him. **'But,'** confesses the apostle, **'I have used none of these things'** (9:15). 'These things' are probably recompense for work (9:7), plus expected courtesies, as well as payment on a par with that given to some unnamed ministers (9:12). The words 'have used' are a subtle declaration that over the years Paul never insisted on remuneration; his mind was made up long ago. Nor did he now have any intention of making hearts bleed, exerting a touching moral pressure to get the church to hurry through an overdue payment: **'But I have not written these things that it might be so for me.'**

Before telling us why he writes in this way he makes a further comment: **'It would be good for me rather to die than...'** (9:15). Just here the apostle might seem to break off his sentence in emotion, resuming with an outburst: **'No man will make my boast empty.'** The NASB paraphrases the whole verse and in the last part connects these independent clauses, perhaps obscuring the feeling with which Paul writes. This 'boast', always the apostle's peculiar joy, would not be denied him; he would rather be dead than lose it.

For Paul to prefer death to the loss of whatever it was he boasted about, and for which money would be no compensation, shows that it must have been extraordinarily important. We strain to catch his meaning.

Nor are we left in suspense for long. But before all is revealed he tells us what this cause for personal exultation was *not*. In plain terms, it was not evangelism. The apostle did not swell with pride because he had been called to office. He proclaimed the gospel, yet did so solely because he was a servant who had no choice in the matter: **'For I am under compulsion; for woe is me if I do not preach the gospel'** (9:16); as time went by the Lord continued to remind him that the man had to proclaim Jesus Christ. It is perfectly true that although evangelism is not a merit-gaining exercise, by his preaching the apostle avoided disaster. But not even this made him jump for joy. The logic is that if he did boast about his work (and he did), there had to be another reason.

4. The apostle's satisfaction (9:17-18)

In 9:17 we are brought a little nearer to an explanation. Whereas a volunteer is pleased to work for nothing and might even flaunt his generosity, the case is different for someone who acts **'unwillingly'**. The reason is that the second man is a servant who does not patronize and who cannot pick and choose what he does.

This is where Paul had always stood: he had a **'stewardship entrusted'** to him. Although his status in the Lord's service was unique, his own wishes, if any, remained unimportant: he had to obey orders. This is a claim that he has made already: 'Let a man regard us in this manner, as servants of Christ, and stewards of the mysteries of God ... it is required of stewards that one be found trustworthy' (4:1-2).

But Paul does not imply that he worked reluctantly and with a grudge. He tells us elsewhere that his activities were his own distinctive offering to his God (2 Tim. 4:6; cf. Rom. 15:16). The emphasis here is simply that his labours in the gospel were never regarded by him as a generous favour bestowed upon Christ, for which Paul could pat himself on the back and for which the Lord and his people ought to have been duly thankful. An evangelist who did not work 'voluntarily', he had been requisitioned by God. Like the industrious slave in the parable of Luke 17:7-10, he only did what he had to do.

Even so, there was something entirely uncalled-for about the way in which the apostle operated and which did yield an abundant reward (9:18). The voluntary activity that gave him so much gratification was the proclamation of good news free of charge to all. Negatively, the reward received by Paul was not the Lord's approval now or later. Positively, it was the joy of a clear conscience, knowing that there was nothing about his person that could be an obstacle, real or imaginary, to others to listen to what he was commanded to tell them. With delightful courtesy the Lord's senior steward reveals that, travelling far beyond the line of duty, he had pre-empted others from putting it about that he wanted to fleece the churches. This was his immense pleasure: **'What, then, is my reward? That, evangelizing, I might deposit the good news without charge, so that I should not make full use of my right in the gospel.'**

'Right' (Greek, *exousia*, 'authority') means the apostle's right to be paid by the people for his work. The NASB brings in 'offer', a clumsy word, instead of 'deposit'. But the writer of this letter never offered the good news to any man. He was an obedient herald of God's commands and promises.

In summary, the apostle refused to demand that the churches pay him. He was humble enough and wise enough to recognize that serving his Master intelligently was an abundant personal reward, even if he had to work with his hands. Oh, and the way in which he went about his duties ought to encourage certain inflated Corinthians to think much more carefully before upsetting their weaker brethren. For this he strove; in this he succeeded — magnificently! 'Paul, thank you!'

Paul, slave yet free (9:19-27)

The apostle's sole concern was to be an effective communicator of the good news of Jesus Christ. To achieve this he had to react wisely to the prejudices and hesitations of the people with whom he came into contact, whether they were Jews or Greeks. Similarly, the Corinthians needed to come to terms with the sensitivities of their fellow-Christians. The difference between the apostle and the church was that whereas he triumphed brilliantly, they failed conspicuously. This is the issue which he continues to address.

In order to win Gentiles Paul had to live among Gentiles; to win Jews it was essential for him to conduct himself as a Jew. Please ponder this because the principle is not quite as simple as it sounds: Paul's statements usually conceal hidden depths, and nowhere more so than here. In the apostle's world his Jewish opponent would have been quick to express abhorrence for someone who discarded the culture into which he was born in order to live like a Gentile. The Greek sceptic would probably have said that he was a fanatical Jew scheming to turn gullible Greeks into Hebrews.[17] Either way, Paul seemed to be a pragmatic and weak man with no fixed principles, a religious entrepreneur who took advantage of the situations into which he precipitated himself.

At a deeper level, the apostle had to be alert to the charge of assimilating his preaching rather than his personality to the local cultures, hammering out one gospel for the Jews and another for the Greeks; one for those who had been reared on the law of Moses and another for those who were guided by nothing higher than the relatively dim lights of nature and darkened conscience. This is why 1 Corinthians sets out to show that Paul's evangel needed, and received, no cultural modification whatever, and that on its own terms it was perfectly adapted for all men everywhere.

Otherwise expressed, the apostle demonstrates for the benefit of certain Corinthians the truth that fixed principles often give rise to flexibility in conduct and relationships, a flexibility that breaks no commandments. But where there is scant knowledge of the truth, or little concern for one's neighbour, whether he be Greek or Hebrew, there remains only a harsh, damaging rigidity which usually descends into sin.

This immense issue is addressed by 9:19-27. Paul's thesis is elegantly simple. In the task of evangelism he was more than willing to accommodate to all and to live alongside those whom he would reach. But — and it is a considerable 'but' — he would be mastered by nothing and by no one, refusing flatly to be dominated by prevailing norms. Not only would he not revert to his former Jewishness to embrace outmoded Jewish feasts, ceremonies and dietary laws as part of his absolute standard; he was unprepared to commit himself to being a Hellene, someone who, even if not a devotee of the gods, might pay court to one or more of the philosophies of Greece. In short, whatever he was in himself, he stepped back from being known as either a Jew or a Gentile. There was one and one only who was his Master (Matt. 23:10): Jesus, whom he knew and preached, dominated him, rather than an inherited ethic. The apostle, to take up his own words, remained **'under the law of Christ'** (9:21).

Outlaws, Moses' law, and the law of Christ (9:19-23)

Bear in mind the reasoning thus far. Beginning at 8:1, the apostle attacks the gross lack of love and consideration shown by not a few of the Corinthians. He presents himself as an example of self-sacrifice in a matter that really does make him wince: the contents of his purse. Now, he expands the principle.

Paul looks after himself (9:19)

The apostle is **'free from all men'**. Because he maintained his financial independence he was no man's lackey and was under no obligation to conform to the practices and opinions of a paymaster. He had turned himself into **'a slave to all'**, which means that he made it his established policy to identify with other men in order to **'win the more'**; the strategy was to bring as many as possible to Christ.

The apostle appreciated that were he unprepared to operate at the level of those among whom he moved with regard to diet, dress, language and general lifestyle he would be far less likely to win them for the Lord. Conversely, were he to adapt happily to different situations he might be perceived to be a friendly, approachable human being possibly deserving an audience.

Old law; no law; new law (9:20-23)

1. Under the law

For this reason Paul behaved as a Jew when he mingled with Jews. He observed the law of Moses **'as under the Law'**, although it was not now his authority in matters of faith and conduct. Hence the rider, **'though not being myself under the Law'**.[18]

The intention is that he might **'win Jews'**, those who, as they saw it, were truly 'under the Law'. The immediate tactic was that when with them (but only then) Paul adjusted to their position so that they might in time abandon Moses and turn to Christ. He knew that the law, grand and good in itself, was never more than a provisional apparatus in God's plan of salvation.[19] Although he never gave any encouragement to his fellow-Jews to abandon the law (the opposite was the case, as Acts 16:3; 18:18 and 21:24 show), he did insist that it was wrong to regard it as a means of justification. It is strictly in this light that he was prepared to observe its regulations in order to identify and empathize with his fellow-Hebrews.

2. Lawless Paul

The apostle also mixed with Gentiles who were **'without law'**, those who are literally 'lawless' (9:21; Greek, *anomos*), a term that

Food offered to idols (8:1 - 11:1)

elsewhere is often derogatory. To appreciate the sensitivity of the apostle's well-chosen word, consider Luke 22:37, which cites Isaiah 53:12 to the effect that Jesus was numbered with the 'lawless', that is, with 'transgressors'. It seems at first sight that Paul confesses to finding his natural place in low society.[20]

Not surprisingly, the matter was not so simple. Basically, the apostle knew that Gentiles were people for whom the law of Moses was unknown or, if acknowledged as an object of Jewish reverence, had no authority. He realized that because his policy statement would make his critics' antennae twitch with anticipation, perhaps fury, an explanation must be forthcoming. Nor did he disappoint them.

3. The 'law of Christ'

His apologia carries both negative and positive qualifications. Negatively, the apostle lived as if he were one of these 'lawless' Gentiles. But he did not live in sin because, positively, he was not **'without the law of God'**. The Lord had made it plain to him both what to do and what not to do, and the apostle honoured his instructions.

This admission is nothing short of revolutionary bearing in mind the statement of 9:20 that the apostle is not 'under the Law [of Moses]'. What 'law' can it be that now dominates the apostle? Specifically, it is nothing other than **'the law of Christ'**. Jesus, Paul's Saviour, has replaced Moses as his great Lawgiver. A further question arises: what is the content of this new Christian 'law'?

It would seem that the 'law of Christ' incorporates three elements. First, there is the whole body of New Testament teaching given by Jesus and his apostles; second, it includes the Lord's personal example and, to a lesser extent, that of the apostles (principally Paul); third — and this is where the law of Christ is unlike Moses' law — it is a law written on the hearts of born-again Christians (Jer. 31:33; Heb. 8:9). In short, it is an absolute code for life that has become the delight of God's people. Seen in this light, the Ten Commandments (Exod. 20:1-17; Deut. 5:6-21), never revoked by Christ, have been honed to the limit by the Lord and his inspired writers. In his day Paul was not unaware of this development. We have already seen a striking example of the principle in his treatment of sexual holiness (6:15-20).

Although the apostle was saturated with the conviction that Christ governs his church through the Spirit, he never taught that freedom from the condemnation of the law means the cancellation of a believer's duty to obey the Lord. Aware that the Christian needs to be transformed by the renewing of his mind in order to 'prove what the will of God is' (Rom. 12:2), Paul knew also that the church was being given propositional teaching to guide it. To take up Ridderbos's words, for the apostle 'Christ ... represents the new standard of judgment as to what "has had its day" in the law and what has abiding validity.'[21]

The kernel of the matter is that Jesus is now King in Zion: his historic example, spiritual presence and written instructions guide his redeemed and responsive people. Read the Gospels, particularly Matthew 5-7. These chapters record the teaching of a legislator who knew that part of his task was to overthrow the false traditions of the scribes and Pharisees *and* to refine to ultimate perfection the commandments of Sinai.

4. Paul's wisdom

A man under law, the apostle strove to **'win'** those of his fellows who recognized no God-given code. As in 8:7-9, the **'weak'** mentioned by 9:22 would almost certainly be those Christians who had not yet made up their minds about certain issues. He wins them by sympathizing with their problems and by seeing things through their spectacles.

We step back in admiration. For Paul it was not enough that these weak people were the Lord's. He wanted them to be strong in Christ, convinced through and through that there are no gods. To succeed in this he would accommodate himself to their sincere but misguided prejudices.

In short, the apostle targeted both unconverted Jews and Gentiles *and* immature believers: **'I have become all things to all men, that I may by all means save some'** (9:22). He lived like this confident that a proportion of those who heard him would convert to Christ and then advance to maturity.

All his activities were geared to the promotion of the gospel (9:23). There was a reason for this: Paul yearned to be **'a fellow partaker of it'**, which means that he desired to share the wonder of

Food offered to idols (8:1 - 11:1)

Christ and the joy of serving him along with his fellows. Although his own salvation was certain, it was not enough. Let there be more and more converts, both at Corinth and elsewhere. For this he was prepared to do anything consistent with 'the law of Christ' whose revealed will was now his rule of duty.

So, strive to excel (9:24-27)

Paul delights to appeal to incontrovertible truth, and does so here in question form: **'Do you not know?'** (9:24). His plan in Corinthian church-building was to encourage the more knowledgeable believers, the ones who had come a relatively long way down the Christian road, to take another step forward and practise intelligent self-denial. As we have seen, his immediate tactic was to offer himself as their example.

'The feast-famed ridge' of Corinth (9:24-25)

Athletics are brought in as an illustration to show what the apostle was seeking for himself and for others. We can easily imagine the young people in the church pricking up their ears when they heard these sentences read out; Paul understood well how to interest a congregation. He knew also that sport was highly popular at Corinth and that Christians could enthuse over a champion sprinter, particularly if he came from their own part of the Greek peninsula.

Five centuries before Christ a Greek poet called Pindar extolled what he termed the 'feast-famed ridge' of Corinth. The feast was the celebration of the Isthmian Games that the city hosted every second year, and the ridge was the Acrocorinth overshadowing the sprawling community.[22] This festival of sport came to attract participants and revellers from the whole of Greece and continued to be celebrated long after Paul's time. The site of the games, the so-called 'gate' of the city, was twelve kilometres east of Corinth and near the bottleneck of land that connects mainland Greece and the deep south. Excavations have shown that the length of the Isthmian running-track was about 181 metres.[23]

To paraphrase, he asks, 'Do you Corinthians not realize that theose who run in a stadium actually run?' Paul concentrates attention upon exertion because he knows that the reason for the athletes being in the arena was competition for honours rather than lounging around. 'Obviously,' the hearers whisper to themselves. 'Well then,' answers the apostle, 'is it not the case that one individual only receives the prize?' 'Of course,' they answer. Paul applies: 'Just so, keep on running that you might receive a garland.' He stresses that the great thing is persistence in the Christian life.[24]

There is no suggestion here, or for that matter elsewhere in the New Testament, that Christians should compete against their fellow-believers. Remember what the Lord said to Simon Peter about being morbidly interested in John's future: 'If I want him to remain until I come, what is that to you? You follow me!' (John 21:22). If we look to Jesus we shall be free from envy, whereas when we stare at others we have to turn our gaze away from the Saviour. Because we do not have eyes in the back of our heads we get ourselves into difficulties. Paul's home-truth is that the individual believer receives his unique prize only if he pushes himself to his limit. What others do is almost irrelevant.

Every man who **'competes'** will endeavour to control himself in all things (9:25). If athletes strive to get rid of anything in their personal habits that could hinder them from receiving **'a perishable wreath'**, how much more should Christians extend themselves to qualify for an **'imperishable'** trophy? At the Isthmian Games such garlands were made of pine fronds or dried wild celery.[25] The apostle contrasts these baubles with what Christ will hand to his champions.

Paul's point is that, like the athlete who surrenders pleasures that in themselves are harmless, believers must sometimes make sacrifices if they want to witness effectively and help others rather than themselves. This is what the Corinthians ought to have been doing. Notice the apostle's emphasis that the occasion of receiving the crown or prize lies in the future. Although Paul does have a species of 'reward' now, a reward in which he rejoices (9:18), he adopts the long view, contemplating the moment when Christians will finally stand before their Lord.

Paul, the athlete (9:26-27)

The apostle is determined to be an example: **'Therefore I run ... I box'** (9:26). He presents himself both as a track-runner and (literally) a 'fist-fighter'.[26] As a runner he is **'not without aim'** (or, 'not

Food offered to idols (8:1 - 11:1)

uncertain'), and has made up his mind to arrive at the finish as rapidly as possible. As a boxer he makes sure that he lands on target rather than flailing empty air. In short, his every movement is in the interests of the ministry. Let the Corinthians learn from him.

Paul is not uncertain about his destiny. Nor, for that matter, is he afraid that certain inconsistent ministers of the gospel will forfeit eternal life. This truth has already been laid down firmly: 'He [the erring but converted leader] himself shall be saved, yet so as through fire' (3:15). Rather, because the apostle is committed to effectiveness (9:27), he will **'buffet'** his body, which means literally that he continues to strike himself 'under the eye' (Greek, *hupôpiazô*): he knocks his body into unconsciousness and then carries it about as his abject **'slave'**. The pictures are vivid.

Because he was a member of the human race, Paul's physical body, although not intrinsically evil, was the seat of much that was sinful. This sad truth is reflected by Romans 8:13, which tells us that 'the deeds of the body' have to be put to death by believers. In 9:27 the sense is that even legitimate desires and activities are to be abandoned should the necessity arise; everything must be available for the altar of intelligent consecration.

The apostle reveals his fear that when life and opportunity are past the Lord would inform him that his activities as a herald had been ineffective, even useless. **'Disqualified'** is given by the NASB, but this is probably not Paul's meaning. 'Unapproved' might be preferable (Greek, *adokimos*). In this last verse the metaphor of the athlete drops away, the apostle writing that it had always been his intense desire to honour the gospel as well as to announce it.

The rationale for this two-stranded approach is that if Paul's personal conduct was not moulded by Christ he would never proclaim the good news effectively to his fellows. In such a situation, although perhaps 'not rejected as regards the faith' (2 Tim. 3:8), the apostle would be perceived ultimately as a servant who had failed, a sober warning which in 2 Corinthians 13:5-7 he throws out to others. To forestall this verdict he was prepared to go to any lengths. The Corinthians should be equally determined.

The lesson of 9:27 for today's evangelists is sharp and to the point: what we are as men is no less important than what we teach. The essential qualification for preaching repentance is to abandon sin in one's own life. The principle is difficult but true.

The evil of idolatry (10:1 - 11:1)

To look back for a moment, the problem addressed by chapter 8 was that some of the Corinthians, relatively naïve and weak in their new-found faith, were confused about realities. They continued to react to the world around as if the gods of Greece possibly did exist. Although they knew in their hearts that this could not be so, they found it difficult to shake off their earlier superstitions. For their sakes more mature believers should give up the custom of eating food they knew had been previously offered to idols.

Paul has also touched upon an aspect of idolatry that was far more sombre (8:5): behind the ornate images and the fabulous deities there were spiritual powers, mini-lords and gods who remained the unperceived objects of the worship of the ignorant people of Corinth. This issue is given particular attention in the present chapter. The doctrine is that Christians must avoid eating such offerings because consumption was tantamount to giving homage to demons. This remained the case even when believers had no desire to indulge in alien forms of worship.

If in chapter 8 the interests of weaker believers were brought to the fore, here the joint theme is the paramount need for the Christian both to protect himself as well as his brothers in the Lord, and also to let the idolater know that image-worship is perilous.

The chapter falls into three principal sections. First, the awful warning provided by Israel in the wilderness must not be ignored by the Corinthians (10:1-13). Second, Paul teaches dogmatically that demonic powers are present in idolatrous worship (10:14-22). Finally, believers are counselled about what they ought to do when invited to eat tainted food (10:23 - 11:1).

Israel in the wilderness (10:1-13)

Paul recalls the journey of Israel in the wilderness fifteen hundred years earlier, showing that what the people of God did then and there must never become a precedent for the churches of Christ. The Israelites belonged to the Lord in name only but did not know him, nor wish to do so. Let Corinth beware.

Food offered to idols (8:1 - 11:1)

The church, the Israel of God (10:1-4)

'For ... brethren' (10:1) carries forward the great issues raised in the two preceding chapters. Sometimes, when introducing a matter of exceptional importance, the apostle warms to his subject by telling the readers that he does not wish them to be **'unaware'**, or ignorant.[27] It is like this in 10:1-4.

The great truth brought to the attention of the Corinthians is the link between the people of God of the Old Testament dispensation and the Christian churches in this final age. The bond between them is the Messiah, the Lord Jesus Christ. None other than the expected 'angel of the Lord' (Mal. 3:1), he was anticipated by the Law and the Prophets as the Prophet/Priest/King of Israel. Now, he is the Saviour of all believers, both Jew and Gentile. Therefore the Christians, rather than unbelieving Jews in their synagogues, are the true Israel.

This being so, the apostle proclaims that those who were brought into a covenant relationship with Jehovah at Sinai remain for the churches nothing less than **'our fathers'**. The description is striking, intended to show that there is a lineal family relationship that has stretched out over the centuries. For this reason the Corinthians needed to ponder their spiritual predecessors. In more detail, they must be humble enough to appreciate the misdeeds of Israel at the time of the exodus from Egypt.

But why does Paul draw attention specifically to the wilderness generation rather than, say, to Israel in the period of the judges, or to the numerous kings of Israel or Judah? There is one magnificent, sufficient reason: when they quit Egypt those who followed Moses were baptized. Moreover, this Old Testament baptism of the people of God was unique: not only had it never happened before; it was never repeated. The Red Sea crossing typified and anticipated the Corinthian situation because the Corinthians had been baptized into the one of whom Moses was a figure (Deut. 18:18).

1. Paul, Corinth and the Old Testament

The principal biblical passages brought to bear in 10:1-13 are Exodus 13:21-22; 14:20-22; 16:4,35 and Deuteronomy 8:3. It is remarkable that the apostle expects the Corinthians, many of whom were Gentiles who, unlike Timothy (2 Tim. 3:15), had no background knowledge of the Scriptures, to be well versed in the Old

Testament. But this seems to be how it was, and it should be so for us.

2. The cloud and the sea

'Under the cloud' means that the people of Israel, collectively the 'fathers' of both Paul and the Corinthians, were guided by the pillars of cloud and of fire (10:1).[28] Additionally, they were **'baptized into Moses in the cloud and in the sea'** (10:2).

Paul knew that when Israel entered the Red Sea the cloud of Jehovah's presence moved to the rear of the column and that the waters took position both to their left and right (Exod. 14:19,22). From where the Egyptians, then in hot pursuit, were watching, the Hebrews vanished completely within these elements. In a way it was an immersion, although not as intimate as that of Pharaoh and his army when they were swallowed up completely by the waves (Exod. 14:28). For Israel the only possible way forward was east, into the howling desert, separating from Egypt for ever and uniting behind Moses, their prophet, priest and leader.

In a similar fashion Christian baptism signals publicly the believer's irrevocable allegiance to the Lord Jesus Christ (e.g., Rom. 6:3; Gal. 3:27). Although this truth by no means exhausts the significance of the ordinance, identification and union are presented in 10:2 as the double point of contact between the baptism of Israel and that of Christians. The implied parallel is as deliberate as it is obvious: Israel, redeemed from slavery, had been baptized; the Corinthians, too, were both redeemed and baptized.

3. Spiritual food and drink

During those forty years Israel shared **'the same spiritual food'** and **'the same spiritual drink'** as the Corinthians (10:3-4). But, we ask, how could their diet have been the 'same'? Israel never broke bread at the Lord's Table and the church was never instructed to pick up manna from the flat, open fields surrounding their city for six days in every seven; nor did the apostle strike the rocks littering Achaia to guarantee the domestic water supply of the local Christians.

The meaning is that, like the bread and wine of the Lord's Table, the nourishment of the baptized people of Israel was 'spiritual' in that it was given to them by the Holy Spirit. Psalm 78:24 tells us that

Food offered to idols (8:1 - 11:1)

'He ... gave them food from heaven', and Nehemiah 9:15 records that 'Thou didst provide bread from heaven for them for their hunger.' That the manna and water were miraculous gifts is not relevant to the discussion. Paul's point is that manna, water, bread and wine are the 'same ... food' because each element derives from God. This consideration is introduced by the apostle to stress that it would be in their own interests for the Corinthians to think about Israel in the wilderness.

Furthermore, just as the manna and the water had been food and drink for the travellers, at the Lord's Table the bread and wine remain bread and wine. The manna and water were not, and the bread and wine are not, transmuted into intangible, spiritual substances masked by the likenesses of these elements yet conveying spiritual life to all who taste. This fundamental truth is assumed by 10:3-4 and is taught explicitly by 10:16-17,21. The food on the table, coming as it does from a baker's oven, looking and tasting like bread and eventually passing through the digestive system, can safely be assumed to be bread, and bread alone. Some venerable church traditions need not be taken as evidence to the contrary.

Paul teaches the Corinthians that because this God-given nourishment declared in the desert, and tells out now, the love of God to his redeemed and baptized people, it possesses a spiritual significance as well as a spiritual origin. This is the truth being brought home to the readers. To illustrate the principle, compare the case of Isaac. Galatians 4:29 records that although he was the natural child of his mother and father, he 'was born according to the Spirit'. Not only did the Lord override the advanced age and barrenness of Isaac's parents; the son and heir was given a spiritual significance that Ishmael, his half-brother by the slave girl, never possessed. Even so, Isaac was never anything other than a normally conceived baby.

4. The rock that followed

The last part of 10:4 insists that the Israelites' miraculous water-supply came from a **'spiritual rock which followed them'**, that is, a rocky mass that travelled behind Israel. The Greek word for 'rock' is *petra*, not *petros*, the latter being a relatively small boulder (cf. Matt. 16:18). **'And'**, Paul adds by way of explanation, **'the rock was Christ.'** Aware that his readers would not realize this to have been the case, he teaches that the Lord was with Israel at that time even as he is with Christians now.

In all probability the apostle identifies the 'rock', Christ, with the angel of the Lord, the messenger who was always with the people of Israel (Exod. 14:19; 23:20,23; 32:34; 33:2). Although Paul was not unaware of the two occasions when Israel obtained water from rocks (Exod. 17:6; Num. 20:11), he probably did not have these events in his mind just here. If so, 'rock' must be taken metaphorically rather than literally.

The principle is that in the wilderness the people drank from the one source from which the Corinthians obtained their blessings: Christ, the divine rock or solid base of Israel. In the great song that he issued before his death Moses referred repeatedly to Jehovah as the Rock of Israel (Deut. 32:4,15,18,30,31), and the theme carries on right through the Old Testament, particularly in the Psalms.[29] It follows that 10:4 implies the essential deity of the one who became a true man at Bethlehem.

The people of God who were not the people of God (10:5-10)

When they were returning from Egypt back home to Canaan nearly all the children of Israel committed idolatry, the sin that sorely tempted some of the Corinthians. Those who offended died. But Paul's teaching is no innovation. Recall the martyr Stephen's indictment of Israel's conduct in the desert and his reference to Amos's denunciation centuries earlier (Acts 7:39-43; Amos 5:25-27). The fathers' gross failure was always a standing embarrassment for following generations of pious Israelites.

'**Nevertheless**', in spite of the blessings bestowed upon Israel, God was not '**well-pleased**' with the overwhelming majority of them (10:5). The proof of his anger was that they were '**laid low** [or, 'spread out'] **in the wilderness**'. When writing this the apostle had Numbers 14:16 hovering before his eyes, visualizing the desert between Egypt and Canaan strewn with the corpses of redeemed, baptized, communicant and rejected Israelites.

1. 'Patterns'

'**Now these things happened as our patterns**' (10:6). 'Pattern' translates the Greek *tupos*, a word which signifies a type, a visible impression, a form, or even a model. Paul's meaning is that those

Food offered to idols (8:1 - 11:1)

tragic deaths stand as a solemn warning for the Christian churches: should the Corinthians imitate the misconduct of the travellers in the wilderness, that is, impress themselves into the ancient mould, they must share their fate. The dismal catalogue of sins is outlined in 10:6-10.

Furthermore, these events occurred **'that we should not crave evil things'**. 'Crave' probably recalls Numbers 11:4 and 34, which recount Israel's longing for the comforts of Egypt at a relatively early stage in the journey to Canaan. Because the truth that Israel remains an awful warning is so important Paul will develop it in 10:11.

2. Apostasy and idolatry

Nor were the Corinthians to become **'idolaters'**, as were **'some'** of the Israelites (10:7). By 'some' is really meant very many: at that time few distanced themselves from the sin of the nation. The apostle refers explicitly to Exodus 32:6, which records Israel's idolatry although not formal apostasy: 'They rose early and offered burnt offerings, and brought peace offerings; and the people sat down to eat and to drink, and rose up to play.'

A subtle truth should not be overlooked, which is that the Bible tends to draw a distinction between the sins of apostasy and idolatry. Apostasy is the formal renunciation of the true God, as in the case of Ahab and Jezebel (1 Kings 16:29-33), whereas idolatry is imageworship, like the adoration of Jehovah under the form of the golden calves made by order of Jeroboam I (1 Kings 12:26-33) or that of deities like Bel and Nebo whose statues had to be carried by donkeys (Isa. 46:1-2).

For all this, there is not much difference. The Ten Commandments show this to be the case when they link idolatry and apostasy (Exod. 20:4-5; Deut. 5:8-9). This is because worshipping Jehovah in a manner that he had not ordained was the same as rejecting him. But Israel did not want to understand this principle. When they idolized the golden calf Aaron justified his action by making out that *this* was the god that had saved them (Exod. 32:4; cf. Ps. 106:19-21). The expressed wisdom was that the people could legitimately worship any object of their choice in the manner of their choosing. Not so, said Moses, and he shattered the tables of the law to manifest his violent disagreement (Exod. 32:19).

3. The nature of idolatry

Paul was aware that idolatry cannot possibly be sincere, serious worship. This is why reference is made to Exodus 32:6. The people did not prostrate themselves in adoration. Quite the reverse: they **'stood up to play'**, by which sexual promiscuity is implied. As Revelation 2:14,20 insist, there is commonly a connection between the two sins: 'Balaam ... put a stumbling block before the sons of Israel, to eat things sacrificed to idols, and to commit acts of immorality'; 'Jezebel ... leads my bond-servants astray, so that they commit acts of immorality and eat things sacrificed to idols.' It was like this in Corinth, a seat of the notoriously immoral cult of Aphrodite. The apostle knew that the church was exposed to danger.

4. Like father, like son (10:8)

Numbers 25:1-9, which states that second-generation Israel also fell into idolatry and sexual immorality, is recalled. It might be significant that Paul employs the present tense: **'Let us not continue fornicating,'** hinting broadly that the Corinthians needed to mend their ways and stand on their guard. Nor was he unaware that Israel had been induced to turn away from the Lord by the women of Moab (Num. 25:1; 31:15-16). The implication here is that carnal allurements in Corinth might well lead on to a surrender of the faith.

Emphasis is given to the dreadful judgement that occurred: **'Twenty-three thousand fell in one day,'** although Numbers 25:9 gives the total as twenty-four thousand.[30] It can safely be assumed that the discrepancy of one thousand is apparent rather than real. First, being round numbers, both figures are probably approximations. Second, the apostle might have omitted those who were subsequently put to death by their fellow-Israelites (Num. 25:4-5).

It is true that Numbers 25 does not declare explicitly that this vast number died **'in one day'**. But Paul does say so, no doubt to remind his readers that sometimes the judgement of God can be as swift as it is terrible.

5. The serpent in the wilderness (10:9)

A specific allusion is made to Numbers 21:5-6. Almost at the end of their forty-year journey the people of Israel complained against God

Food offered to idols (8:1 - 11:1)

and Moses because they were going short of bread and water, lamenting that they would expire in the wilderness. In the event this did happen, but in an unexpected fashion: large numbers of serpents bit large numbers of Israelites. Paul's past-continuous **'were being destroyed'** shows that more and more continued to die from snakebite.

What the Israelites did was to **'try the Lord'**, that is, to test Christ. They challenged him to improve their situation as a precondition for their continuing worship.[31] Paul insists that his readers should never do this. The present tense, **'Do not go on testing'**, is employed because the apostle knows that Christians sometimes resent God's good provisions.

We ought to remember that Christ was with Israel in the desert and that Christ was Jehovah. Parallel this with John 3:14-15: 'And as Moses lifted up the serpent in the wilderness, even so must the Son of Man be lifted up; that whoever believes in him may have eternal life.' The Messiah who sent venomous snakes among the Israelites then provided a way of escape through looking at a bronze effigy of a serpent. In turn, this was a shadow of Christ crucified.

We should never forget that Jesus our Saviour has been appointed the only judge of all men. Peter preached this to the Gentiles, as did Paul (Acts 10:42; 17:31). While time remains we need to look to the merciful Jesus to be saved from the wrathful Jesus.

6. 'Where there is no vision, the people perish' (10:10)

The apostle continues. Believers are not to **'grumble'**. The deliberate allusion is to Numbers 14:2,36 and the murmuring of the people against both Moses and Aaron. This resentment was due to Israel's acceptance of the dismal report of the ten spies to the effect that they were all doomed to perish, either in the desert or if they attacked Canaan.

It might be that Numbers 16:11,41-49 was also in Paul's mind when writing 10:10. This records Israel's rejection of Moses and Aaron during and after the rebellion of Korah. As a result nearly fifteen thousand people died. It is noticeable that the apostle refrains from identifying the targets of Corinthian murmuring, perhaps implying tactfully that the people ought not to be critical of him and therefore of his gospel. That they were frequently more than unkind has been shown by 4:1-5. Here, as ever, Paul is too gentle and wise to name names.

Comfort in temptation (10:11-13)

1. The Old Testament and the Christian churches

Four distinct assertions are made about **'these things'**, judgements that **'were happening'** over a forty-year period of time to Israel in the wilderness (10:11).[32]

First, these events occurred one by one in an ongoing sequence of disasters. It follows that Paul requires us to look at each tragedy as it happened and to take note.

Secondly, they occurred **'as an example'**. This means that they were designed as a pattern to be stamped on the memories of those who should come later. What happened to the people of Israel could happen again.

Thirdly, **'They were written for our instruction'** (or, 'admonition'). 'Written' means that these inflictions were remembered by Scripture specifically to reprove new-covenant believers in later years, and this because we are apt to go astray. Unlike Eli, who failed to admonish his sons (1 Sam. 3:13), the Lord gives us fair warning.

Fourthly, it is added that the record was designed for the apostle's Christian readers as well as for him, upon whom **'the ends of the ages have come'** or 'arrived'.[33]

The double meaning is that all the past ages of mankind pointed to the time of the Messiah and that these epochs have finished their course. Hence, there will be no future preparatory 'age' prior to or following the coming of the Saviour. Because we live in the last time Christians have an immense and unprecedented fund of experience upon which to draw.

It needs to be said that for the apostle these 'ages' were not historical periods such as the so-called 'Middle Ages' or the 'Stone Age'. Paul considered them as specific eras that God set in place for his own purposes. For example, there was the time before the giving of the law at Sinai and after that the waiting period before the first coming of Christ.[34] If we think about it, neither in the Bible nor anywhere else is there, nor could there be, any such thing as 'secular' history. This is because God is God. Nebuchadnezzar may have thought that he had built Babylon, but he was mistaken and suffered for his error (Dan. 4:28-33).

The apostle's message is that all the ages and stages of the work of salvation throughout human history have come to their designated

Food offered to idols (8:1 - 11:1)

conclusions. All, that is, apart from the final advent of Christ. As we shall see in the notes on 15:20-28, this principle is a powerful argument against 'premillennialism'. But this is to anticipate. Here, Paul insists that past eras have reached out to the Messianic churches, their intended beneficiaries, offering their treasures for us to explore. Our experience tells us that without such a resource we would be in very poor shape.

The recall of Scripture in 1 Corinthians is intentional, assuming that Christians ought to study every part of the Old Testament. This has been said already. But it has to be confessed that some parts are difficult. Take Numbers as an example. Young believers might be forgiven for suspecting that it is not directly relevant to their needs. But on the evidence of chapter 10 of this letter alone it is plain that nothing could be further from the truth.

2. As it was, it could be (10:12)

The apostle yearns that believers should be warned by the Scriptures: **'Let him who thinks he stands take heed lest he fall.'** Does this mean that the seriously erring Christian can lose his salvation? We cannot evade the question. The reality is that even though the Lord's people are never free from sin, both in contemplation and in the act (see Rom. 7:24; 1 John 1:8,10), we can never finally fall away from the Lord. This is shown clearly by John 6:35-40; 1 Peter 1:5 and Jude 24. Consider, too, the argument of Romans 6:14 and context: *because* we are not 'under law, but under grace', and *because* our salvation is certain, we are to strive to be holy. It follows that 10:12 must be interpreted in this light.

Perhaps the apostle had in mind an unbelieving professor of the faith who slipped into the church devoid of true repentance. This did happen even in those early days, as witness Titus 1:16; 2 Peter 2 and Jude 4. If this is how he was thinking when he penned these words, and aware that, like the Israelites of old, some Corinthians might show their true colours, Paul issues what is effectively a call to post-baptismal conversion.

But this does not add up: his readers were saints. The truth is that the apostle knew that the Lord's people discover Satan's attacks to be so vicious that they have to cry to God for help. They learn that their hearts can let them down. Although this may sound like a contradiction, it is not, as generations of believers have found out.

We have good cause to assent to the melancholy complaint of Jeremiah 17:9 that 'The heart ... is desperately sick.' Remember Paul's implied warning about what happens when saints do not put on 'the whole armour of God' (Eph. 6:10-17). In short, the apostle would seem to write about the naïve Christian who is blithely confident that 'he stands' so firmly that he can never commit serious sin.

3. The Lord, the believer and temptation (10:13)

Although men should never tempt the Lord to find out what he might do for them (10:9), it remains the case that the people of God are frequently the objects of his trials. James 5:10 and 1 Peter 1:7, not to mention Job, show it to be so. It is this mysterious matter that is considered in 10:13.

Paul declares that **'No temptation has overtaken you** [or, 'has received you'], **but such as is common to man.'** Yes, it is true that because the Corinthians were men they had been, and would be, tested. But it is not true that they had ever been exposed to superhuman trials beyond their endurance. Nor would they ever be.

The reason is that **'God is faithful'**, a truth set out already in 1:9 with a citation from Deuteronomy 7:9. This being so, the Lord **'will not allow'** his people **'to be tempted beyond what you are able'**; he will never permit them to be tested to destruction by some other agent, possibly the devil, so that they curse God and abandon him. Even so, there *is* testing. Difficulties are designed, supplied and monitored by the Lord to show believers that they can and will survive every affliction hurled at them. The end result is that their experience of the grace of God enlarges and they grow in personal faith and godliness (Rom. 5:3-4; James 1:3-4).

Furthermore, the Lord does not permit limited testing to continue indefinitely: **'But with the temptation will provide the way of escape also, so that you may be able to endure.'**

These words are unforgettable: it is none other than God who plans and provides his people's temptations, albeit indirectly, as well as the way out. 'With' suggests that this has to be the meaning: '[together] with the temptation ... the way of escape also'.[35] It is not as if an evil angel or a broken-down providence creates problems for the Christian and that the Lord rushes in at the last moment to pull things together. Everything is organized by him from first to last.

Food offered to idols (8:1 - 11:1)

For example, consider Jesus when he was led by the Spirit into the Judean wilderness to be tempted by the devil. Then there was the godly King Hezekiah, a loyal servant of the Lord left temporarily to his own meagre spiritual devices. What of the apostle's 'thorn in the flesh'?[36] In each of these situations God was in overall charge. But remember that the Lord never invites men to commit sin (James 1:13). Nor does Paul think about such a dreadful thing.

Perhaps 10:13 is deliberately non-specific. The reference to temptations that had at some stage 'overtaken' the Corinthians might be a virtual invitation to them to recall the intimate details of their own troubles, and in this way to confirm the truth of what the apostle says.

Idolatry and demons (10:14-22)

Israel in the desert had been addicted to idolatry; the Corinthians were surrounded by it. Israel suffered because of the addiction; the Corinthians must not fall into the same trap.

Beloved, yes; wise, perhaps (10:14-15)

'**Therefore**' (10:14), the readers, who are Paul's '**beloved**', are to '**flee from idolatry**'. Notice that the apostle is careful to show his affection for the people when he has to take them to task. Because, like the Israelites, his Corinthians were exposed to evil and its consequences and were flesh and blood, they must not tempt God by nibbling at what is wrong. The steward of the Lord instructs them to honour the Lord by running away from the gods in the same way that they were to flee fornication (6:18). The Corinthians are admitted to be '**wise** [or, 'prudent'] **men**', well able to appreciate the argument now to be presented with such immense courtesy: '**You judge what I say**' (10:15). Let them work it out for themselves.

The 'cup of blessing' (10:16)

Explicit reference is made to the Lord's Table, where the church sets the '**cup of blessing which we bless**'. 'To bless' almost conveys the meaning of being thankful.[37] But there is more to the prayer than gratitude: believers ask God to bless the wine so that it might fulfil its intended purpose. It was like this when Jesus 'blessed' bread and fish as a preparation to feeding the five thousand (Luke 9:16).

The truth outlined here is that when Christians meet together and bless the cup they do so as a prelude to displaying their oneness: they are **'sharing** [together] **in the blood of Christ'**. Equally, when they break the bread they demonstrate their fellowship together in **'the body of Christ'**. Paul asks if it is not so and expects the readers to respond with an enthusiastic 'Amen'.

'One bread' (10:17)

'Since there is one bread' it follows that **'many'** individuals are **'one body'**. Individually bonded to Christ, they belong to one another and at the table demonstrate their unity. And it is an astounding unity: they cannot be any less close to other believers than are the numerous members of a single body to one another. Then Paul shows how it is that the Lord's people display their oneness: **'For we all partake of the one bread.'** Notice that 'partake' (Greek, *metechô*) is an emotive yet carefully selected word, meaning to be in a definite partnership with others, rather than eating alone in a sort of religious restaurant where visitors are free to drop in.

Israel's altar, idolatrous sacrifices and the Lord's Table: a common factor (10:18-20)

The Corinthians are requested to **'look at Israel according to the flesh'**. They should consider Abraham's natural family (10:18). We need to bear in mind that when this letter was written the temple of God in Jerusalem was intact and in daily use. Paul himself had been there many times and would return.[38]

The apostle shows that there is an important correspondence between believers at the communion table and Israelites approaching the temple altar. In one respect at least Christians should learn from Jews. Whether it is a case of eating at the table or from what was sacrificed at the Jerusalem altar, the common denominator is a demonstration of interest in the worship of God: Christians are involved in 'a sharing of Christ' and Jews are **'sharers in the altar'** (10:16).[39] Social distinctions become irrelevant in the presence of God. He is all in all.

Food offered to idols (8:1 - 11:1)

This does not mean, of course, that the Lord's Table is a place for sacrifice; here, as in the Gospels, communion is seen as no more (and no less) than the appointed memorial to Christ's self-offering at Calvary.

Paul is bolder still. Even at pagan places of sacrifice the same principle of identification holds good: if Christians might learn from the Jews, let them also contemplate what happens at a heathen shrine.

Because what he is about to say is so extraordinary, the apostle meditates for a moment: **'Therefore what do I mean?'** (10:19). Has **'a thing sacrificed to idols'** actually become **'anything'**? That is, is it the property of real gods? Is the **'idol'**, by which is meant the deity represented by the image, 'anything'? Answering with an emphatic negative, the apostle elaborates on 8:4: 'There is no such thing as an idol in the world, and there is no God but one.' It follows that idolaters do not sacrifice to the gods (10:20). Then Paul makes a positive statement: evil spiritual forces are present in idolatry, although the idolaters are almost certainly unaware of this: **'They sacrifice to demons.'**

Apart from the next verse and 1 Timothy 4:1, which states, 'Some will fall away from the faith, paying attention to deceitful spirits and doctrines of demons,' 10:20 contains the only reference in Paul's writings to such beings. In the New Testament generally a demon is almost always an evil, supernatural personality, even though the devil is never described in this way.[40]

To recapitulate, the apostle teaches that eating at a religious meal is both an identification with others present and with their chosen object of worship. This is the case whether it is the Lord's Table, or the Jerusalem temple and altar, or in connection with idolatrous sacrifices. Therefore it does matter where and what Christians eat.

Suppose that a believer joins with others at a pagan shrine. Because the gods do not exist he cannot have a relationship with any of them. This much is self-evident. None the less, the saint enters into some sort of communion with demonic spirits and their suppliants. This is sinful malpractice. The apostle does **'not want'** the Corinthians **'to become sharers in demons'**, to develop a partnership with the powers of darkness, powers that are implacably opposed to the interests of the Lord's people.

Demons and the Lord (10:21-22)

If the Lord's Table has its wine, the heathen feast has its **'cup of demons'** (10:21). Paul has in mind the Greek version of the Old Testament and specifically Deuteronomy 32:15-21. This passage states that Israel in the wilderness was condemned by Moses for sacrificing to 'demons' (Deut. 32:17). The apostle insinuates that some of the Corinthians were perilously close to imitating the sin that overthrew so many Israelites.

In our twentieth-century world the principle still holds true. If sacrifices to the gods of Greece were offerings to demonic beings, should we not draw a conclusion about modern idolatry? What of the gods of India? Or the Roman mass?

The apostle shows that not only was it wrong to attend both the Lord's Table and the tables of demons, it was morally impossible for the people to continue along this double route. A literal translation might be: 'You cannot continue to drink ... you cannot continue to participate.' Paul warns that if it is maintained the habit must bring the erring people into spiritual ruin.

This needs explanation. Why could not a believer break bread with his church on the first day of the week and on the following day visit unconverted friends at their shrine to enjoy food that he knew had been contaminated by sacrifice?

The reason is simple. If a Christian goes away from the Lord's Table to a pagan shrine he does two things that clash violently. In church he has presented himself to Christ, the Lord who resisted the devil and all his works; a little later he takes it upon himself to reverence beings that are supernatural, evil and the unceasing enemies of the Saviour. In practice he displays a preference for neither Christ nor his adversaries, which means that Jesus is at one stroke degraded to the status of a demon. The tension is impossible and intolerable; Christ and Belial have nothing in common (2 Cor. 6:15).

Paul predicts that the Saviour will not take this lightly: **'Or do we provoke the Lord to jealousy?'** (10:22). Do the Corinthians understand these principles but persist in going both to the Lord's Table and to idol-feasts? There is an unmistakable allusion to Deuteronomy 32:21, which heralds the tragic judgement awaiting Israel in a similar situation: because they provoked the Lord with their idols, the God of Israel proposed to distress them through other

Food offered to idols (8:1 - 11:1)

people's aggression. Yet again Jesus, 'the Lord', is identified as Jehovah in the Old Testament.

Are we **'stronger than he'**? Is it wisdom to ignore the Lord's will? Never. He can overthrow us easily, but we can never prevail against him. This is why opposing allegiances must lead to grief.

Eating with idol-worshippers (10:23 - 11:1)

In chapter 8 Paul showed that participation in idolatrous meals could well bring about the spiritual ruin of naïve believers. Chapter 9 was a parenthesis in which the apostle introduced himself as an example of unselfish behaviour. Thus far in chapter 10 he has developed his condemnation of eating food consecrated to idols. Finally, in rounding off his treatment of the subject he is positive: separation offers its own distinctive bonus in that the one who holds to his principles might become a soul-winner.

All good things around us come from heaven above (10:23-27)

The statement of 6:12, **'All things are lawful'**, and the implication of 8:9, **'this liberty of yours'**, reappear in 10:23. On condition that he remains obedient to 'the law of Christ' (9:21), Paul is permitted to do as he pleases. So are other believers. This includes freedom to eat anything, not excluding food previously sacrificed to idols.

But the practical application is not quite so simple and the apostle presents a major qualification. First, **'Not all things are profitable.'** Secondly, **'Not all things edify.'** Where there is no genuine advantage to be gained by the exercise of liberty there can be no building-up process within the church. For this reason no man should **'seek his own good, but that of the other person'** (10:24).

Again Paul employs present tenses to outline the way ahead: **'Eat anything that is sold in the meat market, without asking questions because of conscience'** (10:25). The Corinthians were free to purchase whatever they wished from butchers' shops and did not need to ask where it came from. When they walked away their hearts need not be disturbed.

There is a reason for this: the world and everything filling it belongs to Jehovah (10:26, alluding to Ps. 24:1). The apostle's intention is to show that this Old Testament principle remains in force: because the meat eaten by the Corinthians derived ultimately from the Lord it was his. Therefore it could not belong to the gods, supposing that they existed, which they did not. It was untainted. It follows that there could be no problem about buying it. In the words of 1 Timothy 4:4, 'Everything created by God is good, and nothing is to be rejected, if it is received with gratitude.'

This rule applies when the Christian takes up an invitation to a meal given by **'one of the unbelievers'** (10:27). Not only may the guest accept innocent hospitality; if and when he enters another man's home he should eat without scruple whatever is offered him. Again, there is no violation of the conscience.

The challenge of tainted food (10:28-29)

Suppose, reasons Paul, that the hospitality is overtly pagan. Suppose that the Christian enters someone's house and is informed explicitly that the food set before him had been offered to the gods. The apostle now gives guidance about this type of embarrassment should it arise.

Left with no alternative, the Christian guest must decline to eat. There are two connected reasons for his (polite) refusal. First, **'because of the one who informed you'**. Secondly, **'also because of conscience; not his own conscience, I say, but because of that of the other person'**. The NASB gives 'for the sake of' rather than 'because of', which reduces the force of the words.[41]

It might be that Paul was considering an unbeliever, perhaps the host, as an informant. If so, the zealous Christian would decline the food with a view to rescuing his unconverted friend from further idolatry. Although such an interpretation is possible, it does not make a great deal of sense. A considerate yet curious host would not want to antagonize his Christian guest by disclosing where his provisions had been, spreading a crude pagan web to catch a baptized fly. The probability is that the other person would be another member of the church who might happen to be present, a believer unsure about the existence of the gods. This would tie up with 8:10, which refers to a weak believer watching a more assured brother eating in an idol's temple.

Therefore, if the Christian guest discovers the origin of what he is about to eat, he graciously withdraws. He does this because he is

Food offered to idols (8:1 - 11:1)

sensitive to the conscientious hesitations of a somewhat weaker brother who is present or who might learn at a later time about the proceedings.

The apostle places himself in the position of the Christian who has to back away: **'For why is my freedom judged by another conscience?'** (not 'another's conscience', NASB). Paul personifies the weak conscience: because it has become prone to fault-finding it sits in judgement on others, almost taking a delight in being shocked and offended.

The argument is that because some in the church *were* like this nothing would be gained if an action, right enough in itself, sent another Christian with an attitude problem into a frenzy of criticism and complaint. It would be folly to allow a small matter of a meal to become a cause of war.

Thankfulness, helpfulness and evangelism (10:30 - 11:1)

'Thankfulness' (10:30) translates the Greek word *chariti*, which, just here, could also mean 'by grace'.[42] The former interpretation is more probable in the light of **'give thanks'** at the end of the verse: Paul contrasts the gratitude of the humble Christian and the grudging behaviour of the fault-finding believer who sees in God's provision no more than idol food.

There is no good reason for the Christian guest to permit himself to be **'blasphemed'** by another saint because he gives thanks. Compare with Romans 14:16, which suggests that tensions of this type were not unique to Corinth: 'Therefore do not let what is for you a good thing be spoken of as evil.'

This is the only place in either 1 or 2 Corinthians where 'blasphemy', an emotive word, is mentioned. Perhaps we are surprised. But we ought not to be, bearing in mind what Christians can be like. Paul highlights the tragedy of a believer being maligned, not by unbelieving Jews or Greeks but by a fellow-Christian: the unstable, ready-to-judge conscience now explodes with a torrent of verbal abuse about a brother's relationship with God.

The opening clause of 10:31, **'Whether, then, you eat; whether you drink; whether you do anything'**, is depreciatory. The NASB gives 'whether' just once, whereas the Greek text has it three times for emphasis. It is as if the people are told that as long as, and so long as, they are motivated by **'the glory of God'**, no restrictions need hedge their behaviour, and certainly not the arbitrary and unjust limitations of the fault-finders.

Be this as it may, Paul is aware that the atmosphere at Corinth is fraught with tension. Because anything and everything that people do can swiftly become an immediate target for ignorant criticism, the glory of God might not be best served by an unthinking assertion of personal liberty. All will be to God's praise when the Christian conducts himself in a way that gives no offence to Jews, Greeks or to the church of God (10:32).

The apostle had learned by harsh experience that the message of the cross remains a scandal and folly to Jews and Gentiles respectively, and that believers will cause offence purely because of their faith (1:23). But he was determined to show that Christians should work hard at not being personally abrasive even if this does mean that actions right in themselves are to be abandoned to avoid strife.

Paul practised what he preached (10:33-11:1); he was more than eager to **'please all men in all things'**, seeking their, rather than his, **'profit'** so that **'they may be saved'**. Repeating 4:16, the apostle indicates that the Corinthians were to be his **'imitators'**, even as he was of Christ. His personal obedience was his qualification for putting himself forward.

6. The covered head
(11:2-16)

Attention is now given to issues that affected the Corinthians when gathering for worship. The first question to be addressed is the way in which women should cover their heads. Paul's treatment may be divided into four sections: first, the principle of headship (11:2-3); second, head-covering as a mark of subordination (11:4-6); third, man, woman and creation (11:7-12); fourth, sanctified common sense (11:13-16).

The principle of headship (11:2-3)

Although the apostle intends to focus upon weaknesses in Corinthian worship, he is keen, as ever, to note what is good: **'Now'**, he praises the people because they had **'remembered me in everything, and hold firmly to the traditions, just as I delivered them to you'** (11:2).

'Tradition' means something that is handed over or delivered. The meaning here is that the Lord's steward had transmitted faithfully to the people what he received beforehand from his Master; in turn, they honoured Christ by retaining what was deposited with them.[1] As we might expect, there is no evidence that Paul was puffed up because he exercised an undoubted influence over the Corinthians.

Having warmed the hearts of his readers, the apostle desires them to be aware that **'Christ is the head of every man, and the man is the head of a woman, and God is the head of Christ'** (11:3).

Notice that the fellowship is not informed that this is how it is; with his customary modesty Paul reveals his desire that they **'understand'**. But his wish is none the less than a command, and he knows that they will appreciate this.

Inevitable questions

Two questions arise. First, why are we given this disclosure about Christ, about Christian men and women and about God? Second, what is meant?

The first question is not difficult. We gather from 11:5 that some women in the church at Corinth prayed and prophesied with their heads uncovered. For Paul this was an important issue that had to be resolved. His reference to men covering their heads in worship seems to be introduced to give force to his teaching about feminine attire.

Secondly, it is not so easy to decide what is meant by the triple references to headship, although there is a clear allusion to Genesis 3:16. After the Fall God tells Eve that 'Your desire shall be for your husband, and he shall rule over you.' In 11:3 Paul has in mind the principle that Adam, subject to God alone, was placed in charge of family life.

Elsewhere the New Testament teaches both that Christ is the 'head of all things', that is, of the created world and of all men and angels, and that he is the 'head of the church' from whom his redeemed people derive their life and strength.[2] It is virtually certain that here the description of the Lord as **'the head of every man'** refers to something else, a third facet of Christ's authority.

The answer to our second question would be that a common element is assumed to be present in three fundamental relationships, each of which is manifested in the church. The apostle insists that women as well as men must be controlled by this common denominator.

The first relationship is the bond that a believing man has with his Saviour; second, there is the oneness that a man's wife has with her husband; third, there is the union between Christ and God the Father. None of these relationships is, of course, held to be the same as the others.

The element common to each of these linkages is subordination: a woman is one with the man, but remains under his authority and

The covered head (11:2-16)

depends upon him; the man is one with Christ, but remains under his authority and serves him; Christ is one with God the Father, but at the present time remains beneath his authority and serves him. Because of this principle of obedience, manifest both in creation and in redemption, Christian women should be careful about how they appear in the congregation. So, too, should men.

Head-covering, a mark of subordination (11:4-6)

The significance of head-covering is that it is a display of respect, even subordination. If we overlook this principle Paul's teaching makes no sense. But if we bear it in mind everything he writes is logical and right.

A man in disgrace (11:4)

Suppose that a man covers his head **'while praying or prophesying'** in the company of other believers. He signifies his subordination to someone other than Christ, someone who would be visually present either personally or by representation. Because, as a man, he is subordinate to no other created being, the action would be a contradiction in terms. The consequence? He **'disgraces his head'**.

The man's 'head' might stand for his natural head. Or it might be Christ or, given Paul's versatility, both. If the former, the man covers his head and makes a woman of himself; he shames that part of his body from which the Lord Jesus takes his title. By acting in this ludicrous way he shames Christ indirectly. If the latter, he veils Christ, as it were; the Lord suffers immediate embarrassment and vexation.

A woman in disgrace (11:5)

On the other hand, should a Christian woman uncover her (natural) head when praying or prophesying she puts it to shame. This is because she takes the place of a man, an attitude contrary to the plan of creation. The Lord ordained that women should be subordinate to men, and men subordinate to none other than God.

Notice that the apostle does not differentiate between married and single people. This is because the proper status of both men and women within redeemed creation is at issue. The principle of solidarity means that at all times every man represents Adam, and every woman Eve.

It follows that if a woman indulges in gender role-reversal, uncovering her head, **'She is one and the same with her whose head is shaved.'** These are strong words and some think that they allude to prostitutes. Perhaps so, but there seems to be no conclusive evidence that Corinthian women of ill-repute shaved their heads. Indeed, reason might suggest that in order to enhance their attractions these ladies would have adorned their hair. The probability, then, would be that the Christian woman with unduly short hair is not being likened either to a Corinthian prostitute or even to an adulteress.[3] Perhaps the best interpretation is that in 11:5 the apostle hypothesizes: if a woman uncovers her head irreverently she ought to take the indignity to its logical conclusion. Let her cut her hair so short that she really does resemble a man.

Paul's point, which is incontestable, is that a short-haired, man-like woman is unnatural. This means that she is unfitted to approach the God who gave her long hair; when praying and prophesying she would expose herself indecently before majesty.

In the Old Testament, although both men and women could take the Nazirite vow, which involved cutting off the hair, women were never allowed to resemble men. Apart from the vow, the shaving of a woman's hair was only permitted as a sign of captivity or uncleanness.[4] This needs to be mentioned because the apostle almost certainly did not have these regulations in mind. His sole implication is that the woman who shortens her hair makes herself out to be a man, a wilful act of self-exposure that cannot be right.

A plea to Corinthian women (11:6).

The principle is repeated for emphasis: if a woman must resemble a man, she should have her hair shaved away. Compromise never satisfies. Off with it all! Let her indulge in complete role-reversal. Conversely, if she deems it disgraceful to pray or prophesy when masquerading as a man, let her cover her head. Words could hardly be more forceful.

The covered head (11:2-16)

The apostle must have known full well that no woman in the church would ever want to part with almost all her hair. Nor, in truth, does he make the suggestion. He must have been aware that some were appearing in the fellowship looking distinctly untidy, by no means presenting themselves as the women whom God had made. With the apostolic tongue well and truly in its cheek, Paul provokes the ladies to appear as dignified sisters in the Lord.

Man, woman and creation (11:7-12)

The principle assumed in 11:4, that head-covering indicates reverent submission, becomes explicit.

Man, the glory of God; woman, the glory of man (11:7)

The man should not have his head covered **'since he is the image and glory of God'**. It is true that God created Adam and Eve at the same time and in the same place, and that Eve was the first woman and the first mother. But it was Adam rather than Eve who was appointed the master of all (Gen. 2:19-20).

Paul extends this principle to the churches. Whether married or single, the Christian man is invested with dominion to the exclusion of the believing woman. Like Adam, he is a glorious being and remains the 'image' of God in a way that no woman can be (Gen. 1:27; 5:1; 9:6); he does not bow to any other created being, not even to his helpmeet. It is for this reason that he carries no sign of submission and appears undisguised before his God as the man that God made him. In this way he honours the book of Genesis and him who inspired it.

Simultaneously, the woman is the **'glory of the man'**. Just as Eve was subordinate to Adam, although not his inferior, in the churches all women remain subordinate to men, although remaining their equals in terms of spiritual blessings and abilities. The woman, whether married or single, must bear the sign of submission. She appears before her God as a glorious daughter of glorious Eve; her head is covered. She honours the book of Genesis and the God who inspired it.

Pragmatism or theology?

Was Paul's teaching conditioned, even framed, by no more than the local culture? That is, were his instructions simply a response to a temporary situation which erupted in Corinth, intended solely for the Christians of that period and therefore capable of modification in later and different cultural situations? Or do they belong to an inspired apostolic tradition binding on all churches until the end of time?

The first view does not stand up. The apostle reasons from Genesis rather than from the social background in which he moved. His perception was that the order of creation, rather than Greek and Corinthian custom, defined the permanent interrelation and attire of men and women in the churches.

Having said this, it does seem that Paul's teaching fits well with his instructions about avoiding idol-worship. When, for example, a Roman sacrificed to the gods he covered his head with his toga, and the wreath of victory worn by an athlete in the Isthmian Games would have had some religious significance. Perhaps the apostle is putting space between the format of Christian worship and the world, a world which invariably rejects the biblical account of creation. If you believe in evolution you will perceive no need for women to cover their heads in worship.

Furthermore, artifacts recovered from the ruins of old Corinth suggest that most women did have long hair, even though it was sometimes fastened up so that it would not flow unimpeded around the shoulders.[5] All this suggests that the Corinthian Christians would not, and certainly should not, have been offended in any way by Paul's teaching. Common sense must have whispered to them that he was right.

Paul and Genesis (11:8-9)

An explicit appeal is made to Genesis 2:18,21-23 to demonstrate the principle that women should cover themselves in the act of worship.

First, **'man'** was not made **'from woman'**; rather, **'woman from man'**. Second, **'Man was not created for the woman's sake'**, but the **'woman for the man's sake'**. Because Eve derived

The covered head (11:2-16)

from Adam to be his helper, no woman, considered as a woman, may be other than subordinate to a man.

Even so, we should never forget that this teaching does not prejudice the standing with God that is the birthright of all believing women. In Christ there is neither male nor female.[6] Here the frame of reference is obviously different.

A woman's interests (11:10)

In church worship a woman is to acknowledge her subordination: **'Therefore the woman ought to have a symbol of authority on her head, because of the angels.'** 'Authority' might refer to a woman's personal status in her family or even elsewhere. Or, it could point to the truth that she is to exhibit man's authority over her. Unquestionably the second interpretation alone does justice to the context.

There is rather more to this than meets the eye. It is implied that the appointed sign of a woman's subordination enhances and advertises her elevated status of helpmeet. That is, she possesses authority because she is under authority. It is this servant-mistress role that she is to display. Because she serves man to the exclusion of any other created being all else bows before her. It follows that an uncovered feminine head represents a wilful abdication of personal dignity and stature.

Furthermore, she must cover herself **'because of the angels'**. This probably means that the holy angels would be shocked, even angered, were they to witness a Christian woman dressing unnaturally, exposing herself in the act of worship. The Bible tells us that these holy beings are intensely interested in the church and exist to serve it.[7] When coming into the presence of God no woman should ever ignore this.

Subordination is not inferiority (11:11-12)

The apostle takes pains to show that woman was not created as a sort of sub-human slave in order to promote the interests of her male lord and master: **'Neither the woman is without the man, nor the man without the woman in the Lord'** (11:11).

The design of the wise Creator was that man and woman should be mutually dependent, never functioning apart from each other. Even as a **'woman is from the man'**, similarly **'man is by means of the woman'** (11:12, referring to Genesis 2:21-23). According to Genesis 3:20, Eve became the 'mother of all the living'. Clearly, had there been no Adam, Eve would not have come into existence; equally, had there been no Eve, Adam would never have become a father.

Further, because **'All things are from God'**, man cannot, so to speak, say to the woman, nor she to him, 'I am better than you, because I made you and you came from me.'

Sanctified common sense (11:13-16)

In 10:15 the Corinthians were invited to assess the truth of what was said. Again an appeal is made, somewhat emphatically, to their own sanctified common sense: **'Judge among yourselves'** (11:13). Let them look at themselves and at their own people. Do they really believe that it is **'proper'** for a woman to pray to God with her head uncovered? A negative response is anticipated.

More questions follow (11:14-15). First, **'Does not nature itself teach you?'** Notice that Paul writes 'you' rather than 'us'; there was no problem here for him. Did not the Corinthians have an instinctive awareness that it is dishonourable for a man to have lengthy, unkempt hair? Recall for a moment that although he had long tresses, Samson did not fall under such a criticism; his flowing locks were kept in place (Judg. 16:13). In any case, his situation was different because he was a Nazirite. Paul continues. Is it not equally obvious that if a woman has long hair it is her **'glory'**? Is it not clear that long hair, although shaming his manhood, enhances, even confirms, her womanhood?

It is then asserted that **'Her hair has been given to her instead of a covering.'** 'Covering' (Greek, *peribolaion*) occurs also in Hebrews 1:12, where it means a mantle, a cloak which wraps around the body and covers it. Similarly, Paul's meaning is that feminine hair has been granted by God 'instead of' or in the place of a covering. This is a powerful expression which is not, perhaps, given due weight by the NASB reading, 'for' a covering. The Greek (*anti* + genitive) can mean nothing less than direct replacement or substitution.[8]

The covered head (11:2-16)

The apostle has shown that a woman must cover her head when she prays or prophesies in the assembly. On such an occasion she is to present herself to the Lord and before his people as a woman. But — and this is critically important — her long hair, whether or not it is secured with a pin or circlet around her head or covered with fabric, is just such an advertisement. A good and wise Lord has not denied this daughter of Eve a natural veil to display her glorious standing as man's appointed helpmeet. Provided her hair is long, there is no necessity for her to wear something to show that she, as a woman, was both created from man and because of him. Her own natural covering is adequate.

The word **'practice'** (or 'custom') in 11:16 refers either to the way in which some women might have uncovered their heads in worship or to incessant quarrels at Corinth about this and other apostolic doctrines. The second view might be preferable: it was not the habit of either Paul or **'the churches of God'** to get themselves tangled up in word-squabbles, particularly where inspired and authoritative teaching was concerned. Let the Corinthians, then, accept what is written and not seek to innovate. Compare this with 14:33,36-38, where the Corinthians are criticized for tinkering with doctrine, and with Paul's attitude to the condescending Athenians (Acts 17:33).

7. The Lord's Table
(11:17-34)

The apostle now probes an issue that must have caused him extraordinary pain: the flamboyant way in which the Corinthians met at the Lord's Table. Their flagrant abuse of the memorial meal was threatening to dismember the church to such an extent that the Lord himself had intervened to terminate the lives of some offenders (11:30).

Paul's treatment of the subject might be said to divide into three parts. First, he reveals how the table was being dishonoured (11:17-22). Then he reminds the people what he had taught them about the original institution of the fellowship meal (11:23-26). Finally, he shows how Christians should and should not approach the Lord's Supper (11:27-34).

Abuse (11:17-22)

Earlier the church was praised because it retained and applied apostolic teaching (11:2). Even so, the way in which the Corinthians disgraced themselves at communion was a cause of grief. Paul proceeds to a detailed exposition of the true significance of the ordinance, giving particular attention to the source of his doctrine.

The Lord's Table (11:17-34)

Divisions (11:17-19)

Apostolic authority (11:17)

'In commanding this I do not praise you.' 'This' is not a retrospective reference to what has been written regarding the place of women in the church. Rather, it is prospective, leading into a number of matters relating to the Lord's Table, an area where the church had fallen down grievously. All these issues are addressed in the light of a prior command from the Lord through his ambassador.

Corinthian divisions and apostolic discretion (11:17-18)

The problem about the Corinthians and communion was that when the people had **'come together'** they did not do this **'for the better but for the worse'**. Because of their behaviour at the Lord's Table they were disadvantaged rather than helped: worship and fellowship had become unprofitable and the people were not building themselves up through the exercise. The discipline of breaking bread was a failure.

'Coming together' is mentioned in this chapter both here and in verses 20, 33 and 34, as also in 14:23 and 26. It is obvious that the Corinthians were committed to meeting as a church. Although this was good, what happened when they were together was frequently bad.

'In the first place' (or, 'first', 'of first importance') shows that the divisions were serious in that they affected the people adversely **'as a church'** when they gathered formally for worship.

The apostle divulges that he had heard about the Corinthian schisms, possibly alluding to information passed on by Chloe's household (1:10-11). Never naïve, he chose to believe **'in part'** what he was told and was reluctant to accept the worst, even when the reports seemed reliable. In his personal attitude to the fellowship he exemplified Christian love, a love which, as he tells us in 13:5, is reluctant to impute evil.

Factions (11:19)

To some extent Paul was resigned to the inevitable: **'For there must also be factions among you in order that those who are approved may become evident among you.'**

Chapters 1-3 condemned unnecessary groupings that apparently had nothing to do with important doctrinal issues. Here the reference is to 'factions' (Greek, *haireseis*, whence 'heresies'), breakaway groups in the church maintaining their own distinctive and eccentric views. Some New Testament examples of this type of sectarianism would be the Sadducees and the Pharisees and even, according to their opponents, the Christians.[1] Notice that in Acts 24:14 Paul refers to 'the way which they [the Jews] call a sect'; he will not admit that the faith that he represents is heretical.

The principle brought out by 11:19 is that disagreements among professing believers must inevitably arise and will of necessity lead to a separation between those who are genuine in their faith and those who are not. This was happening at Corinth.

But perhaps Paul means more than this. Perhaps he indicates that God in his sovereign and surprising wisdom decrees the emergence of heresies, and does this for the advancement of the churches. The divine strategy would seem to be that through adversity and opposition those men of faith and truth whom God has sealed might be recognized and appreciated by his people. Although the Lord does not intend that darkness should permanently overcome light, the former is pressed by him into service as the latter's unwitting herald. It announces the presence of truth and eventually gives way to it.

It might be that in 11:19 there is an allusion to Deuteronomy 13:3, which anticipates that Jehovah will permit false prophets in order to test the discernment of his people. The principle held forth by Paul is exactly the same.

John Calvin could be taken as a relatively modern example. In 1536 Calvin, at the age of twenty-seven, brought out the first edition of his historic *Institutes of the Christian Religion*. The opening address to his monarch, Francis I, King of France, confesses that he was writing to counter 'the tyranny of certain Pharisees', by which he meant the church of Rome.[2] The point is that the Lord employed the corrupt Roman church to make Calvin's ministry a blessing to very many people. Under God, the struggle with the papacy made the Reformer the man that he was.

The Lord's Table (11:17-34)

Back at Corinth the assemblies had split into factions. Tragically, their internal divisions surfaced at the Lord's Table, the place where the saints were supposed to show their oneness and bury their differences. This is why Paul was grieved.

The Lord's Supper (11:20-22)

The indictment is expanded in 11:20, reconnecting with 11:18. The Corinthians **'meet together'**. Their problem was not that of absenteeism. They did gather at the Lord's Table and they did show some semblance of harmony: they ate and drank in one another's company — something which before conversion would have been unknown. But, as Paul sees it, they did not **'eat the Lord's Supper'**. His meaning is that the Corinthians' feast, held formally in honour of the Lord, had little or nothing to do with Christ.

The word 'supper' deserves examination. Perhaps in English it has changed its meaning over the centuries. What we can be sure about is that the background Greek word *deipnon* means a conventional meal, or even a celebratory feast, rather than something to eat at the end of the day.[3] Furthermore, in the New Testament this is the only occurrence of the word in connection with the Lord's Table. It follows that a specific time of day, perhaps evening, for Christians to break bread is not implied. A morning 'supper' would be quite in order.

The imagination staggers at the enormity of the Corinthian abuse of the table. It ought to be noted that even when correctly observed by the church, communion was probably rather more than a token meal. This is implied by 11:21; seemingly, the normal routine was for the worshippers to supply their own food and then to eat together.

If this is what actually happened the practice is not condemned. What the apostle does censure is the habit of the individual believer consuming his apparently pre-prepared meal without waiting to share it with others. Consequently, **'One man is hungry and another is drunk.'**

It is not certain that the use of the word 'drunk' means that Paul had intoxication in mind. What is definite is that considerable differences emerged where there should have been sharing and oneness; having enough for his own requirements, each person was set on enjoying it irrespective of the needs of others. Because the people did not eat together they violated the principle of one cup and one loaf. Remember 10:16-17, which teaches that the single cup means sharing and that the one loaf implies one body.

All this works up to a series of indignant rhetorical questions, beginning with **'Do you not have houses in which to eat and drink?'** (11:22). The implied answer muttered back by the startled people would be that they did not lack in this respect, to which we could imagine Paul retorting in holy indignation that they ought to go home and eat and drink their fill behind their own doors. But the apostle is not so blatant, even though his next words are to the point: **'Or do you despise the church of God, and shame those who have not?'** Yes, they do.

Notice the vivid description of the less affluent Corinthians. They were, in English jargon, 'have-nots', poor folk unable to find food to bring to the meeting-place. Possibly they even lacked their own private rooms in which to eat. The humiliation of these destitute saints was contemptible. As 11:30 shows, it was also dangerous.

A third question shoots forth: **'What shall I say to you? Shall I praise you?'** Although the apostle was never reluctant to give praise where it was due (11:2), did they really imagine that he could commend them in this situation? Repeating the sad statement of 11:17, he insists that **'In this I will not praise you.'** This is in effect a most severe rebuke, and would have been taken as such.

Institution (11:23-26)

The Corinthian church is reminded about the original institution of the Lord's Supper. Gross misbehaviour at the table demanded that plain and authoritative teaching be given.

Paul wrote for all churches in all places and in all times

Before we proceed, let's pause to catch our breath. Bear in mind that this letter was destined for all the people of God in all places and, almost certainly, of all times (1:2). Taking into account the flow of history, can we really doubt that the all-wise God inspired these unforgettable words to protect the saints against that one doctrine

The Lord's Table (11:17-34)

which remains the boast of a false church and the undoing of multitudes of its people: the doctrine of 'transubstantiation'?

This venerable and magnificent superstition, possibly accepted by the majority of the world's professing Christians, maintains that the Lord's Table should properly be described as an altar and that the bread and wine consecrated by a priest become the body and blood of Christ offered in literal sacrifice.[4]

There could hardly be a worse blasphemy. In the words of Thomas Cranmer, an Englishman who sealed his faith with his blood in 1556, the doctrine means in effect that Christ '... either for lack of charity would not, or for lack of power he could not, with all his blood-shedding and death, clearly deliver his faithful, and give them full remission of their sins, but that the full perfection thereof must be had at the hands of antichrist of Rome and his ministers'.[5] Think this through.

The teaching of Jesus, and Paul's application (11:23-26)

The apostle writes that **'I received from the Lord that which also I delivered to you'** (11:23). There is a definite emphasis placed upon 'I': allegedly, the Lord had spoken directly to his apostle about this great matter, and what the apostle heard he has already transmitted to the Corinthians with complete accuracy.[6]

Therefore, because fixed guidelines had been given to the Corinthians, their misbehaviour was all the more deplorable and could not be due to naïve ignorance.

A remarkable claim

We ought to compare the statement of 11:23 with 15:3 and particularly with Galatians 1:12. There the apostle asserts that he received the details of his gospel, in part and in whole, directly from the Saviour, with no human intermediary. This is astounding, bearing in mind that the good news had been heard by many long before Saul of Tarsus was converted, and certainly before he, now the apostle Paul, imparted his revelation about the Lord's Table to the Corinthians. Further, the gospel message being absorbed by the young churches in those very early days would have included teaching about communion. Even if the Gentile believers did not have any, or many, written accounts, the details of the Last Supper must have been widely circulated by word of mouth.[7] This makes the apostle's claim in 11:23 the more remarkable: apparently, his understanding of the memorial meal derived neither from the earlier apostles nor from the churches.

In theory he could have received his information from others, perhaps from Peter when he met him at an early date (Gal. 1:18). It is altogether likely that he did learn much when he travelled to Jerusalem and spent fifteen days with Cephas; we can be sure that the two men did not discuss politics. Even so, notwithstanding these early opportunities given to Paul, the Lord decided to short-circuit the process of transmission.[8]

We can infer that there was a necessary reason for this immediate revelation, a revelation which leapfrogged the witness of those present on the occasion. 1 Corinthians was written about A.D. 57 when the Gospels had not yet been circulated. Nor is it certain that the four were yet complete. Because the churches were in urgent need of guidance the Lord, not to mention Paul, knew that they had to be given immediate and authoritative documentation about this and other matters. Therefore Jesus revealed personally to his senior steward what he had said in Jerusalem some years before. What Paul heard he transmitted orally to the Corinthians (among others) and finally committed to writing.

If what was delivered to the church was precisely what the apostle had received verbatim from the risen Christ, the Corinthians' misbehaviour at the table must be reformed immediately; to bypass Paul would be to continue to disobey the Lord. This is the issue.

'The Lord Jesus, in the night when he was being delivered, took bread.' 'Was being delivered' (Greek imperfect passive, *paredideto*) indicates dramatically that the betrayal was a protracted process that did not happen in a moment. During the long hours when Judas was hatching his evil plot the Lord worshipped at the Passover meal. Even then, in the very late evening when he knew what was afoot elsewhere, Jesus refused to give up the established means of grace.

Furthermore, the Lord, **'when he had given thanks ... broke it'** (the bread), and uttered the words of institution: **'This is my body, which is for you; do this in remembrance of me.'** The breaking of

The Lord's Table (11:17-34)

the bread was for purposes of distribution and sharing only, rather than a symbolic act: the body of Jesus, although tortured dreadfully, was never broken (John 19:36). 'Do' means 'continue doing', from which it is plain that then and there our Lord set up a perpetual memorial for the church. Paul's qualifier **'as often'** (11:26) makes this apparent.[9]

The 'new covenant' (11:25)

The account continues: **'In the same way he took the cup also, after supper, saying, "This cup is the new covenant in my blood."'** The term 'new covenant' recalls both Exodus 24:8 and Jeremiah 31:31. Exodus 24:8 is concerned with the covenant between Jehovah and Israel, that established at Sinai, and Jeremiah predicts a 'new' covenant, better in every way than that inaugurated through Moses.[10]

The two allusions in the recorded words of Jesus are ultra-significant. What Moses rehearsed in shadow form and the covenant to which Jeremiah looked forward was, our Lord knew, being fulfilled through his own ministry.

We look at Moses' and Jeremiah's words more closely.

1. Exodus 24:8

Moses sprinkled sacrificial blood upon representatives of the assembled nation, announcing that this was 'the blood of the covenant, which the LORD has made with you in accordance with all these words'. In ancient times the Greek word *diatheke*, translated as 'covenant', often meant someone's will or testament, as in Galatians 3:15. However, in the Greek version of Exodus 24:8, which was probably floating before Paul's eyes, it stands for the inaugural agreement between Jehovah and Israel.

Moses' sacrifices at Sinai expressed Israel's desire to belong to Jehovah. But their desire was apparent rather than genuine. Gross sins committed there and in Canaan through the following centuries proved beyond all doubt that Jacob's sons had never known what it meant to be true to the relationship; the twelve tribes were never really the Israel of God. In the words of Hosea 1:9, 'You are not my people and I am not your God.'

The irony of the first covenant was that even then, at its inception,

Moses was acutely conscious that his arrangement was incapable of transforming sinful Israelite hearts. Something far better than the blood of bulls and goats would be necessary, and Moses knew that he had not provided it.[11] In this sense the Sinai covenant was perceived to be obsolete or 'old' from the day when it was established.

2. Jeremiah 31:31

Nearly a thousand years after Sinai, in about 600 B.C., it was apparent that the old covenant had been desecrated times without number by Israel and that it was a dead letter. Then, when the people were being carried off to exile in Babylon, the prophet Jeremiah predicted the eventual establishment of a 'new covenant', quite other than the previous arrangement both in its operation and in its designed effects. Not only would Israel be granted the forgiveness of sins; the hearts of the people would be transformed. The church of God in reality rather than in name, the new Israel would never break away from the Lord. At the Passover meal Jesus announced that his imminent death was to be the basis for this new relationship.

3. Confidence

The Lord instituted the symbolic memorial of his death before he died, and did so because he anticipated that his sufferings would be fruitful. He knew that the new covenant could never fade. Not unlike discerning Mary, who prepared Jesus for burial before he was dead, encouraged, no doubt, by the presence of the resurrected Lazarus (Matt. 26:12; Mark 14:8; John 12:1,7), the Lord planned for the future with a sublime and totally justified confidence. His work was far greater than that of Moses, and he knew it.

4. Transubstantiation again

Consider that on the occasion of the Last Supper the body and blood of Jesus were an integral part of his person situated at the side of the Passover table. Our Lord gave thanks, handled the bread and wine and spoke about them. But he did not migrate a metre or so in some mysterious, invisible fashion to become physically one with the elements presumably prepared by Peter and John (Luke 22:8-9). In

The Lord's Table (11:17-34)

other words, he was not in two places at once. If he was at the side of the layout he could not have been in it. The notion of transubstantiation at the Last Supper, the first Christian communion service, is as ridiculous as it is abhorrent. Further, if it did not happen then there is no reason for it to happen now. Nor is there any biblical or other evidence to prove the contrary.

5. Direct inspiration

'Do this, as often as you drink it, in remembrance of me,' are presented as the words of Jesus even though they are not found as such in the Gospels. From this it might appear that they had not been circulated in the churches before they were given to Paul by Christ and handed over by Paul to the Corinthians. The meaning is that whenever Christians 'do this', that is, gather at the Lord's Table, they should think carefully about the Lord's death: the table is a memorial rather than a social occasion.

Paul's application (11:26)

Our Lord's words **'as often'** are applied by his servant: **'For as often as you eat this bread and drink the cup, you proclaim the Lord's death until he comes.'**

It is obvious that Paul rejoiced in the glorious truth that the churches of the new covenant will never pass away and will continue to meet at the table until the day when Christ returns in glory. Further, if Jesus said that the people are to 'remember' his death, his trusted apostle adds that they 'proclaim' it.

'Proclaim' has occurred already in this letter (2:1; 9:14). The contexts show that proclamation is essentially the communication of information to men rather than presenting something to God. So it is here. The burden of these explanatory words in 11:26 is that believers remember the death of Jesus by portraying it, or announcing it visually, to one another, and they need to do this for their own comfort. This is why it is essential to attend the Lord's Table. For the apostle, eating and drinking together in this way declare the death of Christ (**'you proclaim'**). Bread and wine placed in a static position upon a table cannot do this.

Attitudes (11:27-34)

Abuses have been criticized. Now the apostle writes about underlying attitudes at communion.

Unworthy participation (11:27-29)

In 11:26 it is implied that the table becomes a memorial only when it is surrounded by worshippers. This truth is developed in 11:27. Any person who **'eats the bread or drinks the cup of the Lord in an unworthy manner, shall be guilty of the body and the blood of the Lord'**. 'Eats or drinks' does not mean that some Corinthians took bread or wine but not both together. The truth presented here is that an undiscerning and disorderly consumption of either the bread or the wine brings guilt upon the persons concerned and spoils the whole meal; to fail in one area is to fail everywhere.

From Corinth to Calvary (11:27)

Eating and drinking **'in an unworthy manner'** refers to the person who comes to the table with no desire to worship reverently. We know from 11:20-21 that the Corinthians were inclined to treat the Lord's Table as a social occasion, choosing not to see it for what it really is. Instituted by Christ as the joint-memorial of his death, bread and wine were enjoyed by some as if they were at home, or even in the precincts of a Greek shrine.

'Guilty' (Greek, *enochos*) means 'liable to' or 'involved in'. The expression is particularly strong: a participant at the table who sees no spiritual significance in what he eats or drinks makes his own negative declaration about the death of Christ.

If pressed, the man would no doubt admit that Jesus died a number of years earlier at a place called Calvary close to the walls of Jerusalem. He would probably acknowledge that he associates with others who profess to be followers of Jesus. He is admitted to their circle because he personally has been baptized in the name of the Saviour. In spite of this his attitude implies that the one whom the bread and wine represent is of no particular importance to him. So, why does he attend? Possibly because conviviality, not always easy to come by, is not unpleasant.

The Lord's Table (11:17-34)

In short, he is in the shocking position of identifying with those who were immediately responsible for the sufferings of Christ, lacking as they did any idea of who he was or what they were doing to him (2:8; cf. Acts 3:17). Their sin is now his sin; their guilt is his guilt.

Personal self-examination (11:28)

It follows that the professing believer who attends the table should **'examine** [or, 'approve'] **himself, and so let him eat of the bread and drink of the cup'**. Notice the implication of the present tenses: ongoing self-examination becomes the essential condition for ongoing participation.

In practice this means that the worshipper must ask himself some hard questions. Principally, do the bread and wine signify anything to him? Is he truly sorrowful because he is a sinner? Does he want to let it be known that because Christ died for him he desires to be in fellowship with the Lord and with his people? Only his own heart has the answer; only he can tell. He must search himself.

Negatively, self-examination does not imply that the worshipper ought to avoid the table because he thinks he is a failure. Positively, it does mean that when he comes to communion he wants to be told all over again that Jesus died for miserably sinful people such as he is. In a harvest-field ripe corn will hang its head, and this is how it ought to be at the Lord's Table.

The fatal chalice (11:29)

Suppose that an attender eats and drinks with little or no attention to the state of his heart and that Calvary and its significance are far from his thoughts. Paul's analysis of what happens in this type of situation is vivid. The man **'eats and drinks judgement to himself'**, sipping and swallowing his own sentence of condemnation. The reason? He **'does not distinguish the body'**.

By 'body' is meant the Lord's physical body, symbolized by the bread and wine, rather than the church, the spiritual body of Christ. As in 4:7; 6:5 and 11:31, 'distinguish' means 'to make a distinction', 'to appreciate' or even 'to assess'. The unworthy person is blithely insensitive to the vast gulf between this bread and wine and the gastronomic satisfaction offered at home or perhaps at the eating-places that he might frequent. For him it is no more than interesting food and drink.

The heavy hand of God (11:30)

Logically, this **'judgement'** does not have to be eternal condemnation. Nor is it. The explanation is given: **'For this reason** [that is, because of an absence of discernment] **many among you are weak and sick, and a number sleep.'** 'Weak' might mean constitutional weakness, and 'sick' probably refers to physical disablement through illness. Because a sovereign God had smitten them severely a number of the Corinthians were afflicted and others died. Remember Satan's shrewd comment about Job's bodily well-being (Job 2:4-5); health is a man's most prized possession.

In the New Testament death is considered as 'sleep', but with regard to believers only, as we have noted earlier. Here it is asserted that God had seen fit to terminate the lives of some Corinthians because of their attitude to the Lord's Table. Their bodies fell asleep prematurely and their spirits were called away. The privilege of extended service was denied them, although not the promise of salvation.

The need for discernment (11:31-32)

The verb **'distinguish'**, which appeared in 11:29, occurs again in 11:31: **'But had we been assessing** [or, 'distinguishing'] **ourselves we would not have been judged.'** The imperfect tense, 'had we been assessing', brings out the past absence of ongoing self-assessment. 'We would not have been judged' signifies what the grammarians sometimes call point-action: because God had already executed his own sentence it was too late to appeal.[12]

Notice that the apostle identifies with the church although he had not participated in their sin. He focuses on their failure to face up to the matter, pointing out that the consequence of their folly was that the Corinthians as a whole were locked into a process of being 'judged' by the Lord. This judgement was essentially a chastening process: **'We are disciplined by the Lord in order that we may not be condemned along with the world'** (11:32).

The Lord's Table (11:17-34)

Punishment or correction?

Were these inflictions a divine punishment? The answer is that it all depends upon what is meant by 'punishment'.

Punishments are invariably acts of vengeance, paying back offenders what they deserve. Secondly, apart from the death sentence, they can sometimes be chastisements designed to bring guilty persons to their senses. Thirdly, punishments are often meted out by society as warnings to potential offenders.

The chastisements inflicted upon the Corinthians were not punitive. This was because Jesus had died for them: 'Christ our Passover also has been sacrificed' (5:7). Paul knew that a second payment for their sins, this time by the people, was altogether out of the question, as impossible as it would have been unnecessary. Therefore, if some 'slept' they had not gone to perdition. It follows that the discipline was either remedial or a deterrent or, probably, both: surviving offenders were being advised to repent.

The Lord cared for the Corinthians and was shaking them out of their complacency. 'Whom the Lord loves, he reproves' (Prov. 3:12; Heb. 12:6). He refused to allow them to become callous and be condemned along with the ungodly world. Contrast their situation with that of the Pharaoh of the Exodus, a man on whom terminal judgement was inflicted, rather than his being given loving correction. As Exodus 9:16 and Romans 9:17-18 show, the Lord left him as he found him, and the tyrant paid the price for his sins.

Consideration (11:33-34)

'So then, my brethren, when you come together to eat, wait for one another' (11:33). A lesser man than the apostle might have omitted the words 'my brethren' and inserted something like, 'If you are wise...' None the less, such a note of warning is precisely the burden of the introductory 'so then': Paul sounds the alarm rather than merely exhorting the Corinthians to attend to others. If anybody is genuinely hungry, **'Let him eat at home, so that you may not come together for judgement'** (11:34).

Observe once more that apostolic present tenses stress ongoing attitudes, and that Paul allows his own words an authority not less than that of the teaching of Christ. Clearly, immovable guidelines are being laid down for the churches.

In 11:34 the words **'come together'** are truly ominous. If the Corinthians' behaviour at the table does not change for the better they may well gather together, but only to receive judgement. Do they propose to assemble for genuine worship or for chastisement? It is their decision. Given their frivolous attitude to sacred issues, the danger is that the Lord's Table might again provoke divine displeasure.

Further, it appears that there are some other irregularities, concerning which Paul **'will command'** whenever he comes to the city; he is uncertain about when, or even if, he will return. For the moment he anticipates, his provisional itinerary being set out at the end of the letter.

The powerful word 'command' implies authoritative instruction (Greek, *diatassô*).[13] Because the writer is an apostle his words have divine origin and sanction. If the Corinthians failed to take to heart what was required they might do themselves much harm.

8. Spiritual gifts
(12:1 - 14:40)

The spotlight falls upon spiritual gifts. It becomes patently obvious as we read chapters 12-14 that the Corinthians were in a state of almost hopeless confusion about these blessings. Each chapter is a distinct section within the total presentation.

First, the confession of Christ as Lord is the true evidence of the presence of the Holy Spirit (12:1-3). Although there are various spiritual gifts, they all derive from the one Spirit (12:4-11). The human body, a living organism in which every member is interdependent, is a picture of the way in which the church should operate (12:12-31a).

The next main section, 12:31b - 13:13, considers the gifts of the Spirit (Greek, *charismata*) in their true perspective. Although important, they are not all-important, and this for three reasons. First, if unaccompanied by love they are useless (13:1-3). Secondly, Christian love unaccompanied by spiritual gifts is useful (13:4-7). Thirdly, unlike faith, hope and love, they are destined to vanish long before the world comes to its end (13:8-13).

The final section, chapter 14, falls into two parts. The first division (14:1-25) insists that prophecy is superior to speaking in tongues. Why this is the case comes to the surface in 14:1-11. Applications are given in 14:12-19, where Paul's conduct is once again offered as an example to all. In 14:20-25 an appeal is made both to the Old Testament and to Corinthian common sense regarding the relative merits of tongues and prophecy.

The second part of the chapter (14:26-40) is mainly practical. Instructions are given concerning the exercise of prophecy, speaking in tongues and the interpretation of tongues (14:26-33a) and, finally, the role of women in the assembly (14:33b-40).

The Spirit has come (12:1-3)

'Concerning' (12:1) implies strongly that the Corinthians had brought the question of **'spiritual gifts'** to Paul for his counsel. He responds in detail to ensure that the brethren are fully informed about the issue.

Past experience (12:2)

The people, most of whom had been idolaters, are called to ponder their background. The verse is not, perhaps, the easiest to translate. Here is a possible interpretation: **'You know that, when nations, whenever you were being led away to voiceless idols, you were carried away.'** As in 1:23; 5:1 and 10:20, 'nations' could be translated as 'Gentiles'. The NASB's 'pagans' is inappropriate. Three points at least are emphasized by the apostle.

First, the non-Jewish element in the church had formerly been **'led'** away into captivity to worship images. Paul stresses that they were carried off unwillingly and by compulsion rather than being eager disciples of numerous false deities. They were no better than helpless prisoners, and their addiction to idolatry was the consequence of their being overpowered.

Secondly, the false gods remained voiceless (Greek, *aphôna*), the reason being that they were non-existent. Because these figments of the imagination had always lacked the faculty of speech they could not possibly have bestowed it upon Christians who spoke in a variety of new languages.

Thirdly, because the Corinthians were at one time **'nations'** it is implied that their status had changed: no longer Gentiles, they now belonged to the Israel of God. This will be developed by the apostle as an essential element in his chain of reasoning.

But how, and by what or whom, had these converts been carried away? Certainly not by the unreal gods they idolized. The meaning must be that there had been unrecognized, invisible and malignant

Spiritual gifts (12:1 - 14:40)

personalities lurking behind the traditional façade of idol worship. These had overwhelmed the Corinthians.

This is the only occasion in Paul's writings and recorded speeches where the expression **'carried away'** is found (Greek, *apagomenoi*). It is important to note that elsewhere in the New Testament each occurrence of this word presupposes, or is accompanied by, a subject and an object, the meaning being that something or someone is carried away by an agent. This is how it is here.[1] It ought not to be forgotten that in 8:5 and 10:20 the apostle has already made it plain that idolatry is dangerous because it is bound up inextricably with demon-worship.

What the Christian can and cannot say (12:3)

Paul makes known two principles: first, that **'no one speaking by the Spirit of God'** is able to pronounce that **'Jesus is anathema'**; secondly, that no one is capable of confessing that **'Jesus is Lord'** except by the direction of the Holy Spirit. As elsewhere in the New Testament, **'make known'** suggests a first-time revelation of what would otherwise remain hidden from the people of God.[2] It follows that at this point the apostle makes important disclosures that the church needs to understand.

Not only does the living God speak, his Spirit had induced the saints to confess Christ: in so doing they were **'speaking by the Spirit of God'**.[3] No dumb idol could ever have achieved this. Far from being carried away helplessly by a cruel deity, the Corinthians were willingly guided by the Holy Spirit. This is why they gladly acknowledged their Lord, something sullen prisoners would never do. Romans 8:14 brings out the truth: 'All who are being led by the Spirit of God, these are the sons of God.' In short, the Corinthians' situation as believers was fundamentally different to that of the world around. And it was infinitely better.

There is more: the Christian cannot anathematize, or curse, his Saviour. In Old Testament times the Greek *anathema* lying behind the English 'anathema' meant being set apart for God alone. In practice the idiom signified that the beast, or person, put to one side was destined to die; as the NASB indicates it, or he, was 'accursed' by God. It is in this negative sense that the New Testament uses the word.[4]

It follows that because God never blasphemes God, genuine inspiration does not curse Christ. Perhaps the apostle was recalling the time about twenty-five years earlier when he had striven to make Christians blaspheme against their will (Acts 26:11).

The average man of the world who does not know the Lord, nor wants to, is given consideration. A double negative is employed for emphasis. Such a person could not say, **'Jesus is Lord'**, that is, admit that Jesus is God, unless renewed by the Holy Spirit. Neither his sinful heart nor the powers of evil that control him would ever permit such a confession. To put it another way, when the Spirit of God moves a man's heart, that heart impels his lips to make the acknowledgement.

And this admission was upon the lips of the Corinthians, as 1:2 demonstrates: 'the church of God ... at Corinth ... with all who in every place call upon the name of our Lord Jesus Christ'. These people had received the Holy Spirit. Therefore they were no longer the property of evil powers; no longer were they being led away by them to voiceless gods.

The fact that the apostle felt constrained to write in this way might hint at the disorders prevalent at Corinth: apparently, these believers did not know how to cope with spiritual phenomena. It could reasonably be inferred that local versions of the Philippian slave-girl or the Ephesian sons of Sceva had been heard to curse Christ (Acts 16:17; 19:14). If so, because these evil practitioners were vocal and because their spiritual powers were evidently real, the church was confused. The situation needed urgent clarification.

One God; different gifts (12:4-11)

First, Paul shows that it is God alone who is the source of all genuine spiritual gifts. Then he specifies some of them.

Sovereign distributions (12:4-6)

The named *charismata* are considered in each of three different ways: **'There are distributions of gifts ... distributions of ministries ... distributions of activities.'** The NASB gives 'varieties'

Spiritual gifts (12:1 - 14:40)

rather than 'distributions', but this is probably a secondary meaning for the background Greek word *dairesis*. The underlying truth is that God, and God alone, allocated a rich abundance of spiritual gifts to the Corinthians, giving only what he had determined to the objects of his choice, a determination not governed by popular desire.

First, even though there are distinctions in the nature of the blessings, there remains the **'same Spirit'**. Because the people had received all their gifts from the same source they should not boast.

Secondly, although the amazing powers exercised by the Corinthians may be described as **'ministries'**, there is the **'same Lord'**, Jesus, the obedient and self-sacrificing servant of God the Father and of the church. The Corinthians should be keen to minister to one another in the same way that Christ had cared for the disciples.[5]

Thirdly, these blessings are **'activities'**. It is the **'same God who works all things in all persons'**; he alone works miracles through and for the Corinthians. This being so, they should be humble.

Notice that these verses virtually present the doctrine of the Trinity: all the three persons of the Godhead had distributed gifts to the saints.

The principal charismata (12:7-11)

Spiritual gifts everywhere (12:7)

'But to each one is given the manifestation of the Spirit for the common good.' The initial 'to each one' is emphatic: apparently, every member of the Corinthian church had some spiritual gift and nobody had been overlooked. If we think about it we shall see that Paul is making a remarkable statement about the presence of the Holy Spirit in the church.

'Manifestation of the Spirit' is unusual. One possible meaning is that the Spirit had made himself known to the Corinthians. Another could be that gifted people showed plainly that God was with them (= 'manifestation about the Spirit'). Perhaps the first interpretation is better because elsewhere in Paul's writings believers are never said to manifest or show forth the Spirit. As in 2 Corinthians 2:14, the Spirit discloses himself through them.

Either way, numerous spiritual gifts had been entrusted to individuals for the benefit of the assembly. For this reason there must be no question of rivalry. Further, Paul employs the present tense: **'is given'**. He knew that even as he wrote charismata were being bestowed.

The gifts of the Spirit (12:8-10)

Now comes a presentation of some spiritual gifts. If we compare this carefully with 12:28 and with Romans 12:4-8 we notice that the list does not appear to be complete.

Even granting this proviso, it seems that there is a deliberate classification. I have tried to demonstrate this by departing from the NASB text and splitting the passage into three sentences which parallel the three principal families of gifts. I would suggest that this procedure is true to the background Greek because these groups are introduced respectively by **'to one'** in 12:8 and **'to a different person'** in both 12:9 and 12:10b.

> **For *to one* is given a word of wisdom through the Spirit; to someone else, a word of knowledge according to the same Spirit.**
>
> ***To a different person*, faith by the same Spirit; to someone else, gifts of healings by the one Spirit; to someone else, workings of powers; to someone else, prophecy; to someone else, assessments of spirits.**
>
> ***To a different person*, families of tongues; to someone else, interpretation of tongues**
>
> (12:8-10).

Within each division there are related sub-species of gifts, each gift introduced by 'to someone else'. But how can we be sure that there is such a classification? The answer is that Paul employs two significantly different words, both of which, probably unfortunately, come across in the NASB as 'another'. **'Different'** (Greek, *heteros*, whence 'heterodox') is implied at the beginning of 12:8, and in 12:9 and 10b it introduces the second and third groups. **'Someone else'** (Greek, *allos*), a less forceful term, stands for distinctions within a particular class (12:8,9,10a,b).

The arrangement seems to go like this:

Spiritual gifts (12:1 - 14:40) 233

1. Gifts that have reference to the intellect (12:8)

A word of wisdom
A word of knowledge

2. Gifts that depend upon faith (12:9-10a)

Faith itself
Healings and the workings of powers
Prophecy
The assessment or discernment of spirits

3. Gifts that relate to the faculty of speech (12:10b)

Tongues
The interpretation of tongues

Although this scheme seems obvious it might be unwise to ask why it should be so. Perhaps the apostle brings to the fore the fact that the charismata were saturating the young churches.[6]

1. Wisdom and knowledge

In our first category there were **'a word of wisdom'** and **'a word of knowledge'**. 'Word' (Greek, *logos*) occurs twice in 12:8, each time without the definite article 'the'. As such, it means no more than utterance or speech. Similarly, in English we might refer to 'a word of encouragement' or to 'a word of warning'. The Greek is probably not much different, and this could be how we are to understand the two gifts.

It is not easy to identify them. Perhaps they were almost the same in that some people spoke with 'wisdom' (Greek, *sophia*) and others with 'knowledge' (Greek, *gnôsis*). The former blessing might have been the capacity to declare new revelations from God, as distinct from the antiquated, stale wisdom of the world, a wisdom roundly condemned in 2:5,6,13. To judge by the order of gifts mentioned in 12:28-29, 'a word of knowledge' may have been a teaching ability. If so, some of the people were gifted to explain both the meaning and the application of apostolic doctrine. Or it could have been related to prophetic disclosure, as 14:6 possibly implies: 'I speak ... in revelation or in knowledge or in prophecy or in teaching.'

2. Faith, healings, powers, prophecy and the discernment of spirits

In the second category the gift of **'faith'** is mentioned first. We need to remember that every saint, exactly like those at Corinth, is by the mercy of the Lord a believer. Ephesians 2:8 makes this abundantly clear: 'For by grace you have been saved through faith: and that [faith] not of yourselves, it is the gift of God.'

Unquestionably more than common saving faith in the Lord, this charismatic faith seems to have been an enhanced, more intense faith of a quality not granted to everybody. Maybe there is an allusion to this in 13:2, where the apostle speaks of having 'all faith'.[7]

Mention is made of **'gifts of healings'** in the plural rather than a single 'gift of healing'. Is the reference to a cluster of different healing miracles performed by one person (**'to someone else'**)? Our minds stagger at what seems to have been happening at Corinth and elsewhere.

What **'workings of powers'** were remains uncertain, except that they appear to have been other than healing miracles. The deaths of Ananias and Sapphira could have been an earlier example, as also the temporary blinding of Elymas the sorcerer (Acts 5:1-11; 13:11).

In those times **'prophecy'** was extraordinarily significant, as witness 14:1 and 39. Unlike the syllabuses of established Christian teachers, such as Aquila and Priscilla (Acts 18:26), the prophetic word was always new, inspired and infallible. In 2:12-13 the apostle, we remember, implied that he possessed this gift in an extraordinary measure.

It is important that we understand what prophecy was. Nowadays some Christians pick up the word 'prophet' and use it as a convenient label, no doubt doing this innocently enough but in a loose fashion. Just by way of illustration, a brochure listing taped sermons preached by Dr Martyn Lloyd-Jones announces that he was an 'apostle and prophet of the 20th century.'[8] But this was not the case at all. Minister of the gospel and a means of blessing to many, the 'Doctor' was not an apostle of Christ who declared hitherto unknown prophetic revelations; nor did he ever make such a claim.

Back in New Testament times it appears that genuine prophecy displayed at least four unfailing characteristics.

First, because it came immediately from the Spirit, prophecy was *without error*. The Old Testament prophets of the Lord were never

Spiritual gifts (12:1 - 14:40)

mistaken. Deuteronomy 18:21-22; 1 Kings 22:28 and Jeremiah 28:9, to take just three examples, make this plain. There is no reason to suppose that the principle did not hold good for the Christian prophets of the first century A.D. Because the Spirit is truth, he guides into all truth (John 16:13).

Secondly, flawless prophecy was *authoritative*: the prophets who spoke from God were always able to say with perfect confidence, 'Thus saith the Lord...' Their own human weaknesses were not permitted to distort the accuracy, or to detract from the authority, of what they said.

Thirdly, prophecy was always *predictive*. This needs to be emphasized. Upon careful investigation, every genuine prophetic utterance recorded in the Old and the New Testaments refers at some stage and in some way to future events. There are no exceptions. '"Write therefore ... the things which shall take place"' (Rev. 1:19).

Finally, prophecy always *unfolded something more about the plan of redemption centred upon Christ*. Even Agabus' prophecies concerned future events that would help shape the apostolic mission (Acts 11:28; 21:11).

The **'assessments of spirits'** must have been the ability to distinguish between Spirit-given prophecies and artificial, uninspired utterances.[9] If we take into account the background situation suggested by 12:2 we need not be surprised that such a gift was essential.

3. Tongues and their interpretation

Now we come to the third category, in some ways the most remarkable of all the three groups. It leads with the gift of **'tongues'** (sometimes referred to as 'glossolalia', from *glôssa*, Greek for 'tongue').

At the outset something needs to be said about this charisma. Tongues are not considered by 1 Corinthians as ecstatic sounds that could mean nothing to those who uttered them, even if at times the hearers were mystified. Quite simply, *glôssa* was virtually a functional synonym for the Greek *dialektos*, whence 'dialect' or 'language', and — as we shall see immediately — also for the Greek *phône*, whence 'phone' or 'voice'.

According to Acts 2:4-11, on the Day of Pentecost the disciples praised God in a variety of foreign languages which, it seems, bore no resemblance to one another. This is shown by Luke's employment of *heteros* in Acts 2:4, 'other [different] tongues'. Further, each 'tongue' was recognized immediately by individuals in the listening crowd as 'his own language' (Acts 2:6,8). Communication is emphasized by Acts 2:11, which reveals the unanimous judgement that the crowds heard their 'own tongues'. On this momentous occasion the brethren spoke in understandable languages.

Nor is there any evidence to show that the Pentecostal gift of glossolalia was anything other than the gift of tongues experienced at Corinth or anywhere else.

That the meanings of these words in the New Testament are precisely what they were in the Greek-speaking world of the time is beyond doubt. Dio Chrysostum wrote about the singing of Homer's epics in India and observed that poetry composed originally in his own 'tongue' *(glôtta, = glôssa)* was being reproduced by the Indians in their own 'language' *(dialektos)* and 'voice' *(phône)*.[10] Only a rash man would attempt to show that New Testament 'tongues' were ever anything other than conventional languages then in use even though they were gifts from the Spirit. It might be noted that the 'new tongues' of Mark 16:17 are said to be 'new' not because they are something other than languages, but because they would be new in the experience of both speakers and hearers. There is no clash.

The apostle's claim is astonishing for a second reason. Apparently, this gift enabled the favoured recipient to utter **'kinds'** of tongues. In its singular form, 'kind' (Greek, *genos*) means 'race', 'family', 'species' or 'class'. For instance, in the Greek Old Testament, Genesis 11:6 portrays mankind before the time of the tower of Babel as one 'people' (literally a 'kind') that possessed one universal language understood by everybody. The same word, 'kind', can also stand for distinct divisions among living things.[11] In 12:10 *genos* occurs in the plural because after God's intervention at Babel humanity divided into families with very many 'kinds' of language.

It was not that the Lord had given somebody a single foreign tongue with which to praise God to his heart's content whether at Corinth or elsewhere. Rather, the favoured individual was granted a whole range, or 'kinds', of distinct languages. The NASB expresses this helpfully: **'to another, various kinds of tongues'**. As it had been some years before in Jerusalem on the Day of Pentecost, a broad spectrum of languages was appearing in the young churches (cf. Acts 10:46; 19:6).

Spiritual gifts (12:1 - 14:40)

The Lord never failed to provide for his people. If one believer could speak at choice from a range of unlearned languages now at his disposal, another would be enabled to interpret each and all of them for the benefit of the assembly, and this in order that all might understand the inspired utterances. The relevance of this gift is made plain in chapter 14.

Many gifts; one Giver (12:11)

Reference is made to these wonderful gifts to emphasize that the **'one and the same Spirit works all these things'**. Although it is true that 12:6 states that God (the Father) 'works all things', there is no contradiction because the Spirit is from God; what the Spirit does, God does, and what God does is made real by the Holy Spirit. Here, as in many other places in his letters, Paul contributes to the doctrine that there is one God who subsists in three distinct but not separate persons.

Furthermore, the sovereign God spreads his gifts among believers in an unpredictable manner: **'distributing to each one individually just as he wills'**. There is no question of the people gazing at good things stacked upon the heavenly shelf, as it were, and taking from it the blessings which intrigued and fascinated them the most, and which they felt might enhance their personal status.

It follows that neither should the Corinthians glow with pride if they exercised spectacular abilities, nor be envious of other fellow-beneficiaries, nor feel they were higher up the scale than less favoured individuals; God had made his own distribution with no reference to the merits of the recipients. The tongues-speaker was not necessarily a more spiritual Christian than the brother who was not gifted in this way. Nor were the gifts of prophecy or of healing given, say, to the more saintly saints.

The body of Christ (12:12-31a)

The apostle shows that although the church is composed of many people with differing personalities and gifts, it remains true that each saint is connected with all the others and that he needs them. There can be no exceptions to an interdependence as deliberate as it is unavoidable. In the words of Alexandre Dumas's D'Artagnan, uttered in a somewhat different context, it is a matter of 'All for one, one for all'.[12] Let the people rejoice in this and exploit it.

The body: diversity in unity (12:12)

The human body is a single working unit composed of many dissimilar parts. Just so with Christ and the church.

Inspired 'body' language

'For' introduces 12:12-31a in order to illustrate and apply the principle of variety in unity taught in 12:4-11. The picture Paul takes up is that of the human body, consisting as it does of a vast number of members operating in perfect harmony. Hippocrates, the celebrated Greek physician of the fifth century B.C., observed that in the anatomy of a man, 'All the parts form a whole, and severally the parts in each part, for the work [of the body].'[13] In those distant times men perceived the extraordinary co-ordination among the elements of the human frame. The principle is obvious, which is why it is used; the apostle never went out of his way to be difficult.

From Christ to the church, or via the church to Christ?

Notice that 12:12 reads, **'So also is Christ,'** rather than 'So also is the church.' The apostle's doctrine is that because believers are united individually to Christ they are **'members'** (or 'parts') of one another. The principle was foreshadowed in 6:15, where the Corinthians were reminded that 'Your bodies are members of Christ.'

But the glorious diversity within the oneness that Christians enjoy is of gift and function rather than of status. Text and context assume that there is one received faith, a unique instrument of salvation incapable of modification and in which all believers share.[14] Perhaps it would not be too harsh to say that Paul's teaching is quite unlike the posturing of ecumenical Christianity, which embraces, not without tension, churches and men who might do well to stop, stoop and think for a moment. Were they to do so they might realize that, if unleashed, their distinctive beliefs have sufficient

Spiritual gifts (12:1 - 14:40) 239

potential to cancel one another out. Of course, it is possible that such churches are not entirely unaware of where they stand. If so, they compound their problems.

Further, in describing the church as the **'body of Christ'**, 12:12 takes for granted the truth that we can belong to God's people only when we have become one with the Saviour, and that we unite with him by repentance and personal faith.

This needs to be shouted from the housetops for at least two reasons. First, multitudes of people are tragically ignorant that salvation is by faith in Christ alone. Secondly, this doctrine has shaped European and, if we ponder the matter, world history. To be specific, here is the difference between Rome and the Reformers and, at a more fundamental level, between the religion of the Bible and all other historic 'faiths'.

Rome has always demanded that men give her their allegiance and by this route come to Christ. The Reformers and others, such as the orthodox Anabaptists, read their Bibles and disagreed. What they did was to urge men to call directly upon the Saviour and find peace with God. There was not, is not, and can never be, any common ground between Rome and the Reformation.

To put it in another way, Christ is the only mediator between God and sinful men (1 Tim. 2:5). But can we be received by Christ when we are aware of who he is and what we are? Or do we need a back-up organization such as the papacy to endorse our faith and in effect to plead for us? The answer given by the Bible and true Christian experience is that we need no representative to introduce us to Christ. This is because he gives an immediate welcome to all who come to him on his terms. A long time ago even his enemies had to admit that 'This man receives sinners' (Luke 15:2). It is at this critical point that Rome has always been in error, making herself out to be the essential intermediary between men and Christ.

The baptism of the Spirit (12:13)

How it is that Christians relate so intimately to Christ and therefore to one another is demonstrated with a vivid picture: **'For in one Spirit we were all baptized into one body.'** The importance of a correct understanding of the metaphor will be obvious to all.

Baptism 'in' or 'by' the Spirit?

Some would deny that the preposition **'in'** shows the Corinthians to have been baptized 'in' the Spirit. The argument is that whereas baptism necessarily takes place 'in' something, the Holy Spirit is a person and not a thing, and certainly not a fluid into which men can be dipped. In his exposition of Romans 6, Dr Lloyd-Jones insists that the baptism mentioned in 12:13 is baptism *by* the Spirit into the body of Christ and that the same teaching surfaces in Romans 6:1-11.[15] But there is a problem: were we to follow this lead and suggest 'By one Spirit we were all baptized into one body,' as the translation we would in effect be likening the Holy Spirit to an officiating minister when baptizing suitable candidates. It doesn't seem to fit.

No doubt Dr Lloyd-Jones was right in claiming that the baptism of 12:13 has nothing to do with water, but is it true that the Spirit is the *agent* of baptism? In 12:13 the Greek is *en eni pneumati*, which admittedly can be translated as *'by* one Spirit'. Equally, *'in* one Spirit' is grammatically correct. It is just as obvious that 'by' is not at all the same as 'in', from which it follows that grammar does not seem able to decide the issue. We need to make a judgement on other grounds.[16]

The second part of 12:13 states that all Christians have been given a drink: **'We were all made to drink of one Spirit'** (not 'We were all made to drink *by* one Spirit'). Without dispute, the third person of the Trinity is compared to a liquid. So, why not with regard to baptism? Why cannot believers have been 'baptized in one Spirit'?

It seems better to side with Calvin, who understood Paul to mean that by definition all believers have been baptized 'in' the Holy Ghost, the Spirit being the medium rather than the agent of this particular baptism, in just the same way that water is obviously the medium of water-baptism.[17] Paul insists that the consequence of this common baptism in the Spirit is that believers discover themselves to be encapsulated within the body of Christ, which is his way of saying that they know that they belong to both Christ and to the saints.

Is Spirit-baptism connected with water-baptism?

According to this interpretation, believers have been baptized 'in' the Spirit. If this is correct an unavoidable question arises: is there

Spiritual gifts (12:1 - 14:40)

a link between water-baptism and Spirit-baptism? This needs to be thought through with some care for at least two reasons. First, because of the tragic doctrine of baptismal regeneration.[18] Secondly, the Gospels compare as well as contrast the water-baptism of John the Baptist and the Spirit-baptism given by the Messiah; at first sight there does seem to be a biblical connection between the two.[19]

Let's submit the question in a different way. If the baptism mentioned in 12:13a is specifically 'in' the Spirit, does this mean that the experience is something other than baptism in water? Or is it implied by the apostle that the Corinthians' water-baptism had been accompanied by Spirit-baptism, or even that their water-baptism was Spirit-baptism? If either alternative is intended it would seem that converts are born again when they are baptized.

This approach has not been uncommon among British Baptists, although not those of a reformed persuasion. G. R. Beasley-Murray claims that, according to the New Testament as a whole, adult baptism is the true context of regeneration.'[20] This is another way of saying that the candidate is born anew in the baptistery. But is this so? Surely true conversions do not happen in this way.

Before we decide upon the connection, if any, between water- and Spirit-baptism, we should concentrate upon the main issue. The Corinthians and the apostle were united in the body of Christ because they and he (**'we ... all'**) had been **'baptized'**. Compare this with 10:2, which refers to the baptism of Israel: in the same way that the Hebrews were united by their baptism 'into Moses', the Corinthians had been brought together by being baptized 'into one body'. But a qualification is necessary: although in the overall context the medium appears to scale down to a secondary issue, its identity is crucial to Paul's argument.

1. The medium of baptism

Throughout the New Testament baptism is assumed to be 'in' water unless a different medium is identified by the context. Apart from water-baptism we read about baptism in the Spirit and/or fire, baptism into death and baptism in the sea and the divine cloud.[21]

Moreover, on the rare occasions when a contrast is made between baptism in water and baptism in the Spirit or in fire, water *is* specified in order to make the distinction obvious. The point is that it is these exceptions that prove the rule. To repeat, baptism is invariably assumed to be in water *unless* another medium is definitely mentioned. Nor is there any undoubted instance of water and Spirit appearing as joint media for baptism. John 3:5, 'born of water and the Spirit', is no disproof.

It is like this in Paul's recorded sermons in Acts and in all his letters. As we would expect, baptism as an event and baptizing as an action are mentioned often.[22] With just two significant exceptions, 'in water' or some such qualifier does not appear because it is obvious that water is involved. The two exceptions are 10:2, which we have just mentioned, and 12:13. In the former the joint media are the cloud and the sea; in the latter a single medium is mentioned, the Spirit of God.

2. The exceptional statement of 12:13

Therefore the qualified statement, **'In one Spirit we were all baptized,'** has nothing to do with water. The apostle is not referring to his own baptism by Ananias, or to the baptism of the Corinthians, whether administered by his colleagues or by himself.

If water-baptism were meant the apostle would almost certainly have written, 'For we were all baptized into one body', leaving out any reference to the Holy Spirit. This outward baptism into the fellowship of the church would have been recognized immediately for what it was. It follows that 'the baptism of the Spirit' must be something else, nothing other than the great, initiating work of the Holy Spirit that had brought the Corinthians into new life. Repentance and water-baptism followed.

Belief in the Trinity flows from our experience of the Trinity

In summary, God the Father had baptized his people into the Spirit so that they would remain united with Christ as his body. From this we can infer a fundamental principle: only those who have discovered the grace of God will ever truly believe in the Trinity.

But Paul did not pen 12:13 and the surrounding context as a theological treatise aimed against, say, archetypal Unitarians or Jehovah's Witnesses. It was his burning desire to eliminate misunderstanding and conflict in the church and to bring the saints together. To do so he had to convince them about the unique origin of spiritual gifts. Even as God had brought all the Corinthians to

Spiritual gifts (12:1 - 14:40)

faith, similarly the same God in three persons had bestowed gifts upon them (12:4-6). In brief, all that they had was from God. He remained everything; they were nothing.

A shared experience

It follows that the ethnic, social and cultural backgrounds of the Corinthians, **'whether Jews or Greeks, whether slaves or free'**, had been rendered perfectly unimportant.

To emphasize this God-given oneness it is stated that **'We were all made to drink of one Spirit.'** The figure of speech changes dramatically. Not only had the Holy Spirit become the external medium of baptism; he had also been given to the Corinthians as, so to speak, an internal drink: he entered into their innermost beings. This statement can be compared directly with the teaching of Jesus (John 4:13-14; 7:37-40). For the Lord and for his steward the picture is that of desperately thirsty people who are given water and whose lives are saved. Paul stresses that the survivors share their restored life and that the church is essentially one because every member is indwelt by the Spirit.

Remember that even as Spirit-baptism is not water-baptism, this corporate experience of drinking has no connection with the wine of the Lord's Table.

Don't feel inferior (12:14-26)

There is more. Unity is by no means drab uniformity (12:14). The truth is driven home that although a single **'member'** or organ of a human body possesses one principal function, the complete frame is not one part but **'many'**. Because each member serves the common interest the body possesses an extraordinary versatility and can perform a wide and exciting variety of functions. Similarly, because Christians are personally united to Christ they belong to one another and are able to achieve much for the Lord.

Being sulky (12:15-16)

The apostle had an irrepressible yet sanctified sense of humour. He deploys it here with startling effect: an imaginary foot complains that it does not belong to the body, the sole ground of complaint being that it is not a hand. Paul's point is that the argument is fallacious. If it should be the case that the foot is separated from the body, the reason cannot be because it is not a hand: **'It is not because of this that it is not of the body'** (12:15).

Common sense acknowledges that there can be no other possible reason for separation. It follows that, yes, the foot is as much a part of the body as the hand. Truth to tell, the foot's silly complaint shows that the limb is perverse. Because it is patently not a hand it wants to quit.

Similarly (12:16), the reader is asked to contemplate an ear which has a colossal but misplaced inferiority complex. It moans that because it is not an eye it is not a part of the body. The folly of such talk is countered with a question: **'It is not for this reason any the less a part of the body** [is it]?' Of course it belongs.

Realism (12:17)

The metaphor is extended: **'If the whole body were an eye, where would the hearing be?'** Imagine that God had created the body to perform one function only, to see. Where and what would the ear be in such a grotesque scenario? Nowhere and nothing. Further, this surrealist 'body' would be deaf to the sounds of earth and heaven alike.

Again, **'If the whole were hearing, where would the sense of smell be?'** Suppose that the human frame were no more than a gigantic ear. What about the nose? With nowhere to go and nothing to do, it would be just like all the other organs: irrelevant and redundant. Imagine the gross inadequacy of such a ludicrous mismatch: unable to sense fragrance or stench, the 'body' could do nothing but listen. The designer who might have thought this up obviously had an untidy mind and fumble-fingers!

What the Lord has done (12:18-20)

These negative illustrations lead to a positive affirmation (12:18). As in 12:20; 13:13 and 15:20, **'but now'** (Greek, *nuni de*) is emphatic, referring to the current state of affairs: **'But now God has placed the members, each one of them, in the body, just as he desired.'** This is how it is. Designer distinctions within the human frame have given rise to a rich and balanced corporate existence. Looking at it the other way, a rich corporate existence proves mutual relevance stemming from creation: God did not design, manufacture and integrate the numerous parts of the human body so that they could operate in inglorious jangling or ineffective isolation.

If **'all'** the parts of the whole body were just **'one member'**, not only would the others be irrelevant, but **'where would the body be?'** (12:19). Like the aforementioned ear and nose, it would have nothing to do and nowhere to go. It would probably not exist at all, even as a fantasy of a weird imagination.

Looking behind these verses to the real-life situation that Paul addresses, it is not hard to see that this and the earlier questions are nothing less than a devastating broadside aimed at certain arrogant Corinthians. The apostle's burden is that evangelical self-importance will complain that there is something unfair about not being gifted in the same way as other Christians. The apostle knew that, unchecked, this attitude could destroy a church.

'But now there are many members, yet one body' (12:20). The immense number of elements interlocking in the human body give rise to its perfect efficiency.

Equality and mutual need (12:21-24a)

One of the amazing attributes of the body is that the individual parts minister to the whole by serving one another. It is not as if each answers privately to some sort of a central control that monitors each sector. Thus the eye does not inform the hand that it must reluctantly acknowledge its usefulness because it has no alternative; it admits cheerfully its direct dependence upon the hand. The head does not encourage the feet with a sulky affirmation of their relevance; it confesses that it cannot do without them (12:21). In sum, each member realizes that it depends upon every other part. Perhaps the apostle was aiming this particular shaft at those who valued the church yet objected to the presence of certain individuals in it.

Interdependence is particularly relevant when some parts of the body **'seem to be weaker'** (12:22), a weakness that is apparent rather than real. Perhaps Paul had in mind the hand and the feet mentioned in the previous verse. In that the eyes and the head display character and perhaps beauty, they have a capacity denied to fingers and toes although the latter have their place. The picture is apt. Consider a too-wealthy ageing woman who hires expensive surgeons to give her a face-lift. Even if their efforts gratify her because she knows that she makes an impression of sorts on others, her hands will always give her years away. Beauty is only skin-deep, and an attractive face needs bodily dexterity and mobility far more than freedom of movement requires flashing eyes and wrinkle-free cheeks.

'We bestow more abundant honour' upon those parts of the body that we consider to be **'less honourable'** (12:23). That is, we clothe the body with great care to make it look attractive, the consequence being that **'Our unseemly members come to have more abundant seemliness.'** 'Unseemly' means 'indecent': whereas clothes dignify, nudity is disgraceful. Adam and Eve acknowledged this when they sewed fig leaves together (Gen. 3:7). On the other hand, those parts of the body that radiate a natural nobility do not need garments (12:24a). Paul does not specify, but the face would probably be an obvious example.

A perfect design from the all-wise Designer (12:24b-26)

Although it is true that 'we' adorn the less honourable parts of the body (12:23), according to the last part of 12:24 it is God, not we, who **'so composed** [or, 'blended'] **the body, giving more abundant honour to that member which lacked'**. The fact that we clothe ourselves reflects the divine purpose.

In brief, God has arranged the human frame so that there might be **'no division in the body, but that the members should have the same care for one another'** (12:25). Because the organism is a unit no part of it can function successfully in isolation. Therefore illness is never localized. Conversely, the health of one organ implies that the whole system is sound: **'If one member suffers, all the members suffer with it; if one member is honoured, all the members rejoice with it'** (12:26).

'Honoured' is unexpected. We, in our wisdom, might well have written something like, 'If one member is healthy, then all the members are strong.' But not Paul. Perhaps the sense is that when one part suffers, all suffer, and that when one part is honoured the other members can and do rejoice even though the honour cannot be shared. The principle is that universal joy because of a local honour banishes resentment. 'A joyful heart makes a cheerful face' and

Spiritual gifts (12:1 - 14:40)

'Bright eyes gladden the heart' (Prov. 15:13,30). If the king's head is crowned his whole person is decked with dignity.

One practical application would be that when Christians indulge in pride and self-assertion they advertise an unnecessary and perverse inferiority complex. The truth is that none of the Lord's people is ever inferior. 'All things belong to you' (3:21). Let us be content to remain what the good Lord made us.

The body of Christ: priorities (12:27-31a)

The analogy of Christ's body, a body that possesses many members, was introduced by 12:12. That Christians belong to one another because they belong to Christ via the baptism of the Holy Spirit was explained by 12:13. The metaphor of the body was developed in 12:14-26. In 12:27-31a the illustration is brought to bear upon the church.

The grand application (12:27)

'You', the saints considered as a fellowship, are **'Christ's body'**. This means that individual believers are **'members'** of it: all that has been written about the human body relates directly and immediately to the Corinthian situation.

It is important to observe that notwithstanding their faults these people were the body of Christ and possessed a fundamental, God-given oneness. The apostle's plea is that they must develop and mature their unity rather than having to generate it.

The Lord assembles the church (12:28-30)

Even as God the Creator has arranged the different parts of the body, so it is with the church (12:28-29). Notice that certain gifts are personified. For example, **'gifts of healings'** are assumed to be 'members'. This is deliberate, showing that a believer lives for Christ only when he shares with others what the Lord has given him. Nominal attachment is an empty contradiction.

We need to evaluate the enumeration implied by **'first ... second ... third ... then ... then'** in 12:28. It would appear that apostles are deemed to be more important than prophets, and prophets more significant than teachers. Because **'various kinds of tongues'** occurs at the end of the sequence it might be that last in line means least in relevance.

In 12:7-10 priority among the gifts is not implied. This is the case, too, in Romans 12:4-8 and Ephesians 4:11-12. Here it has to be otherwise. To anticipate, 12:31 will make it plain that some spiritual gifts are 'greater', which means that they are more useful to the community. The principle surfaces again in 14:1,5.

In the overall context Paul is saying that all the members belong both to the church and to one another because of a built-in interdependence. Further, the least obvious members of the body of Christ do not lack their own honour and relevance. But Corinth was a deeply disturbed fellowship in which many entertained the fallacy that the more spectacular gifts were the most useful and for that reason were the most desirable. The congregation was sensitive, too, to the fact that apostles and travelling prophets came and went, and in the case of some, such as Paul, were frequently somewhere else. They were aware that this was not the case with the phenomenon of speaking in tongues. Never absent, the gift was an amazing verification of the Spirit's presence among them, capable of immediate exhibition and, they believed, guaranteed to fascinate all who heard.

In short, the Corinthian tongues-speakers were suffering from an acute bout of inflated ego. Knowing that he had to apply therapy, Paul's method is to list various offices and gifts in descending order of significance. Anticipating the argument of 14:20-25, he implies that glossolalia was overrated because its function was not appreciated. Because the mini-catalogue is designed to point out priorities it is not exhaustive.

More gifts

'Teachers' would possibly have been non-inspired men able to explain the recently revealed truths of the gospel to other Christians. **'Helps',** or 'helpful deeds', their actions standing for the persons concerned, might have been supportive church members. **'Administrations'**, or 'governments', the function standing for the person, represent those who guided the church. Who these administrators were at the time of writing is hard to say; perhaps they were elders.

If we accept that some of these roles and functions are permanent, we would need to admit that others are not. For instance, Paul

Spiritual gifts (12:1 - 14:40)

handed over to the people both in written form and by word of mouth what he had received from the Lord (11:23; 15:3). Although the apostles vanished from the face of the earth many centuries ago, their inspired writings remain with us; being dead, Paul yet speaks. He did his work, contributed to a treasury of teaching that will guide the churches until the end and then went to be with the Saviour. His office is closed.

This cannot be said of administrators and helpers, who in the nature of the case always need successors. Their role carries through from one generation to the next. Hebrews 13:7 and 17 acknowledge this with their respective references to those, now with the Lord, who 'led' and those, now with the people, who remain as 'leaders'.

A remorseless apostolic interrogation appears in 12:29-30. First, **'All are not apostles, are they?'** No. Similarly, the Corinthians are required to concede that not all of them are prophets, that not all are teachers, that not all work powerful miracles, that not all are healers, that not all speak in languages and that not all can interpret.

Following on from this, if the members contribute in various ways, two mutually hostile attitudes must be seen to be as foolish as they are wrong: personal pride in the exercise of a specific gift and resentment if one does not have that particular ability.

Greater gifts

A startling command appears in 12:31a: **'But earnestly desire** [or, 'be jealous for'] **the greater gifts.'** The words 'earnestly desire' seem to be a command rather than a statement: Paul is not admitting that the Corinthians were coveting the more useful charismata; rather, he tells them that they should be doing so. The sentiment is repeated in 14:1 and 39.

We need to reconcile this with 13:4: 'Love ... is not jealous.' But there is no contradiction: whether jealousy is a vice or a virtue depends upon attitude. Jesus displayed a holy jealousy; the Corinthians were rightly jealous for Paul's welfare; above all, God is jealous (John 2:17; 2 Cor. 7:7; Exod. 20:5).

The meaning is that if the Corinthians were genuinely concerned for their church they should be sufficiently humble to ask the Lord to give them the gifts of his choice, not theirs, and be satisfied with what he decided. If they could achieve contentment with their lot, they would be in a position to cherish and support the fellowship.

Evangelical church unity

Even if — as this commentary seeks to show — spiritual gifts are no longer bestowed upon the Lord's people, 12:27-30 has much to say to us now. All true believers are essentially one because we belong individually to Christ. That this is how it is remains beyond dispute. What, then, of the Eldorado of visible inter-church unity among broad-spectrum evangelicals? Conversations, conventions, contentions and conferences about this vexed matter have sometimes been known to generate more heat than light. Darkness can thicken rather than clear. My own view would be non-committal: maybe it is worthwhile to burn money, time and talk in yet more come-together exercises; maybe not. Much depends upon personalities and the needs of the hour.

What is clear is that genuine togetherness can never be achieved by the sacrifice of fundamental doctrines among those who *do* know the Lord. A case in point would be charismatic Arminians and 'cessationist' Calvinists (forgive the jargon). Friendly debates might remind them that their irreconcilable differences would torpedo the idea of co-operation at street level.

This does not mean isolationism. We want to learn from others with whom we sometimes disagree strongly. In truth, we need to do so. We certainly appreciate Christians who see important matters in different ways. Sometimes we are in a position to help others on the opposite side of the usual boundaries of inter-church fellowship, and this never fails to satisfy. Local problems and situations come and go, and so do demarcation lines. It follows that where they are to be laid down must always be subject to review.

But remember that Paul never invited the Corinthians to sweep vexed doctrinal issues under the carpet where they would not be noticed. Nor did he suggest that in their assemblies they should vote about what to believe and then be carried along by a majority view. Rather, he expected them to hold tenaciously to the traditions that he had taught them. He might, one dares suspect, have had a problem with the idea that some biblical truths could be of secondary importance.

Because the sixty-six books of the Bible and their teaching are still with us we ought to relax a little. We might take to heart apostolic advice to the Philippian jailor and do ourselves no mischief (Acts 16:28).

Spiritual gifts (12:1 - 14:40)

Love, the more excellent way (12:31b - 13:13)

The last part of 12:31 leads into chapter 13: **'And I show you a still more excellent way.'** Wistfully, Paul turns from the spectacular gifts of the Spirit. Although in his day they were essential he was not blind to their inadequacy. 'More excellent' (Greek, *kath' hyperbolen*), a traditional reading, is good — even excellent! But it demands an explanation. We have seen already that the burden of the chapter is the church's need for an accurate appreciation of spiritual gifts. This is why the apostle reveals that there is an upward way for the Corinthians that is incomparably better than their obsessive pursuit of spectacular charismata. Should they take his lead they can only ascend to higher levels of usefulness.

The expression 'more excellent' occurs elsewhere in the New Testament, and a comparison is able to uncover the force of the meaning here. In Romans 7:13 sin is said to be 'utterly' sinful, and in 2 Corinthians 1:8 the apostle tells his readers that he had been burdened 'excessively', to the extent that he thought he would die. According to 2 Corinthians 4:17, the future glory of the people of God will be 'far beyond' any comparison with present troubles, even though the latter give rise to the former. Galatians 1:13 confides that the apostle had persecuted the church 'beyond measure'.

The various ways in which the NASB translates the expression, as quoted above, show us 'more excellent' in different guises. The meaning in 12:31b is that the proposed vista for the Corinthians lies utterly, excessively and in its immeasurable bounds far beyond anything that the people could ever imagine. In contrast, their frenetic search for astonishing charismata, needful though the latter may well be in their chuch, is almost a waste of time.

As yet, the Corinthians are ignorant of this new road. Knowing them, they will probably want to be told; certainly, they must be told; equally certainly, they will be told. Their apostle/prophet/pastor/ spiritual father knows, and will reveal, all.

Imagine the emotional shock wave caused by these words when they were first read out to the Corinthians. After all, they lacked no spiritual gift. Miracles were usual in their community (1:7; 12:10,28-29). What could be greater than healing, or the performance of powerful signs, or than being a prophet, or leading or teaching the church, or speaking in other languages? Now appears the promise of something much more wonderful. For a fleeting moment the church is held in suspense.

The people must have trembled with anticipation when they heard Paul's, **'And I show you a still more excellent way.'** 'What', they whisper the one to the other, 'can this marvel be?'

The apostle does not tantalize one moment longer. Astonishingly, the alternative route for the Corinthians is not new at all. It had always been with them, overlooked because it seemed to be unspectacular.

The 'more excellent way' is, in one word, **'love'** (Greek, *agape*). The climax disintegrates, leaving, perhaps, an aftermath of frustration and disappointment for the overweening Corinthian charismatics. Some of them must have seethed.

Preliminary matters

In order to understand the **'more excellent way'** we need to define **'love'** and then examine a brief outline of Paul's argument. We shall also try to take into account the relevance of chapter 13 for today.

What is agape?

The Bible has much to say about agape. First and foremost there is the love that God has for the people of his choice. There is the love that men should have for God and that redeemed saints do have for him. Furthermore, Scripture has much to say about the love that Christian believers ought to have, and frequently do have, for one another in their churches. We know that we must love both our enemies and our neighbours.

Here, the context shows without a doubt that the apostle has in mind the love of Christians for their fellow-believers.[23] Employing the first person singular, 'I', in 13:1-3, Paul presents himself yet again as an example to the Corinthians. Treading thin ice, he asks them to compute his usefulness were he to descend to their arrogant superficiality.

The argument of chapter 13

The burden of 13:1-13 is that love is as indispensable as it is excellent. The whole chapter is nothing less than a carefully articulated and

Spiritual gifts (12:1 - 14:40)

reasoned explanation of why this is so, and reaches its climax in three stages. For the record, one would disagree with the idea that whatever else these verses might be, they are a celebratory hymn in praise of love, a view that has been held by not a few expositors. A psalm in honour of nothing in particular, chapter 13 is a summons to a loving attitude in the church, a rather different matter notwithstanding the charm and finish of the apostle's carefully chosen words.[24]

The first part of Paul's thesis is that gifts which are not exercised graciously are useless, of advantage neither to their exponents nor to their beholders; nothing good can be achieved without agape (13:1-3).

Secondly, Christian love is preferable to spiritual gifts because it has a far superior potential (13:4-7). The loving person, personified by 'love', has qualities that outperform the display of any spiritual gift. Although the charismata, when seasoned with love, are profitable, agape, even when unaccompanied by gifts, can do much more good.

Finally, the gifts of the Spirit will eventually cease to function. Paul predicts specifically that prophecy, tongues-speaking and knowledge are to vanish from the churches. But Christian love, together with faith and hope, will never fail (13:8-13).

The discussion reduces to a question of priorities. The Corinthians ought to be much more concerned about the long-term situation of the people of God than about phenomena never planned by the Lord to remain within the pilgrim, earth-bound churches.

The relevance of 1 Corinthians 13

A further preliminary question arises. As this exposition aims to show, the apostle shares with the Corinthians his anticipation that the gifts of the Spirit were destined to disappear very soon.

Suppose, for a moment, that this prediction proved to be accurate. Suppose that for many hundreds of years, since about the end of the first century A.D., neither genuine prophets nor prophecies have emerged in the churches. Suppose, too, that tongues-speaking and new God-given revelations ('knowledge') have not manifested themselves during this long period of time. Although I believe that this has been the case, some might well disagree. In truth, an argument to the contrary would not appear to lack merit.

For instance, if spiritual gifts were withdrawn a relatively brief time after they were given, it might be objected that, like the outdated rituals of Moses' dispensation, 1 Corinthians 13 cannot relate to the needs of the saints now; if what is being said here is right this golden chapter remains a museum piece, addressing a situation that long ago ceased to be. The critic would flourish his complaint by pointing out that the difference between 1 Corinthians 13 and the tabernacle system is that, belonging as it does to the New Testament, the former must be a guideline for today's Christians. How can part of the New Testament not relate to New Testament believers? Confessedly, it is almost enough to take one's breath away; the criticism looks good.

Now consider the problem in another way. Chapters 12-14, dealing as they do with spiritual gifts, are part of Scripture. Amen! When we read them we sense that they are God-breathed. Does it not follow that the gifts of the Spirit should be sought and exercised by Christians now? Why would God in his providence have caused these blessed chapters, particularly chapter 13, to remain in our Bibles if they speak to a temporary, long-gone situation? Surely it follows that the view about to be developed must be mistaken?

There is a satisfactory and essential response to this. Let's go back to our earlier supposition, that Paul did anticipate the early withdrawal of the gifts of the Spirit. Would he have been wise to conceal what he knew would happen? Can you imagine the apostle coyly permitting the delusion that prophecy and miraculous powers would function indefinitely in the assemblies?

If this approach is, broadly speaking, correct, what would have been the consequence of such a cover-up for the post-apostolic churches? During the course of two millennia generations of sincere believers would have coveted spiritual gifts, yet all in vain because, like Rachel's children, they had been taken away and are no more (Matt. 2:18). But, unlike Rachel, most of the people of God would have been unaware of the deprivation, and this because in the earliest days no apostle cared sufficiently to place himself on record about the truth. Ultimately, one higher than the highest apostles might seem to have been at fault.

Blissful ignorance would not have been the lot of all. Discerning souls recognized from sad experience that alleged signs and miracles invariably turned out to be fake. Refusing to abandon hope, they persevered in their relentless quest for the real thing. For many the procedure was to join the queue waiting to see the newest

Spiritual gifts (12:1 - 14:40) 255

miracle-worker in town. Others delved hopefully into church history, ancient and modern, orthodox and esoteric.

Again, all in vain. Never did they light upon the crock of gold at the foot of the charismatic rainbow. Asking themselves a few semi-serious questions, the more gullible concluded that somewhere and somehow something had gone badly wrong, probably with themselves, and that for their sins God had denied the churches needed revival. What the hindrance had been they could not say — an anomalous and tragic state of affairs.

Happily, this is not the real situation; the churches have never been abandoned by their God to a limbo-land of uncertainty about spiritual gifts. It will be maintained that chapter 13 spells out what the Corinthians, and all of us, need to know.

I would claim also that any approach other than the general outlines of this exposition generates insoluble problems. In my view, chapter 13 becomes impossible if looked at in any other way. But this is something which you need to work out for yourself, and you probably will.

Spiritual gifts by themselves are useless (13:1-3)

Tongues of men and of angels (13:1)

'The tongues of men' are known languages that men speak. Those **'of angels'** would be languages employed by God's ministering spirits. That angels do speak is shown by Hebrews 2:2, 'the word spoken through angels', and by the numerous angelic communications in the book of Revelation. Angels spoke to Joseph, Zachariah and Mary, and on one occasion sang in the presence of certain poor shepherds in a way that they could understand.[25] There are a thousand other references. 'Angel', of course, means 'messenger' (Greek, *aggelos*, pronounced 'angelos'), and a messenger is supposed to communicate. But here Paul seems to refer to distinct angelic dialects beyond human ken.

Notice that the apostle does not claim to speak in the languages of angels, or in all the tongues that men employ. He merely asks his readers to take up an imaginative challenge. Suppose that he could express himself in these languages, yet doing so without any tender affection for his listeners. As far as they are concerned he, the great apostle, would come across like a bronze or brass disc resonating when struck, or like a clanging cymbal. Strident, pompous and eager to display his ego, the steward of the Lord would repel other Christians. The principle is that when we deign to address someone we dislike our feelings inevitably come across even if, or especially if, we use 'angel-speak'.

The picture would have impressed the Corinthians, whose city was famed for its bronze manufactures. Dio Chrysostum claimed that craftsmen there were able to give their castings a realism that suggested 'the power of flight'. The great gate of the temple in Jerusalem, possibly the Beautiful Gate of Acts 3:2,10, was manufactured from Corinthian bronze and was said to be more valuable than other gates made of silver and gold.[26] Paul's selection of the metaphor was as deliberate as it was skilful. Compare with Mark 5:38, where the same Greek word for 'clanging' *(alalazô)* refers to the incoherent 'wailing' of a crowd. The apostle's point is that even God-given language, if exercised arrogantly by the Corinthians, becomes altogether repulsive. We can infer that some of them were as brassy as their local goods.

Paul the pompous (13:2)

The apostle begs leave to consider his effectiveness as a Christian servant were he to know **'all mysteries and all knowledge'**, and yet to remain proudly devoid of love. 'All mysteries' would mean a perfect and comprehensive understanding of the way of salvation, and 'all knowledge' would be the ability to communicate this revelation (cf. 12:8; 14:6). Such a teaching syllabus would omit nothing, Paul being in effect like the authors of all the books of the Bible put together.

The apostle asks us to suppose that he possesses **'all faith'**, sufficient **'to remove mountains'**, an illustration that he must have known our Lord employed during his ministry.[27] In the tenure of such capacities he becomes suddenly the greatest of the servants of God, the most marvellously endowed of the prophets. But, were he to have no love for his fellows he would be **'nothing'**, an encumbrance and an embarrassment.

Paul, philanthropist and hero (13:3)

We are invited to stretch our minds a little further to contemplate the apostle giving his possessions to feed other men and leaving nothing

Spiritual gifts (12:1 - 14:40)

for himself. Imagine, too, Paul being willing to deliver his body to the martyr's fire to be burned to ashes because of his faith.[28] Should his generosity or sacrifice be for personal reasons only, lacking love for others, **'it profits me nothing'**. His inherent selfishness could not fail detection. No heart would melt. All would turn their backs and walk away. The world would not want to know.

Love has immense potential (13:4-7)

The second strand of the apostle's exposition of the superiority of the way of love is presented by 13:4-7. Whereas the gifts should be exercised lovingly or not at all, we learn here that agape can function excellently even if it exists in splendid isolation.

Love is all you need

In contrast to the spite and boastfulness of the Corinthians who exulted in their spiritual gifts, love achieves; these vainglorious saints have failed because they repel their fellows.

Love is **'long-suffering'** (13:4). This might mean that it is prepared to bear with imperfections in other Christians in the confidence that one day they will grow to maturity. It is **'kind'**, or gentle and helpful. Negatively, love is not **'jealous'** in an unworthy sense. It does not **'brag'**, seeking personal applause from others. It is not **'inflated'** (or 'puffed up'; 'arrogant', NASB), unlike some in the church. We recall that in 4:6,18,19 and 5:2 Paul referred to this sad state of the heart — many of the Corinthians must have been burning with spiritual bravado.

Nor does love **'act unbecomingly'** (13:5): the loving Christian does not indulge in rude or crude speech and behaviour. Agape does not **'seek its own'** because it is more concerned for the interests of the fellowship, a claim that the apostle has already made about himself (10:33).

Love is not **'provoked'** or, almost literally, 'does not go into paroxysms'. Remember the two recorded occasions when Paul virtually lost his temper. Allowances can be made for how he felt when he gazed at what went on in Athens (Acts 17:16), but possibly not for his row with Barnabas, even though his judgement about the irresponsible John Mark was almost certainly right (Acts 15:39). If we go about it the wrong way an argument won can mean a heart lost. Compare Hebrews 10:24, which in literal terms advocates 'a paroxysm of love and of good deeds'.

Christian love does not **'attribute evil'** (not 'does not take into account a wrong suffered', NASB). That is, agape is heartily reluctant to accuse others of sin, or even to suspect that they plan wrong. Scribes, who reckoned they knew much, were eager to think evil of Jesus (Matt. 9:4).

Love **'does not rejoice in unrighteousness, but rejoices with the truth'** (13:6). 'Truth', the opposite of 'unrighteousness', probably means doing what is right (cf. John 3:21; 1 John 1:6). Or, the meaning might be that the sincere Christian will not rejoice when he sees the gospel distorted. After all, Jesus is himself 'the truth' (John 14:6).[29] Either way, love rejoices together 'with' truth. Truth is eager to share its joy and the loving heart will be quick to take up the invitation.

We have been told much that love can and cannot do. But the exposition of its amazing potential is not yet ended. First, love **'bears all things'** (13:7). 'Bears' might mean to 'carry' or endure, as in 9:12 and 1 Thessalonians 3:1,5, or even to 'tolerate', to pass over in silence: the loving Christian will not publicize the known failings of others.

Additionally, love **'believes all things'**. Perhaps this statement is a complement to that in 13:5, which tells us that love does not impute evil. Here, we learn that love takes men at face value unless there is positive evidence to discredit them. Note that this grace is not implied to be naïve, accepting as true everything that it hears.

Love **'hopes all things'**, refusing to take failure as final; no easy discipline, it looks for the best possible outcome in any event or situation. We remember that the apostle Thomas was not the best exponent of this virtue (John 11:16; 20:25). Finally, love **'endures all things'**. To 'endure' means to accept hardship or even persecution, as in 2 Timothy 2:10-12, Hebrews 12:3 and 1 Peter 2:20.

Why love is much more effective than spiritual endowments

Paul's logic is as elegant as it is simple. To recapitulate, the abilities catalogued in 13:4-7 lie infinitely beyond the grasp of spiritual gifts. But they are not impossible for agape. So, when love flows from the heart of the devoted Christian he can achieve. For this reason agape is more to be desired than the charismata.

Spiritual gifts (12:1 - 14:40)

By now this exposition of the 'more excellent way' must have brought certain inflated Corinthian egos near to a state of collapse. But Paul has more to say — much more.

The charismata must soon pass away (13:8-13)

We come to the third part of the chapter, six brief verses that are critical. They predict that, whereas the gifts of the Spirit must soon vanish, Christian faith, hope and love abide. The application is that the Corinthians should enthuse about **'these three'** (13:13) rather than about short-term, temporary phenomena.

The gifts will fail (13:8)

Love **'never fails'**, or 'does not fall', 'is never falling' (a Greek present tense, *oudepote piptei*). Because love among Christians is essential the Lord will take no action to remove it. Agape will always stand in position.

'But whether there are prophecies, they will be done away.' 'Whether' is repeated three times in this verse, emphasizing that the apostle is, and that the Corinthians ought to be, largely indifferent to the possible existence of temporary gifts.

Compare this with 'whether' in 3:22; 8:5 and 10:31. Paul was always keenly aware of the distinction between what is necessary and what is not. The emphasis here is that even if there are prophecies in the churches (and, it is implied, there might not be), they are not all-important. For this reason God will ensure that they are to be 'brought to nothing'; were they of lasting value they would last. Just like self-important people (1:28), great leaders (2:6; 15:24), food and the stomach (6:13) and even death itself (15:26), they are to be put out of commission and must pass from the scene.

We must be clear about what Paul does *not* mean. Although he believed it, he is not suggesting here that false prophecies in the churches will eventually fall to the ground, rather like the erroneous prediction of Zedekiah that Ahab and Jehoshaphat would conquer at Ramoth-gilead (1 Kings 22:11),[30] and that true prophecy is to continue indefinitely. In acknowledging that the Holy Spirit does raise up genuine prophets, the apostle speaks as one of their company. His prophecy is that one day the blessing of prophetic utterance will discontinue. The implied reason, to be opened up in 13:10, 12, is that all the prophecy that the churches need would soon be on record and in their possession.

Redundancy will also be the lot of Spirit-given languages if (**'whether'**) they are present. The grammar is forceful (Greek: *pausontai*, future middle from *pauô*, 'I cause myself to cease'). The apostle implies that tongues must come to their end because they accept early retirement, to be replaced immediately by something else. That is to say, Spirit-given human languages will respond to an irresistible summons from the Lord. They depart politely and not reluctantly from the churches, never to be heard again. But love will never be asked to bow out, and will never do so.

Supernatural knowledge might be granted to some in the church. If so, it too must **'be done away'**. If 'a word of knowledge' was a gift that incorporated new revelations about Christ for the Lord's people, Paul writes that in God's good time the Lord will see to it that there are no further disclosures.

Why this must be so (13:9)

There is a grand double reason for the cancellation of these three spiritual gifts, prophecy, tongues and knowledge. First and negatively, current prophecy and knowledge are said to be incomplete. Secondly and positively, they are to be replaced by something that in its own way will be complete (13:10).

'For we know in part, and we prophesy in part,' suggests that tongues, not mentioned here, were no more than a vehicle for the other two gifts. A comparison with 14:2 and Acts 2:11 tends to establish the matter: tongues-speakers uttered 'mysteries' and at Pentecost believers gifted in this way told out the 'mighty deeds of God'. Because glossolalia is no more than a carrier it is destined to vanish along with knowledge and prophecy.

'In part' is quantitative, suggesting something good in itself but which is incomplete, like a section of a jigsaw puzzle or part of a manuscript. The apostle's claim is that charismatic knowledge and prophecy do not tell out, nor can tell out, all that needs to be told.[31]

Does **'we'** in 13:9 (and 13:12) refer to an average cross-section of the church, or to the acknowledged apostles and inspired Christian prophets who, as is the case in 12:28; Ephesians 2:20; 3:5 and 4:11, might be singled out for special reference? It is important to

Spiritual gifts (12:1 - 14:40)

note that in 1 Corinthians 'we' can sometimes stand for the apostles and prophets only and at other times for all believers.[32]

Here the apostles and prophets probably have the edge. The 'I-you' tension in chapter 13 suggests that **'the partial'** (13:10, NASB) or 'the thing that is in part' was a body of incomplete revelations granted to, and through, one element within the churches — the non-apostolic prophets. Paul's meaning is that even if all the prophets' disclosures were to be combined there would still be no full exposition of the way of salvation. Because these revelations had failed through no fault of their own to convey all that needed to be known they themselves must vanish. Likewise the prophetic transmitters were about to be decommissioned because they had no further verbal messages to transmit.

Their immediate replacement (13:10)

Paul discloses the occasion when prophecies and prophets are to vanish: **'But when the perfect thing comes, the thing that is in part will be done away.'** This is a most important statement.

First, the appearance of 'the perfect thing' is promised, something real and objective, having its own independent existence. Complete in itself and 100 per cent effective, it will need no supplement. The NASB's 'the perfect' is far too vague and fails to give us the apostle's meaning. The Authorized Version's 'that which is perfect' gives the sense well.

1. The meaning of 'perfect'

The Greek behind 'that which is perfect' is *to teleion*. The definite article, 'the' (*to*), is followed by a noun, *teleion*, meaning 'full-grown', 'mature', 'complete,' or 'perfect'. But the idea is not that of a state of perfection that is to supervene. To enlarge upon what has already been said, Paul anticipates a specific entity, complete and total in itself, that will come to the churches here, in this world.

A brief but excellent definition of 'perfect' was given by the Greek philosopher Aristotle, who flourished in the fourth century B.C. For him a 'perfect thing' lacked nothing, to the extent that it would be impossible to find 'even one part' of it anywhere else. There was also the remark of Cicero, whom we have met already: 'Man himself ... is by no means perfect, but he is "a small fragment of that which is perfect". The world on the contrary, since it embraces all things and since nothing exists which is not within it, is entirely perfect'.[33]

When we come to 13:10 we find that the meaning of the word is exactly the same although the frame of reference is quite different. The apostle knew that there would be no shift in function between the thing that is 'in part', currently in the possession of the churches, and 'the perfect thing' which, when he wrote this letter, Christians did not have; the distinction would be solely that of quantity and content. Just as for Cicero there was nothing inherently inadequate with man as man except that by himself he remains incomplete, no more than part of a greater unity, so for Paul the temporary gifts were adequate as far as they went, but they did not tell the whole story. They foreshadowed and demanded something else yet to arrive, something that would make up their shortfall. This ties up neatly with 13:12, where it is predicted that 'the perfect thing' will in the event give a much plainer ('face-to-face') revelation of the plan of salvation.

We remind ourselves that 'the thing that is in part' is by definition a specific vehicle, albeit incomplete and therefore relatively ineffective. If we think about it, this 'partial thing' can be nothing other than prophecy and knowledge, charismata said in 13:9 to be 'in part'. This identification is confirmed beyond doubt by the prediction of 13:8 that prophecies and knowledge are to end.

No date is given by the apostle for the arrival of 'the perfect thing'. Nor does he indicate if its coming is to take place instantly, or over a period of time. But he indicates that its introduction is certain, or as we might say, 'as good as done'.[34]

2. A summary

It is necessary to take into account the background to 13:10 and its context. In the churches of Paul's time there were prophets who received and transmitted revelations concerning the scheme of salvation. As with Philip's daughters who prophesied (Acts 21:9), what they said was unrecorded. Therefore their words have been lost to posterity. Essentially, their relevance could have been no more than local and temporary. These inspired saints did not offer, nor were required to offer, a perfect exposition of the faith to be accessed by the churches until the end of time.

Spiritual gifts (12:1 - 14:40)

Because of the inherent limitations of such prophetic ministry the apostle anticipates its complete cessation. But the people of God are not to be deprived of infallible revelation: the inadequate medium and message will be replaced in their entirety by something else, an apparatus conveying a revelation able to satisfy the needs of all. The disappearance of the first occurs when and because the second emerges; as the sun rises, the moon disappears. Paul intends us to infer that this ultimate channel of communication will bring with it the definitive presentation of the Christian mystery.

Two illustrations are introduced to show what this final and perfect vehicle is to be. First, the picture of the apostle's own growth to adulthood (13:11); second, a contrast between sight by means of a mirror and direct perception (13:12).

Childhood and adulthood (13:11)

Paul confides that **'When I was a child, I used to speak as a child, think as a child, reason as a child; when I became a man, I did away with childish things.'**

1. The future in terms of the past

The action words 'did away' have exactly the same meaning as 'done away' in 13:8 and 10 (Greek, *katargeô*, 'cancel', 'nullify'), with the exception of the tense transferring to the past. The reason for the time-switch is that the apostle explains what is going to happen in terms of time gone by when he personally had to move forward.

In detail, he likens the anticipated replacement of 'the thing that is in part' by 'the perfect thing' to his own experience of growing up, a process involving a willing advance from things appropriate to Saul the child to the expanding interests of a young man. Perhaps his triple reference to speaking, thinking and reasoning 'as a child' reflects the initial learning experiences that filled his mind in his very early life; since those days his horizon had become far wider.

The apostle alludes to his own childhood to show that years earlier he had adapted willingly to inevitable changes. The Corinthians should imitate his philosophy and have no regrets when spiritual gifts were phased out, as they must be. What he really means is that because they had no superior medium of revelation the young churches needed the gifts and could not function without them. But time does not stand still. Soon enough, the limited educational equipment of the first years would have done its work. Paul's obvious implication is that a complete and permanent deposit of teaching much more extensive than local and unrecorded prophecies would be essential. Nor would the Lord deny this to an expanding constituency of believers soon to be separated permanently from the synagogues, that would possess its own distinctive theology and, under God's guidance and control, work out its own destiny.

2. Childlike or childish?

In chapter 13 infancy is projected neither as childishness nor as immaturity of character. This needs to be recognized. Some Corinthians were childish and even infantile in their behaviour, and others were mature or 'grown-up'. This did not mean that the former were necessarily young in years or that the latter were their seniors.[35] The apostle, a versatile writer, employs the child-metaphor in two distinct but related frames of reference: elsewhere, personal immaturity; here, principally the development of the church from its period of infancy towards settled adulthood. A failure to perceive this would lead to serious confusion.

3. The presence or absence of gifts is no indicator of maturity

Although Paul himself spoke in tongues more than anybody else (14:18), he was by no means childish. Nor does he make out that the Corinthians who exercised glossolalia were necessarily spiritually mature or immature. In the overall context, and particularly in chapter 12, his message is that it is one's attitude to the temporary gifts of the Spirit, rather than possession or non-possession of them, that signals either spiritual growth or the lack of it. But individual spiritual development is not to the fore in 13:10 or the immediately surrounding verses.[36]

The apostle was aware that he lived in a unique period when the gospel was being proclaimed for the first time without the back-up and encouragement of what we know as the New Testament, but with the back-up and encouragement of the gifts of the Spirit. This is the concern of chapter 13. To repeat, Paul anticipated that the

Spiritual gifts (12:1 - 14:40)

churches would soon receive a comprehensive and permanent exposition of the plan of redemption. For this reason they should be ready to pass beyond the stage of wanting to depend upon temporary and incomplete revelatory gifts.

Even so, the theme of personal maturity or immaturity is not entirely absent. It is as if Paul says that when, years before, he had grown physically there was a corresponding psychological and mental development. Had this not been the case he would have remained an adult in body yet with the mind of a child, a distortion of the person he was supposed to be. He dreads that the Corinthians might find themselves spiritually and emotionally in a not dissimilar situation.

This is why they should be big enough to put away **'childish things'**, good and exciting gifts from the Holy Spirit that sustained them in their corporate infancy and that hitherto had engrossed their interest. Soon enough these charismata would no longer be appropriate for them. The immediate prospect was that the churches were to travel beyond the horizon of this infant stage in their history. When they did so they would receive **'the perfect thing'**, an ever-present apparatus showing them all they needed to know this side of heaven.

But suppose that the people failed to respond to the challenge of the years. Should they not adjust to the moving scene they would look backwards, stretching out childishly for unattainable gifts lying further and further behind them. Worse, their concentration must be deflected from the ideal thing that at last they have permanently before their eyes and that yields so much more.

The mirror (13:12)

Paul confirms the matter: **'For just now we see in a mirror dimly, but then face to face; just now I know in part, but then I shall recognize even as I have been recognized.'**

'Just now' (Greek, *arti*) signifies the immediate present rather than the NASB's ambiguous 'now'.[37] The apostle asserts that he and the Corinthians saw for a few fleeting moments, as it were, via a polished metal disc. The picture is apt: just like nocturnal dreams or mirror-reflections of brief duration, unrecorded prophetic visions and words hover momentarily before they vanish for ever. Paul's point is that because the charismata afford no more than transient and enigmatic pictures of the mystery of Christ they are strictly temporary; the Lord has something better in store for the churches. Even so, there is a common factor: both media enable the people to see.

1. Spiritual sight

Spiritual vision is an Old Testament thought-form. Before Christ came the prophets brought to the attention of Israel what they were shown by the Lord. See, for example, Numbers 12:6-8, which is definitive; 1 Samuel 9:9: 'For he who is called a prophet now was formerly called a seer'; and Isaiah 2:1: 'the word which Isaiah ... saw concerning Judah and Jerusalem'; not to mention the visions of men such as Daniel, Ezekiel and Zechariah. There are many other references illustrating the principle. Paul's words are exactly what we would expect from a Christian apostle and prophet steeped in the Old Testament. How else would he have expressed himself when discussing the content and media of revelation?

2. Numbers 12:6-8

Most commentators have taken the view that 13:12 recalls Numbers 12:6-8.[38] I side with the majority and am persuaded that Paul makes here a deliberate allusion to this crucial chapter from the book of Numbers. It would appear that the apostle intended his readers to ponder carefully Jehovah's rebuke to Aaron and Miriam concerning their brother Moses:

> And he said, 'Hear now my words. If there shall be your prophet Jehovah, in a vision to him will I make myself known; in a dream will I speak with him. Not so my servant Moses; in all my house he is faithful. Mouth to mouth I speak with him, and plainly, and not in enigmatic sayings, and the form of Jehovah he will see. And why were you not afraid to speak with my servant, with Moses?'
> (Num. 12:6-8).

The Hebrew, 'if there shall be your prophet Jehovah' means 'if your prophet be Jehovah'. This is probably a vivid way of showing that the prophet came from the Lord and was literally his mouthpiece.[39]

Spiritual gifts (12:1 - 14:40)

There are unmistakable similarities between this passage and 13:12. The adverbial 'mouth to mouth' in the Septuagint translation of Numbers 12:8 is basically the same as Paul's **'face to face'**, both meaning direct and unambiguous speech communication. 'Enigmatic sayings' are equivalent to the apostolic **'dimly'** or 'enigmatically': revealed truth is clothed and presented in suggestive imagery, imagery that conceals yet reveals underlying truth.[40]

As we have observed, the apostle frequently employed the Greek version of the Old Testament as well as the Hebrew text, and I would propose that both are woven together in 13:12. Paul was an expositor rather than a photocopying machine, and in his numerous quotations and allusions never bound himself arbitrarily to the original consonantal text or to Greek.[41]

Numbers 12:6 also refers to the typical prophetic 'vision', which, it seems, Paul interprets flexibly but not inaccurately as **'mirror'**. To anticipate, this would appear to be the key to the riddle of 13:8-13. Further, there are parallels between the situation of Aaron, Miriam and Moses and that of the Corinthian church. We shall return to this shortly.

3. Face-to-face sight

The apostle states that **'We see in a mirror dimly.'** As we have already seen, Corinth was famous for its bronze-wares, among which were polished metal mirrors. In contrast to our modern reflectors these objects were relatively ineffective, yielding hazy images. Josephus notes that the silver mixing bowls contributed by the Egyptian Ptolemy to Herod's temple in Jerusalem shone more brilliantly than mirrors, so much so that worshippers could see their faces in them,[42] a remark that does not say much for the mirrors of the period! In the same way, **'just now'** — by which Paul means the time in which he lived — what God's people could see of themselves within the scheme of salvation was at best obscure. Nor did they behold everything.

Matters were to change. **'Then'**, when **'the perfect thing'** comes, **'we'** (Paul, the Corinthians and others) shall **'see face to face'**. The churches' understanding of salvation would derive from something to be set before their eyes, telling everything in the clearest possible fashion. Because 'mirror' is obviously an illustration, so also is 'face to face'. Paul would never wrench the imaginations of his readers by switching in the space of a brief sentence from a metaphorical to a literal description.

We go back to the Old Testament, the concepts of which dominated the apostle. There, 'face to face' means direct, mouth-to-mouth communications, but communications that were never accompanied by the unimpeded sight of God in all his glory. This distinction between complete communication and incomplete visual experience is fundamentally important. Jehovah spoke with Moses 'face to face', holding nothing back, yet at no time was the latter permitted to behold the face of God (Exod. 33:11,17-23). Similarly, Jehovah spoke with Israel 'face to face' at Sinai, but Israel never actually saw the Lord (Deut. 4:12; 5:4; cf. 34:10). By analogy, it follows that Paul does not refer to the advent of Christ when, as 1 John 3:2 and Revelation 22:4 promise, we shall see his face.

Wayne Grudem, in his important study of prophecy in 1 Corinthians, seems to be confused at this critical point. He remarks that 'face to face' in the Greek Old Testament 'is clearly used to speak of seeing God personally, as in a theophany'. From this he infers that Paul's anticipated 'face-to-face' revelation, based as it is upon Old Testament precedents, must be nothing other than 'seeing God at the consummation'.[43]

Here is the eye of the storm. Upon the resolution of this question depends the overall interpretation of 1 Corinthians 13, a true theology of spiritual gifts and, last but certainly not least, our approach to the red-hot question of whether the charismata are with us now. When the initial skirmishing is done it is here that charismatics and non-charismatics must lock swords in brotherly conflict, a stuggle from which one side only would be able to march away with any semblance of victory.

To repeat, it is true the Lord met Israel directly. But the people never at any time beheld Jehovah face to face, even though they undoubtedly saw something of him. There were also other theophanies (e.g. Judg. 6:22; 13:21-22), but no man ever gazed upon the fulness of God. With particular reference to Moses and Israel, the expression 'face to face' designates unimpeded verbal communication rather than full, unclouded vision; speaking, not seeing.[44] I suggest that this cannot be controverted. Therefore (*pace* Dr Grudem) Paul was not thinking about the consummation.

Putting aside the obvious fact that the apostle knew about Corinthian mirrors, we need to ascertain why he refers to reflected

Spiritual gifts (12:1 - 14:40)

sight. Not a few commentators consider that he had creation in mind: God is mirrored, as it were, by the world that he made.[45]

If we think about it, this cannot possibly be the case. Romans 1:20 teaches that men understand and take note of the unseen things of God by contemplating his marvellous works. But this does not mean that the creation is an image of God. He is not like, say, the hot sun, or a cow. Plutarch, a prolific author of the late first century A.D. who was born not far from Corinth, exemplified these as reflected images of God. Such degraded thinking would have been foreign to the apostle.[46]

4. Visions and mirrors

This exposition would suggest that the interpretation of 13:12 lies in Numbers 12:6, which specifies the medium of typical prophetic insight. Here we find the conceptual background to Paul's mirror metaphor. The rationale is that in the apostle's time there was a Hebrew word *(mar'ah)* that meant both 'vision' and 'mirror'. It is precisely this word that we find in the Hebrew text of Numbers 12:6. Paul seems to be telling the Corinthians, in language which they could readily appreciate, that their spiritual gifts were akin to Old Testament prophetic visions, at best dim and incomplete reflections of the way of salvation.

Now a plea to you, the reader, to be tolerant. Because this working assumption controls the approach adopted here to 13:8-13 evidence must be submitted in its favour. This is attempted in Appendix II, which you might care to read. For the moment there is one essential point to be emphasized: during and long after the Old Testament period it was usual for prophetic visions to be thought of by Jewish people in terms of relatively hazy mirror-reflections. This understanding was traditional by the middle of the first century A.D., so much so that it seems almost obvious that Paul would have coaxed it into service. The thesis of this exposition is that it is this analogy which he takes up in 13:12. In detail, whereas other explanations for the appearance of 'mirror' in 13:12 fall down, this approach harmonizes exactly with both text and context.

5. Back to Numbers 12:6-8

According to the proposed interpretation we have here a subtle play on words. The apostle is gently ironic, likening prophetic visions, then in the churches and long before in Israel (Num. 12), to imperfect mirror-reflections. He parallels Corinthian hyper-enthusiasm for spiritual gifts with the sinful aggressiveness shown by Aaron and his sister Miriam.

Remember that Israel's journey in the wilderness featured prominently in 1 Corinthians 10. Bear in mind also that Paul's overarching doctrine in this letter is that the Christian churches constitute the Messianic Israel. Again, although not for the last time, the apostle applies the principle of 10:6,11, according to which the events at and after the Exodus were recorded specifically for the benefit of the new-covenant saints.

The background to the incident recorded in Numbers 12 was Moses' own complaint that the burden of leadership had proved too great for him. Graciously, the Lord gave his Spirit to seventy elders to assist his servant. Joshua was uneasy about this, albeit as a supporter of Moses. On the other hand, Aaron and Miriam resented their brother because they thought far too highly of their own leadership capacities (Num. 11:14-30; 12:1-2).

Jehovah's words of rebuke to Aaron and Miriam (Num. 12:6-8) insisted that there were two distinct forms of revelation. First, from time to time, there may have been prophetic visions ('if', Numbers 12:6). The problem with these obscure disclosures was that they were unrecorded and lacked permanent authority. Secondly, God's word through Moses was 'mouth to mouth', definitive and plain and in the event recorded as written law by which the Israel of the old dispensation had to live. In short, Moses' revelations were uniquely and permanently authoritative. The remainder of the Old Testament bears this out. According to the summary given by Deuteronomy 34:10, 'No prophet has risen in Israel like Moses, whom the LORD knew face to face.'

Just so, implies Paul, at Corinth and elsewhere. The infant Christian churches did experience prophecy. But the phenomenon was strictly temporary, to be replaced by a complete and enduring revelation of the plan of God for his people in the final dispensation. Therefore the Corinthians must stand where Aaron and Miriam stood when rebuked by Jehovah. They must recognize that their prophets did not offer a complete ministry and that their prophecies possessed at best a local and temporary usefulness. This is the burden of the first part of 13:12.

6. Knowing because known

In the second half of 13:12 Paul asserts that **'Just now I know in part, but then I shall recognize even as I have been recognized.'**

Again the apostle refers to himself. His words are a counterpart to 13:9 ('for we know in part'), yet with a development. Not even Paul had received a total revelation of the Christian mystery. In time, when 'the perfect thing' arrived, the churches would escalate to a new, adult stage of existence. 'Then' even the apostle would 'recognize'. A medium expounding the programme of salvation definitively in all its splendour was to be made available. The verb **'I shall recognize'** is, in terms of Greek grammar, in the middle voice (*epignôsomai*, from *epiginôsko*). Paul's probable meaning is that he would be in a position to find out for himself what 'the perfect thing' had to tell.

Further, the measure by which he would be enabled to appreciate the revelation of God in Christ would be **'even as I have been recognized'**. 'Even as' probably means 'because': because the Lord knew him he would know about the Lord.[47]

Recognition is developing awareness, the experience of coming to see something for what it really is.[48] Once again Paul parallels both his own and the Corinthian scene with that of Israel in the desert. In more detail, Exodus 33 and 34 might well have been in his mind.

Following the incident of the golden calf, Moses expressed concern for his future and for that of Israel. Because he believed that Jehovah knew him, the servant of the Lord prayed that he might know the ways of Jehovah; he yearned to understand the plan of God for his people, to comprehend because he had been comprehended. His prayer was answered: not only did his face shine; to him, rather to than any other prophet, was given the complete revelation of the law (Exod. 32; 33:12-13,20; 34:28-29).

This fits exactly with the episode in which Moses was criticized by his brother and sister (Num. 12) and with the 'now' and 'then' scenes of the first part of 13:12. In the words of Psalm 103:7, the Lord 'made his ways and deeds known to Moses, his acts to the sons of Israel'. In his subtle recall of Numbers 12:6-8 the apostle implies that the tension between Moses and the prophets was typical and that the Lord is about to grant the churches a revelation superior to those transmitted to them verbally by their own prophets. The saints will soon know even as they have been known.

Faith, hope and love (13:13)

The exposition of love concludes: **'But now abide faith, hope, love, these three; but the greatest of these is love.'** The Greek for 'but now' (*nuni de*) means 'now therefore', often signifying the end of a movement or process and a revised state of affairs (cf. 5:11; 12:18 and 15:20). It is not the same as 'just now' (*arti*) in the preceding verse, but suggests an ongoing, stable situation.

The meaning is that before, during and after the displacement of spiritual gifts by 'the perfect thing', faith, hope and love remain in the churches. It is significant that the verb 'abide' is singular, as if faith, hope and love are in some sense partners which never split up and which never bid farewell to the people.

Moreover, the trio are mentioned elsewhere in the New Testament and in early Christian literature. It is almost as if, prompted both by Scripture and by experience, some sub-apostolic writers reckoned **'these three'** to be fundamentally important, perhaps much more so than spiritual gifts. They knew that faith in Christ generates a firm hope in salvation, and that faith and hope are manifested by love for the church.[49]

Of these three agape is said by Paul to be the **'greatest'**. That is, love is more important than faith and hope in exactly the same way that some spiritual gifts are 'greater' than others (12:31; 14:5).

A 'New Testament' canon?

The thesis presented here is that 'the perfect thing' predicted in 13:10 can with hindsight be recognized now as our New Testament, a set of inspired books complementing the Old Testament. Nor is it unreasonable to believe that Paul was not unaware of this development even though he could not have known that there were to be four Gospels plus twenty-three other books.

Being out of step

In all honesty, it must be admitted that this approach flies in the face of nearly every commentator, ancient and modern. Lenski could speak for most with the remark that even the Scriptures are 'able to convey to us only a part of the full reality which we shall at last come

Spiritual gifts (12:1 - 14:40)

to know'. John Calvin took a similar view: 'I say that the ministry of the word is like a mirror ... it is not so clear as it will eventually be at the Last Day.'[50]

Surely, observations like these go badly astray. Paul was concerned with an imminent, rather than an impending, 'perfect thing' which, relative to unrecorded prophecy, would be comprehensive and final. There is no contrast in 13:8-13 between prophecy, whether verbal or written, and the glory that is to be. The end of all things is not on the agenda.

The Corinthians and the Old Testament

Could the Corinthians have detected cryptic allusions in 13:12 to the books of Exodus and Numbers (if they were considered cryptic)? If, of course, the apostle knew that identification would lie beyond his readers' capacity there can be no such allusions; he never asked the impossible. But consider again 10:6 and 11, and also Romans 4:23 and 15:4. Those to whom Paul sent 1 Corinthians were expected to come to grips with the Old Testament even though they were unable to purchase modestly-priced printed editions from a local Christian bookshop. (This is not a frivolous comment. Opportunity for quietly studying the Law, the Prophets and the Writings would have been rare.) Because of his rigorous demands it follows that the introduction of such allusions by the apostle can be anticipated.

Was the apostle aware of emergent 'New Testament' Scripture?

The revelation through Moses was nothing less than the written Law. This suggests, via the recall of Numbers 12:6-8 in 13:12, that 'the perfect thing' was expected by Paul to take the form of inspired and authoritative writing. Further, there is considerable evidence within the New Testament itself to indicate that the early churches were conscious of the emergence of God-breathed Scripture. Consider, for example, 2:13; 14:37; 1 Timothy 5:18 (Luke 10:7); 2 Timothy 3:16 and Revelation 22:18-19. In his second letter to believers living in what is today northern Turkey, a long way from Jerusalem, the apostle Peter acknowledged that 'all' the letters of Paul were included in 'the rest of the Scriptures' (2 Peter 3:16). He would not have made this statement had he not believed it personally, had he not known his readers to be aware of a developing body of inspired documents, and had not the apostle Paul, the author of some of these 'Scriptures', been conscious of the dignity and calibre of what he was writing.

It is difficult to approach Hebrews 2:1-4 in any other way. Confirmatory miracles are considered to lie in the recent past, history rather than news, marvellous wonders that had been overtaken. But by what? Seemingly they had been superseded by the letter and by other documents; the author reveals that others also had received truth from those who heard the Lord.

The works and purposes of God

Furthermore, reason suggests that if God revealed himself historically in Jesus Christ he would expound that revelation in the form of an infallible record. Nevertheless, modern liberal theology usually finds the concept of a written and inerrant 'Thus saith the Lord...' impossible to digest, conceiving the Bible in both its parts to be no more than a unique but fallible recital of the acts of God. In recent years a jargon word for the idea has been developed, *Heilsgeschichte,* German for 'the story [or history] of salvation'. But evangelicals believe that the Bible is certainly not a story and that it is far from being simply a history.

Surely, first principles must tell us that the liberal approach cannot be good enough. If God has granted no inspired and accurate explanation of how he saves his people, how can we know that we have been known? Equally, were not the apostles in error when they affirmed that their account of Jesus Christ was the Word of God? Take, as just one example, Acts 10:36, which falls within Peter's bold address to Cornelius and his family: 'The word which he [God] sent to the sons of Israel, preaching peace through Jesus Christ (he is Lord of all).' Peter was either a sober, Spirit-filled apostle of God or a charlatan whom Cornelius should have packed off to Joppa without more ado. But he did not do that, and we know why not.[51]

That the transition from 'the thing which is in part' to 'the perfect thing' is akin to growing up, a relatively gentle process which cannot happen instantaneously, is shown by 13:11. Suddenness is absent from the growth process. In the words of Daniel 9:24, vision and prophecy were being sealed up. Paul can be reasonably interpreted as claiming that in his day the train of events was already on the move. His message is that the Corinthians ought to share his

Spiritual gifts (12:1 - 14:40)

enthusiasm for a new, exciting situation rather than remaining dull and childishly immobile.

A word of caution is necessary. The apostle could not have imagined that he would survive to see the complete collection of the twenty-seven books of the New Testament as we know them. He must have been aware that he would soon enough depart for glory, a journey that he took some ten years after writing 1 Corinthians. But he knew that already God was granting his final word to the churches through inspired penmen and that he was one of them; with others he had begun to comprehend even as, or because, he had been comprehended.[52]

Not all would see it like this. Gordon D. Fee states blandly that this approach to 13:10 and its context is 'an impossible view of course, since Paul himself could not have articulated it'.[53] Why not? Arguably, the apostle does do so, albeit in veiled terms and with becoming humility; he would never push himself forward. Anyway, because Fee's assertion appears without benefit of argument it seems to lack weight.

The early church

It needs to be said that the early churches did believe in the appearance of a definitive canon of New Testament writings. Of this there can be no question. Here is one slender piece of evidence from the available patristic texts.

Ignatius, who died in Rome as a martyr about the end of the first century A.D., wrote letters to a number of churches. The epistle to the Philadelphians criticizes some Judaizers who would not accept an enlarging Bible. Apparently, one of them said, 'If I find it not in the charters I do not believe in the Gospel.' 'Charters' is significant because the background Greek word *archeia* means 'archives' or even 'public records', authoritative documentation placed on deposit.

The best interpretation of Ignatius' report would be that the Judaizers refused to believe anything that was not taught plainly by the 'archives', what we would call the Old Testament, and declined flatly to accept the authority of the written Gospel record. Ignatius tells us that he counterattacked immediately with the retort that 'It is written,' by which he meant that there were Scriptures other than those of the Old Testament. Not unexpectedly, they answered 'That is the question.' His concluding reply was: 'To me the charters [written archives] are Jesus Christ, the inviolable charters are his cross, and death, and resurrection, and the faith which is through him.' It seems that Ignatius, writing only forty or more years after the death of Paul, held that the 'gospel' was enshrined in God-given writings telling out the way of salvation.[54]

Although this and a mass of similar evidence does not establish the approach adopted here to 13:8-13, it is consistent with it. Here is precisely what we would expect to see in copies of early writings that in the providence of God have come down to us.

A final word about a 'canon'

Near the north-east shore of the Dead Sea there is a ruined site known as Khirbet Qumran. Close by are some caves in which the celebrated 'Qumran' or 'Dead Sea' scrolls and other miscellaneous fragments have been brought to light. Some bits of papyrus were found in Cave 7, scraps that have been dated to not later than about A.D. 50, and that *might* have been included in copies of a few of the books of the New Testament. One fragment seems to reproduce Mark 6:52-53; another, 1 Timothy 3:16 - 4:3. If the dating of these scraps is accurate and if New Testament material was deposited at Qumran before the end of the Roman-Jewish War in A.D. 70, we have evidence for an early development of a body of canonical Christian books.[55]

Will there be faith and hope in heaven?

It has been argued that the expected 'perfect thing' (13:10) cannot be the final, glorious coming of our Lord, and that it has to be something else, something that the apostle knew was imminent.

By far the most important reason for this approach is that faith and hope are always understood by the New Testament as disciplines for God's people in this world only. Scripture in general says nothing about the glorified church in heaven believing in and hoping for a final release from tension. The fact that the souls of the martyrs cry out, 'How long, O Lord?' (Rev. 6:10) does not disprove this.

This eloquent absence of any reference to post-mortem and post-advent faith and hope has always been a stumbling-block for the many commentators who hold that 1 Corinthians 13:8-13 points to the coming of Christ. The truth is that biblical faith and hope never

Spiritual gifts (12:1 - 14:40)

stretch out to anything lying beyond the coming of the Lord.[56] Further, the speculative notion of an undefined celestial faith and hope does real damage to the truth that death and then the final advent of Jesus usher us into the splendour of the King's house where 'The first things have passed away' (Rev. 21:4).

Admittedly, if faith and hope and their associated struggles continue after the Second Coming, there is no problem about 13:8-13. On this understanding, the arrival of Jesus must be 'the perfect thing'. Then the gifts of the Spirit cease and faith, hope and love endure eternally. But there is an insuperable difficulty with this scenario: it does not fit. When Christ returns we shall obtain the 'outcome', or end, of our faith, 'the salvation of our souls' (1 Peter 1:9).

To illustrate the problems of those who succumb to the eschatological approach to 13:8-13, Ridderbos's solution could be mentioned. He argues that although faith and hope cannot exist after Christ appears, they are to be represented in the glory. This is because they constitute our present bond with the Saviour, a bond that is to endure in a perfected form following the advent. He stresses that this cannot be said for spiritual gifts. As he sees it, faith and hope will remain, but in a strictly relative sense.

This type of argument is so tortuous that it ought to be abandoned. It is like saying that the scaffolding used in the construction of a house remains as a permanent feature after the building has been completed.[57]

It may be concluded that Christian faith as presented by the New Testament is to become suddenly redundant. From this it follows that in 13:8-13 the apostle Paul, who cannot disagree with the Holy Spirit, with other sacred penmen, or even with himself elsewhere, does not take us beyond the final advent of Christ.

'The perfect thing' and the second advent of the Lord

Here are some more reasons which appear to clinch the argument that 'the perfect thing' (13:10) does not refer in any way to the Second Coming.

1. 'The greatest of these is love' (13:13)

If faith and hope are supposed to function along with love after the coming of Christ, it is hard to see in what respect agape would be the greatest of the three. On the other hand, if the coming of 'the perfect thing' is other than, and prior to, the appearance of the Lord, 13:13 fits neatly into place.

Paul's meaning is not that faith, hope and love last for ever, but that these are blessings that the churches need — and possess — throughout the present age, and that within the trio love is the most important.

2. The scope of 1 Corinthians 12-14

Positively, these chapters concern themselves with spiritual gifts. Negatively, as we have already seen, they are not concerned either with the interim blessedness of the saints when they fall asleep or with the resurrection state.

As Judisch helpfully observes, 'The "complete thing" cannot be the state of eternal bliss ... such an identification is foreign to the context. Paul makes no other reference to eternal bliss or death or the parousia in this section of 1 Corinthians (chapters 12-14, which constitute a discourse on the use of spiritual gifts).'[58]

An eschatological reference for 13:8-13 would be an illogical shift in Paul's flow of thought.

3. The difference between 'the thing that is in part' and 'the perfect thing' (13:10-12)

The two entities are alike in that both are media of revelation. Whereas 'the thing that is in part' (prophecy, tongues and knowledge) reveals something of the mystery of redemption, 'the perfect thing' is presented as a complete exposition, complementing and completing what had been ministered through non-writing Christian prophets.

If 'the perfect thing' points to the introduction of the heavenly scene which, even in the interim experience of God's departed people, will be 'far better' (Phil. 1:23), it collapses as a meaningful contrast to the strictly quantitative thing that is 'in part' (13:9,12). On this understanding, the glory to be would be no more than an indefinite expansion and extension of the present degraded state of things.

Elsewhere in Paul's writings the distinction between this world and the age to come is essentially qualitative. Consider, for example, 15:42-55; Romans 8:21-25; 2 Corinthians 4:17; Philippians 3:21

and Revelation 21:4. When the Lord appears tears will bow before joy, weakness before strength, bondage before liberty, faith before sight and corruption before incorruption. The momentous event is to bring in a metamorphosis quite dissimilar to the simple replacement of one medium of communication by another. Our Lord described the end as 'the regeneration' (Matt. 19:28). The frames of reference are different.

4. Christ is not a 'thing'

Had Paul wished in 13:10 to describe Christ as the perfect Saviour he might well have written 'the perfect man' (Greek, *ho teleios*, masculine) instead of 'the perfect thing' (Greek, *to teleion*, neuter). The grammar is revealing. A medium of communication, whether limited or total, is a 'thing'. We are required to draw our own conclusion.

5. Is 'the perfect thing' the same as 'the end'?

'The end' (Greek, *to telos*) occurs in 15:24 with reference to the advent of Christ. Both in the interests of consistency and clarity, why should the same word not have been introduced in 13:10 if the Second Coming of the Lord and the end of the world are under consideration? The expression 'the perfect thing' does appear awkward if Paul intended to refer to the winding up of this age.

As we shall note with reference to 15:24, 'end' suggests a climax, or the final issue of a matter. To illustrate, Romans 6:21-22 employs *to telos* in describing death as the 'outcome' of sin and eternal life as the 'outcome' of faith in Christ. Compare with 1 Timothy 1:5: 'The goal [*to telos*] of our instruction is love ... and a good conscience and a sincere faith.' We can easily see that the sense of the word is not at all the same as the Greek *to teleion*, 'the perfect thing', something that is in itself independent and complete.

6. 'The coming' of what?

The apostle was not in the habit of referring loosely to the advent of Christ as 'the coming'. We do so; he, never. Paul trembled with awe and anticipation at the thought of the appearance of the Saviour, and always qualified it carefully as the coming 'of Christ', of 'our Lord Jesus', of 'the Lord', or of 'our Lord Jesus Christ'. Sometimes, in stark but reverent simplicity, he wrote about 'his' coming.[59] This blessed truth is couched by the apostle in the most august language.

If 'the perfect thing' is related somehow to this great occasion, we might expect a clarification of the matter. Because there is none we may conclude that it is something different.

7. Growing up

The change from childhood to adulthood, mentioned in 13:11, is necessarily gradual. A process rather than an event, it cannot happen instantaneously. Paul teaches that the objective replacement of 'the thing that is in part' by its perfect complement should be accompanied by a developing attitude within the churches. He presents himself as an example.

It is doubtful whether such a gradual process could illustrate the resurrection of the dead, a universal miracle that will occur 'in a moment, in the twinkling of an eye, at the last trumpet' (15:52). The frames of reference have nothing in common.

8. 'Knowledge'

Because Paul's references to 'knowledge' (Greek, *gnôsis*) and 'know' (*ginôskô*) elsewhere in his letters are never linked to the blessed state of the church when and after Christ comes, it is virtually certain that no such datum appears in 13:1-13.[60] In short, 'knowledge' refers to our present understanding of the revealed mysteries of the faith, mysteries which, had they not been revealed, would remain unknown. It follows that an escalation from prophetic revelations to 'the perfect thing' is an essentially this-world matter.

9. The 'mirror'

Sight by means of a mirror (13:12) would seem to parallel 13:9, which refers to incomplete prophetic revelation. Paul does not, of course, mean that the Corinthians stare into polished metal plates when in the act of worship. As we noted in our earlier consideration of this verse, consistency demands that expected face-to-face sight has to be as figurative as mirror-vision. In turn, this means that 13:8-13 compares and contrasts two vehicles of revelation, one of which is present, hazy and incomplete, and the other imminent, perfect and direct. The passage says nothing about literal sight now or in the heavenly scene.

10. Christ, the reflection of God's glory

In travelling through this world Christian pilgrims become more and more like the Lord Jesus, although at times it seems hard to believe and on occasion hard to discern. 2 Corinthians 3:18 claims that 'We all, with unveiled face beholding as in a mirror the glory of the Lord, are being transformed into the same image.'

Some think that the Greek word for 'beholding', *katoptrizomenoi*, should be translated as 'reflecting'. This is grammatically possible. On this construction the believer is said to reflect Christ continuously. But Paul's fundamental contrast is between unbelieving Jews who do not see and Christians (whether Jews or Gentiles) who do, their reflecting medium being the Saviour. God has bestowed 'the light of the knowledge of the glory of God in the face of Christ' (2 Cor. 4:6).[61]

It might be supposed that 13:10-12 is an anticipation of 2 Corinthians 3:18. If this is so, 'the perfect thing' becomes the advent of Christ when we shall dispense with the mirror and see face to face.[62] But such a parallel would be superficial and inconsistent. The reflected vision of 13:12 is dim whereas that of 2 Corinthians 3:18 lacks nothing, a metaphorical reflection by which we gaze upon the fulness of the glory of the Lord: Christ is the perfect mirror-image of the Father.

It would seem that what we have in 1 and 2 Corinthians is a good example of the versatility of Paul, with the mirror-metaphor being employed in two different frames of reference. First, 13:12 anticipates the replacement of variously distributed gifts by 'the perfect thing'; secondly, 2 Corinthians 3:18 is concerned with the more fundamental status of all who have received the revelation of God in Christ.

To put it another way, 13:12 takes for granted that all believers behold God through Christ. 2 Corinthians 3:18, we may assume, must have been conceptualized in its author's mind when he wrote 1 Corinthians. But 1 Corinthians 13 is not concerned with this great principle. That God's mirror-revelation through the Saviour is something imperfect, incomplete and dim would have been unthinkable for Paul. For him, Christian experience involves walking by the light of the divine glory as perceived in the face, or person, of the God-man, and not under the guidance of blurred, shadowy reflections. It follows that the mirror-metaphor of 13:12 falls within another, more restricted framework.

Moreover, whereas the context of 2 Corinthians 3:18 addresses a bitterly hostile Jewish opposition, that of 1 Corinthians 13:12 does not. The two verses should not be placed in tandem.

11. Will Christ ever cease to reflect the glory of God?

No. According to Revelation 22:4, in the resurrection state the people of God are to behold the face of Christ rather than that of the Father. Bear in mind that our Lord prayed that those given to him might eventually see his, that is, Christ's, glory (John 17:24). Nowhere in the New Testament is there any evidence to suggest that the face of the Father will be the object of direct sight. This is not contradicted by Matthew 18:10, according to which the angels in heaven behold God directly.

It follows that the dim mirror, destined for redundancy, cannot be Christ. Therefore it is something else. Therefore its replacement, 'the perfect thing', points to something other than the final advent.

12. 'Knowledge ... will be done away' (13:8)

We assume that the faculty of knowledge is to persist after the coming of Christ and that the resurrected saints will know what is happening. If so, 13:8 does not stretch out towards the end of the world but to the cessation of limited revelation at some time prior to the appearance of our Lord.

Conclusion

If you have waded through these observations you might well hesitate about giving an 'Amen' to this thesis. Quite apart from the sensitivities of those who believe they exercise spiritual gifts, many who make no such claim will find it almost impossible to accept that the charismata vanished from the churches nearly two thousand years ago.

Such reservations and hesitations are to be respected. Further, let it be said that this exposition of 1 Corinthians 13 is a rough-hewn thing. Others, no doubt, have done better. Others could do better. Yet others, it is earnestly to be hoped, will do better.

Spiritual gifts (12:1 - 14:40)

But pause for a moment and consider carefully. Perhaps you believe in all sincerity that the gifts of the Spirit are meant to remain indefinitely in the churches. If so, you must come to terms with 13:8-13. Here is a challenge you cannot avoid and would not evade. To maintain your cause you are under obligation to wrestle with text and context, and with questions such as those that have been raised. Here lies your dilemma: to back off is capitulation, whereas if you take up the gauntlet you must in time acknowledge that there is a more excellent way.

For my own part, I think that this chapter is the stone of stumbling for Pentecostalism and that the 'non-eschatological' approach, if it can be so described, explains Paul's words in a way beyond the reach of any other.

The anticipated sequence of events

Let's sum up this examination of 13:8-13 by dividing the apostle's expected programme into three stages:

1. At the time when 1 Corinthians was written, faith, hope and love were universally active. Additionally there was a wide range of spiritual gifts and some God-breathed apostolic writings that were increasingly accepted as additions to the Scriptures (that is, to the Old Testament).

2. Paul predicts that faith, hope and love, 'these three', will remain indefinitely, by which he means until, but not after, the world's end. Not so the charismata; at a very early time they will cease to be granted by the Spirit because they must fade away in place of the emergent 'perfect thing'. The apostle prophesies about prophecy, tongues and knowledge in order to show that long-lasting Christian graces are so much more important than short-term spiritual gifts.

3. This 'perfect thing' will never be withdrawn. Rather, in the ongoing pilgrimage of God's people in this age it is to co-exist permanently with faith, hope and love.

It follows of necessity that 'the perfect thing' cannot be linked to the final advent of the Lord.

Prophecy first; tongues last (14:1-40)

When 1 Corinthians was written tempers were running high in Achaia about those who did and those who did not possess extraordinary spiritual gifts. It remains for the apostle to deal with an aggravated situation in which many who spoke in tongues strove for pride of place in the life of the church. Dividing into two parts, chapter 14 shows that their enthusiasm was as misguided as it was misapplied.

That prophecy was the most valuable of all the temporary gifts of the Spirit, bar none, is established by 14:1-25. In 14:26-40 there are rules for prophesying and speaking in tongues when the people come together.

Prophecy, the important gift (14:1-19)

First, prophecy is shown to be superior to uninterpreted tongues (14:1-12a). Secondly, the truth is applied (14:12b-19).

A principle stated (14:1-12a)

The apostle has made it obvious that faith, hope and love are far more important than the gifts of the Spirit. Now he demonstrates that one spiritual gift, that of speaking in foreign languages, is remarkably less significant than all the other charismata, and certainly less desirable than prophecy.

Corinthian priorities were wrong. Perversely, the people majored upon the least useful of the gifts. This imbalance meant that other blessings, plus the need to develop Christian character, were being marginalized.

The fellowship, then, is to **'pursue love'** (14:1). 'Pursue' is a strong word, meaning to persecute or chase (Greek, *diôkô*).[63] The idea here is that of a determined pursuit for a loving attitude in church relations. But although the various charismata are not to be hunted down and seized, the fellowship as a whole is to **'desire earnestly spiritual gifts, but especially that you may prophesy'**. These blessings are by no means to be despised, the reason being that they come from God. Of these, prophecy is the most useful, one of the 'greater gifts' to which 12:31 made allusion.

A reason is given for this supremacy. Although the man who **'speaks in a tongue'** does, it is true, address God, he is unable to

Spiritual gifts (12:1 - 14:40)

communicate effectively with fellow-Christians: **'No one hears.'** Apart from the speaker, only God deciphers what is said (14:2).

1. Tongues

As has been suggested, in the New Testament 'tongue' stands for language, a language being an organized system of encoded sounds designed for communication. At Corinth and elsewhere a God-given tongue would not have been a synthetic thing, a random and incomprehensible mix of pre-learned linguistic building-blocks. It could not have been incoherent noise.

Human speech always comes across in the form of words, whether spoken or written. To illustrate, in the New Testament those who are said to 'speak' are Scripture itself, God, men, angels, demons, stones and, on one celebrated occasion, a donkey.[64] The miraculous gift of speech in 'tongues' can be no exception to the general rule. It might be that chapter 14, with its cluster of references to the practice of *speaking* in tongues, intends to make this point in a way that cannot be misunderstood by the disinterested reader.[65]

2. The overriding need: the edification of the church (14:1-5)

Notice that in 14:2 **'tongue'** is singular: apparently, the person who rose to speak confined himself to one language even though he probably had others at his disposal. Compare with 12:10, which refers to 'kinds of tongues'. In worship the speaker addressed God rather than the congregation because (to repeat) 'No one hears'. The failure to communicate to others was because **'By the Spirit he speaks mysteries.'**

The NASB gives, helpfully, 'in his spirit' rather than 'by the Spirit' (14:2). But there is a problem. On the face of it the verse seems to suggest that the tongue-speaker was given words to utter that he may or may not have understood, the apparent reason being that his speech was generated by his inner spirit rather than the fruit of a sanctified intellect. The interpretation is plausible.

My contention is that it was not like this, nor could it have been. The data given in this chapter indicate strongly that the tongue-speaker always knew exactly what he was saying. The assertion of 14:14 that 'My spirit prays' does not, as we shall see, disprove the principle. In any case, it may be doubted whether the mind and spirit of a rational person can ever operate independently of each other.

'**Mysteries**' are revelations of God's plan of salvation.[66] This means that in dispensing mysteries the tongue-speaker was a prophet (14:2). So too is the man who '**prophesies**' (in a known language) because he '**speaks to men edification and exhortation and consolation**' (14:3). At a later date Paul would 'commend' the elders at Ephesus to 'God and to the word of his grace, which is able to build you up' (Acts 20:32). Prophecy had this capacity. An inspired and intelligible word from the Lord, it could not fail to be a benediction to God's people. But unknown tongues were useless in this respect.

The matter is summed up by 14:4. The man who '**speaks in a tongue edifies himself**' but the one who '**prophesies edifies the church**'. Who is more useful, and therefore more important? To this question there can be only one possible answer: the prophet who speaks intelligibly. For this reason the apostle desires '**you all**', every person in the church, to '**be speaking in tongues, but rather that you would continue prophesying**' (14:5). We depart from the NASB here in an attempt to bring out the significance of the provocative present tenses. They indicate that within the congregation glossolalia should never cease, the only proviso being that pride of place be given to prophecy.

Go back to chapter 13, according to which love is said to be greater, functionally more useful, than faith and hope, all three being more important than prophecy and knowledge. Now it transpires that prophecy is '**greater**' than tongues-speaking. Seen in the overall framework of chapters 13 and 14, the order of precedence and relevance is love, followed by faith accompanied by hope, then prophecy and, last and decidedly least, tongues.

If, in spite of this, the tongue-speaker interprets he is not regarded as less great than the prophet. This is because the church would '**receive edification**'. Notice that interpretation should be ongoing and that every single word of a tongue must be made intelligible to the people. From this it follows, once again, that tongues were languages.

3. Numbers 11 and 12

In the exposition of 13:12 it was proposed that Numbers 11 and 12 were in Paul's mind. This suggestion is given considerable support by 14:5. These chapters from the book of Numbers disclose that a surge of prophecy in the camp of Israel, followed by domestic tensions, led to Aaron and Miriam defying their brother Moses.

Prior to the confrontation, Numbers 11:28-29 records Moses' response to Joshua, a servant jealous for his master's position. The problem was that the younger man had urged Moses to restrain Eldad and Medad, two of the seventy elders, from prophesying in public. Moses responded vigorously: 'Are you jealous for my sake? Would that all the Lord's people were prophets, that the Lord would put his Spirit upon them!'

Moses knew well that he was transmitting written law from the Lord. Harbouring no dark suspicions about an undermining of his unique ministry, he yearned that each and every Israelite might be a prophet. Paul found himself in an analogous situation. It is not difficult to see why there is a definite recollection in 14:5 of Moses and Joshua, Eldad and Medad. Well aware that something far more enduring than verbal prophecy was being granted to the churches, the apostle could not, and would not, bring himself to suppress genuine prophetic ministry. This is why he desired that the Corinthians might prophesy rather than speak in unknown tongues.

4. Sensible sounds (14:6-12a)

Whenever possible Paul is affectionate. Here, he speaks to **'brethren'** (14:6). As in 13:13, **'but now'** means: 'This is how things are.' Because alien languages without interpretation are useless, of what value to the Corinthians would even Paul the apostle be if he came to them speaking in several tongues? None at all. Conversely, would he not profit the church were he to address them **'either by way of revelation or of knowledge or of prophecy or of teaching'**? Certainly.

In 14:6 we have the first specific reference by the apostle to a 'revelation' considered as a Spirit-given disclosure. He has stated already that certain great truths concerning salvation had been 'revealed' to others and to him 'through the Spirit' (2:10).[67] Now, revelation is associated with personal knowledge, the former giving rise to the latter. Similarly, prophecy is linked to teaching because the former presumes the presence of a prophet, someone who instructs others. Overall, there is a relationship, perhaps a sequence, connecting all four: revelation leads to knowledge, and the possessor of Spirit-given knowledge becomes a prophet who enlarges the minds of the people.

But only if the Spirit's revelations are shared with the church can they be effective. Paul's irrefutable assertion is that if *he* is no exception to this principle, the Corinthians certainly cannot be.

This is borne out by 14:7. If the inanimate flute or harp do not give a **'distinction in the tones, how will it be known what is played'** on them? The illustration is simple: sounds that mean nothing can communicate nothing and cannot help the hearer. What is true musically is true for spoken language.

Similarly, if a **'bugle produces an indistinct sound, who will prepare himself for battle?'** (14:8). No one at all. Adrenalin will not flow because there is no signal to take up arms; neither will the courageous stir nor the cowardly blanch. Nothing happens.

Let's focus our attention upon the immediate issue. Paul does not claim that tongues are non-languages. His assumption is that all intelligent communications, including languages, operate according to established rules. It follows that organized sounds that are not understood are tantamount to a jumble of meaningless, irritating noises. The application here is that uninterpreted languages are irrelevant and irreverent.

'Unless you utter by the tongue speech that is clear, how will it be known what is spoken?' (14:9). 'Clear' means 'significant': the utterance is important because it says something. Again, it is accepted that because he issues meaningful words the Corinthian tongue-speaker speaks. Even so, although the potential to communicate is inherent in glossolalia, if the man is to serve the saints a way must be provided for them to understand him. Should this not happen, **'You will be speaking into the air.'** Just as an ineffective ministry is like slapping space (9:26), speaking in a mysterious tongue is a useless exercise.

The apostle assumes that the principle of understanding is universal, from which it follows that the tongue-speaker has no licence to be an exception. **'There are, perhaps, a great many kinds of voices in the world, and none of them is voiceless'** (14:10). As also in 14:11, NASB gives 'of languages' instead of 'of voices' (Greek, *phônôn*). This is not inaccurate, except that it obscures the truth that a 'voice' emits nothing but intelligible speech: if there is no voice there is no speech, and vice versa. Thus,

Spiritual gifts (12:1 - 14:40)

'voiceless' means 'dumb' in the same way that idols are dumb (12:2), and even as Jesus was like a silent lamb (Isa. 53:7; Acts 8:32).

Further, in 12:10 and 28 reference was made to 'kinds of tongues', a construction like 'kinds of voices'. Paul's deliberate parallel shows beyond a shadow of doubt that a 'tongue' was reckoned to be a 'voice', an uttered language. The apostle continues. A voiceless voice would be a contradiction in terms: **'If then I do not know the power of the voice, I shall be to the one who speaks a barbarian, and the one who speaks will be a barbarian to me'** (14:11).

'Barbarians' were non-Greeks. The Hellenes prided themselves that they were the only people in the world who could speak intelligently, choosing to believe that others, racially and culturally their alleged inferiors, could do no more than splutter out, so to speak, a nonsensical 'bar-bar'. The term passed into general use, which is why Luke in Acts 28:2 calls the Maltese 'barbarians', even though he praises their unexpected kindness. All that is meant by the missionary doctor is that the islanders were not of Greek origin. Romans 1:14 is bolder when it links the Greeks and the barbarians. This might just be a subtle apostolic hint that the former may not have been as far ahead as they made themselves out to be.

In 14:11 it is assumed that a voice or language had **'power'** (Greek, *dunamis*). This means ability, as in Matthew 25:15, where the departing lord dispenses money to his slaves, to each according to his 'power'. The voice has strength to communicate.

Be this as it may, what, asks Paul, if intelligent words in the God-given voice are nonsense to a listener who thinks and speaks in another tongue? Whereas the speaker congratulates himself because he has a superior endowment, his hearer concludes that the man is a fool. Barriers are set up by both sides and fellowship is destroyed. Repeating **'so also you'** from 14:9, 14:12a shows that this is how it was at Corinth.

The importance of the principle (14:12b-14)

Some who could, and others who could not, speak in tongues were at loggerheads. The NASB joins 'so also you' (14:12a) to **'since you are zealous of spiritual gifts'**, but this is an unnecessary repetition.

The unfortunate state of affairs in the church had to be corrected. Because the people were keen to show off their endowments (literally, 'spirits'), the apostle allows them to do so provided always that they **'seek to abound for the edification of the church'**.

We should compare with 12:7, where Paul contemplates the Spirit individualizing himself in different people, and also with 'the seven Spirits of God', by which is meant the third person of the Trinity (Rev. 1:4; 3:1; 4:5; 5:6). It is exactly like this in 14:12, which teaches that the one Spirit of God is the source of tongues, prophecy and all other gifts.

'Therefore let one who speaks in a tongue pray that he may interpret' (14:13). Only if this prayer is answered will the man's God-given language ever become intelligible to the people. Should he be denied this further gift he must remain silent.

Paul always constructs his sentences with the greatest care, here no less than elsewhere. The present tenses that he builds into 'speaks', 'pray' and 'interpret' mean that continual tongue-speaking demands ongoing prayer with a view to ongoing interpretation. Notice, too, that tongues are not reckoned to be the ultimate gift. The person blessed in this way should always be praying for something more effective, that is, for the key by which his otherwise ignorant hearer can comprehend this miraculous speech.

In 14:14, as in 14:6, Paul hypothesizes. He imagines himself worshipping in a tongue, yet lacking the power of interpretation: **'For if I pray in a tongue, my spirit prays, but my mind is unfruitful.'**

This verse raises four questions. First, what is the difference between praying with the spirit and praying with the mind? Secondly, what does Paul mean when he says that it is possible for his mind to be unfruitful? Thirdly, did the tongue-speaker understand what he said? Most important of all, why did the person speaking in a tongue have to ask for interpretation if he understood what he was saying?

1. Praying with the spirit and with the mind

'Spirit' almost certainly stands for the conscious inner self, the essential person, rather than the Holy Spirit. Compare this with the reference in 2:11 to the inner spirit of a man.[68]

Although the Spirit of God within us intercedes continuously for the saints (Rom. 8:26-27), this is not the truth presented here. The apostle refers to intelligent prayers ascending from a worshipper's human spirit, prayers verbalized in a tongue recognized by nobody. The point is that because the worshipper does not intend others to hear there is no problem.

But the speaker understands. The man praying in a tongue does not bid farewell to his wits. There is no question of some sort of pseudo-ecstatic, jumbled utterance meaning nothing to the worshipper and therefore signifying nothing to the God to whom prayer is made. We know from Matthew 6:7 that the Lord does not appreciate the meaningless repetitions to which Gentiles are addicted and never leads his people to pray like this.

Consider Mary's song of praise: 'My soul exalts the Lord, and my spirit has rejoiced in God my Saviour.' She certainly understood what her 'spirit' was saying to God and about him (Luke 1:46-47).[69] On the other hand, 'mind' stands for the thoughtful intellect, particularly when interacting with other people. Compare with 1:10, 2:16; Romans 1:28; 12:2 and 14:5. This is not to say that a man's spirit and his intellect are different things. Ephesians 4:23 brings this out clearly with the summons to 'be renewed in the spirit of your mind'. Nor is the mind ever inactive when prayer is made.

To pray with the 'spirit' means to address prayer to God without being heard by others. To pray with the 'mind' or intellect is to address God publicly with the needs of others in mind.

2. The unfruitful mind

The reference in 14:14 to prayer with an **'unfruitful'** mind means either that the apostle does not know what he says, and consequently is no help to himself or to anybody else; or that he knows well enough what he says, but is unintelligible to his hearers and does not help them.

The first interpretation is impossible. As we have just seen, prayer is a conscious and intelligent act; at no time is the connection lost between a worshipper's heart, his thinking processes and his vocal chords. The meaning has to be that praying in an uninterpreted tongue is unprofitable for the hearers.

This finding is borne out by the uniform emphasis of this word 'unfruitful' in the New Testament. Mark 4:19 explains how worry, wealth and wanting things make the word unfruitful; they are no help to the progress of the gospel. Similarly, the mysterious tongue-speaker is no use to others.[70] Further, the context of 14:14, and particularly 14:6 and 14:16-17, are about contributing to the needs of the church rather than self-gratification.

3. Did the tongue-speaker understand what he said?

This question has been answered already. Nevertheless, let's delve a little further because it is important. Was it the case that the person who spoke in a tongue did not understand what he said? Apparently, yes; in reality, no. Surely he remained in control of his speech, saying what he wanted to say. Further, 'interpretation' means translation from one language to another, as in John 1:38,42 and 9:7, Acts 9:36 and Hebrews 7:2. Occasionally the word can signify explanation, as in Luke 24:27, which states that the Lord unfolded the Scriptures.[71] Corinthian interpretation implies that glossolalia *was* rational language.

There is more. The gift of a tongue was not merely the ability to speak in a different language. According to 14:2, inspired words in the God-given tongue gave rise to mysteries revealed by God. Remember 2:13, according to which God's gifts were explained accurately with words taught to the prophets by the Spirit rather than expounded by speculative human wisdom: the words of the Word of God were Spirit-given in their entirety.

It was like this with glossolalia. The tongue-speaker was granted three blessings. First, he spoke in a foreign language and knew what he was saying. Secondly, the precise words that he employed were taught him by the Holy Spirit. He was not at liberty to pick and choose his own expressions to expand God-given thoughts. Thirdly, he disclosed truths about the way of salvation otherwise inaccessible to the church and to him.

None of this can possibly be reconciled with the modern misapprehension that the tongue-speaker blessed God, all the time remaining blissfully unaware of the meaning, if any, of what he 'said'.

4. Why the necessity for interpretation?

If a tongue is to carry edification and exhortation and consolation to the church (14:3) it must be translated with perfect accuracy. Only then will the church lose nothing of what the Lord wants it to hear.

Even though the tongue-speaker knew what he said, we cannot assume that he was able to interpret accurately what could well have been a somewhat extended utterance. Nor can we take it for granted that he usually restricted himself to a few brief sentences in a tongue, pausing to follow up with a translation for the benefit of others, halting again to revert to the language, then translating some more sentences, and so on.

The reality must have been that, obedient to Paul's regulations, the gifted man stood up to speak in the confidence that the Lord had answered his prayer already. He knew that he or someone else would be granted an inspired block interpretation of his equally inspired words. Without such a conviction he would have remained quietly in his place. Knowing that he could say something in the vernacular, he dared not trust his own meagre resources in giving the fellowship a fallible translation. For this fundamentally important reason he applied to God for a further spiritual gift before opening his lips in public. There had to be inerrant interpretation, and he knew that only God could make it happen.[72]

The practical application (14:15-17)

'What is the outcome then?' (14:15). There must be translation. Paul intends to **'pray with the spirit'** and to **'pray with the mind also'**.

Notice the important word **'also'**: when interpreted, the prayer ascending from the spirit of the Christian to God becomes a product of the mind capable of encouraging the people. It is now two-dimensional, possessing horizontal and vertical co-ordinates. Similarly, when Paul purposes to **'sing with the spirit'** he will **'sing with the mind also'**, that is to say, singing intelligibly so that others might understand his lyrics.

If, as we know, the apostle could participate in a duet in a dungeon (Acts 16:25), he must have been eager to benefit others by singing to the Lord anywhere. We should not be less optimistic in our churches, even though singing in tongues is an impossibility in this post-charismatic age. But music, although a gentle servant, can be a bad master. It has a wonderful capacity to soothe and to excite the imagination, as once it did to two very different men, King Saul and the prophet Elisha (1 Sam. 16:23; 2 Kings 3:15). For all this, it must never be more than a servant. Worship and entertainment cancel each other out.

Reverting to the text, what if an individual Corinthian continues to **'bless in the spirit'**, that is, praises God in a tongue which he alone understands? (14:16). Notice that Paul employs the present tense because he is probing the settled habit of individual readers. What would be the reaction of the man who **'fills the place'** of an **'ordinary person'**, someone with no special ability, who is (NASB) 'ungifted'?[73] How could he possibly identify with another man's **'giving of thanks'**?

He cannot because he does not know what is being said. The apostle implies that even if the man might be ordinary he is no fool. He refuses to say 'Amen' and shrinks back from putting his signature to a blank cheque. Incidentally, if we think the matter through it seems obvious that a tongue could not have involved 'giving of thanks' if the tongue-speaker remained ignorant of what he said. After all, how would he have known that he was being grateful? Were there a divorce between mind and mouth he might, for all he knew, have been possessed by some unclean spirit driving him to say that Jesus was anathema (cf. 12:3). The apostle's assumption here, as everywhere, is that the Spirit-led worshipper addresses God intelligently.

The individual Corinthian who gives thanks **'well'** in an uninterpreted tongue senses that he is heard by God (14:17). In Authorized Version terms, he is conscious that the Lord has been 'intreated' for him.[74] None the less, excellent though this blessing is, it is not good enough for Paul. The reason is that the hearer does not understand and is not edified. Because the interests of the church are paramount, and because these interests have not been served, the unknown tongue should not have been uttered.

Paul, tongues and the church (14:18-19)

Now follow words that must have cut the Corinthian church to the quick. Paul, like the tongues-speakers, gives thanks to God; he is never anything other than grateful. But in his case he blesses the Lord for the scope of the gift: **'I thank God, I speak in tongues more than you all'** (14:18).

Perhaps we are meant to consider this disclosure in both of two ways. First, the apostle thanks God because he is able to thank God in other tongues; secondly, he thanks God that he can thank God in this fashion 'more than you all'. The latter assertion is truly astounding.

We know that Paul was at least bilingual (Hebrew/Aramaic and Greek; Acts 21:37,40). The disclosure in 14:18 is that, in addition to the languages that he had learned, he spoke in very many other tongues with which he had been endowed miraculously. Were all the Corinthians to count up all the undoubtedly large number of languages given to them by the Spirit for their use their sum would be considerably less than those placed by the Lord at Paul's disposal; he outstripped the whole church by far. In this respect the Spirit had blessed him to a quite exceptional degree.

The next statement is no less remarkable: **'However, in the church I desire to speak five words with my mind, that I may instruct others also, rather than ten thousand words in a tongue'** (14:19).

The apostle claims that each of his formidable array of languages had a vocabulary of not less than ten thousand words. The significance of ten thousand, a 'myriad', is that it was the largest numerical unit in use at that period. Paul means that he could at will speak countless words in any language of his choice, but that he did not choose to do so. **'However'** is emphatic: although he had been given so much he refused to parade even one of these languages when in the company of other Christians. The reason for this holy unwillingness is that there would be no advantage for the church; no one would learn anything from him.

What Paul was ready and eager to do was to speak in a language understood by the people. Further, he was prepared to restrict himself to just five words (no doubt well-chosen) in a common tongue so that the whole church might be able to understand quickly and easily. For him clarity was all-important. This is why he brings in **'instruct'** (Greek, *katecheô*, whence 'catechism'), suggesting a teacher-pupil relationship. The brethren must be taught and uninterpreted tongues must give way.

The language of the pulpit

Interestingly, that five brief words can carry a great deal of meaning was shown in the early history of Christianity by the employment of *ichthus*, Greek for 'fish', as a logo. Most of us know that it was a five-letter acronym for 'Jesus Christ, Son of God, Saviour'. Even though the apostle would probably have been unaware of this development it illustrates something we need to remember. If a genius like Paul could restrict himself to five words to get his message across we should not parade language others will find difficult. How, then, does this principle affect long pulpit prayers and sermons? What do we make of sanctimonious jargon and tones of voice supposed to be appropriate for the pulpit but which the servant of the Lord would not use elsewhere? Sometimes preachers need to unlearn. Like Paul, the dedicated teacher will have no desire to show how gifted he is. He will drop all affectation because he has something to say to people who matter.

Tongues, prophecy and the Old Testament (14:20-25)

As with just about everything else mentioned in this letter, the Old Testament is brought to bear upon the issue of speaking in foreign tongues.

Childlike or childish? (14:20)

It appears that Paul considered not a few of the Corinthians to be like children. Well, what of it? Our Lord taught that unless men strain to be childlike they cannot enter the kingdom of heaven (Matt. 18:3; Mark 10:15; Luke 18:17). The word which these three Gospel references employ (Greek, *paidion*) is exactly that used in 14:20.

But there is a shift in meaning. To be childlike is far from being childish. It is essentially in this second respect that Paul saw the Corinthians: they were regressive and even puerile in that they refused to develop a balanced, mature view about certain essential matters.

Although small children are not unaware that they must grow up, for them the day seems so distant that it is almost unimaginable. Being without mother and father, leaving home, having to earn money, possible marriage, caring for a family and eventually dying are matters about which they have little conception. To attain the age of twenty means becoming old. Their family, their toys, their friends, their presents and their school make up their world. They know no other and want none other. When adults inform them that

Spiritual gifts (12:1 - 14:40) 297

they must grow up they soon shrug the idea off and go back to playing. Their fleeting childhood years are the substance of all that is important.

Nor is this wrong. Youngsters ought to enjoy their childhood. They need time — not too little and not too much — without the cares of the wide world thrust upon them. Burdens will arrive soon enough. But imagine a situation where the years have passed and the adult is not even a late developer. The one-time child is seriously retarded, exhibiting the mentality and affections of a badly-behaved infant. This is how things were at Corinth.

Therefore, **'Brethren, do not be children in your thinking; in evil be babes, but in your thinking be mature.'** The Greek behind 'mature' is *teleioi*, 'complete' or 'perfect', and 'thinking' means the ability to see a situation in its true light. For example, this was decidedly not the case with a foolish youth who preferred not to think about what he was doing and who got into trouble with women (Prov. 6:32; 7:7; 9:4). For him the present was all that mattered. Childishly, the Corinthians considered the temporary gift of tongues far more important than it was, not choosing to see beyond their immediate situation. Perhaps this superficial evaluation carried with it a malicious sense of superiority; some who were gifted with glossolalia must have been horrible.

The apostle teaches that there has to be an attitude reversal. First, the people are to abandon the notion that tongues-speaking is some great matter. Second, they must cease to be condescending, even unpleasant, to believers not endowed in this way. Third, they must develop a mature, adult appreciation for what is really essential. By way of illustration, although he was never a Christian, the Roman emperor Marcus Aurelius (A.D. 161-180) wrote concerning his late father that 'He was a man mature, complete, deaf to flattery, able to preside over his own affairs and those of others.'[75] This is what Paul desired for the Corinthians; they did not know how to handle themselves and those around them.

Paul, Deuteronomy 28 and Isaiah 28 (14:21)

There is a grand reason for this necessary change in outlook. The apostle refers to **'the Law'**, by which is meant the Old Testament as a whole.[76] A specific quotation from Isaiah 28:11-12 is introduced, although it is probable that Deuteronomy 28:49 is in mind as well.

It will be helpful to consider what Moses, fifteen hundred years before Christ, and Isaiah, eight hundred years after Moses, did say, and then to try to understand Paul's application of these Scriptures.
Moses said:

> The Lord will bring a nation against you from afar, from the end of the earth, as the eagle swoops down, a nation whose language you shall not understand
>
> (Deut. 28:49).

Isaiah 28:11-12 shows the prophet's realization that this sad prediction was coming to pass:

Indeed, he will speak to this people
Through stammering lips and a foreign tongue,
He who said to them, 'Here is rest, give rest to the weary,'
And, 'Here is repose,' but they would not listen.

Moses warned that if Israel remained unfaithful to Jehovah, God would in time evict them from the land of promise, doing so through foreign invasion: barbarian soldiers with strange languages would overrun their inheritance. It is a sombre picture.

History records that this happened. Isaiah 28:7-10 presents a dreadful spectacle of drunken priests ridiculing what was for them the infantile prophetic word. Very well, retorts Isaiah, God will speak to Israel through a people of another tongue, that is, a foreign enemy, and through the destruction brought upon Judah by this other nation. An unknown and seemingly childish language, that of an alien army heard in the heartland of Judah, is to be the outworking of God's curse upon Israel (Isa. 28:15).[77]

Paul gives his own free translation of Isaiah 28:11 and of the last part of 28:12. His point can be grasped easily. What uninterpreted languages, or 'tongues', were in past time, they remained in the Corinthian situation: a sign of God's holy anger, although not directed to the Christians. Whatever the faults of the latter, they *did* believe. Again, the history of Israel is taken as a background pattern for the churches.

The Corinthians imagined that uninterpreted tongues signified the blessing of God upon the tongues-speakers. The apostle knew

Spiritual gifts (12:1 - 14:40)

that this understanding was not wholly erroneous. But because the issue was much more complex he teaches that the people would do well not to indulge in a facile oversimplification.

A dual role for tongues

Paul's meaning is that in his day the gift of tongues served a secondary role in addition to its obvious first task. The primary function was to demonstrate that Christ is the Saviour of the world, with all its multitude of languages, rather than of Abraham's family alone. This truth comes to the fore in Acts 2:1-13; 10:46 and 19:6, where we read about both Jews and Gentiles speaking in tongues. But glossolalia served also to prove that the blessing of God was being withdrawn from disobedient Israel, a 'perverse generation' (Acts 2:40), to be transferred to the Gentiles. Strangers unwelcome to the Jews had, as it were, entered into occupation.

In short, Paul indicates that a revived sign of judgement upon a disbelieving people should not be seen through charismatic rose-tinted spectacles solely as a sign of the grace poured out on the young churches. When the Corinthians praised God in innumerable languages they were showing beyond a shadow of doubt that the true Israel extends around the world. But they were also shaming Abraham's natural children for the latter's gross unbelief. Let the Corinthians exult, but not overmuch, in such an extraordinary gift.

In retrospect

The first Christian century witnessed the historic establishment of the Gentile churches and the dispersion of Israel. Because these events, marked by tongues-speaking, were milestones in what is for us the distant but not dim past, it is no surprise that the sign itself became redundant long ago. Before the Day of Pentecost no one, not even Christ or John the Baptist, spoke in tongues. All in all, it is perfectly reasonable to believe that following that event glossolalia appeared suddenly among Jewish and Gentile Christians in churches dotting the eastern Mediterranean seaboard, made itself heard in spectacular fashion for a few brief years, and just as abruptly obeyed the summons to depart.[78]

The effect of tongues upon visitors (14:22-25)

The principle laid down in 14:21 is applied in the following verse: **'So then tongues are for a sign, not to those who believe, but to unbelievers; but prophecy is for a sign, not to unbelievers, but to those who believe.'**

The Corinthians were saints, from which it followed that uninterpreted languages were not appropriate for their situation; the people needed intelligible prophecy to build them up. But tongues were designed to mean something to unbelievers. This was in spite of the fact that historically the sign had always been ineffective because of the spiritual blindness of those exposed to it. In past centuries Israel refused to perceive the judgement of God behind the invading armies, armies which were a word from God meant specifically for them.

This is why in 14:22 the apostle indicates that it must be like this at Corinth and elsewhere and why 14:21 remoulds the condemnation contained in the final part of Isaiah 28:12. The prophet's original 'but they would not listen' is now predictive: 'and even so they will not listen to me'.

Suppose that **'the whole church'** assembles, that **'all speak in tongues'** and that **'ordinary people'** and **'unbelievers'** join the congregation (14:23). Our imagination might well stagger at the thought of each person in a large fellowship speaking in other languages. Apparently, this was not an impossibility at Corinth. Perhaps Paul exaggerates, although it is unlikely. Because he always said what he meant and meant what he said, we need to accept his words at face value. What effect, asks the apostle, would this remarkable phenomenon have upon visitors?

We are told. As in Israel, similarly in Corinth; the wheel had turned full circle. Foreign languages in their profusion achieved then, and achieve now, nothing useful: **'Will they not say that you are mad?'** Unconverted visitors would discern neither the supernatural origin of tongues, nor the fact that they were true languages, nor their significance. Rather, they would attribute what they heard to the speakers' apparent mental imbalance. Of course, this appreciation would reflect negatively upon the visitors for whom the gift was meant to say something rather than upon tongues and their exponents. But for Paul the needs of the unconverted visitors came first.

The situation changes dramatically if all prophesy and an individual unbeliever or ordinary person enters. What he hears are

Spiritual gifts (12:1 - 14:40)

inspired words from God himself, words that concern his own personal situation and, most important of all, words that he understands (14:24).

'He is convicted by all, he is assessed by all.' Compare with 2:15, 'The spiritual man appraises all things,' and with the prediction of John 16:8 concerning the Holy Spirit: 'He ... will convict the world concerning sin, and righteousness and judgement.' Remember 6:2: 'The world is judged by you.' At Corinth the visitor learns about God and about himself through the ministry of Spirit-filled Christians. It is as if he realizes that he has been condemned by a court of law. He is ashamed of himself.

Paul teaches that prophecy is hugely significant for someone who is not a Christian, at least, not when he enters the assembly. How can this be if, as 14:22 asserts, prophecy can mean nothing to such people? The probable answer is that the visiting unbeliever would not be quite in the sad situation of apostate Israel in Isaiah's day, or like the hostile Jews in the first century A.D. His presence in the Christian assembly demonstrates a degree of personal interest, perhaps a measure of sympathy. Although tongues remain a meaningless nonsense, prophecy might well speak to someone not entirely hardened.

That this is the case is suggested by 14:25: **'The secrets of his heart are disclosed.'** The man prostrates himself, worships and acknowledges that **'God is certainly among you.'** When he wrote these words the apostle might have remembered what he did when the Lord revealed himself to him on the Damascus road: he fell to the ground (Acts 9:4; 22:7; 26:14).

There is an allusion in 14:25 to Isaiah 45:14, and possibly to Zechariah 8:23. Both are Messianic. Isaiah portrays Egypt, Ethiopia and the Sabeans, the last possibly an African nation, seeking admission to Israel. They desire this because they know now that God is with his people. Zechariah's prophecy is similar. For the apostle, what was predicted centuries before is coming to fruition. Once again the fellowship at Corinth is seen as a representative of the expanding, Messianic Israel.

Concluding directions for the conduct of worship (14:26-40)

Having concentrated upon various aspects of congregational worship, chapters 11-14 now end with applications of the principles laid down. The church is to take into account the need for order, the true role of women, the fact that apostolic teaching is authoritative, and that tongues are of limited value.

Tongues, interpretation and prophecy (14:26-33a)

These verses are important because they shed considerable light on how an early Christian church was supposed to conduct its worship.

Notice that mention is made of a plurality of prophets (14:29,31-32). There must have been elders in charge, even though we never read about them in the Corinthian letters. Acts 14:23, Philippians 1:1 and Titus 1:5 show that elders, or overseers/bishops, were appointed in each church where Paul had an interest, and it is inconceivable that it should not have been so at Corinth. But in this part of chapter 14 the apostle is concerned with the regulation of inspired speech rather than with leadership.

'**What is the outcome then, brethren?**' (14:26). As in 14:15, the Corinthians are required to apply what has been said. '**When you assemble**', or 'are assembling', implies a routine of worship currently shaping itself into a definite pattern.

1. The church first (14:26-27)

It is acknowledged that many, perhaps all, of the Corinthians were gifted. Because '**each one has**' something from the Lord every member should contribute (14:26). A teaching would be the exposition of some truth and a revelation would be an entirely new message to and through a prophet. The guiding principle is that everything must be done with a view to the edification of the fellowship, to the extent that even if an individual felt himself being moved by the Spirit the good of the church remained more important than his own proper desire for self-expression.

In any particular gathering of the church only two or at the most three persons are permitted to exercise their gifts (14:27). Further, they speak in succession, not simultaneously, and each tongue is to be given an immediate interpretation. There is no delay. Apparently, one person only, either a tongue-speaker or someone else, is authorized to interpret for the group of two or three.[79]

2. Self-control (14:28-32)

The tongue-speaker is assumed to be completely self-controlled, able to speak or to remain silent as he desires. No man may claim afterwards that he had to speak because he was impelled by the Holy Spirit against his will.

Secondly, the maximum permitted number of contributions approaches vanishing point (again, three at the most). The intended implication is that speaking in tongues was of strictly limited importance.

Should there be no interpreter, the tongue-speaker has to be **'silent in the church'**; he must control himself although he is permitted to speak in his heart **'to himself and to God'** (14:28). Yet again it is assumed that in tongues-speaking the mind and tongue were co-ordinated, the speaker knowing exactly what he said.

The procedure is the same for the prophets (14:29): two or three at the most are allowed to speak. Although more important than tongues, prophecy is not deemed to be all-important. **'The others'** are required to **'discern'**.

We need to consider 'the others' and to establish why discernment was necessary. We know from 12:10 that the capacity to distinguish spirits was a gift other than prophecy. According to Deuteronomy 18:20-22, the whole congregation of Israel was required to test prophetic utterances. By analogy, it might be that the Corinthian assembly is instructed to assess prophecies. 1 John 4:1 appears to back this up: 'Test the spirits to see whether they are from God; because many false prophets have gone out into the world.'

But if we bear in mind 12:1-3 and the reference to the possible anathematizing of Jesus, it might be asked if a large and somewhat immature church would have been in a position to make a responsible assessment? Because the context focuses here upon prophecy it might be better to consider 'the others' as other prophets. If so, the principle is that individual prophetic utterances were not to be accepted uncritically by those who were gifted in this way.

That the Holy Spirit was active in an extraordinary fashion at Corinth, and presumably elsewhere, is demonstrated by 14:30. When one prophet was delivering an inspired utterance (by implication, in a standing posture), another seated prophet might have been given a **'revelation'**. Undoubtedly the latter would have indicated that the Spirit had disclosed something to him. When this happened the prophet already speaking must **'keep silent'**.

Here we have a truly amazing scene in which it was by no means unusual for numerous revelations and inspired utterances to burst upon a single church meeting. Since the age of the apostles there has, surely, never been anything remotely like this. But there does not need to be. The Bible, which is all prophecy and beyond which there is no prophecy, expects and deserves neither addition nor subtraction. Revelation 22:19 makes this plain. Based upon Deuteronomy 4:2 and 12:32, it practically places the Apocalypse and other Christian writings on a level with the law of Moses.

The prophets were prohibited from speaking simultaneously because there was no necessity for such a confusing procedure: **'For you can all prophesy one by one'** (14:31). Each of the maximum number of three prophets has his opportunity to unburden himself of all that the Lord told him. And there is a grand reason for this way of doing things: **'so that all may learn and all may be exhorted'**. Nothing that the Lord had revealed need fall to the ground. Notice, too, the present tenses: because learning and encouragement are always necessary this is how matters are to continue as long as immediate and local prophecy endures.

The apostle shows that his regulations are practical as well as desirable: **'And the spirits of the prophets are subject to the prophets'** (14:32). When they deliver their messages the prophets are never taken beyond themselves by God so that they rant and rage uncontrollably. Rather, they are well able to govern themselves.

3. Heathen and Christian prophecy

In this crucial respect these inspired people were quite unlike, say, the Philippian slave-girl of Acts 16:16 who had 'a spirit of Python'. The latter was a mythical serpent slain by Apollo, the god for whom she allegedly spoke when in a trance. Far from the girl being in control of the spirit, it dominated her, although not for long. In fulfilment of the promise of our Lord (Luke 10:20), the spirit submitted to Paul.

It seems that mental imbalance was accepted generally as part and parcel of Gentile 'prophecy'. Four centuries earlier, Plato wrote that the inspiration of the prophetess at Delphi was a type of divine madness. He even claimed that no one could utter divinations when he was in his right mind, but only when his intelligence was chained up, perhaps by disease or by some form of divine inspiration. Cicero described prophecy as a state of frenzy (Latin, *furor*) in which the soul abandoned reason. Plutarch insisted that predictive prophecy was essentially 'irrational' (Greek, *alogon*) although the voice heard by others was the prophet's. 'Irrational', an emotive word, occurs in 2 Peter 2:12 and Jude 10 in their descriptions of animals as senseless, and in Acts 25:27 in connection with the absurdity of sending Paul to Caesar for no good reason.[80]

The apostle must have been well aware of how the world summed up its mad prophets, and he outlines with careful precision the phenomenon of genuine utterances given by God. In 14:32 it is clear that the reference cannot possibly be to evil spirits nor, in all probability, to the Holy Spirit. The 'spirits' would almost certainly have been the human spirits of the prophets. Compare with 14:15: 'I shall pray with the spirit.' On the other hand, Hodge argues powerfully that 'the spirits' must have been manifestations of the Holy Spirit, who cannot strive with himself. This approach cannot be entirely ruled out.[81]

4. The Lord's paths are peaceful (14:33a)

If, as seems likely, 14:32 refers to the human spirits of the prophets, the apostle has in mind inspired men and women who conclude prematurely that their urge to speak out should not be discouraged. Their favoured tactic would be the pre-emptive strike: because something had been laid upon their hearts by the Lord they just have to stand up. Not so, claims Paul; the Lord never deprives his servants of self-control, not even when their words are genuinely God-breathed.

This is backed up by 14:33a: **'For God is not a God of confusion, but of peace.'** A number of overlapping prophecies, each given by inspiration, become jumbled and unintelligible, in our terms something like the effect of several taped sermons being played at the same time. In such a situation the speakers would sound like a group of chattering monkeys having their Christmas party. Apparently it was sometimes like this in Corinth. Paul's point is that disorder has to be wrong because the Lord is never confused and never confuses. Rather, he delights in tranquillity. It is just so, we recall, with marriage: God has called Christians to live in peace (7:15).

The silence of women in church worship (14:33b-36)

The apostle draws his remarks almost to a close in 14:33b with **'as in all the churches of the saints'**. Either these words conclude 14:26-33a, dealing with the exercise of tongues and prophecies, or they lead into 14:34-36. Two reasons, at least, suggest that it is better to take them in the second sense. First, the observation that God is the God of peace (14:33a) is an adequate conclusion to 14:26-33a. Secondly, the reference to other churches would parallel 11:16 within a context also concerning women.

Paul was anxious to show that ladies were to be **'silent in the churches'** and were **'to subject themselves'** (14:34). That he wrote to one church, Corinth, concerning women in 'the churches' suggests that this particular fellowship was influential and had a responsibility to care for others. Or, which is more likely, the apostle intended this letter to be circulated because he wanted his instructions to be accepted everywhere.

Three reasons are given for the silence of women. First, as stated by 14:33b, this was the prevailing custom in the emerging churches. Secondly, **'It is not permitted'** (by apostolic authority). The *Textus Receptus* gives 'has not been allowed to them [other churches]', which means that the restriction, by no means an innovation, was of some long standing and remained in force. Third, this prohibition is **'just as the Law also says'**.

Questions arise. How can church custom be binding? The answer must be that the anonymous fellowships mentioned by Paul were good examples because they honoured his instructions. Further, does the apostle refer to married women, or to all women? The answer would be that he takes into account all women, as does 'the Law', his original authority.

According to 11:3-16 women are to cover their heads. This is because of the order prescribed by Genesis 3:16 where Eve was informed that Adam would rule over her. In chapter 14 it becomes evident that the uncovered head is not the only way in which a woman can subvert the order laid down in Genesis. She is able to achieve role-reversal, and with good effect, by taking charge in church. In order to assume command she must raise her voice, and it is this which Paul finds objectionable.

The reason for his prohibition is that in the fellowship the men are meant to lead and the women to follow. Therefore if a woman,

Spiritual gifts (12:1 - 14:40)

whoever she might be, is heard submissively by men, the order of Genesis collapses and disorder triumphs. Compare this with 1 Timothy 2:11-15 and Titus 2:5.

What is meant when Paul denies women the opportunity to speak, or even to raise questions in the assembly? Does the apostolic ban extend to women preachers? What, for example, of women reading the Bible in public? What about open prayer, or prophecy, or subordinate leadership-roles assumed by women?

Hodge admits that women were endowed with the gift of prophecy but insists that within Paul's sphere of influence they were never permitted to exercise their charisma in public.[82] Consistently with this view he denies that women should pray openly in modern churches. Many of us would, with respect, disagree strongly.

First, 11:5 refers to women praying and prophesying, presumably in the church. The whole section, 11:2-34, is set within a major division of the letter (11:2 - 14:40) concerning itself entirely and exclusively with congregational worship. To limit 11:5 to private prayer, as Hodge does, seems artificial. Apparently, Paul assumes that women do pray and prophesy in the assembly.

Secondly, although the Law insisted that the woman should be governed by the man, there were prophetesses. They appear, too, in the New Testament.[83] How would these inspired saints have been perceived to be prophetesses if their words remained unknown and unrecognized by the people of God? The reality is that their utterances were often placed on record for the benefit of all; God spoke through them as well as through their male counterparts. And even when there was no lasting, written record of their declarations they must have exercised an immediate and local ministry to both women *and* men; we do not read about women prophesying for the benefit of women only. It transpires that in neither the Old nor the New Testament is the proper submission of women to men held to be incompatible with such participation. Nor does 1 Timothy 2:12 issue such a ban.

'If they desire to learn anything, let them ask their own husbands at home' (14:35). The concern is with self-assertion, not with prayer and prophecy. If married women have questions about the content of an interpretation or of a revelation they should ask their husbands to explain matters to them privately. Their silence shows their holy subordination: **'For it is improper for a woman to speak in church.'** This is a dramatic assertion: if a woman strains to make her voice heard in the meeting she behaves indecently.

A robust challenge is thrown out: **'Was it from you that the word of God first went forth? Or, has it come to you only?'** (14:36). Apostolic irony is undisguised. The Corinthians cannot really believe that they are the mother church of Christendom, holding what they imagine is a patent to define and declare the gospel. Paul knows that if, for the sake of the argument, they had been the original assembly, even so they would possess no legislative authority any more than did the Jerusalem church in the crucial matter of the terms of admission of Gentile converts (Acts 15:23-29). They must realize, too, that they were not the only church that had ever received the truth, a principle already brought to light in 11:16. Because this is how matters stand they must listen.

Women in leadership roles

It appears that 14:34 prohibits any activity that places a woman in a leadership role in the church. This would include the pastoral ministry and its associated activities, the office of elder, occasional or regular preaching and teaching in the assembly, and even the public reading of the Bible. But it would not prevent women from being servants ('deacons') in their churches. Phoebe was one such (Rom. 16:1), and 1 Timothy 3:11 probably refers to ladies who were given office in Timothy's pastorate. Nor is there anything to prevent women from giving reports to church meetings, recording minutes or taking part in open prayer. Experience shows that the last is especially valuable and often a means of blessing for a fellowship. Women, like men, are unable to prophesy, the reason being that the gift is no longer with us.

What about women priests? Quite apart from the fact that women should never be appointed as ministers of the gospel, the notion begs the question of a separate, ordained priesthood in the churches. The truth is that no one should ever accept the title 'priest' because Christ is exclusively the great High Priest of all his redeemed people. As the letter to the Hebrews teaches eloquently, we neither possess nor need another. This being so, it is not easy to agree with evangelical episcopalians that a clerical priest is no more than a presbyter or elder.[84]

Sectarianism

In Paul's time the Corinthian congregation suffered from overweening delusions of grandeur. Since then there have been other triumphal churches, the most august being Rome. Because the papacy has always asserted that it is competent to define the received faith it is in the tragic situation condemned by 14:36. But very early church history shows that authority to establish doctrine was never the property of any one communion, part of the reason being the congregational order of the churches. In particular, what Christians held to be true never depended upon ecclesiastical or conciliar imposition. It is surely this species of megalomania that distinguishes the sects from the saints. A sect is a group, large or small, ancient or modern, that makes itself out to be the sole purveyor of truth. The Jehovah's Witnesses and the Mormons are two recent exponents of the error. Evangelical churches never think like this.

Paul's authority (14:37-40)

The apostle tells the Corinthians that his instructions are binding upon the churches. Even though his word might be unpalatable, the prophets at Corinth must recognize it.

Although he does not say as much, Paul virtually places himself in the situation of Moses *vis-à-vis* Aaron, Miriam and the other prophets of Israel in the wilderness (Num. 12:6-8). He realizes that he participates in the generation of a written body of revelation that will overtake and eventually replace the ad hoc and unrecorded prophecies welling up within the emerging churches. This ties up precisely with chapter 13, which anticipates the early disappearance of unwritten prophecy in favour of 'the perfect thing'.

That women were actually speaking out in the Corinthian assembly is suggested by 14:37, where it is acknowledged that some of the saints probably differed from the apostle on the matter. Considering themselves as prophets or, at the least, as spiritual people, they were extraordinarily reluctant to show Paul the respect due to his office.

Let such folk recognize that **'The things which I write to you are the Lord's commandment.'** Although this assertion refers back to chapters 11-14 and the subject of orderly worship, there is no need to restrict it to this one matter only. In all probability 14:37 takes the whole letter into account, including chapters 15 and 16;

everything that Paul writes is nothing less than a single, unified 'commandment' from Jesus. If the reading of the *Textus Receptus*, 'commandments', is original the sense remains the same. Therefore the Corinthians must give strict attention to the complete epistle. It would hardly be possible to make a more explicit and emphatic claim to full inspiration and infallibility. We are surely allowed to draw our own conclusion about how Paul estimated his words.

Even so, the apostle was less than confident that everybody in Corinth would take to heart what he said: **'But if a person is ignorant, let him be ignored'** (or, perhaps, 'let him make himself ignorant', 14:38). Refusing to argue with anyone who spurns his apostolic authority, Paul courteously informs the dissident that he may leave. These genteel words are a diplomatic but quite definite 'Be gone!'

The present tenses of 14:39 bring to the fore the need for the church to remain in the habit of distinguishing between prophecy and tongues. A more literal translation than that given in the NASB may help to bring out the neat verb-object/object-verb sequence employed in differentiating between the two gifts. The turn of phrase is masterly: **'Therefore, my brethren, desire earnestly to prophesy, and to speak in tongues do not forbid.'**

Joshua had used this harsh word 'forbid' when complaining to Moses about the prophets Eldad and Medad in the camp of Israel (Num.11:28). Paul has alluded to this already (14:5). It is probable that he does so again at this point: like Joshua, the Corinthians must not forbid God-given prophecy. In effect, the exposition of chapters 13-14 concerning both the appreciation and the abuse of spiritual gifts is based almost completely upon the precedent set by Numbers 11 and 12.

Far from the Corinthians' enthusiasm for charismata being restrained, they are urged to yearn for the gift of prophecy. The apostle repeats 12:31 and 14:1, 'desire earnestly', although a shade more explicitly.

He concludes. **'All things'** are to be **'done properly'** (literally, to be 'well-formed') and **'in an orderly manner'** (14:40). When the people worship their God there must be dignity and harmony.

Modern 'tongues-speaking'

William Samarin, in his comprehensive and sympathetic study of modern tongues-speaking, has been a formative influence in my

Spiritual gifts (12:1 - 14:40)

attempt to come to terms with Pentecostalism. Samarin claims that the average Pentecostal or charismatic 'tongue' is essentially non-language, even pseudolanguage, rather than a supernatural phenomenon. Equally, he would maintain that glossolalia cannot be gibberish. Rather, upon careful examination modern tongues-speaking turns out to be exactly similar to other speech-patterns occurring in more or less normal circumstances.

The justification for his negative appreciation is that the so-called 'tongue' is nothing other than a random but not irrational interweaving of elements of previously learned language(s), an interweaving that is inevitably and invariably deliberate. He believes that anyone can indulge in this sort of 'speech' if he is uninhibited.

Samarin concludes that although contemporary speaking in tongues is not inspired, it is definitely not the product of psychological imbalance, far less of demon possession.[85] To illustrate his meaning, the practice would be akin to a comedian imitating the accents and syllables of a language that for him remains foreign. But what he says might come across to the naïve listener as the real thing. All it amounts to is an entertainment, a man babbling skilfully in an amusing but deliberately disorganized fashion. Someone acquainted with the genuine language would know.

If these findings are valid, modern tongues-speaking might appear to be a shallow, fake imitation of the miraculous gift mentioned in Acts and 1 Corinthians, and a poor fake at that. It goes without saying that it could not be a blessing from God the Holy Spirit.

May one be yet more vile? Perhaps there are not a few modern tongues-speakers who find themselves in the unfortunate situation of Hans Christian Anderson's fairy-tale emperor, a splendour-seeking monarch who was offered some very special robes for an important procession. His avaricious weavers made out that the material for these golden garments was so fine that it was virtually transparent, and so light that one could not weigh it. The king's vanity was tickled. Deluding himself that he could see through the fabric yet declining to see through the trick, he placed an expensive order. In the event the procession set off even though the robes did not exist. Nor would the monarch hide himself when a child in the crowd let out that he was unclothed and when all the townsfolk jeered.

Sometimes Christians are *so* complicated. We press on regardless even when we are unhappy about the procession.

9. The resurrection of the body
(15:1-58)

Paul turns to a completely different subject, the doctrine of the resurrection of the body. In Corinth the matter was no less controversial and serious than the numerous questions addressed already.

Some within the church held that it was impossible for the bodies of the dead to come alive again. Had the anti-resurrectionists desired a slogan, 'Once in the grave, always in the grave,' might have suited them. Their sullen conviction clashed violently with Paul's preaching, and they knew it. So did he.

These people were heretics, although the apostle did not raise the temperature by labelling them in this way. Perhaps he had them in mind when he penned 11:19: 'There must be factions among you.' Nor do we know if they had worked out the overall implications of their denial, yet had elected to keep a low profile. Perhaps they were not clever enough to see the downward path along which they were dragging others as well as themselves. Again, we cannot tell.

Nor does it matter. What is important is that sympathy for the heralds of eternal death is said to be misplaced. The apostle was convinced that deviant doctrine is never well-meaning and that it is usually strident, as witness the reproachful **'you say'** in 15:12; these people made no pretence of trying to guard the church. Paul does not pull his punches, and the drastic consequences of their denial of the resurrection of the body are spelled out in considerable detail.

It was perfectly obvious to the apostle, and probably to the sceptics, that the doctrine of the resurrection of the dead was vital. It was not the case that both parties, orthodox and heretical, could share in dialogue to hammer out some sort of compromise in order

The resurrection of the body (15:1-58)

to bolster a superficial church unity. Truth and error were engaging in mortal combat. Paul knew that the anti-resurrection faction in the church was waging total war against him, against his message, against his mission, against all Christians and ultimately against the risen Christ. Here was no sincere disagreement among brethren about some lesser issue. Whatever they thought, and whatever others thought about them, these people were far from being misguided souls devoted to the Lord. They were evil (15:33-34).

We do not know the names of these purveyors of error. Possibly they were, like Hymenaeus and Alexander, converts of Greek extraction who remained too fond of the world (2 Tim. 2:17-18). If so, this could have been their real reason for attacking the faith. But identities are irrelevant. One issue was all-important: that the good news of the risen and triumphant Saviour be restated, defended and applied. This is the burden of chapter 15.

The Sadducees also denied the same great truth (Matt. 22:23; Mark 12:18; Luke 20:27; Acts 23:8). But the immense difference between the Jewish sceptics and these Corinthian heretics was that the latter had been baptized; with their lips they had acknowledged the risen Saviour and had joined the church at Corinth. To repeat, 15:12 reads 'you say', not 'they say'. These people must have made a confession something like that of Romans 10:9: 'If you confess with your mouth Jesus as Lord, and believe in your heart that God raised him from the dead, you shall be saved.' How could they remain within the community of the risen Christ, yet blatantly deny the possibility of resurrection? Not only were they in error; they were grossly hypocritical.

This great chapter might be said to fall into three principal divisions. First, the apostle recalls events that demonstrated beyond all doubt that the Lord Jesus rose from the dead (15:1-11). Secondly, he shows that the resurrection of Christ is indispensable to his preaching; it *is* the gospel. In more detail, if Christ rose from the dead there can be no logical objection to belief in the ultimate bodily resurrection of every believer; the former anticipates the latter and is its pattern (15:12-34). Thirdly, the nature of the resurrection body is discussed, although specific details are not given; curiosity remains unsatisfied. Stale old arguments often levelled against the resurrection are shown to be unreasonable. This being so, the sceptics are not to be believed (15:35-58).

The historic resurrection (15:1-11)

Paul knows that Christ rose from the dead because the risen Lord explained the good news to him, an action beyond the capacity of a dead man. Moreover, many others saw Jesus in his risen glory during the interval of time after his death and before he ascended to heaven.

Jesus: Lord and Teacher (15:1-4)

The apostle introduces the discussion by explaining how he had received the message he proclaimed. There is no logical connection between this new chapter and chapters 1-14; the little word **'now'** (Greek, *de*, 'but', 15:1) leads into a quite new subject.

'I make known to you' might be a gentle rebuke, as if the Corinthians, who had heard Paul often, did not really understand the gospel even though they had **'received'** it from his lips. On the other hand, as in 12:3 and elsewhere, the formula might introduce a subject of exceptional importance.

Very good news (15:1-2)

The apostle was convinced that his preaching brought nothing but good to men. This is emphasized deliberately by the repetition of **'gospel'**, both as noun and verb. 'Gospel' (Greek, *euaggelion*, pronounced 'evangelion') is a precious word which literally means 'good message': **'the good message with which I evangelized you'**. The truth underlining Paul's word-selection is that the resurrection is good news, and nothing but good news, and that without it all is gloom.

Not only had the Corinthians received this truth; they now **'stand'** in it. The message that Jesus rose from the dead has become the permanent foundation of their lives: Christ lives for them and they live for Christ. Paul can say this because he is aware that only some of those within the church deny the doctrine.

Moreover, it is **'by'** this gospel that the Corinthians **'are saved'**, that is to say, are being carried along by a rescue process. The tense is present continuous, and we could compare with 1:18: 'to us who are being saved'. Elsewhere in his letters Paul insists both that believers are in principle already saved *and* that their final salvation lies in the future (e.g., Eph. 2:5,8; Rom. 5:9,10; 8:24). Redemption is a matter of yesterday, today, tomorrow and eternity.

Here, salvation is described as incomplete because all depends on whether or not professing believers are prepared to hold on to the apostolic message. A lifeline cannot save those who after a time let it go deliberately. In spite of the tremendous spiritual peril in which they were placing themselves, a peril that they probably did not appreciate, some Corinthians were slackening their grip. They allowed themselves to be deluded into believing that the apostolic line was, in truth, rotten. Suppose, Paul implies, that the heretics were right. Suppose that he was a charlatan. Suppose that the doctrine of Jesus' resurrection was a bluff, a key element in a perverse confidence trick.

In this situation the Corinthians would have **'believed in vain'**. Paul is subtly ironic: they should not have listened to him in the first place. In doing so they were dragging themselves towards eternal ruin rather than salvation. Because this evaluation is important it is repeated in 15:14: 'If Christ has not been raised ... your faith also is vain.'

The apostle does no more than hypothesize; he concedes nothing. The Corinthians had not been deceived — at least, not by him. If, then, they were to discard the authorized gospel in favour of those who proposed error they really would be lost. Notice that good news is mentioned again for emphasis in 15:2, **'through which you also are being saved ... the word which I evangelized you'**. A challenge is being thrown out: the Corinthians reject the apostolic message at their peril. What could be more foolish? The scorners and all who give ear to them are being scorned.

Fundamental truths (15:3-4)

The people are reminded that their apostle delivered to them matters of **'first importance'**, truths he personally received from a supreme authority. 'First importance' in the NASB is a good translation because it signifies 'principal things' rather than 'first of all' — the latter implying a ministry that would have been in some sense a chronological first.[1] As is clear from Acts, the gospel had been delivered to many others before ever it came to Corinth. Further, as in 11:23 and Galatians 1:12 ('For I neither received it from man, nor was I taught it'), Paul insists that he had not contrived his good news; he had never been more than an accurate relay for what he received from Christ.

This is astounding. Everything he told the people about the cross was handed over to him by the Lord. Obviously, a dead Saviour could not communicate. Therefore, Jesus must have been raised from the dead. Because this is how it was, the apostle can proceed to define the core and kernel of his evangel and lead into a record of some of the appearances of the risen Christ.

To die **'for'** sins means that Christ gave up his life for the benefit of sinners.[2] Although the concept of substitution is not explicit here, it is implicit and undeniable. The claim is then made that what happened to Christ and what the Lord explained to the apostle were all **'according to the Scriptures'**; apostolic preaching about Jesus was true because, exactly like the ministry and sufferings of the Saviour, it had its roots in the sure word of Old Testament prophecy.[3]

Further, the living Lord confirmed to Paul personally that he had been buried and that his resurrection occurred three days after death, all according to the Scriptures. Why, it might be asked, the three-day time-lapse? And were the three days predicted specifically by the Old Testament?

Quite apart from the experience of Jonah, a shadow of the Christ who would be the Saviour of the world,[4] the historic three-day interval between death and resurrection demonstrated two truths. First, it proved that Jesus was not taken down unconscious from the cross; he actually expired and was then buried. Paul's words are emphatic: **'Christ died'**. It is as if the apostle anticipated that men would teach otherwise, as has been the case. The Koran (*Sura Al-Nisa*, 4:157-8) maintains that Jesus swooned upon the tree and was revived later: 'They declared: "We have put to death the Messiah, Jesus the son of Mary, the apostle of God." They did not kill him, nor did they crucify him, but they thought they did.'

Secondly, had the Lord remained in the tomb for a longer period, his body must have suffered corruption. Martha was sure that decomposition was well advanced when her brother Lazarus had been in his tomb no more than four days (John 11:39). God did not permit this to happen to Christ (Ps. 16:10; Acts 2:27,31; 13:34-35). In principle as well as in detail, the Old Testament anticipated the three-day interval affirmed by the Lord to Paul.

As elsewhere, the interment of Jesus is associated somewhat more closely with his resurrection than with his death: **'He was buried ... he was raised.'** That is, the tomb was not so much a grave as a cradle, even a womb, a theatre of life (cf. Ps. 2:7; 16:11; 89:27; Acts 2:26-27; 13:33).

The statement that our Lord **'was raised'** (or, 'has been raised'; Greek, *egegertai*, perfect passive from *egeirô*) occurs again in this chapter six times, always with reference to Jesus (15:12,13,14,16, 17,20). With some rare exceptions (Matt. 11:11; Mark 6:14; 2 Tim. 2:8), the expression occurs nowhere else in the New Testament.

The intentional significance of Paul's 'has been raised' is that the living Christ remains in a state of what could be termed 'risenness': what happened early in the garden tomb was not, cannot, and will not be reversed. The truth is driven home vigorously that he whom God raised from the dead is by definition the *risen* Saviour. Therefore he is Lord of all.

Historic witnesses (15:5-11)

The apostle shows that Christ must have been raised from the dead because after his burial he was seen alive by a large number of people. Corpses lying in their graves neither talk nor walk.

Christ's appearances before the ascension (15:5-7)

Paul's list of witnesses is chronological, **'then'** occurring no less than four times, although not comprehensive. We can only speculate why the appearances to the women, or even to Stephen, are unmentioned (Matt. 28:5-7; Mark 16:9; John 20:14-18; Acts 7:56). Perhaps the apostle restricts himself to witnesses who were accessible when he wrote the letter: if asked, they would have been able and willing to verify the resurrection. The apostle's argument seems to be that because the raising of Jesus is beyond all dispute and capable of confirmation through a little diligent research, the sceptics must be perverse.

First, the Lord **'was seen by Cephas'** and then **'by the twelve'** (15:5).[5] 'Seen by' emphasizes that men who were in Jerusalem when Jesus died were granted a sight of him soon after his decease; he revealed himself to them deliberately rather than being by coincidence where they were. The number twelve must be ideal, standing for the whole college of the apostles: even though there were only eleven of them at the time, Judas being dead, Jesus was seen by those who would establish his church.

Afterwards the Lord was seen by **'more than five hundred brethren at one time'** (15:6). Although no record about this is given either in the Gospels or in Acts, the sequence of the narrative shows that the event occurred after Jesus was seen by Peter on the evening of the first day of the week but before James saw him (15:7). We may conclude safely that the James mentioned here was the brother of Jesus and that this meeting was the occasion when he passed from obstinate unbelief to humble faith, as can be inferred by a comparison between John 7:5 and Acts 1:14. He soon became one of the principal leaders in the Jerusalem church.[6]

Paul insists that **'most'** of the five hundred who saw the risen Saviour were alive as he was writing the letter. 1 Corinthians was written over twenty-five years after Christ rose, and during this interval the five hundred must have testified repeatedly about the resurrection of their Lord. How could they forget it? The apostle is saying in effect that such an accumulation of reliable testimony cannot be shrugged off by certain clever Corinthians. They should consult these men; there is still time because most of them **'remain until now'**; the Lord had permitted the majority twenty years or so to encourage the infant churches.

But some of the five hundred had **'fallen asleep'**, by which is meant that they were believers (unbelievers die; believers fall asleep).[7] Notice that the risen Lord appeared exclusively to disciples, refusing to expose himself to a world that would have ridiculed him even in his glory.[8]

Following the appearance to James, the Lord **'was seen ... by all the apostles'**. The reference could be to the day of ascension (Acts 1:2-10). Yet again, the eleven who survived to see Christ might be considered ideally as the representatives of those whom he would send. Or does Paul refer to them and to Matthias (Acts 1:21-26), a man who saw Jesus alive from the dead before he was appointed the twelfth apostle in place of Judas Iscariot? This interpretation would avoid a needless restatement of 15:5 concerning 'the twelve'.

The resurrection of the body (15:1-58)

Five years later: Christ's appearance to Paul (15:8-10)

Finally, the Lord manifested himself to the apostle: **'And last of all, as it were to one untimely born, he was seen also by me'** (15:8). The ex-Pharisee confesses that he had seen the living Jesus with his own eyes some five years, no less (about A.D. 34), after the historic resurrection. The apostle was deeply conscious that as time goes by Christ remains a risen Saviour.

'Last of all' could mean either that Paul was the last of the apostles, or that he was the last man to see the Lord. The second view is difficult because in later years the apostle John was to see Christ (Rev. 1:17). But perhaps Paul indicates that he was the last person to whom the Lord revealed himself specifically to prove that he had risen from the dead. This would fit with Acts 26:16, where the apostle recalls what Christ said to him years before: 'For this purpose I have appeared to you, to appoint you a minister and a witness.' Either way, the conversion of Saul remains without parallel in that there is no record of the risen, ascended and glorified Christ ever appearing to anyone else in order to generate faith. Perhaps there was no other occasion. Perhaps Paul is claiming that his conversion experience was as unique as it was remarkable. For this reason the Corinthians ought to hear him.

In the Greek Old Testament the word for **'untimely born'** *(ektrôma)* signifies a stillborn baby, or a foetus ejected prematurely because it is dead. It also stands for a premature child who survives but whose appearance is scarcely human.[9] The latter is probably the sense here. In describing himself in such a dramatic fashion Paul may mean either, or both, of two things.

First, he became an apostle without the months and years of experience and instruction given to the earlier apostles. Think again about Matthias. He received his office because he had been loyal to the Lord during the three-year ministry and because he had seen the risen Saviour (Acts 1:3,21-26).

It was not like this for Saul of Tarsus. A matter of hours, or even minutes, before Christ appeared to him the Jew was filled with a fanatical hatred for the disciples. A few days after his renewal by the Spirit and baptism, he was proclaiming Jesus as the Son of God (Acts 9:1-20). In this respect the transformation was like a premature birth.

Secondly, until the time when the Pharisee came to know the Lord he was a moral monstrosity. His personality had been deformed by malice. In later years he never forgot what he used to be, as is made plain by Galatians 1:13, Philippians 3:6 and 1 Timothy 1:13,16. For this reason Paul, the last man to be made an apostle, believed that he remained the **'least'** in dignity among his colleagues (15:9). Further, he did not accept that he was **'fit to be called an apostle'**, a statement that demands attention.

Paul was always conscious of his authoritative position, and in 1 Corinthians he makes it plain that in a demanding situation he would be ready to exercise his office.[10] Even so, he felt that he should never have been granted this status, the reason being that he **'persecuted the church of God'**. This negative appreciation is evidently not an implied criticism of the wisdom of God in calling him. All he means is that, as he saw it, the sin of being an arch-foe of the churches had become a permanent stigma.

'But' Paul had come to be what he was **'by the grace of God'** (15:10). The unmerited favour of God was not **'vain'** (or 'empty'). It was full, full of power to transform Saul of Tarsus into the apostle to the Gentiles. The direct consequence of this transformation was that over the years he had **'laboured even more than all of them'**. 'Labour' means hard, toiling work, as in 4:12: 'We toil, working with our own hands.'

This assertion is extraordinary. Each apostle, no doubt, worked hard. Paul does not imply anything else. Nor is he a megalomaniac when he claims that his exertions had far outstripped the combined toil of all the others. Confessedly, because each had done so much, their joint labours must have been immense. For all that, in contrast to Paul's endeavours, their mountain of hard, grinding toil displayed the magnitude of a molehill.

Even the excellency of his labours was no ground for self-esteem; the apostle qualifies himself immediately: **'yet not I, but the grace of God with me'**. 'Grace' is mentioned no less than three times in 15:10. First, Paul shows that his office and message had been backed up by his own consistent hard work even though he was dust. Secondly, even his capacity for toil derived from God; in hindsight there was nothing that he could say he had achieved in his own strength. Because God had called him and had used him, what he proclaims about the death and resurrection of Jesus must be given the utmost respect.

These principles are permanently relevant. If you are a minister of the gospel, work as hard as possible for the Lord; do not urge your people from behind. If you are not known to be laborious your flock might be disinclined to hear you. Even so, there is more to the ministry than diligence; neither is work everything, nor is it the chief thing. Do not sacrifice prayer for perspiration. Pace yourself and learn how to worship awhile. Always take your shoes off in the presence of the Angel before you contemplate your assault upon the next Jericho (Josh. 5:15). Because the law of diminishing returns operates among the Lord's people as well as elsewhere we often achieve more when we attempt less. If and when we have achieved we realize that it was he, not we, who succeeded.

The message, not the messenger, is vital (15:11)

Paul's office and situation were unique but his message was not. **'Whether'** is depreciatory, as in 3:22 and 13:8. The apostles, 'whether' Paul or the others (**'they'**), speak with one voice: the message is all-important whereas the identities of the preachers are irrelevant. It had been through more than one minister of the gospel that **'you'**, the Corinthians, **'believed'**. If some rejected the truth of physical resurrection they clashed with all the apostles, men who had seen Christ (15:5,7). Therefore the situation of the minority sceptics was anomalous; they were misfits in the church of God. They ought to have taken this into account.

Recapitulation

Before continuing, let's sum up the apostle's four reasons why the Corinthian waverers needed to give attention to his message.

First, Paul had been exposed to a marvellous medium of revelation: Jesus came to the persecutor and explained his death and resurrection.

Secondly, there had been a marvellous transformation: the risen Christ made a new man of the wretched Saul of Tarsus and did it in a moment.

Third, the Lord empowered the regenerated Pharisee to undertake a marvellous ministry. Over the years he had achieved far more than all the other apostles put together.

Fourthly, there was a marvellous doctrinal unity among the apostles and their colleagues: all spoke with one undivided voice.

The significance of Christ's resurrection (15:12-34)

The second division of chapter 15 expounds the truth that apart from the resurrection of Jesus there can be no good news from God. First, the Corinthians are asked to imagine the consequences if the Lord did not rise from the dead (15:12-19). Secondly, and almost as a digression, matters are presented as they really are: because Christ has been raised the sceptics are wrong (15:20-28). Thirdly, readers are invited again to contemplate what it would mean for some professing Christians were Jesus dead, and are challenged to come to their senses (15:29-34).

Suppose, for a moment, that Jesus is dead (15:12-19)

Some at Corinth denied flatly the possibility of the resurrection of the body (15:12). Their unbelief was aggravated by manifest hypocrisy, hence the acidic **'among you'**: they were in the acutely embarrassing situation of belonging to a baptized community confessing formally as a condition of admission that Jesus rose from the dead. How could they bring themselves to **'say'** what they did about the dead in general, and by inference about the Lord in particular?

'From the dead'; 'of the dead' (15:12-13)

The qualifier **'from the dead'** occurs often in the New Testament and almost always with reference to the Lord.[11] The plain meaning here is that the entombed Jesus, so to speak in the society of all dead people, came alive, stood up and abandoned their company.

'But if there is no resurrection of the dead, not even Christ has been raised.' The logic in this statement is that the alleged impossibility of resurrection denies a particular example, that of Jesus: not even *he* could have been a positive exception to the negative rule.

Empty faith (15:14)

'And if Christ has not been raised, then our preaching is vain, your faith also is vain.' 'Vain' means 'empty'. Here the preacher-convert relationship is given consideration: because the 'preaching'

The resurrection of the body (15:1-58)

or heralding forth (Greek, *kerugma*, as in 1:21 and 2:4) was sheer emptiness; the preachers gave out nothing and gained no one. Nor did the converts receive anything of value.

Slander and libel (15:15-16)

Why it is that the resurrection of Jesus is important will be made plain in 15:17, which spells out the sombre truth that a dead Jesus cannot save. As Paul leads up to this statement he makes the observation that if the heretics are right, **'We are even found to be false witnesses of God.'** The reason for this dramatic claim is that **'We witnessed against God that he raised Christ, whom he did not raise, if in fact the dead are not raised.'**

To understand the force of these words compare directly with Mark 14:55: 'The chief priests and the whole council kept trying to obtain testimony against Jesus.'[12] The operative word in Mark's record is 'against' (Greek, *kata* + the genitive, exactly as in 15:15): the leaders of Israel had set themselves quite deliberately in opposition to Jesus.

Similarly, if the Corinthian sceptics were in the right Paul would have been indulging in false allegations, the intended object of his slander and libel being none other than Almighty God. The train of thought is that if the dead do not rise, Christ did not rise. Because the apostle knew this, as he must have done, yet persisted in preaching the resurrection of Jesus, he would have been a conscious and conspicuous liar — and necessarily an unsuccessful one, because, as Rabbi Gamaliel, tutor to Paul in the latter's youth, observed in a not dissimilar situation (Acts 5:39; 22:3), who can fight against God?

It is obvious that this disagreement about the resurrection was no sincere difference of opinion in which a spirit of Christian love and mutual respect should have prevailed. Paul's opponents accused him of fighting against God. If their charges were true, the apostle was lost. If untrue, the Corinthian sceptics were in the process of destroying themselves.

The argument is developed to show the consequences of Corinthian unbelief. Paul repeats for emphasis the inexorable logic of 15:13: **'For if the dead are not raised, not even Christ has been raised.'** What is universally impossible could not have happened in the case of Jesus, notwithstanding the preaching of the apostles and others.

Fruitless, unprofitable faith (15:17)

'And if Christ has not been raised, your faith is worthless; you are still in your sins.' Paul states that if the apostles trafficked in falsehood their silly converts must have damaged themselves seriously. 'Worthless' means 'fruitless' (Greek, *mataia*). Gullible faith in a dead Jesus was stated by 15:14 to be 'vain' but here it is said to be unproductive: because the deluded Corinthians had trusted in something that was nothing they derived nothing from it and were advantaged in no way. Hence, they remained guilty sinners. Effectively (although this is not mentioned), they would have found themselves in the same position as those Jews warned by Jesus that they would die in their sin (John 8:21).

We need to be clear why the resurrection of Jesus is essential for the salvation of the believer. Let Scripture interpret Scripture. Romans 4:25 tells us that 'He who was delivered because of our transgressions ... was raised because of our justification.' This implies that the resurrection of Jesus was necessary for at least two intimately related reasons.

First, it demonstrated that God acknowledged the sufferings of Jesus to be exactly what they were meant by the Lord to be, an intentional and acceptable sacrifice for the sins of others. Had Jesus not been raised it would have been as if God verified the condemnation passed upon him by both Jews and Gentiles. The prisoner from Nazareth would have been detained by his heavenly Father in a perpetual prison.

Secondly, the empty tomb anticipated Jesus' ascent into heaven to present himself triumphantly before God on behalf of those for whom he died. In the words of John Owen, the Puritan, 'For whom Christ offered himself, for all those, and only those, doth he intercede.'[13]

Therefore, if Jesus does not appear at the throne of God as our High Priest we remain lost; if God does not accept him, why should he accept those who rely upon him? There is no reason at all. But the glorious truth is that he was raised, that he has ascended, that he does intercede, that we are accepted and that he will come again.

The blessed dead ?(15:18)

Further, queries the apostle, if the Lord is not (by definition) a 'risen' Saviour, what about those who have **'fallen asleep in Christ'**? We

The resurrection of the body (15:1-58)

know from 11:30 that some of the Corinthian Christians passed into heaven when they fell asleep physically.

Paul hypothesizes. If Christ never rose, these dead Christians perished when they breathed their last. At the moment when, as they and others naïvely trusted, they should have entered through golden gates into heavenly life, they found themselves confronted by the gaping jaws of hell, precipitated into a state of condemnation to await the final judgement.[14] Instead of their bodies falling asleep, these foolish believers perished in sin. Death, shocking in itself, introduced them to an infinitely worse, unexpected shock.

In a context like chapter 15 **'to perish'** does not mean the annihilation of body and soul. Here, as in the New Testament generally, perishing is the opposite of being saved, the conscious experience of permanent separation from God with all its attendant miseries.[15] Scripture neither implies nor teaches explicitly that final judgement leads to the obliteration and non-existence of the unforgiven sinner. Nor is there any logical reason why destruction has to be an instantaneous event leading to oblivion. It could as easily signify eternal alienation, which is what the Bible teaches.

Wasted lives (15:19)

Thus far Paul has countered the charge that he was slandering God. Particular thought has been given to the plight of believers, whether living or sleeping, should Jesus be dead. Now the apostle ponders again the dismal situation in which he and his colleagues would find themselves if the Lord had not risen: **'If we have hoped in Christ in this life only, we are of all men most to be pitied.'**

This hypothetical admission is concerned solely with the apostle's activity in the world as it is. For Paul 'to live is Christ' (Phil. 1:21). If Jesus is dead it follows that the situation of the average Christian is deplorable because he worships a fiction. Unfortunate as this would be, what about the apostles, the pioneers of this supreme fallacy? If they preached something that they did not believe they would have remained guilty men. Conversely, if they were fools enough to have swallowed the colossal fantasy their wretchedness would have remained beyond measure. This is because their present, earthbound happiness, quite apart from their expectation of salvation, had been established upon an error. Because the resurrection was recognized by right-thinking men to be a mirage, the 'apostles', who could not have been sent by dead

Jesus, a non-Christ, would have attracted nothing but the ridicule, disgust and just condemnation of society. Nor would God help them.

The logic of unbelief

We go through Paul's chain of reasoning again to make sure that we understand it.

Suppose, it is argued, that dead people do not rise. It follows that Jesus remains dead. Therefore the ministry of the apostles and the faith of their converts are equally empty. The apostles have been slandering God, a dangerous procedure. Because their faith leads nowhere, Christians remain guilty, unsanctified sinners. Those believers who have died did not fall asleep; rather, they perished in their sins and remain for ever beyond redemption. Finally, the apostles have made a shipwreck of their lives on earth; they can be neither happy nor useful. Worse, they have thrown away any hope of peace with God and of heaven at the end.

The packaged argument is that these must be the tragic consequences for all believers if the shameless Corinthian sceptics are right.

Matters as they really are (15:20-28)

Unnecessary and illogical heresy wearies Paul. Let others think what they want and go their own way. For his part he will not allow the Corinthians to wallow a moment longer in the hopeless unbelief to which they had been enticed by some of their own people.

'But now,' means, 'This is how matters continue to be' (15:20). The apostle is always concerned with reality, in this case the glorious truth that Christ was not left dead in the tomb. Proofs have been advanced already (15:5-8). Therefore the schismatics are wrong. Therefore the negative inferences which flow necessarily from their wicked, groundless assumption can be discarded. In that **'Christ has been raised from the dead'**, he remains permanently in a state of risenness.

We should not overlook the neat way in which the tables are turned on the sceptics. They chose to persuade themselves that the resurrection of the body (anyone's body) was an impossibility, from which it followed that Jesus remained dead. They brazenly discounted the mass of evidence to the contrary.

The apostle reasons in the opposite direction. The resurrection of Jesus actually occurred. If one man can rise, others may — others must. The reality is that the living Lord Jesus is **'the first fruits of those who are asleep'**. The reference, again, is to the sleeping saints rather than to those who die in their sins. The apostle is not concerned just at this point with the general resurrection of all men, although he did believe it (Acts 24:15).[16]

First fruits (15:20)

In the Old Testament the formal presentation of the 'first fruits' of the land by the people of Israel had a dual significance. First, the act consecrated the coming harvest to God. Secondly, consecration was based upon the expectation of a coming harvest from God; a pledge to the Lord from the people flowed from their belief in the Lord's pledge to them. In Paul's letters both principles are advanced.[17]

With regard to the resurrection, after he rose from the dead and ascended to heaven the Lord fulfilled his earlier promise and sent the Holy Spirit to his people (Luke 24:49; Acts 1:4). Paul teaches that the Spirit has become the indwelling pledge that they, too, must eventually be raised from sleep and be like the Saviour. Romans 8:23 is explicit: 'Having the first fruits of the Spirit, we ourselves groan, waiting for the redemption of our body.'[18]

It is true that in 15:20 there is no explicit reference to the Old Testament ordinance of first fruits. Yet because Passover and first fruits were associated historically (Exod. 23:15-16; Lev. 23:5-10), Paul might well have had them both in mind. He has already expounded Christ as 'our Passover' (5:7), and the resurrection of the Saviour is seen here as the commencement of the harvest. The association would not have been lost upon Jewish believers at Corinth.

Adam and Jesus (15:21-22)

The truth that the resurrection of Christ promises that of the church is expanded by 15:21: **'For since by a man came death, by a man also came the resurrection of the dead.'** As in 15:12, 13 and 42, we are pointed to the resurrection 'of the dead'. But now there is a difference. Well aware that Christians continue to fall asleep, the apostle indicates that this process is to end: the final resurrection will not be *'from'* the dead, those who rise leaving others behind them in the sleep of death; it will be **'of'** the dead — that is, of all God's people. Not one saint remains in sacred slumber because resurrection will be the experience of the whole church.

These two verses compare and contrast Adam and Jesus, anticipating Romans 5:12-19, part of a letter sent from Corinth not long after 1 Corinthians was written at Ephesus. Important truths bear repetition.

The apostolic reasoning is that just as Adam affected all his people permanently, Jesus has a lasting effect upon those who belong to him. This is the parallel drawn by Paul between the two men. But there is also a profound contrast bound up within the parallel: whereas Adam was the point of origin of death, both spiritual and physical, Jesus has become the source of spiritual and physical resurrection.

All who are **'in Adam'**, that is, the whole of humanity, die (15:22). Because mankind without exception was contained, so to speak, in its first parent, death in every form became universal and ongoing when Adam apostatized. We know that experience shows this to be the case. Notice Paul's consistency: he does not write that Adam's race 'sleeps', a description reserved for believers only.

It might be supposed that here we have some sort of a doctrine of universal salvation, the apostle making out that even as 'all' die, 'all' (that is, the same human stock) will be made alive. The supposition would be fallacious because Paul clearly draws a parallel between all in Adam and all in Christ rather than identifying them. Two separate constituencies were in his mind, not one. Romans 5:17-19 shows this to be so.

1. The fall of Adam

The assumption of 15:21-22 is that Adam did something which brought about both his own personal ruin and that of his children. Again, we have to turn to the letter to the Romans to find out what the deed was.

According to this great epistle, men deserve and suffer death, that is, alienation from God, with all its consequences. This is because they participate in the guilt of Adam's original sin in Eden (Gen. 3). Romans 5:12 is specific and is incapable of any other

The resurrection of the body (15:1-58)

interpretation: 'Therefore, just as through one man sin entered into the world, and death through sin, even so death spread to all men, because all sinned.'

The inspired reasoning is: first, that Adam sinned; secondly, that the penalty was death, a penalty *following* rather than preceding the offence; thirdly, that all men 'sinned' ('sinned' implying a single, only-one-of-its-kind apostasy perpetrated by humanity as a whole at one place and at one point in time);[19] fourthly, that mankind was sentenced to death as a result of its corporate offence.

The verse teaches that what Adam did, his descendants did on that occasion in Eden and they did it in his person. Because he was the legal representative of the family as well as its natural head they all without exception sinned through him and with him. Romans 5:19 makes this plain: 'Through the one man's disobedience the many were made sinners.' Because of the solidarity shared by Adam and his children they turned from God *en bloc*, in consequence of which they were delivered to death.

There is more. The letter to the Romans shows that this estrangement was by no means the end of the human tragedy. As if original sin were not enough, men everywhere have compounded their predicament by heaping up their own offences, offences for which they must pay (Rom. 1:32; 2:2,6-8; 3:9-19).

2. The righteousness of Christ

We return to 1 Corinthians. If there is an intimate bond between sinful Adam and his fallen people, there is an equally strong union between Christ and all who are 'in' him. This very different bond leads to a dramatically different effect: all who belong to Christ **'shall be made alive'**, by which is meant bodily resurrection following spiritual reconciliation with God through Christ.

Let's pause. It might be suggested here that if believers are given life, unbelievers lose it, a positive surely implying a negative. If so, it could be argued, the unrepentant dead must be annihilated or obliterated either at death or at the Day of Judgement.

As we have seen, 15:18 shows that this cannot be. Furthermore, in the New Testament 'to be made alive' means entrance into living fellowship with God through Christ (15:45; John 5:21; 6:63). It would be illogical to infer that those who do not experience this cease to exist. Like the rich man in the parable (Luke 16:19-31), they remain consciously separated from God. Theirs is death indeed.

The resurrection and the 'millennium' (15:23-24)

'Order' (Greek, *tagma*) in 15:23 means 'turn', 'succession' or 'sequence'. The apostle shows that Jesus' resurrection leads to similar physical resurrections for all who belong to him, but at a later time. Although the resurrections of Christ and of believers are in principle one single, great event, it is an event considered sequentially in two stages: first, the glorification of Christ and **'after that'** (or, 'then') that of his spiritual body, the church. The analogy of the first fruits and the coming harvest is exact.

The second and final stage in the resurrection of the church will occur **'at his coming'**. The Greek word for 'coming' (*parousia*, 15:23) often means the arrival of someone important. In the New Testament it usually, although not always, refers to Christ.[20] The apostle's doctrine is that our bodies are to emerge from their long sleep and stand up when the Lord arrives in person in this world. Our resurrection gives rise to the ultimate and eternal church meeting, the elect of God assembling together in blessed fellowship with the Lord and with one another. Death cannot withhold us from him. Nor does it mock the Saviour as it did just once outside the walls of Jerusalem.

Now to 15:24, which demands the most careful consideration. It can easily be misinterpreted: **'Then comes the end, when he delivers up the kingdom to God, even the Father, when he has abolished all rule and all authority and power.'**

The NASB reads a little awkwardly that Christ is to surrender the kingdom 'to the God and Father'. Perhaps this tends, albeit unwittingly, to mask Paul's trinitarian emphasis, which is that the kingdom will be surrendered specifically to the 'Father' rather than to 'God'.

Three related questions must be raised. First, what is the 'end'? Second, when will the 'end' be? Finally, how do we interpret the statement that at the 'end' Christ is to deliver the 'kingdom' to the 'Father'?

1. What is the 'end'?

'End' (Greek, *telos*) means a conclusion or a finish or, with a slightly different nuance, a goal or target, the intended outcome of an issue, the hoped-for completion of a programme. This has already been mentioned in our discussion of 13:10.

The resurrection of the body (15:1-58) 331

Both emphases are probably combined here. Although Paul does not specify what the 'end' is, there can be no doubt as to his meaning: the programme of redemption is destined to reach a climax leading directly to Jesus' transfer of the 'kingdom' to the Father.

2. When will the 'end' be?

The solution of the first question leads to an answer for the second: the 'end', the final, consummated salvation of the church, brings about the immediate end of this world as we know it.

Remember 2:6, which teaches that 'the rulers of this age' are being brought to nothing. But the context of 2:6 says more: in the brief time given to each of them before passing into oblivion these men operate blindly in the interests of God's elect.

The Bible gives many examples of this magnificent truth. There were two Egyptian Pharaohs, the benefactor who exalted Joseph and the enemy who drowned in the Red Sea (Gen. 41:41-42; Exod. 15:1-21; Ps. 136:15). The common denominator between them was that the Lord raised both men to power in order to benefit Israel. Then there was Nebuchadnezzar of Babylon, a cruel and arrogant man who destroyed the city of Jerusalem and its temple. For all that, he was the Lord's servant (Jer. 25:9; 27:6). Can we forget Cyrus of Persia, who allowed the Jews to return home (2 Chron. 36:22-23; Ezra 1:1-4) and who is described as the Lord's 'shepherd' and 'anointed one' (Isa. 44:28; 45:1).

But they remain lesser figures when contrasted with those murderous individuals who crucified Jesus. Even so, had the latter not sinned there would be no salvation for Jews or Gentiles. Romans 11:11-12 teaches this clearly: through their wickedness Christ was despatched to Calvary. The principle is that although the welfare of the church sometimes appears to be subject to the caprice of evil men, it remains safe in the hands of God. He, and none other, is the Lord of heaven, the great King who rules the age in which we live. He and none other leads his people on.

This truth surfaces in 15:24. When the gospel has done its work Jesus will lay down his **'kingdom'**, his provisional government of the entire world of rebellious men and evil spirits. His enemies pass from the scene. The old, sinful universe ends.

Look at this in a slightly different way in order to establish the matter. We know from 15:23 that the resurrection of the church occurs when Christ comes. Further, the New Testament teaches plainly that the world must end at the final advent of the Lord. Consider, for example, the three related parables of the faithful and unfaithful servants, of the ten virgins and of the talents (Matt. 24:45 - 25:30): history winds up when the one who is the master, the bridegroom and the slave-owner returns.

It follows that the resurrection of the church takes place at the end of the world rather than at some earlier time. Compare with John 6:39-40 and 11:24, which refer to 'the last day'.

3. What is the 'kingdom'?

The question has been answered already: the **'kingdom'** is Christ's kingship of a passing world order. But two subordinate matters must be thought through: first, the meaning of **'then'** (Greek, *epeita*, 15:23, or *eita*, 15:24, both meaning 'after that' or 'next'); secondly, the destruction of death.

It is obvious from 15:23 that Paul assumes a time-lapse between the historic resurrection of Christ and that of the church: Christ rises and 'then', at a later date, he appears. When he does come his people rise up to meet him. The point is that this important little word, **'then'**, occurs again in 15:24, suggesting that there is to be another interval, on this occasion between the arrival of the Lord and **'the end'**: **'those who are Christ's at his coming, then comes the end'**.

To put this into perspective, if the time interval implied by 'then' (15:23) between the first and the second advents of our Lord is obviously not less than almost two thousand years, why should not the interval implied by 'then' (15:24) be of a similar magnitude? Admittedly, on the surface, it might appear that the apostle predicts the coming of Christ and then the Lord's ongoing presence in this world for a period of time.

There are many godly Christians who believe that Jesus will reign on earth for one thousand years after his second advent, yet before the world comes to its end. This, it is said, is part of the true interpretation of Revelation 20:1-10. It is claimed, too, that 15:24 fits nicely into such a 'premillennial' scheme ('premillennial' meaning that Christ comes back *before*, pre-, the millennium). In his excellent New Testament commentary, Henry Alford wrote that although Paul was aware that there would be such an interval its duration was never revealed to him. Later on, the figure of one thousand years was made known to John on Patmos.[21]

The resurrection of the body (15:1-58)

This approach is plausible but seems, logically and exegetically, more than dubious. There is also another factor which has never failed to sway this writer. Premillennialism would appear to be vulnerable to the truth that when our Lord ascended into heaven he separated permanently from all contact with sin and death, never again to be humiliated by the presence of mortality and never again to be insulted by the contradiction of sinners. Three years of ministry at the end of his earthly life completed that unique ordeal.

The basic thesis of premillennialism is that the glorified Christ is to return to a scene in which, as one advocate has it, there will be 'no deaths during this thousand years, *except* those which occur by reason of transgression and disobedience' (italics added).[22] This means that the world would be populated by both undying saints and dying sinners jostling together in a one-thousand-year tension. This is surely impossible. Nor is it necessary to believe that Revelation 20 teaches it. Upon reflection, the idea would seem to propose a contradiction and degradation rather than a triumph. When the Lord comes all his work will be ended.

It seems better to infer that 'then' in 15:24 introduces 'the end' as the logical termination of a series of interconnected events, which may or may not coincide.[23] In context, Paul's principal concern is to outline cause and effect, to stress that one element in the programme of salvation leads necessarily to another. Seen in this light, the death of Christ precedes his resurrection, and the Lord's resurrection leads to his eventual return and to the simultaneous resurrection of the church. The resurrection of the church precipitates 'the end', and 'the end' brings in the surrender of the 'kingdom'. Unquestionably, the whole programme takes time, but it is neither said nor implied that each distinct event *must* take place at its own individual, separate moment in history.

By analogy, 15:54 tells us that 'when' the corruptible body clothes itself with incorruption 'then' the predictions of Isaiah 25:8 and Hosea 13:14 will be fulfilled.[24] One occurrence brings about another. This is how it appears to be in 15:24.

Imagine a housewife entering her dark kitchen or utility room at the end of the day. 'Then' she snaps on the light switch and 'then' proceeds to fill and programme her timed washing/drying machine to operate during the night hours. When she depresses the switch on the appliance a light tells her that the system is ready to function. Notice that the lady is involved in at least four related operations:

entering and lighting the room, programming the appliance and then (via her instructions) washing and drying her laundry. In the sequence the first action leads to the second, the second to the third and the third to the fourth: when she does one thing something else is set to happen and, in the case of the washer-dryer, sooner or later according to her inclination.

It seems to be rather like this in 15:23-24. The resurrection of Christ, his return, the resurrection of the church, 'the end' and the transfer of the 'kingdom' to the Father are considered as distinct but inseparable elements that work in sequence. They are parts of a single programme dedicated to the glorification of God through Christ and his church. But the time-intervals, if any, between these events and how long the complete operation is meant to take are not under consideration.

What, then, of the destruction of death? The coming of Christ and the resurrection are to be the joint occasion for the permanent overthrow of death, the last remaining enemy of the people of God (15:26). Because, by definition, no enemies remain after the advent of the Lord, there need be, and cannot be, any time-interval between the resurrection of the church and 'the end'. When Christ appears death dies. Hostilities are over. This is just another way of saying that 'this present evil age' will be no more (Gal. 1:4).

When a conflict comes to an end soldiers abandon their weapons. Whether theirs is victory or defeat, fighting finishes. It will be like this when the Lord appears. For the second time he comes from the throne of God to a scene of death and hostility, not now to die but to gather in his church and to eliminate his last struggling foe. He succeeds. No enemy remains to ride out against him.

We are now in a position to think further about the 'kingdom' that the Saviour is to hand to his Father at the end of the world. When Christ makes the transfer he will **'abolish all rule and all authority and power'** (15:24); the surrender of the 'kingdom' occurs when, and not after, the Lord finally puts down all other, lesser powers. The two events merge; there is no time interval.

Jesus, we know, is the universal Lord exclusively in the interests of God and his people. Furthermore, the spiritual kingdom of Christ, the church, lasts for ever. Daniel 7:14 is explicit:

And to him was given dominion...
That all peoples, nations, and men of every language
Might serve him.

His dominion is an everlasting dominion
Which will not pass away;
And his kingdom is one
Which will not be destroyed.

That Daniel's everlasting kingdom is the church is indicated by the use of the word 'serve', for the world does not consciously obey the Saviour. The second part of the verse was applied by Jesus to himself because he expected to establish a universal and eternal church with himself as its Lord.[25] Before our Lord was born Gabriel informed Mary that her son's kingdom would 'have no end' (Luke 1:32-33).

It is with reference to his headship over the church that Christ exercises a strictly this-world dominion over those whose hearts he does not choose to transform. The latter constitute the 'kingdom' of 15:24. If 'kingdom' had been intended by Paul to describe the church a qualification would almost certainly have been added, such as 'kingdom of God', or 'kingdom of Christ', or 'his kingdom', as is *always* the case elsewhere.[26] This is a most important point. The qualification is absent here because the reference is to the sovereignty of Christ in the world at large rather than to the elect.

Christ's reign (15:25-26)

That 15:24 focuses upon the mediatorial lordship of Christ in this provisional scheme of things is proved by 15:25: **'For he must reign until he has put all his enemies under his feet.'** Jesus controls the entire world, but only until every enemy is vanquished. When this happens there will be no sinful world to control. Just as David's enemies fell beneath his feet (1 Kings 5:3), Jesus will stand over every prostrate opponent. Because war is no more the Warrior-Prince returns his rod of iron to the Father who commissioned and sent him.

There is a deliberate recall in 15:25 of Psalm 110, and particularly of verse 1 of the psalm. Jehovah guarantees to David's 'lord' that he will sit at the right hand of the throne of God 'until' all his enemies become his footstool. Historically, this promise of exaltation was fulfilled when Christ ascended into heaven.[27]

Observe that, whereas the psalm states that Jehovah subdues these enemies, 15:25 asserts that Christ conquers. There is no inconsistency: the Son of God acts as executor for the Father until the footstool is fully in place. Then the Son's provisional kingship is wound up.

In the next verse death is said to be **'the last enemy'**. The meaning is that even now, as time goes by, our Lord progressively overthrows his opponents. Death holds out only because it is permitted by God to remain in the world until Jesus comes back. Then it, too, vanishes.

A new heaven and a new earth (15:27-28)

Psalm 8:6 is recalled to show that **'all things'** must submit to Christ the King. The psalm looks back to creation when the natural order was subjected to Adam and his children. Paul, moved by the Spirit, implies that the psalm also looks ahead to the Messiah, the one who, in terms of 15:45,47, is equally the 'last Adam' and the 'second man'.

The apostle asks the reader to allow his imagination to race towards the end of the world: **'He** [the Father] **says, "All things are put in subjection** [to Christ].'"' 'Says' is best understood as that which the Father will say at the end, rather than what he says now, even as 'delivers' (15:24) concerns the final surrender of Christ's kingly authority to the Father.[28]

Then the Father will acknowledge that all things have been subjected to Christ, the Lord of all, but with one exception: **'it is** [that is, 'will be'] **evident'** that God the Father is not, nor was, subjected to the Son. When the former acknowledges Christ's complete subjugation of all things it remains apparent to the saints and to the angels that the Father is the sole exception. It might be put in this way: in the glory of heaven Jesus will be subordinate to his Father even as Joseph, confessedly lord of all Egypt, remained subordinate to Pharaoh (Gen. 41:40; Acts 7:10). This is the reason why **'When all things are subjected to him,'** that is, to the Son, **'then the Son himself also will be subjected to the one who subjected all things to him, that God may be all in all.'**

This statement parallels 15:24. Neither there nor here is Jesus said to surrender his lordship of the church. He gives up no more than his administration over 'all things' in an evil world which, after his advent, ceases to exist. He yields himself to his Father. What the Son set out to do he has done. He has fulfilled his Father's pleasure and bows before him. He sees the travail of his soul (Isa. 53:11). No longer does Jesus need to exercise dominion in heaven and earth, alike in judgement and in salvation. He wields the sceptre of iron no more. All is at an end. The programme has finished. Christ remains both the eternally divine Son of God and the human head of his body, the church. The Father, the Son and the Holy Ghost, the one triune God, are worshipped by adoring angels who never fell into sin and by a church restored fully and eternally from sin. Nothing can disturb the glory of the new creation. Never again will the Son be commissioned to seek and to save, to bleed and to die, to reign and to judge.

The resurrection of Christ and personal self-control (15:29-34)

It was reasoned in 15:12-19 that if it is impossible for dead bodies to rise Jesus is assuredly dead. This means that believers remain in their sins and are lost. That such fears are groundless was demonstrated by 15:20-28: Christ remains a risen Saviour. Further, the historic resurrection of Christ leads to the restoration of the created universe.

Now Paul gives more thought to his own situation and that of some other believers should resurrection be an impossibility. Balancing and arranging his emphases perfectly, he makes the point that the risen Christ alone can bring about the sinner's spiritual and moral renewal.[29]

In 15:29-32 'what?' or 'why?', represented by the same Greek word *(ti)*, occur four times for emphasis. The apostle's questions are rhetorical: would the various believers to whom he refers behave as they do unless they were confident about the resurrection? Certainly not.

Baptism for the dead (15:29)

At Corinth and probably elsewhere some converts were being baptized **'for the dead'** (or, 'with reference to the dead'; 'on behalf of the dead'; Greek, *huper* + genitive). Who these dead people were and what the Corinthians' interest was are not specified by Paul. His sole concern is that if the dead remain dead there can be no possible connection, neither now nor at some time in the future, between them and living, in-this-world Christians. Then he shows that death is not annihilation and that those who were being baptized with reference to the dead had not taken leave either of their senses or of the deceased. The passage is remarkable: **'Otherwise, what will those do who are baptized for the dead? If the dead are not raised at all, why then are they baptized for them?'**

Although we do not know as much as curiosity might crave, we know something. First, the definite article, 'the', before 'dead' implies that specific Corinthians who had passed away are in mind. Second, 'are baptized' (present tense) suggests that baptisms for this reason were currently taking place with something of the dimensions of a practice. Third, it was believed by some baptismal candidates that these 'dead' people would be raised. From this it follows that the deceased were believers, as is suggested by 15:18, 'those who have fallen asleep in Christ'. Fourth, the dead are not described as 'asleep' because the apostle looks at them as if he were one of the sceptics for whom the grave is the end of all things.

The central issue is that if these Christians had breathed their last and had passed out of existence, how could the ones who were being baptized 'for' them explain themselves? What were they to do? Their baptisms must be absurd if there is no bodily resurrection.

There have been many conjectures, ancient and modern, about the nature of these baptisms. One not unpopular interpretation is that the baptismal candidates were, at least in the matter of baptism, unorthodox and possibly heretical. If so, 15:29 indicates that for such people a denial of the resurrection must compound the error and folly of their ways. In support of this approach we note that Paul uses the word 'they' twice, as if he distances himself from the practice. A parallel might be 8:10 and 10:20-22, where he looks askance at Corinthians who frequented idol-temples. Perhaps he disapproved in the matter of baptism for the dead.

But the apostle never failed to condemn what he knew to be wrong. Compare with 11:17-34, in which he castigates the Corinthians' abuse of the Lord's Table. Nor is it likely that he would allude tactically to a perversion of baptism in order to demonstrate a principle. Since no explicit condemnation of baptism for the dead appears, we may assume that Paul did not necessarily object. So what was this baptism?

It is altogether probable, even certain, that many deceased Christians had left glowing testimonies behind them. Paul himself never forgot Stephen (Acts 22:20; cf. Acts 26:10; Heb. 2:3-4; 11:4;

The resurrection of the body (15:1-58)

13:7). Nor is it impossible that some converts came to their baptisms with the understanding that at the resurrection they would be reunited with those who had finished their pilgrimage. Even if this was not the basic motive for baptism it might have been part of the incentive. We can easily sympathize.

Let's take our interpretation down this path. Suppose, Paul argues, that there can be no resurrection. Obviously deceived by gross apostolic superstition, these unfortunate converts realize too late that they pursued a mirage. Their error is beyond redemption and their life's investment has evaporated. What will they do? Nothing except rend their hearts and their garments. The souls of the dead are no more, and when these living Christians come to their turn to die they too will cease to exist. It would have been better had all alike, both living and dead, never heard about Christ. This is the undeniable thrust of the heretics' denial of the resurrection of Jesus in particular and of the church in general.

On balance, the present commentary would opt for this type of approach: the apostle insists that the Corinthians who were 'baptized for the dead' are not to be denied their hearts' desire. He reassures them: they were not mistaken. The blessed dead must rise, which is why they are blessed.

Bad doctrine leads to bad behaviour (15:30-34)

Paul returns to his own situation and that of his colleagues (**'we'**, 15:30, as in 4:9, 'us apostles'), although it is possible that he refers to all Christians. Why should they endure danger **'every hour'** if there is no future resurrection? Would they be so incomprehensibly foolish? No.

1. An apostolic oath (15:31)

The apostle sheds light upon his sufferings: **'I protest, brethren, by the boasting in you, which I have in Christ Jesus our Lord, I die daily.'** This is a mild oath assuring the Corinthians that what is said is the truth. A similar affirmation occurs in the Greek version of Genesis 42:15, where Joseph swears to his brothers 'by the life of Pharaoh'.[30]

Although this letter shows that he criticized the Corinthians when necessary, Paul gloried in them when he worshipped his

Saviour. He swears that it is so, giving the exalted King his full title, 'Christ Jesus our Lord'. May such a one act against the apostle should he lie or exaggerate about the statement that each new day brings with it the likelihood of imminent death. It is because evangelism and the certain resurrection of his converts are so glorious that he is ready to face inglorious suffering day by day. He shares this with his Lord and he shares it with the people as he details his incentive for ministry.

Clearly, dying daily was no way for Paul to live. The apostle's claim is that because he was a reasonable man who needed at least some creature comforts he would never expose himself to perils of this magnitude were there no risen Saviour and no resurrection.

2. Isaiah's Jerusalem; Paul's Ephesus (15:32)

These sufferings are sketched in bold contours to startle the complacent church over the sea at Corinth: **'After the manner of men I fought with beasts at Ephesus.'** Paul means that he was compelled to struggle against beastly people devoid of spiritual sensitivity, men who probably had never heard about the resurrection of the Lord and who would not believe it even if they were told. Compare with what Jesus said about his enemies' perverse attitude to the possibility of someone rising from the dead (Luke 16:31).

In 15:32 there is no reference to wild animals as such. Nor do we read elsewhere, not even in the catalogue of sufferings in 2 Corinthians 11:23-33, that the apostle ever found himself facing lions in a stadium, although there was a time when it almost happened (2 Tim. 4:17). Ignatius, whom we have met, wrote that once he had to fight with 'wild beasts' and 'leopards', by which he meant soldiers.[31] Perhaps the bishop had this verse in mind. Psalm 22 likens the enemies of God to animals, including the lion, and Titus 1:12 reminds a minister that the people of Crete were 'evil beasts'.

If the words are figurative the meaning must be that the hostility shown by some unbelievers had been animal-like and ferocious in the extreme. Should there be no resurrection the apostle has lost everything. He is a fool.

'If the dead are not raised' in 15:32, repeating from 15:29, connects directly with the immediately following **'Let us eat and drink, for tomorrow we die,'** rather than with the remark about the

The resurrection of the body (15:1-58)

Ephesian animals. Isaiah 22:13 is alluded to in order to bring out the gravity and folly of this death-wish. The prophet addresses the residents of the 'valley of vision', Jerusalem, where there ought to have been genuine spiritual sight but was not (Isa. 22:1). Many refused to take to heart the truths of God's Word and preferred to believe that death was the end. For this reason they indulged in revelry to burn up what little time remained to them.

The apostle supposes that the Corinthian sceptics are the latter-day counterparts of the cynics of Isaiah's Jerusalem. If the incredulous do hold the root of the matter he and his colleagues might as well abandon themselves to unrestrained lust. There is nothing else. There will be no meeting with God even if he does exist.

3. Paul and poetry (15:33)

'Do not be deceived: "Bad company [literally, 'evil associations' or 'evil speeches'] **corrupts good morals."'** Having quoted the Hebrew prophet, Paul introduces a line from a Greek poet, Menander, which had possibly become a proverb. The apostle must have been an exceptionally well-read man with an immense capacity for recall. Elsewhere he cites from two other Greek poets, Aratus (Acts 17:28) and Epimenides, who had a low view of Cretans (Titus 1:12).

Some Corinthian believers were favourably disposed to those among them who denied the resurrection. Paul claims that those who live as if there is no world to come inevitably set temptation in the way of naïve converts. His appeal to a worldly proverb could be a subtle hint that in this matter the Corinthians lacked common sense as well as spiritual insight. In today's jargon they were not even 'streetwise'. Jesus said, 'Take care what you listen to' (Mark 4:24).

4. Come outside into the cold air (15:34)

The section ends with an exhortation which, even by apostolic standards, is strong: **'Awake rightly, and stop sinning; for some have no knowledge of God. I speak this to your shame.'**

To 'awake' means to rouse oneself from a stupor, as when Noah and Nabal recovered from their fits of drunkenness (Gen. 9:24; 1 Sam. 25:37). The application is that falling under the influence of those who deny the resurrection is like participating in a drunken bout. The only thing to do is to grope towards the exit and recover one's senses. It is as if Paul says, 'Do what is right: go outside and wake up.' To remain inside must mean more sin, in plain terms either holding error, or propping up evil men, or both.

Those Corinthians who had no knowledge of the resurrection were perverse. A direct comparison should be made with the Sadducees, men ignorant both of God's Word and God's power (Matt. 22:29; Mark 12:24). The fact of the matter was, and is, that those who decline to turn to the Lord never do appreciate what the Bible says. How could it be otherwise?

As in 6:5 in the issue of going to court, so here; Paul writes these things so that the Corinthians might be conscience-stricken. Contrast his attitude in 4:14 where he denies that he wishes to make his adversaries feel small. In the matter of the resurrection the situation is entirely different: the people should be thoroughly ashamed of tolerating those who reject the doctrine.

The rebuke should be considered by churches led by ministers who play fast and loose with this vital truth. It is shameful to retain them. The congregation that supports such a pastor shares his guilt.

Resurrection completed (15:35-58)

The apostle has shown that because there had been a historic resurrection, that of Jesus, there must be many more when the Lord comes again. But acceptance of this truth raised some important and difficult questions that Paul knew had to be addressed. What is to be the nature and appearance of the bodies of the risen saints? How will they rise? The apostle was aware that he could not avoid such matters, and he would not evade them. We can imagine numbers of the Corinthians hanging upon every word as the letter was read out, hardly able to conceal a reverent impatience as they waited for an expansion of Paul's teaching. But others would scarcely have concealed their scorn for this supreme folly.

The apostle has the sceptics in mind and anticipates uninformed and unintelligent questions. Like the Sadducees, some of the Corinthians believed that the resurrection body, were there to be such, would be similar to the body that we now have. For them the notion of a resurrection was as dubious as it was revolting.

The resurrection of the body (15:1-58)

This fallacy needs consideration. Were the supposition correct we would nod our heads in reluctant agreement. Who wants to be raised from the dead to begin again the weary process of growing-up, ageing and dying? If the resurrection means this we discard it. But Christ taught that the resurrection will not be like this: those who rise will be 'as angels in heaven' (Matt. 22:30; Mark 12:25; Luke 20:36). Their bodies are to be of a different quality altogether. Although chapter 15 does not introduce the angels as a background for Paul's reasoning, his doctrine is essentially the same as the Lord's.

The section divides into two principal parts. The splendour of the resurrection body is expounded in 15:35-49 and 15:50-57 reveals how the whole church of God is to rise triumphantly from death. The chapter closes in 15:58 with an encouragement to believers to work hard.

The glory of the resurrection body (15:35-49)

First, the principle of resurrection is shown not to be unreasonable: creation gives its 'Amen' to the truth (15:35-41). Secondly, Paul considers the nature of the resurrection body (15:42-49).

Look around; look up (15:35-41)

Irreverent questions are expected: **'But someone will say, "How are the dead raised? And with what kind of body do they come?"'** (15:35). The apostle's response is substantially a preemptive device, by no means unusual in his letters, designed to stifle ignorant criticism before it has a chance to get a word in edgeways. Compare Romans 6:1,15; 7:7,13; 9:19.

If the cynics could have been introduced to his study, supposing that Paul enjoyed such a facility, they would have endeavoured to tie him up by asking just how a rotten corpse is supposed to emerge from decomposition. And if, for the sake of both the argument and the opportunity of bear-baiting the great man, they conceded that it might just happen, they would have quizzed him further about the appearance of the living dead. Paul expects that 'someone' will always emerge with such queries.

1. A foolish question and a wise answer (15:36-37)

The questioner is a **'fool'** (Greek, *aphrôn*, 'senseless', 15:36). These typical and inevitable arguments against the resurrection are worthless, and are so for one elegant and simple reason: the future resurrection is certain. It is almost as if Paul says, 'Be silent. Be patient. Believe. All will be revealed.' We could compare his words with the ring of truth in God's solemn promise to a wealthy but godless man when informed that against all probability something drastic would happen. Specifically, the 'fool' must die (Luke 12:20). Here, the Corinthian sceptic is reminded that he speaks rashly about matters beyond his understanding.

Paul concedes that the spiritual ignoramus does not lack some sort of know-how about field and garden: **'You, that which you sow does not come to life unless it dies.'** Obviously not. This is an uncompromising challenge, leading with 'fool' and continuing immediately with an emphatic 'you'.

Consistent with the teaching of Jesus (John 12:24), death is presented as the essential condition for new life. Does the fool not realize this when he plants his own seed in the soil? Of course he does. Let him apply the principle to the grand doctrine he ridicules so blithely.

Another truth appears: physical death is disorganization leading to reorganization rather than annihilation. Paul reminds the fool that **'You do not sow the body which is to be, but a bare grain, perhaps of wheat or of something else'** (15:37). The meaning is that when the man plants a garden he knows that his seed, of whatever vegetable species it happens to be, does not cease to exist. It disintegrates but only to be reshaped at a later stage. This universal rule never fails and is well-understood: the full-grown plant stems from the original seed even though there is no obvious resemblance. Paul's point is that death leading to bodily resurrection is like this. Although physical disorganization is the necessary preliminary for future life, the resurrection body will neither look the same nor be the same as the present body.

Benjamin Franklin (1706-90), the celebrated American statesman, printer and inventor, believed this. His epitaph, composed by himself, tells out his hope:

> The body of
> Benjamin Franklin, printer,
> (Like the cover of an old book,

> Its contents worn out,
> And stript of its lettering and gilding)
> Lies here, food for worms!
> Yet the work itself shall not be lost,
> For it will, as he believed, appear once more
> In a new
> And more beautiful edition,
> Corrected and amended
> By its Author![32]

Exactly!

2. Vastness and variety (15:38-41)

We are told by the apostle why the resurrection body must be different: **'But God gives it a body just as he wished, and to each of the seeds a body of its own'** (15:38). The allusion is to Genesis 1:11 and the creation of different kinds of plants and trees. Whatever grows at the present time does so because long ago the Lord decreed growth. It will be just like this for God's people when they rise.

Stop reading for a moment. If there are trees, bushes or flowers outside your window, look at them now. Consider that God enables them to blossom in strict accordance with specifications originally laid down long before Genesis was written. If this were not so the trees and flowers would not be there for you to admire. Similarly, if you are a believer, the God who works now in forest, field and garden will one day refashion your body according to a blueprint already drawn up. This is Paul's great doctrine.

Turning from vegetable life to the animal world, 15:39 introduces a universal negative: **'All flesh is not the same flesh, but there is one flesh of men, and another flesh of beasts, and another flesh of birds, and another of fish.'** Although all flesh is flesh, each life-form is distinct, and no two are identical.[33] Further, notwithstanding the apparently infinite range of distinctions in vegetable and animal life to be seen on this diminutive sphere, they are no more than a tiny part of creation: there are **'heavenly bodies'** as well as **'earthly bodies'** (15:40).

For Mediterranean people the night sky is blacker than it seems for Europeans. This has the effect of making the stars appear far more vivid and numerous. As the apostle gazes upwards he is aware that although they are many, these bodies share a peculiar

'glory' in that they are extra-terrestrial. They hang in space. They are different.

He proceeds. On planet Earth there are, it is true, an amazing number of dissimilar bodies. In spite of this they share a common 'glory' in that they have their being in the only habitat ever created by God; life-forms exist nowhere else in the cosmos. Because the earthly and the celestial are different the two orders defy comparison.

There is more (15:41). Each heavenly body has its own distinct 'glory', sun, moon and stars being specified as obvious examples. Although in a class of their own because unlike anything found on earth, they, too, exhibit startling dissimilarities.

The transformation of the body (15:42-49)

Let's recapitulate. Each living plant and creature in our world is unique (15:38-39). In the different environment of space there are innumerable bodies of which no two are the same (15:40-41). In short, creation is majestic in its dimensions and awesome in its variety.

1. *The analogy* (15:42a)

Paul insists that this splendid analogy teaches a profound truth: **'So also is the resurrection of the dead.'** Variation in creation demonstrates beyond a shadow of doubt that the doctrine of the transformation of the present, natural body into a new, resurrected body is eminently reasonable and by no means absurd. What is absurd is the notion that a resurrection would reintroduce the existing state of things, a state characterized by death.

Notice again that whereas the Lord rose 'from' the dead leaving others behind him (15:12,20), when the end comes none remain in their graves. Here the discussion turns upon the resurrection 'of' the dead: all the Lord's people without exception are to rise.

The apostle does not digress by describing the resurrected body of Jesus. No doubt he could have done so because on one occasion he saw the Lord (9:1; 15:8). His solitary point here is that when it is raised from death the body of the believer is to be like that of Christ (15:48-49). Perhaps Paul's veil of reverence is deliberate, designed to excite our faith and hope.

2. Continuity yet contrast (15:42b-44)

The continuity yet immense contrast between our dying frame and the glorious thing destined to rise from the dust are expounded in four ways.

First, the body **'is sown in corruption'** but is to be **'raised in incorruption'**. The meaning is that the believer has one body, not two. After it has decomposed it is to be refashioned rather than discarded. Again, the picture is that of the field. The seed buried in the earth lives on as the full-grown plant rising from that same earth. But Paul's metaphor incorporates a factor that he knew is no part of the natural growth process. In the present scheme of things the flower that develops from the seed must itself fade away (Isa. 40:7; 1 Peter 1:24); death generates death. With the resurrection of the body the pattern is wonderfully different: a dead thing gives rise to that which cannot die. Considered as a seed, the corpse rots in order to rise. When it does it will be imperishable.

In the New Testament 'corruption' sometimes means moral degradation, as in 2 Peter 1:4; 2:19. 'Incorruption' can signify moral purity, as in Ephesians 6:24. Although the two might seem to be different there is an inseparable connection in that the corruption of sin leads to the eventual decomposition of the body (Rom. 6:23). This is why 15:42 contrasts our pre- and post-resurrection frames. Now, we perish; then, never. Where there is no sin there is no death.

Second, **'It [the body] is sown in dishonour, it is raised in glory'** (15:43a). 'In dishonour' and 'in glory' are adjectival, describing the state of the body rather than the manner of burial or (for the Christian) how it is subsequently raised. Josephus records that the terminal illness of Herod the Great, the monster who tried to kill the baby Jesus (Matt. 2:16), was so repulsive that the sages considered it a divine judgement. Yet the monarch planned a funeral 'such as no other king had ever had'.[34] Even if a deceased person is given a splendid burial, his body is a lifeless, decomposing thing, lacking beauty and fit only for covering up. Although in life there might have been some degree of physical attraction, all vanishes at death. Notwithstanding the ceremony, Herod's body was 'sown in dishonour'. In the case of the believer, when he is raised he will live for ever with a glory similar to that of his Lord.

Third, **'It is sown in weakness, it is raised in power'** (15:43b). 'In weakness' and 'in power' describe the condition of the body respectively at death and later at the resurrection, rather than how it is buried and how is to be lifted up. The point being made is that a dead body, so weak that it cannot bury itself, will become immensely powerful.

We have been told that the body of the Christian is to be imperishable, glorious and dynamic. But Paul has not finished. The resurrected frame is to possess a fourth characteristic: **'It is sown a natural body; it is raised a spiritual body'** (15:44). Justification for this statement follows at once: **'If there is a natural body, there is also a spiritual body.'** Wavering believers are encouraged with the assurance that it is so: if God has given us bodies adapted to this scene, we can be confident, writes Paul, that he will grant us bodies fitted for the world to come.

By **'natural body'** is meant the conventional, human system adapted to the world as we know it. We might compare with the reference in 2:14 to the 'natural man', an ordinary person.[35] The characteristics of the **'spiritual body'** are not disclosed, apart from what is written in 15:42-44. This information is filled out by the teaching of the New Testament elsewhere concerning the risen Saviour (principally, Luke 24:15-51; John 20:19,26,27; Acts 10:41). From this data we can infer that the 'spiritual body' will not be immaterial, a thing lacking physical being. Luke 24:37,39 show that, far from being pure spirit, the body of the risen Jesus possessed flesh and bones. This is Luke's way of saying that our Lord was a complete human being after his resurrection as well as before his death.

3. The natural body and the spiritual body (15:45)

The truth that there is an immense distinction as well as continuity between the natural and spiritual bodies is expanded in this verse: **'So also it is written, "The first man, Adam, became a living soul." The last Adam became a life-giving spirit.'**

Two awe-inspiring assumptions appear. Not only is the resurrection body to be like that of the risen Christ, the spiritual body of the believer will also be **'life-giving'**. To understand exactly what is meant here we have to compare scripture with scripture. When the body of Adam had been fashioned God breathed into its nostrils the breath of life (Gen. 2:7); 'it' became 'he'. Later, although Adam was sinless he learned from God that he was capable of dying (Gen.

The resurrection of the body (15:1-58)

2:17). In the event this happened; because he was alienated from his Creator his soul and body parted company (15:22; Gen. 3:19; 5:5). Fallen Adam was neither able to resist the onset of death, nor to cancel it once it supervened.

Not so the sinless Lord Jesus. He never received life from an external source. Rather, it was given to him 'to have life in himself' (John 5:26), even though he could die, and did die. The context of this verse from John's Gospel shows that because he possesses life the Lord grants it to sinners now, in this world — something Adam could never do. Moreover, Jesus will resurrect the saints physically (John 5:29). In 15:45 the Saviour is described as 'the last Adam': even as the original man communicated death to his fallen children, so Christ, the God-man, transmits his resurrection life to the church.

The apostle's meaning is that because the glorified body derives from Christ it will not die. Perhaps John 7:38 provides a parallel. Here our Lord describes the blessed state of the pilgrim believer: 'From his innnermost being shall flow rivers of living water.' Paul applies the same principle to the saints at Christ's coming: when raised, life streams out from them rather than, so to speak, having to be injected.

4. The train of events (15:46-49)

That there is a definite sequence in the plan of God for his people is shown by 15:46. **'The spiritual'** body does not appear first. Rather, **'the natural'** body is followed by 'the spiritual', even as the seed precedes the full-grown plant. The meaning is that believers must not be despondent because we have not set our eyes on what is to be. Perhaps Paul was attacking those at Corinth and elsewhere who held that seeing *is* believing and that what is invisible has to be unreal. The resurrection must be, says the apostle, but not yet.

Further, the folly of some Corinthians' denial of the gospel is brought out by the reference to the timing of the respective appearances of Adam and of Christ in this world (15:47) — Adam in Eden and Jesus at his incarnation: **'The first man [Adam] is from the earth, earthy; the second man is from heaven.'** The *Textus Receptus* refers to 'the second man, the Lord from heaven', but the sense is the same.

This is a further recall of Genesis 2:7, which tells about the formation of Adam from the dust of the earth. The apostle's reasoning is that even as Adam preceded Christ in time, our own resurrection cannot take place yet; death always comes before life. 'We walk by faith, not by sight' (2 Cor. 5:7).

Our Lord became a true man with a true body (Luke 24:39; 1 Tim. 2:5; Heb. 2:14,17). Further, according to John 3:13, 'the Son of Man' 'descended from heaven'. In company with his apostolic colleague, Paul asserts that the man Jesus had his origin in heaven, although his body did not somehow exist there before coming into the world. Whereas Adam was created without his prior agreement (because he did not exist), the human life of Jesus began when the eternal Son of God voluntarily took our nature upon himself.[36] It is in this sense that he is said to have come down from heaven. Menno Simons, the eminent sixteenth-century Anabaptist leader, believed that at his incarnation our Lord 'did not become flesh of Mary, but in Mary', implying that Christ brought his humanity down with him to Bethlehem.[37] It would seem that Menno, although very far from being a heretic, was slightly off-track at this point. Philippians 2:7 shows that our Saviour 'emptied himself, taking the form of a servant, and became in the likeness of men'. Jesus was born a baby, looked like a baby, sounded like a baby, had to be cared for like a baby and, as time passed, proceeded to develop from babyhood to full manhood. This was because he derived his true humanity from Mary.

As Adam is, literally, **'the earthy'** (person), similarly his descendants are **'earthy'** (15:48). Essentially dust, we have no enduring substance in this passing scheme. Even as Jesus is **'the heavenly'** (person), so are those who are **'heavenly'**. Because of the fundamental importance of this truth Paul is explicit: in the same way that every member of Adam's race derives his physical being from him, the spiritual body to be given to the believer will be exactly like the resurrection body of his Lord. Philippians 3:21 and 1 John 3:2 make this plain.

'Borne' in 15:49 means 'to have worn' or 'to have carried about' (Greek, *phoreō*). The word occurs in connection with courtiers who wear delicate clothes (Matt. 11:8) and the officer who bears the sword of justice (Rom. 13:4). Even as the people of God have borne, or worn, **'the image of the earthy'**, that is, have resembled Adam, so **'We shall bear the image of the heavenly'**, that is, Christ. Some early manuscripts read, 'Let us wear the image of the heavenly.' If this was Paul's meaning he would seem to be encouraging the Corinthians: 'Come on, let's be eager to put on the image of Jesus.'

The resurrection of the body (15:1-58)

At Bethlehem the eternal Son of God became the human Son of God, although he did not lay his deity to one side. In the words of the statement issued by the Council of Nicaea in A.D. 325, he who was 'true God of true God ... came down and was made flesh, and became man'.[38] Further, the New Testament teaches that our Lord remains for ever what he became. When he returns he will be seen as man as well as God (Acts 17:31; Titus 2:13). If not there would be no glorified humanity for us to inherit.

The necessity of the resurrection (15:50-57)

Paul teaches that the resurrection of the church is to occur at the second coming of Christ (15:23). Because his advent must be an instant event rather than a process, the resurrection of the church must also be instantaneous.

Even though the logic is indisputable, the inference itself is quite extraordinary: the people of God, as numberless as the stars, are destined to rise simultaneously. The imagination reels.

'Flesh and blood' (15:50)

An introductory statement explains why it is that the resurrection of the church is indispensable: **'Now I say this, brethren, that flesh and blood cannot inherit the kingdom of God.'** When Paul says something he expects to be heard. It was like this with his teaching about marriage and the Lord's Table (7:29; 10:15,19), and it is so here.

In the New Testament the expression 'flesh and blood' stands for the human frame rather than man's sinful nature (Matt. 16:17; Gal. 1:16; Eph. 6:12; cf. Heb. 2:14). The apostle was perfectly aware that the kingdom of God, although not the rule of Christ over a temporary, unbelieving world, is eternal. Here he insists that the human body as it exists now cannot possibly participate in the coming glory.

There is a fundamental reason for this restriction: **'Nor does the perishable inherit the imperishable.'** Like most of the apostle's great statements, this requires careful consideration. We know from experience that our flesh is not inherently sinful. To illustrate, when the Christian exposes himself to temptations he is aware that he ought not to blame his body even though it is the vehicle of natural desires that sometimes go out of control. It is the heart that lets him down. The body eventually becomes dust because the heart is sinful (Rom. 6:23). The reasoning in 15:50 is that because the body bears the consequences of moral corruption it is barred permanently from entering a realm where sin is unknown.

Words are selected with the utmost care, in this case nouns rather than adjectives. The human frame is not pictured as a normally healthy thing that is prone to corruption; it is essentially 'the perishable [thing]', incarnate 'corruption'. Every organ, every nerve and every fibre of our being is rottenness. Juxtaposed to this is 'the kingdom of God'. This kingdom is not said to be incorruptible; rather, it is characterized by its name and title, 'the imperishable [thing]'. The King himself, his people and their habitat are perfectly holy and therefore eternal.

If, then, 'the perishable' might somehow secure admission to what is by definition 'the imperishable', the latter would be no more: the eternal plan of God would collapse, darkness would supervene and in its presence light would capitulate. But it cannot be. God will act. Christians who have fallen asleep will enter the eternal kingdom of God because their bodies become imperishable, freed from every taint of physical and moral corruption. It is precisely this prospect which is presented as a certainty rather than a vague hope.

A 'mystery' (15:51-52)

'Behold, I tell you a mystery.' Not even the Corinthians, with their spiritual gifts (1:7), had ever been remotely aware of what is about to be shared with them.

A 'mystery' is a secret revealed openly by God rather than remaining behind locked doors (as in 2:7; 4:1; 13:2; 14:2). Compare with 1 Thessalonians 4:15, where Paul writes about the coming of Christ, and does so 'by the word of the Lord'. There he claims that his message is from God and that it is transmitted through inspired words; the Lord guides Paul as he writes.

1. Did Paul expect to see the Second Coming? (15:51)

The mystery presented here is that **'We shall not all sleep, but we shall all be changed.'** In mentioning 'we' the apostle does not suggest that he, among others, would remain in this world until Christ's arrival. First, had he believed this it is obvious that he would have been seriously in error. He did die, and we in our time know that the Lord has not yet returned. Because inspiration is never wrong something else is meant.

Further, Paul often associated himself with others without implying that he was necessarily one of their number (e.g., 6:15; 10:22; 1 Thess. 4:15-17; and perhaps 2 Cor. 5:1). This is probably the meaning here. More importantly, this letter was written as conscious Scripture rather than as an ad hoc message meant exclusively for the Corinthians at that time (1:2). Because **'we'** refers effectively to the whole church of Christ, the most that is claimed is that death is not to be the experience of all believers: 'Not all sleep.'

The apostle knew that in his day some Christians had left this world, and that they would not be the last to do so. He knew also that some will be alive when the Lord appears. His message is that because deceased and surviving believers cannot enter the kingdom of God in possession of their natural bodies, **'all'** are to be **'changed'**.

In detail, the revealed mystery of 15:51 is that those who do remain in this world to welcome Christ will not fall asleep as a necessary precondition for resurrection; as living persons they are to be transformed physically. Bypassing death, their earthly bodies will be changed instantly into their resurrection form.

2. When are resurrection bodies formed? (15:52)

Exactly when do the resurrected bodies of the sleeping saints come into being? Are they to develop gradually, just as a seed changes into a plant over a period of time? It is true that Paul's metaphor of sowing does seem to imply gentle development (15:36-38,42-44). Alternatively, are these new bodies formed instantaneously when their predecessors die, perhaps to be stored in the heavens to await the second advent? Or is there some other procedure?

We are not left in doubt. The change will occur immediately when Christ comes: **'in a moment, in the twinkling of an eye'**. The selection of words is dramatic in the extreme. Although the church of God embraces 'a great multitude, which no one could count' (Rev. 7:9), each and every one of God's people is to be transformed in no more time than it takes us to blink an eye or to glance at something.

Moreover, the transformation of the church will be one single event occurring **'at the last trumpet'**. Then, the saints of both dispensations and of every age in the history of the people of God must all rise together. In short, the resurrection is to be universal, instantaneous and final.

This is a truly astonishing revelation. In the Scriptures generally trumpets would seem to perform two functions, calling people together and sounding warnings. Our Lord spoke of 'a great trumpet' that is to summon the elect (Matt. 24:31), and 15:52 refers to this.[39] On this great occasion there are to be no further warnings given to men. Time will have run out. The last of all trumpets sounds from heaven rather than from earth, heralding the resurrection of the dead and the overthrow of the final enemy, death.

Inevitability (15:53)

There is a profound reason for this universal change: resurrection is inevitable because it is necessary: **'This perishable must put on the imperishable, and this mortal must put on immortality.'** The operative word is 'must'.

The argument goes like this. Death, which disorganized the union between body and soul, is no more; the believer's physical frame and his spirit now reunited, the saint lives for ever, although not with the old, mortal body: he does not rise in order to revert to the pre-resurrection state. This is because sin and corruption cannot trespass upon the eternal kingdom of God (15:50). Compare, too, Revelation 21:27: 'Nothing unclean, and no one who practises abomination and lying, shall ever come into it.' Now we learn more: because the plan for the body-soul union of Genesis 2:7 is not to be suspended indefinitely there *must* be a completely new phase of existence for redeemed humanity.

It is for this reason that the dying body is to clothe itself with incorruption and immortality, in a sense acting for its own immediate benefit. The grammar is vivid, the three occurrences of **'put on'** in 15:53-54 implying self-interest (the Greek middle voice). It is almost as if Paul reveals that our human dust will whisper to itself, 'It's time to wake up for a new, everlasting day,' and proceeds to do so.

Are men 'immortal'? (15:54)

It is God in Christ alone who possesses 'immortality', as 1 Timothy 6:16 makes plain. This truth needs consideration. Immortality means much more than that the Almighty exists for ever, or even

The resurrection of the body (15:1-58)

that he is immune to death. The word is rich and full, signifying everlasting blessedness, a quality of being inherent in God alone. It is this blessedness which is graciously given by God to the church.

Let's stray from the subject for a moment. What of unbelievers? Is it true that they are immortal? Is it even true that all men possess immortal souls? Strictly speaking, the answer to such questions is negative, the reason being that immortality and eternity are different concepts. The first suggests quality and the second duration, which is why the Bible speaks about eternal rather than immortal judgement. But the fact that the condemned are not said to be immortal does not mean that they face obliteration.

To come back to 1 Corinthians 15, when our human dust 'puts on' corruption and deathlessness, prophecy (**'the saying that is written'**) will 'come about': ancient predictions — Isaiah 25:8 and Hosea 13:14 — are to be realized (15:54-55).

Isaiah 25:8 appears in a section of the prophecy (Isa. 24:1 - 27:13) expounding the sovereignty of Jehovah in both judging the wicked and saving his people. Death, with all its attendant miseries, is seen to have covered up all men (Isa. 25:7). In response, the Lord will swallow up the veil of death for all time, but for Israel only (Isa. 25:8); universal salvation is not predicted.

In a little more detail, **'in victory'**, Paul's flexible variation of Isaiah's 'for all time' preserves the sense of the basic Old Testament text: life is victorious in that it survives its conflict with death.

The sting of death (15:55-56)

Hosea 13:14 is a grand promise from Jehovah that he will ransom his people from the power of Sheol and redeem them from death. By 'Sheol' is meant the abode of the dead generally, a situation in which the people of God will not remain. Having effected this resurrection, the Lord exults in the spectacle of the downfall of death: 'O Death, where are your thorns? O Sheol, where is your sting?'

Paul knew that the prophets expected the Messiah to conquer death,[40] and was confident that when the Lord does come again these two ancient predictions must be fulfilled. For these reasons the apostle introduces the writings of the past to give added weight to his own revelation. He stands consciously and deliberately as a new-covenant prophet in direct succession to the prophets of old-covenant Israel.

1. Sin brings death

Death is an awful thing, and 15:56 explains why: **'The sting of death is sin, and the power of sin is the law.'** The background word for sting *(kentron)* can also mean 'goad', a pointed rod used for driving cattle. Although at his conversion Saul was told that he was like a beast pushing against its goad (Acts 26:14), the meaning here must be sting: death is described as an excruciatingly painful experience for its victims rather than an instrument prodding them on in their evil path.

Verse 56 has in view the situation of a man, now dead, who did not know Christ. During his lifetime he neither sought nor found peace with God. Having passed from this world, he is brought into final and irreversible ruin. This is why death is like a stake that had been driven through his heart and soul. The deceased individual is left with one prospect and one only, the final judgement (Heb. 9:27). Until then he remains incarcerated in a spiritual prison not of this world and with no one to plead on his behalf (2 Peter 2:9; Jude 15). When the time arrives, as it must, not only will Christ refuse to be his Saviour, none other can be.

2. The difference between right and wrong

That sin must lead to condemnation has been demonstrated historically by a unique event. This was the occasion when God placed himself on written record concerning what is right and what is wrong, confronting evil men as the implacable enemy of all that is contrary to his holy will.

When this revelation happened, and where, and to whom the mind of God was revealed are all set out with just one word, a word as fearful as it is majestic: **'law'**. We can imagine the apostle's pulse quickening as he wrote it down. By 'law' is meant the body of the commandments and the intricate pattern of conduct and worship given to Israel at Mount Sinai fifteen hundred years before Christ was born.

This law, later refined to perfection by the example, the teaching and the work of our Lord (9:21; Matt. 5:17), crystallizes the principles by which men should live. Law is said to give 'power' to sin in that the latter is isolated and identified as the malignant and potent bias of foolish men who choose to break the commandments and who bring upon themselves the wrath of God (Rom. 1:32; 5:20; 7:5,8,11).

It follows that sin is not a psychological aberration, an emotional weakness, or a social malaise that can be countered, say, by superior education or a more adequate standard of living. It is a powerful and unrelenting anti-God attitude that harms and degrades. Unless it is checked through obedient faith in Jesus Christ it leads to hell itself.

Imagine for a moment (but only for a moment) what the world would be like had not God given his law. There would be no absolute standard of conduct for men to follow and therefore no rules to break (Rom. 4:15; 5:13; 1 John 3:4). Neither holiness nor evil would exist. No deed would be right or wrong. Not even Satan could be condemned.

We need to be clear about this. In a context insisting that Christ has conquered the grave, 15:56 concerns itself with sin, death, the law and judgement. The presentation is deliberate so that 15:57 can bring into relief the prospects of the Christian.

Death, a solemn servant (15:57)

The believer who does not study his Bible might, it is true, suspect that death still frowns at him. But he would be wrong. For the child of God the role of death has been reversed dramatically. The universal tyrant has become a friendly and altogether harmless servant, his new charge being to lead dying saints to their risen Saviour rather than to the execution chamber.[41] Deceptively gloomy, the servant does no more than furrow his eyes respectfully before the privileged believer whom he must serve.

Therefore, **'Thanks be to God, who gives us the victory through our Lord Jesus Christ,'** a victory nothing less than the believer's personal triumph over death and the grave. Because all condemnation has vanished (Rom. 8:1), death brings the saint nearer to his God. His body might sleep, but his soul is consciously with the Lord Jesus. Then, when the Lord returns to this world, the believer's body is transformed and he remains with Christ for ever.

God **'gives'** us the victory. This implies that for Christians there are two movements currently operating in tandem. At the same time as this world is steadily being reduced to nothing (1:28; 2:6; 6:13; 15:24,26), the people of God approach their final, irreversible triumph.

Please turn to Colossians 3:1-2. Here we read that we have already been raised spiritually with Christ and are exhorted to fix our attention upon him. Read. Ponder. Now put your Bible down for a moment. Close your eyes, think about heaven, where the Lord Jesus is. Open your heart to him in thankfulness and prayer. In particular, bless God for the victory he is giving you today.

An encouragement and a guarantee (15:58)

Because triumph is certain the Corinthians are to be **'steadfast'**, that is, resolved about what they believe. The same word (Greek, *edraios*) occurs in 7:37 in connection with the father who has made up his mind about an important family matter.

Further, the people are to be **'immovable'**; the apostle's **'beloved brethren'** must not be swayed by false teachers who deny the resurrection or contradict any other part of Paul's teaching. The implication is that such predators are to be resisted.

They are to be **'always abounding in the work of the Lord'**. Consider this statement alongside 16:10 and Philippians 2:30, referring respectively to the consecrated labours of Timothy and Epaphroditus. The analogy suggests that each and every Corinthian is expected to be a keen supporter of the ministry of the gospel — always, and with enthusiasm.

A double negative

The apostle has claimed already that he is a hard-working labourer (3:8; 4:12; 15:10; cf. 2 Cor. 11:23). Given his passionate belief in the truth of the gospel, it is not hard for us to see that he would have spent himself. To his considerable delight he knew that there were at least some in Corinth who also stretched themselves as much as possible. He gives them an incentive: they are to go to the limit, **'knowing that your toil is not in vain in the Lord'**. This is a typical apostolic double negative. The claim that toil is not vain or empty means that there is something in it. Because it cannot be useless it must be useful.

The resurrection of the body (15:1-58)

For the Lord, and with the Lord

There is a wonderful justification for this holy optimism. Notice that Paul is not writing about labour 'for' the Lord. Rather, his concern is for what is done **'in the Lord'**. That is, if and when Christ works through the hard-working Christian the Lord has no intention of wasting his own energies; he guarantees the outcome of what he does through the efforts of the consecrated toiler.

By implication this concluding encouragement attacks the Corinthian cynics. Those who reject the doctrine of the resurrection have no certain beliefs. Nor have they ever received a commission from the Lord. Therefore they will never be hard workers. In the unlikely event of their ever being resourceful, they can achieve nothing of abiding value for Christ, for the church, for the world, or for themselves.

Workers or toilers?

Before we move on to chapter 16 and the question of the financial commitments of the Christian, let's consider the challenge of 15:58. Does our faith make us toil laboriously for the Lord rather than for enhanced personal prosperity? Many believers will work themselves to near-exhaustion to maintain attractive houses but are not always too keen to give time, perspiration and money to the **'work of the Lord'**. If your income happens to exceed your expenditure by a reasonable margin, read 1 Timothy 6:17-19.

Furthermore, are we consistently busy for the Saviour, or do we give up easily when things are difficult? Even if disappointment is no sin, the luxury of discouragement might be. In church life there will probably be more workers than toilers, more who give sincerely than sacrificially and more who resign than remain. Paul implies that unmitigated toil rather than work is a channel of blessing.

10. The conclusion to the letter
(16:1-24)

Thus far the apostle has dealt with doctrinal and practical issues of extraordinary importance and has done so with an assumption. All the way through his long letter Paul has either insisted or implied that the saints who make up the Corinthian and other churches belong to the Messianic Israel. This is the case whether they are Jewish or Gentile.

For this reason the experiences and particularly the sins of Israel in the earlier dispensation are referred to repeatedly. It would not be an overstatement to claim that if we fail to recognize the principle much of the epistle loses its meaning. The point is repeated because now, at the end of the letter, it is this continuity between the old and the new that leads Paul to broach an intensely practical matter, one no less vital than anything mentioned in the previous fifteen chapters: financial help for the saints in Jerusalem (16:1,3).

The chapter seems to fall into two main parts. The first concerns money and the apostle's impending travels (16:1-9). The second refers to some trusted colleagues and gives final admonitions and greetings (16:10-24).

The collection (16:1-9)

Elsewhere the formula, **'Now concerning...'** introduces issues about which the Corinthians certainly (7:1) or probably (7:25; 8:1; 12:1) had sought guidance. Here also the formula seems to imply a previous request for clarification of a sensitive matter (16:1).

The conclusion to the letter (16:1-24)

The question of giving is dealt with in considerable detail in 2 Corinthians 8-9. In both passages the apostle gives expression to his burning desire to see the Gentile fellowships identify with Jewish congregations by transferring needed money to them.

Supporting other churches (16:1-4)

Good examples encourage as well as provoke. Here the Galatians are held up to the Corinthians as patterns. Elsewhere the Corinthians are proposed as models for the Macedonians and the Corinthians and the Macedonians together for the Romans (2 Cor. 9:2; Rom. 15:26). The apostle was never reluctant to let the churches know that others were ahead of them in certain ways. He shows himself a wily pastor who knows all the tricks even though his artifice is, as ever, loving and his motivation pure.

Perhaps the intensity of persecution in Jerusalem (Acts 8:1; 11:19-20,29; 26:10) had reduced many Jewish Christians to abject need. Even so, for the apostle there was more to sending money to Judea than the relief of poverty. He was moved by the awareness that the Gentile churches had a special duty to help their Jewish brethren. As Romans 15:27 makes plain, this was because the Gentiles had received much spiritual blessing from them. In point of detail, persecution in Jerusalem had been the occasion for the establishment of the church at Antioch. Should not the receivers give and the givers receive? Although this much is not said here it must have been at the back of the apostle's mind.

Notice that in this sensitive matter the Corinthians are to fall into line: **'As I directed the churches of Galatia, so do you also'** (16:1). But money matters are never simple. There was the thorny question of how much the brethren should donate. **'Each one'** in the church, apparently without exception, was to calculate intelligently and responsibly what he could, rather than would, give, the amount being worked out privately **'as he may be prospered'** (16:2). The NASB reads 'as he may prosper', translating the background Greek passive verb as an active. This does not reflect the true meaning, that the believer is obliged to give in proportion to how the Lord might be prospering him, rather than in the light of his apparent success in making money. God controls the purse-strings.

Responsible Corinthian giving is to be handled by responsible stewards, including Paul when he arrives at Corinth (16:3). The principle laid down is that because money given for the Lord's people remains the Lord's property it must be handled with care by givers and administrators alike. The church at Corinth was to choose its own men to transfer the collection to Jerusalem. Determined to remain above suspicion, Paul flatly refuses to handle the matter by himself. The principle is repeated in 2 Corinthians 8:19-21. Further, he will send letters with the messengers to the Jerusalem church, no doubt to clarify for whom and for what purposes the money was being sent. Rigid safeguards were necessary to prevent hard-earned and generous gifts being frittered away in a far-off land.

Acts 19:21 gives us Paul's final itinerary at about the time when he wrote 1 Corinthians. He had decided to leave Ephesus to travel to Macedonia, onwards to Corinth and from both regions through to Jerusalem. The last sector would be attempted only if the financial contribution was sufficiently large: **'And if it is fitting for me to go also, they** [his colleagues] **will go with me'** (16:4).

Perhaps the apostle had mentally quantified the Corinthian income and had a fairly good idea of what they were capable of giving. He issues a firm warning to the people: they are to give responsibly. If not, he will abandon plans to travel to Jerusalem. Should he make this negative decision, his own failure to convey an appropriate sum would signal to all the churches that the Corinthians had not come up to expectations. In plain language, it would not be 'fitting' for him, the apostle to the Gentiles, to make an arduous journey to the mother church in order to hand over a paltry amount. Let the Corinthians do their duty or be put to shame. Paul writes with such remarkable boldness because he loved these people dearly and was committed to them. They knew it and he knew that they knew. Hence he threw down the gauntlet.

Christians and giving

Because the whole subject of how and why believers should give is important we digress a little from the commentary to think about some practical implications of 16:1-4.

Principally, these verses are not concerned with what we might term the regular 'Lord's day offering', contributions usually di-

The conclusion to the letter (16:1-24)

rected towards the expenses of one's own church. Paul's concern was with relationships between Jewish and Gentile believers living in different parts of the world at a time when the churches were young. We should bear this in mind even though some lasting principles are laid down.

Giving is a duty

Although financial contributions to the Lord's work must always be voluntary, giving a proportion of our money is a positive obligation. Although the New Testament never requires believers to give a specified amount of their income (not even, say, ten per cent, or a 'tithe'), it requires all of us to give something. How much, when, where and to whom we give are additional matters that ought not to obscure the principle.

Give to believers

Christians should be generous to fellow-believers and particularly to those needy saints who have been a blessing to the potential givers. Consider Galatians 6:6 and 1 Timothy 6:18. Although philanthropy is not wrong, how much better it is, and how much more in accordance with the spirit of the New Testament, to give to the kingdom of God! Remember the parable of the dishonest steward (Luke 16:1-9). We give now to the Lord's needy people so that they will welcome us when we join them in heaven. Let's take the long-term view about our money.

God gives us all we have

Paul assumes that God controls our income: either he gives or he withholds material benefits. If the Lord helps us materially we are to give to others a significant and responsible proportion of what we earn. If we are not prospered financially we should not feel obliged to give or pledge what we do not have. This is made plain by 2 Corinthians 8:12 even though in 16:2 the apostle appears to suggest that at Corinth 'each one' has been blessed to some extent. Nor did a certain poor widow reckon that her slender means absolved her from contributing to the temple of God (Mark 12:41-44; Luke 21:1-4).

Why we should give

The incentive for giving is expounded by 2 Corinthians 9:6-11. Those who contribute responsibly can expect to be granted more money by the Lord. Even so, and this is really important, their monetary blessings are not rewards.

In summary, there is such a thing as a cycle of blessing: generous believers attract more benefits in order to increase their giving. Money is like seed producing food given out by the generous farmer: the more seed he spreads the more food he produces, and the more food he produces the more relief he gives. Increased relief for others attracts more seed at source. This is quite unlike the notion that if we give to the Lord's work God will give us more for ourselves. The New Testament knows nothing about what is sometimes termed the 'prosperity gospel'.

When to give?

The believer is to put money aside regularly on each **'first day of the week'**, our Sunday (16:2). The day is indicated specifically by the background Greek 'first from the sabbath'. It seems obvious that in apostolic times this day was regarded by all believers as sacred (John 20:19,26; Acts 20:7; Rev. 1:10). The principle here is that the occasion of the Lord's day sanctifies gifts for the Lord.

Notice that there was to be an ongoing **'collection'** at Corinth. This implies strongly that money was to be handed in by the worshippers when they assembled together. Although the pressing needs of the churches in Judea were uppermost in Paul's mind, it is hardly likely that he intended the Lord's day offerings to peter out when those particular gifts had been collected and sent on. Giving money in the context of fellowship was, and should be, an essential element of the worship of God.

Planned contributions

The needs of the Lord's people ought not to be met by hurried giving. Paul desired that there might be no collection if and when he arrived at Corinth. This was because he was keen to avoid ill-considered and unworthy contributions made under pressure. If we do not plan our giving we will never give adequately. We dishonour ourselves, the church and the Lord.

The conclusion to the letter (16:1-24)

Be grateful for help received

The Corinthians' giving is described in 16:3 as a 'gift' (Greek, *charis*), probably meaning a 'favour'. If we receive material assistance from other Christians we should never think that it was their duty to help us, or that we deserved it. Say 'thank you', whether by word or, preferably, by letter.

Bring it to the Lord in prayer

The writer of this commentary once sat under the ministry of a zealous pastor who had worked out his theology of giving, a theology conspicuously better than his mathematics. 'Give,' he urged his flock, 'a tenth, if that is what you think the Lord wants from you.' 'But,' he added thoughtfully, 'perhaps you might give even more, maybe an eleventh. Pray. Don't be legalistic.' Amen.

Plans for travelling to and from Corinth (16:5-9)

The original travel-plan had been to move directly from Ephesus to Corinth, from Corinth northwards to Macedonia, back to Corinth, and thence to Judea (2 Cor. 1:15-17). Subsequently the apostle changed his mind. Writing from Ephesus, he reveals that he is about to tour the Macedonian churches before coming to Corinth, a journey he eventually made (16:5; Acts 19:21; 20:1). Effectively, the Corinthians were given notice that they had been demoted in the apostolic list of priorities. No wonder that some of them were upset and that they were not reluctant to air their opinions. From the apostle's point of view there was an excellent reason for his revision, and we learn about it in 2 Corinthians. Suffice to say that there he defends himself vigorously against being inconsistent and irresponsible.

In anticipation of this new itinerary he writes that he will perhaps stay for a while, or even spend the winter at Corinth (16:6). In the event, he remained there for some three months, as against eighteen months for the first visit (Acts 18:11; 20:3). His travel plans after staying at Corinth were rather uncertain, hence his comment, **'wherever I might go'** (16:6). This is in spite of his expressed hope to arrive eventually at Jerusalem. The reference to the Corinthians sending him on his way shows that he expected the visit to their city to be fruitful and happy.

In 4:19 the apostle indicated that his stay at Corinth would only be 'if the Lord wills'. Here he reaffirms the principle, but employs a slightly different expression, **'if the Lord permits'** (16:7). Paul had worked through his arrangements and now shares what he hopes to do, aware that heaven might have other plans, as had once been the case in Asia (Acts 16:6-10). On the other hand, perhaps the wind of the Spirit will fill the sails of his vessel and drive him to his desired haven. Time will tell. In any event, all is subject to a higher intelligence.

Although the apostle was reasonably certain about where next he ought to move in his work for the Lord, he was always ready to rethink his arrangements. He displayed flexibility as well as faith. Much can be learned here about the tactics of Christian service. We should refer everything to the Lord for his final permission and want what he makes clear he wants. Read James 4:13-16.

The intention was to remain at Ephesus **'until Pentecost'** in the following year when the weather would be good enough for Paul to set out on the long journey (16:8). There were, it is disclosed, two other reasons for staying in Asia (16:9). First, **'a wide door for effective service'** had been **'opened'**. That is, there were golden opportunities for presenting the gospel, opportunities not to be left unexploited. We know that when he finally left Ephesus the apostle found another door opened for him at Troas on the European side of the Dardanelles (2 Cor. 2:12). As ever, the Lord led him on.

Secondly, there were **'many adversaries'**, probably unconverted Jews and Greeks and possibly Christian Judaizers (Acts 19:9,13-16,23-28; 20:29-30). Paul would not leave Ephesus until he had made every effort to safeguard the church there.

Final remarks (16:10-24)

Concerning Timothy and Apollos (16:10-12)

According to Acts 19:22, Erastus and Timothy had been sent ahead of Paul to Macedonia, the plan being that Timothy would proceed to Corinth (4:17). In 16:10 the apostle refers to the reception the young man ought to receive should he come. Bearing in mind that the autograph of 1 Corinthians was dispatched from Ephesus after

The conclusion to the letter (16:1-24)

Timothy's departure, it might be that Paul provides back up for the younger man: time needed for him to attend to problems in the Macedonian churches plus the hazards of travel could lead to his delayed arrival at Corinth. Hence the comment: **'if Timothy comes'**.

Timothy was relatively young, somewhat timid and probably less than physically robust. Furthermore, he was Paul's subordinate (1 Tim. 4:12; 5:23; 2 Tim. 1:6-8; 2:1-7). The apostle was well aware that if some of the Corinthians had already challenged his authority, electing not to regard him as a servant of Christ (4:1), they would undoubtedly give his junior colleague a difficult time. Therefore, upon arrival the latter must be **'without fear'** (16:10), assured of the respect due to someone who works 'like a child serving with his father' (Phil. 2:22).

Either **'the Lord's work'** (16:10) was work that the Lord undertook personally through his servants, or the labour to which he had appointed Paul and Timothy, or both. In the light of 15:58, 'abounding in the work of the Lord', the first view might be better.

The psalmist wrote that 'I am small and despised, yet I do not forget thy precepts' (Ps. 119:141); tender years can attract ridicule. For their part, the Corinthians were not to despise Timothy (16:11). Even as they were required to send Paul on his way (16:6), so they should dispatch Timothy in peace, in this case back to his superior.

It appears that Timothy was to return to Paul in the company of some brethren, possibly Titus and an unnamed co-worker (perhaps Erastus, if we compare Acts 19:22 and 2 Cor. 12:18). On one occasion Paul went by himself to Corinth (Acts 18:1), and he knew how arduous and lonely travel could be. Therefore he was reluctant to allow a young man to attempt a somewhat longer solo journey.

Apparently the Corinthians had asked that Apollos might be sent back to them. The opening of 16:12, **'But concerning...'**, suggests that Paul is alluding to sensitive issues relayed to him from the church. Nor was the apostle unsympathetic to the needs of the people: **'I encouraged him greatly to come to you with the brethren,'** possibly with Timothy and others, or even with the returning three-man delegation from Corinth to Paul at Ephesus (16:17).

During his first visit to Achaia Apollos was an enormous help to the church (Acts 18:27-28). For some unexplained reason he had left to go back to Ephesus. From 16:12 it transpires that later he declined flatly to return to Corinth, considering himself free to stay where he was. Presumably this was because he was not under Paul's authority. For his part, the apostle was unable to insist that the Alexandrian must make the journey.

Why Apollos was unwilling to return must remain a matter of speculation. Was he discouraged by the factions at Corinth, one revolving around his name (3:4), or, which is more likely, was there local business that took priority? Even so, promises the apostle on the word of his fellow-worker, he will come **'when he has opportunity'**. Paul, eager that Apollos should be with the church in his absence, knew neither fear of, nor jealousy for, a highly-talented, God-blessed and popular colleague.

An exhortation to the church (16:13-14)

The people were asleep and needed to wake up (16:13). They were to stand in the faith because they were tottering to and fro with few solid beliefs to hold them up. They were to act like men because they seemed to be cowardly. They were to allow themselves to be strengthened because they had become spiritually and morally weak. Further, all their activities were to be performed in love (16:14). The preceding chapters reveal just why this advice was so necessary.

Concerning the delegation sent by the Corinthians to Paul (16:15-18)

The apostle urges the whole church to be at peace, referring specifically to some of their best people (16:15-16).

What a joy Stephanas and his family must have been to Paul! Not only were they the first of the Achaians to profess the faith, but their conversions led to lives well-spent for Christ. With people like this in Corinth hope was not extinct. The apostle's meaning is that voluntary helpers of their calibre (**'such men'**) generate their own authority within a fellowship and that such authority should be recognized and honoured. The household of Stephanas has much to teach us.

A specific example of Stephanas' commitment to the Lord and the saints was his sea-journey, accompanying Fortunatus and

The conclusion to the letter (16:1-24)

Achaicus, from Corinth to visit Paul at Ephesus (16:17). In those times travel was no light matter. That the three men probably brought the letter mentioned in 7:1 is a tribute to their devotion. Because the well-being of their home church was a matter of first importance the perils of land and sea were not reckoned to be an insuperable problem.

The apostle had been thrilled about the arrival of the delegation; these men compensated him for the absence of the church. Notice that Paul writes **'rejoice'** rather than 'rejoiced'; the glow remains even as he pens these words. Moreover, they had supplied **'what was lacking on your part'**. The apostle loved his Corinthians and made no attempt to disguise his joy at the arrival of their representatives. When the delegation reached him it was almost as if he were back at Corinth. The apostle had a remarkably large heart.

'What was lacking' might be interpreted as a failure by the Corinthians to share their news and needs. Alternatively, it could have been a shortfall in missionary support. Perhaps the former interpretation is the better: Paul was delighted to be in touch with the church again, albeit indirectly; what he had missed were the people rather than their cash.

Moreover, the three men had **'refreshed'** both the apostle's **'spirit and yours'**, by which is meant his own morale and that of the Corinthian church (16:18). It might be that Paul, as their spiritual father (4:15), had been restless in the absence of news from Corinth. Also, when intelligence arrived it had not been uniformly good (1:11). Now, because he knew how matters stood, he could unwind a little.

We can easily see how these three men were a blessing to Paul. But how could the arrival of this delegation have given rest to the home church? One answer might be that the decision to send the men to Ephesus must have been a refreshment for them; Paul understood that the fellowship that shows an interest in others helps itself. Maybe he knew also that the eventual reception of this letter, bringing positive news about the delegation's visit to Ephesus, would uplift the congregation.

Greetings from the Asian churches; Paul's final word (16:19-24)

'The churches of Asia greet' the Corinthians (16:19). Ephesus was the principal city in an area that included the seven churches of the

Apocalypse (Rev. 1:4,11). The apostle knew that the Lord was multiplying his people rapidly.

In the Greek Old Testament 'to greet' *(aspazomai)* is equivalent to the background Hebrew 'to seek for peace'. According to Exodus 18:7, Moses and his father-in-law wished each other peace when they met. Paul employs this expression forty times in his letters because he was always concerned to encourage healthy relationships among the churches.

Aquila and Priscilla (16:19)

Aquila and Priscilla, resident also at Ephesus with Paul (Acts 18:18-19), sent particularly warm greetings. This is understandable because when they lived for a time at Corinth they opened their home to the apostle and witnessed the rapid development of the infant church in the city (Acts 18:2-3). They were well loved. To judge from Romans 16:3, they went back to Rome not long after 1 Corinthians was written. For reasons which are not usually plain this apparently affluent and independent couple were often on the move.

Not surprisingly, the church in their house identified with their greetings. Aquila and Priscilla made it a practice to extend hospitality to congregations whenever they were able. They gave shelter to Apollos (Acts 18:26) and to some of the Ephesians, and at one stage accommodated a fellowship at Rome (Rom. 16:5). According to 2 Timothy 4:19, it appears that they travelled again to Ephesus (supposing that to have been the letter's destination). We cannot imagine them not serving the Lord's people whatever their circumstances. That they were involved with house meetings was not because of a desire to be different. At that time Christians had to meet in this way because they did not possess church buildings.

The kiss (16:20)

'All the brethren' salute the Corinthians. Paul speaks for everybody at Ephesus because he was trusted by everybody. The **'holy kiss'** commanded by the apostle could not have been more than a sign of affection, or even of submission. Contrast the false kiss of Judas Iscariot (Matt. 26:49; Mark 14:45; Luke 22:47). This pattern of kiss is mentioned also in Romans 16:16; 2 Corinthians 13:12 and 1 Thessalonians 5:26. 1 Peter 5:14 refers to the undoubtedly similar 'kiss of love'.

The conclusion to the letter (16:1-24) 371

The adjective 'holy' shows that there were no unworthy undertones. Presumably, men and women would not have been allowed to kiss one another. Compare Paul's caution with the statement of 2 John 1, acknowledging that John loved an elect lady *and* her children, and John 11:5, recording the love of Jesus for two women *and* their brother.

In Paul's own hand (16:21)

It appears that the apostle's normal practice was to dictate his letters to a secretary, yet ending them himself (Rom. 16:22; Col. 4:18; 2 Thess. 3:17). That he wrote the whole of the letter to the Galatians in his own hand was exceptional (Gal. 6:11). These last verses, 16:21-24, written by Paul personally, are typical of the man. They display a concern and a winsomeness that could not have failed to win the hearts of many. Love and consideration can achieve when cold argument, be it ever so convincing, must repel.

Love for the Lord and for his people (16:22-24)

For Paul, to **'love the Lord'** (16:22) was the same as loving God, the reason being that the Saviour is God. This is why he indicates that if someone in the church fails in this highest duty, **'Let him be accursed.'** 'Accursed' translates 'anathema', a word that has occurred in 12:3 in a very different context. Because the apostle would never employ unintelligible expressions (14:19), the Corinthians must have heard this formula before. They knew what he meant.

The apostle could not write about loveless believers with unruffled composure. He indicates that it is a dreadful matter to be a professing Christian within a church and in spite of this not to know the Lord. Evidently there were such people at Corinth, which would explain why 2 Corinthians 5:20 urges the fellowship to 'Be reconciled to God' and why 2 Corinthians 13:5 instructs the readers to 'Test yourselves, to see if you are in the faith.'

'Maranatha' should possibly be read 'marana tha', two Aramaic words which in combination mean, 'Our Lord comes' or 'Our Lord, come', a cry often upon the lips of Christian people (Rev. 22:20). 'Maranatha' is effectively an urgent warning to those who may not love the Lord that they need to consider their ways before Christ does appear. The expression occurs also in the early second-century A.D. *The Teaching of the Twelve Apostles,* 10:6, in a context that exhorts those who are not holy to avoid the Lord's Table because their presence would attract present and future judgement. The Corinthians' notorious abuse of the communion meal might have been in the anonymous author's mind.

Again and again in his letters the apostle begins or ends, or both begins and ends, by referring to **'the grace'** that Jesus gives.[1] It is like this in 16:23. Although there might be some who never came to love the Lord and who crept into the church under false pretences, this is not the position of the overwhelming majority of the Corinthians. Therefore, may this grace **'be with you all'**.

The apostle concludes with an assurance to the church that his love is with **'you all in Christ Jesus'** (16:24). This is in spite of the sad fact that some of them had been extraordinarily hurtful. Remember 4:8-10, which contrasts the affluence and arrogance of the Corinthians with the poverty and humiliation of the apostles. Paul loved his neighbours as himself.

Apart from **'Amen'**, which is omitted by a few manuscripts, the final word in the letter is **'Jesus'**. The author was acutely conscious that no one is as important as the Saviour. The Lord remains alpha and omega, beginning and end, first and last. In him we have all things; without him there is nothing.

Appendix I
1 Corinthians and the Old Testament

The first letter to the Corinthians assumes that the Christian churches are the Israel of the Messianic age. This is why the epistle is saturated with allusions to, and quotations from, the Old Testament. Although no claim is made to complete accuracy, here are what appear to be the allusions, both certain and possible, and the quotations:

Allusions

1:9	Deut. 7:9
1:20	Job 12:17-18; Isa. 19:11-12; 33:18; 44:25-26
1:23	Isa. 8:14-15; Hosea 14:9
2:6,8	Ps. 2:2,10
2:16	Isa. 40:13
3:11	Isa. 28:16
4:4	Job 27:6
5:7	Exod. 12:21; 13:7
5:8	Exod. 12:14
5:13	Deut.17:7; 19:19; 22:21,24; 24:7
6:2	Dan. 7:22
6:17	Deut. 10:20
7:30-31	Ezek. 7:12
8:4	Deut. 4:35,39; 6:4
9:7	Deut. 20:6
9:13	Lev. 6:16,26; Num. 18:8,31; Deut. 18:1-3
10:1-2	Exod. 13:21-22; 14:20-22

10:3	Exod. 16:4,35; Deut. 8:3
10:4	Exod. 17:6; Num. 20:11
10:5	Num. 14:16,23,29-30; Ps. 78:31
10:6	Num. 11:4,34
10:8	Num. 25:1,9
10:9	Num. 21:5-6; Ps. 78:18
10:10	Num. 14:2,36; 16:41-49
10:13	Deut. 7:9
10:18	Lev. 7:6,15
10:20	Deut. 32:17; Ps. 106:37
10:21	Mal. 1:7,12
10:22	Deut. 32:21
10:26	Ps. 24:1; 50:12; 89:11
11:3	Gen. 3:16
11:7	Gen. 1:27; 5:1; 9:6
11:8	Gen. 2:21-23
11:9	Gen. 2:18
11:19	Deut.13:3
11:25	Exod. 24:8; Jer. 31:31; Zech. 9:11
13:5	Zech. 8:17
13:12	Num. 12:6-8
14:5	Num. 11:29
14:25	Isa. 45:14; Zech. 8:23
14:34	Gen. 3:16
14:39	Num. 11:28
15:3	Isa. 53:8-9
15:4	Ps. 16:10
15:21	Gen. 2:17; 3:17-19
15:25	Ps. 110:1
15:32	Isa. 22:13
15:38	Gen.1:11
15:39	Gen. 1:21,24-25
15:47	Gen. 2:7
15:49	Gen. 5:3
16:8	Exod. 34:22; Lev. 23:15-21; Deut. 16:9-11

Direct quotations

1:19	Isa. 29:14
1:31	Jer. 9:24

Appendix I

2:9	Isa. 64:4
3:19	Job 5:13
3:20	Ps. 94:11
6:16	Gen. 2:24
9:9	Deut. 25:4
10:7	Exod. 32:6
14:21	Deut. 28:49; Isa. 28:11-12
15:27	Ps. 8:6
15:45	Gen. 2:7
15:54-55	Isa. 25:8; Hosea 13:14

Appendix II
Visions and mirrors

The Hebrew alphabet has always been composed of consonants with almost no vowels. This meant that as long as the traditional pronunciation and spelling of words were kept alive there was no problem about reading the Old Testament. But after the dispersion of Israel in the first century of the Christian era matters changed; it was perceived that Jews who spoke little or no Hebrew or Aramaic would be unable to understand the Scriptures in the original language unless they were given reading aids.

That the ancient vocalization of the sacred texts was preserved for posterity was due largely to the dedicated labours of the Massoretes (literally, 'transmitters'), a school of Jewish scribes operating from about A.D. 500 to 1000. They devised an elaborate but logical system of vowel signs inserted into the jealously guarded script to fix its pronunciation. Although their apparatus was noninspired it has always proved essential for the reading of the Hebrew Bible by both Christians and Jews.[1]

Mirrors and the vocalized text

In the Massoretic Old Testament there are two principal words for 'vision'. One of these, *mar'ah*, which appears in Numbers 12:6, is relatively rare, occurring elsewhere eleven times only (Gen. 46:2; Exod. 38:8; 1 Sam. 3:15; Ezek. 1:1; 8:3; 40:2; 43:3; Dan. 10:7 (twice),8,16). Perhaps *mar'ah* emphasized the mode rather than the content of a revelation, although this should not be pressed too much. The boy Samuel had to 'tell the vision [*mar'ah*] to Eli' (1 Sam. 3:15). The other word, *hezyôn*, is much more common, stressing the actual content of prophetic revelation.[2] With regard to the consonantal *mrh*, there can be little doubt that the Massoretic *mar'ah* preserves the traditional articulation and meaning.

The point to be made is that because the occurrences of *mar'ah* are so few it might be that this Hebrew word sustained what for Westerners are two distinct meanings: 'mirror' and 'vision'. That is, the evidence appears to show that *mar'ah* was not simply a homonym for 'vision' and 'mirror', but that the former was conceptualized in terms of the latter.

There is considerable evidence in favour of this suggestion. From at least the time of Moses, about 1500 B.C., prophetic revelations were considered to be indirect, obscure and incomplete. Often they were held to be mediated through dreams, phenomena which, if we think about it, are indirect pictures. Numbers 12:6, alluded to in 13:12, states categorically that when they were asleep the prophets were granted revelations from God. Compare, too, Joel 2:28, cited by Acts 2:17, in which prophetic visions (*hezyônôt* rather than *mar'ôt*, plural of *mar'ah*) are connected with dreams.

This was true for others besides the prophets of the Lord: 'Pharaoh awoke, and behold it was a dream' (Gen. 41:7). The royal idolater knew that what he had seen was a picture of something real, and he wanted to find out what the reality was.[3] Cuneiform tablets from Ugarit (now Ras Shamra) in northern Phoenicia and dated to about the fourteenth century B.C. employ a single word (*drt*) for both 'dream' and 'vision'.[4]

To recapitulate, it has been suggested in the body of the commentary that 13:12 recalls *mar'ah*, Numbers 12:6. That is to say, prophetic visions are portrayed by Paul somewhat ironically as hazy and inadequate mirror-images. The task now is to present evidence to sustain the thesis.

Exodus 38:8

Translated without exception elsewhere in the Old Testament as 'vision', here *mar'ah* definitely means a metal mirror: 'Moreover, he [Bezalel] made the laver of bronze with its base of bronze, from the mirrors of the serving women who served at the doorway of the tent of meeting.' This is the earliest available evidence we have in favour of the vision-mirror parallel.

Ezekiel

Centuries after Moses, about 600 B.C., the prophet Ezekiel saw visions. These impress the reader of his book as virtual reflections. Certainly, the word the prophet almost always employs is *mar'ah* (Ezek. 1:1; 8:3; 40:2; 43:3). Ezekiel emphasizes repeatedly that the chariot of fire and its intricate details appeared to him as a series of likenesses rather than as an objective reality (Ezek. 1:1,4-28; 8:1-2; 10:1-22; 43:3). The pattern fits, particularly if, as has been suggested, the crystal firmament was a reflecting surface.[5]

Between the Testaments

With the passage of time the concept of the prophetic vision as a species of reflection took firm root. The apocryphal Ecclesiasticus, written originally in Hebrew about 200 B.C., states that 'The vision of dreams is as this thing against that, the likeness of a face over against a face' (34:3). The vision comes via a dream and a dream is a reflection. Because the original Hebrew is unknown there is no real proof that Sirach, the author, employed *mar'ah* even though there can be no doubt about the parallel he draws between mirrors and visions. With reference to this verse, R. H. Charles noted that 'Dream and mirror are alike in this, that the image in both is a mere reflection as contrasted with the reality. There may be the further idea that as a mirror merely reflects what is placed opposite, so a dream merely portrays what is read into it.'[6]

The analogy was evident to other peoples. Aristotle remarked that 'The most skilful judge of dreams is the man who possesses the ability to detect likenesses ... by likenesses I mean that the mental pictures are like reflections in water.' Philo of Alexandria, in some ways more a Greek than a Jew, wrote that 'In deep sleep the mind ... fixing its gaze on truth as in a mirror discerns in dreams absolutely true prophecies concerning things to come.'[7]

In Israel this particular word for 'vision', *mar'ah*, took on 'mirror' as its first meaning. The shift will be documented below. We are told, too, that during the inter-testamental period prophecy was perceived to be extinct (1 Maccabees 4:46; 9:27; 14:41). Could later generations have remembered that the prophets had seen things, albeit indirectly

Appendix II

and never with perfect clarity? No great leap of the imagination might have been needed to consider visions as mirror-reflections.

Later Hebrew

Qumran

1. The War Rule

Among the 'Dead Sea' scrolls found at Qumran there survives a lengthy manuscript known as *The War Rule,* perhaps written in the last decades of the first century B.C. or at the beginning of the first century A.D. It is basically an account of a predicted final conflict between the 'sons of light', Israel, and the 'sons of darkness', Satan's army. Lines 5 and 11 of column 5 are relevant. They insist that the swords and metal shields of the sons of light are to be polished to such an extent that each resembles 'a vision [*mar'ah*] of a face'. Note that the mirror and its image, reflecting agent and reflection, are considered as one: a polished shield *is* a reflected image, a representation of something else.

2. The Angelic Liturgy

This is a document concerned with heavenly worship, the main background source being Ezekiel, especially chapters 1 and 10 for the throne-chariot and 40-48 for the heavenly sanctuary. On general grounds the composition is thought to belong to the first century B.C. Significantly, Ezekiel is said to have seen likenesses rather than objective reality. The liturgy states concerning the throne that 'From between his glorious wheels there is as it were a fiery vision [*mar'é ésh*] of most holy spirits. About them, the appearance of rivulets of fire in the likeness of gleaming brass.'[8] Reflections come immediately to mind.

The Mishnah

The same word, *mar'ah*, occurs in the Mishnah, a compendium of oral law that, as has been remarked, was in existence by the end of the second century A.D. Here *mar'ah* signifies a metal mirror rather than a glass reflector (Kelim 14.6; 30.2), although it must have been appreciated that 'vision' was the other primitive meaning of the word.

The rabbis and Ezekiel

That Jewish scholars considered Ezekiel's visions to have been like reflections is suggested by a document entitled *Visions of Ezekiel*, originating in the fourth or fifth centuries A.D. The rabbis often displayed an intense interest in Ezekiel's chariot, and this work might be the earliest known text on the subject, preserving early traditions about visions. The prophet is said to have beheld reflections from the surface of the river Chebar, and to have seen God in the same way that a man might behold a king indirectly by means of a mirror.[9]

From Greek to Hebrew

I have been struck by the translation of 1 Corinthians 13:12 in the Hebrew New Testaments published by the Trinitarian Bible Society and the British and Foreign Bible Society. Both give: 'For ... we see in a mirror [or, 'in a vision', *mar'ah*] and by riddles,' reproducing quite unmistakably, although no doubt unintentionally, the Hebrew text of Numbers 12:6. These versions are not, it should be said, conclusive proof of the point being made.

The imagination travels back two millennia to Ephesus where the bilingual Paul, with mirror-like visions on his mind, thought out what he wanted to say in 13:12 in terms of the Hebrew of Numbers 12:6, even though he was writing in Greek.

These illustrations have been selected from a wealth of material to show that the shift in the primary emphasis of *mar'ah* from 'vision' to 'mirror' was well-established in Paul's time and he could hardly have been unaware of it.[10]

A rabbinic red herring

How did the rabbis grapple with Numbers 12:6-8? What was their appreciation of the distinctive media of revelation granted respectively to the prophets and to Moses?

Appendix II

The fallacy

1. The face of God

Their surviving writings show that these Jewish scholars were almost, if not always, controlled by the flat statement of Exodus 33:20 that no man can see the face of God and live. Nor were they wrong. But it may be suggested that their inference was off track, laying a trail that has misled not a few modern investigations into the provenance of Paul's mirror-metaphor.

What the rabbis did was to misinterpret Moses' sight of Jehovah 'plainly' (E. J. Young's translation of *mar'eh*, 'form', Num. 12:8).[11] They made out that in company with the prophets the legislator saw what he saw 'in a vision'. Nor did the rabbis innovate. They probably expressed a long-standing tradition about how Moses, for them the greatest of men, was permitted to see something of the Lord. A liturgical prayer from Qumran, necessarily dated pre-A.D. 70, addresses the God who at Sinai renewed his covenant with Israel 'in a vision [*mar'ah*] of glory.'[12] The problem here is that the Bible never describes the Sinai theophany as a 'vision'.

Because the Jewish evaluation of how Moses saw the Lord is fundamentally important it needs exposition. To illustrate the point I have remoulded Numbers 12:6-8 after what might have been the fashion of the rabbis. The italics and parentheses are mine:

> *v. 6.* And he said, 'Hear now my words. If there shall be your prophet Jehovah; in a *vision* [*mar'ah*] to him will I make myself known, in a dream will I speak with him.
> *v. 7.* Not so my servant Moses; in all my house he is faithful.
> *v. 8.* Mouth to mouth I speak with him, and by *vision* [*mar'ah*], and not in enigmatic sayings, and the resemblance [or, 'similitude', 'apparition', but not 'form'] of Jehovah he will see. And why were you not afraid to speak with my servant, with Moses?'

Whether or not some of the rabbinic commentators disapproved of the much earlier Septuagint differentiation (12:6, Greek *en oramati*, 'in a vision'; 12:8, *en eidei*, 'in a form') is uncertain. What seems definite is that they tended to understand consonantal *mrh* in 12:8 as *mar'ah* ('vision'), deliberately duplicating *mar'ah* in 12:6.

In this way they usually backed off from what would turn out in time as the Massoretic *mar'eh* ('form') in 12:8.

From their point of view there was a perfectly good reason for this procedure: they could not accept that Moses saw anything of God, let alone the divine face, with his naked eyes. For this reason they concluded that, together with the other prophets, the lawgiver received visions.

2. Moses and the prophets

The difficulty with this avenue of interpretation is that Numbers 12:6-8 insists that Moses was *not* like the other prophets: he did *not* see visions. Nor were his revelations in any way enigmatic. What he heard he heard plainly, and what he saw he saw clearly. One presumes that Paul was perfectly aware of the difference and that he based the theology of 1 Corinthians 13 upon it. Had he not perceived the distinction between the media defined by Numbers 12:6-8 he would have summed up Moses as another, albeit extraordinary, recipient of hazy revelations, thus demoting him to the level of the non-legislative prophets. This he could not have done.[13]

The rabbis erred in confusing face-to-face verbal communication with direct, unimpeded vision. But the two were by no means the same. To enlarge upon what has been said, Moses heard God speaking to him directly. Moreover, he understood all that he was told. Yet with his eyes he saw something of the being of God rather than everything. Paul appreciated this and comes across as a better student of Torah than the rabbis (and some moderns).

Evidence for the rabbinic fallacy

There is an abundance of material which shows that post-destruction Judaism never got away from the idea that Moses as well as the prophets received visions. The only perceived difference was the number and/or the quality of the visions given respectively to Moses and the prophets:

1. Siphre Bemidbar

Included in the oldest commentaries of a biblical kind embodied in Jewish literature and in their original form possibly predating the

Appendix II

Bar Kokba revolt (A.D. 132-135), Siphre Bemidbar ('Numbers in the wilderness') considers Numbers 12:6-8.

Whereas in the biblical text consonantal *mrh* occurs in each verse, Siphre replaces *mrh* in verse 6 with another word, *hezyôn* ('apparition'), implying perhaps that prophetic visions were ecstatic and hallucinatory, inferior to the sight enjoyed by Moses.[14] But the author guards himself, Exodus 33:20 being introduced into the discussion to show that not even Moses could have seen anything of the Lord directly.

2. Targum Onkelos

'Onkelos' was Aquila, a Jew of the second century A.D. who translated the Old Testament into literal Greek, although his name became associated with the Aramaic version. The *targum*, originating about A.D. 145,[15] relates that the prophets saw 'in visions' (Num. 12:6), while Moses saw via a single 'vision' (Num. 12:8). It ought to be noted that the Aramaic noun for vision is not identical to that behind mirror in Exodus 38:8. Apparently, Aquila would not make a flat identification of 'vision' as 'mirror'.

3. Targum Neophyti

This dates from the fourth or fifth centuries A.D. but is thought to have a pre-Christian origin.[16] Both the prophets and Moses saw *'en visiones'* (Macho's Spanish translation), the media being the same in each case. As in Onkelos, and perhaps for a similar reason, the Aramaic word for 'vision' is not quite the same as that translating 'mirrors' in Exodus 38:8. Nevertheless, the fallacy persists.

4. The Babylonian Talmud

This massive work dates from not earlier than the sixth century A.D. In Seder Nashim I ('Order of women'), Yebamoth 49b asserts that each of the prophets looked into a dim glass, whereas Moses looked through a clear glass. Like theirs, his visual perception was a reflection of reality. The footnote to the printed text observes that 'In his prophetic insight he [Moses] knew that the deity could not be seen with mortal eye.'[17]

5. Leviticus Rabbah

Dated to the seventh century A.D., this work equates 'mirror' and 'vision' (1.14). The document approves the view of one rabbi that although Moses and the prophets were alike granted *'specularia'* as visual aids, Moses saw by means of one polished mirror whereas the prophets, exemplified by Ezekiel *par excellence*, through nine blurred mirrors. The media of revelation were identical even though the degrees of reflection were different.

Modern scholarship

The unfolding of 13:8-13 is made more difficult by those commentators who recognize that Paul could not have anticipated the rabbinic approach to Numbers 12:6-8. But it may be suspected that some moderns go off at a tangent in proposing that the apostle derived his mirror metaphor from an extra-biblical source, probably from Greek thought.[18] In the commentary it has been suggested that this route leads nowhere.

What almost all researchers, Protestant and Roman Catholic, do *not* do is to acknowledge a possible connection between Paul's mirror in 1 Corinthians 13:12 and *mar'ah* in Numbers 12:6. It is here that we come to the crux of the matter. Why, then, does scholarship avert its gaze from something so obvious? Could it be because 'the perfect thing' might turn out to be other than, and prior to, the coming of Christ — even a canon of new-covenant writings?

A mirror and its image

Let's go back to the idea of a reflecting surface considered as, in effect, a vision: we glance at the metal and see something else (possibly, but not necessarily, our faces). What is the difference between the burnished metal and the vision it displays? From the point of view of ordinary spectators, not much. Perhaps nothing at all.

In our modern, scientifically orientated world we refer to mirror-reflections or mirror-images, but never to 'mirror-visions'. If we did speak like this we might be considered quaint. Further, we

Appendix II

distinguish between the mirror and its reflection; for us the one is not the other.

But consider. 'Reflect' means to bend or throw something backwards (compare 'flex' and 'reflex'). The word is virtually a scientific term because it assumes that mirrored light travels to and fro. Now suppose that we are Hebrews living at the turn of the ages when Paul wrote 1 Corinthians. There is no such word as 'reflection' in our language and we may not be not aware of the physics of light. This does not mean, of course, that we are ignorant or ill-informed. Because we live in a different age the mirror *is* its image and the image *is* the mirror.

We know that in earlier times prophets had been sent from God and that these prophets saw things indirectly. Furthermore, *mar'ah*, a word for 'vision' employed in our Scriptures and often in later literature, is precisely that which we employ for a piece of highly-polished metal, an object that in itself becomes from time to time virtually a picture or a vision.

The evidence suggests strongly that this is how it was. Interestingly, modern Hebrew tells us that this is how it is now: *mar'ah* still means (first) 'mirror' and (second) 'vision'. This commentary postulates that here, in the semantic equivalence between 'mirror' and 'vision', lies the provenance of the mirror metaphor of 13:12.

In short, because dreams were like mirror-images and because prophetic visions often came through as dreams, the prophets were thought to behold dim but suggestive reflections. This was often the case, too, when these servants of the Lord were not asleep. The probability is that versatile Paul, mindful of Corinthian bronzeware and clanging Christians, employs the ancient analogy in his refutation of charismatic pretensions.

Notes

Preface
1. In making this claim I am flying in the face of much modern scholarship. For example, it has been claimed with regard to 1 Corinthians that 'It is crucial ... to recognize that Paul is not writing a timeless tractate. His witness is addressed to a specific historical situation and participates in the contingency of that movement... To the extent to which historical critical research can aid in illuminating Paul's witness, it provides an invaluable interpretive tool' (Childs, *New Testament as Canon*, pp.273-4).

This apparently 'either/or' approach is typical. But surely it is perfectly legitimate to take a 'both-and' view of the matter. If so, Paul addressed a contemporary situation and the needs of all the churches in the complete period between the first and second advents of Christ.

The background to 1 Corinthians
1. Rom. 15:24,28. The First Epistle of Clement to the Corinthians, usually dated about A.D. 95, was sent to Corinth on behalf of the church in Rome. It states that Paul 'reached the limits of the west' (5:7). This suggests a point far west of the imperial city.
2. Acts 16:37; 22:3,25; 1 Tim. 2:7.
3. Matt. 27:24; Mark 15:15; Luke 23:25; John 19:12-16; Acts 3:13.
4. Josephus, *Wars* 3.540.
5. Alexander Pope, *An Essay on Criticism*, lines 215-18.
6. Dio Chrysostum, *The Corinthian Oration* 4.8.36.
7. Dio Chrysostum, *On Virtue* 4-5.
8. Horace, *Epistles* 1.17.36.
9. Dio Chrysostum, *The Corinthian Oration* 4.34; Pindar, *Eulogy* 12 (87); Pausanias, *Corinth* 5.1.
10. Pausanias, *Corinth*, 1.5.
11. Dio Cassius, *Book 21*.
12. Dio Cassius, *Books 21,43*.
13. Philo, *The Embassy to Gaius* 281; Murphy-O'Connor, 'The Corinth that Saint Paul saw', p.153.

Notes

14. Seneca, *Epistle 104*; Dio Cassius, 61.35; 62.25; Acts 25:11-12; 27:24; cf. 2 Tim. 4:16.
15. As suggested by Murphy-O'Connor, 'The Corinth that Saint Paul saw', p.154.
16. The NASB reading. Some manuscripts read 'mystery' instead of 'testimony', 2:1. 'Mystery' is probably better.
17. Romans 16:5 in the *Textus Receptus* refers to Epaenetus as the 'first-fruits of Achaia'. But this reading is questionable.
18. The all-important 'Delphi inscription' helps to date Paul's time at Corinth. For example, see Morris, *Epistles of Paul to the Thessalonians*, pp.14-15.

1. The introduction to the letter

1. Hence 3:10-12; 2 Cor. 12:12; Eph. 2:20.
2. Acts 2:21; 7:59; 9:21; 15:17; 22:16; Rom. 10:12-14; 2 Cor. 1:23; 2 Tim. 2:22; Heb. 11:16; James 2:7; cf. 1 Peter 1:17.
3. Cf. Gal. 6:16; Eph. 2:19.

2. Divisions within the church

1. Cf. 2 Cor. 5:16.
2. Cf. Acts 18:8; Rom. 16:23.
3. Cf. Acts 15:1,5; 17:32; Gal. 1:8-9; 1 Tim. 6:20; 2 Tim. 4:3.
4. 2 Kings 16:7-20; 2 Chron. 28:16-25; Isa. 7:1-25.
5. Cf. Acts 14:15-17; 17:23-29; Rom. 1:20-28; Eph. 2:12.
6. Cf. Matt. 24:13; Mark 13:13; Heb. 3:6,14.
7. Cf. Matt. 12:38; 16:1,4; Mark 8:11-12; John 6:30.
8. Cf. 9:19-22.
9. Cf. Acts 10:42; 13:41; 17:31.
10. Cf. 1:2; Rom. 1:7; 8:28; Jude 1; Rev. 17:14.
11. Cf. Eph. 2:4,8.
12. Cf. Rom. 8:23; Eph. 1:14; 4:30; Heb. 9:12.
13. Gen. 6:9; Job 1:1; 2:3; Gen. 17:1; 2 Sam. 22:26-27; Ps. 18:25. There are many other such references. The approach adopted here is not innovative. Brown writes that 'This meaning of *teleios* fits very well with the LXX use of it as a translation for Hebrew *salem* in the expression "keeping one's heart perfectly true to the Lord"', and cites 1 Kings 8:61; 11:4; 15:3,14 ('The Semitic Background of the New Testament,' p.438).
14. There are thirty-five occurrences of *archôn* in the New Testament (apart from this verse): twenty-six times with reference to men and eight to demonic powers. Revelation 1:5 refers to Christ as 'the ruler of the kings of the earth'.

In the eight references to demonic powers the word is in the singular. There is no evidence for the plural of *archôn*, as found in 2:8, having a demonic reference, whereas the sixteen occasions of the plural form refer to human rulers. Of these sixteen, thirteen, no less, allude to the authorities involved directly in the historic death of Jesus (With acknowledgements to Ling, 'A note on 1 Corinthians ii.8', p.26).
15. E.g. Matt. 8:29; Mark 1:24; Luke 4:34; cf. Acts 16:17; 19:15. (*Pace* Guthrie, *New Testament Theology,* p.143).
16. Kaiser, '1 Corinthians 2:6-16', p.312.
17. E.g. Dan. 2:18-47; 4:9; cf. Rom. 11:25; 16:25; Eph. 1:9; 3:3-4,9; 6:19; Col. 1:26-27; 2:2; 4:3; Rev. 1:20; 10:7; 17:7.

18. Cf. John 18:38; Acts 3:17; 13:27.
19. Cf. Ps. 24:8-10; Acts 7:2; Eph.1:17; James 1:17.
20. Cf. Acts 2:23; 3:14-18; 4:10; 5:30-31; 7:52; 13:28.
21. Cf. Rom. 8:27; Rev. 2:23.
22. Josephus, *Wars* 6.38.
    Hodge takes the 'active' view (*1 & 2 Corinthians*, p.40); Lenski the 'passive' (*Interpretation of I and II Corinthians*, p.112).
23. In the Septuagint, Gen. 40:8-22; 41:12,13,15; Num. 15:34; Dan. 5:12,16; cf. 2 Cor. 10:12.
24. Cf. 2 Sam. 23:2; 2 Peter 1:21.
25. For example, Hanson, *The New Testament Interpretation of Scripture*, p.74.
26. The word 'natural' occurs again in 15:44,46 as a description of our present human bodies.
27. Judith 8:14. Paul cites Isaiah 40:13 in Romans 11:34 also, but for a different purpose.
28. For jealousy as a virtue, cf. John 2:17; 2 Cor. 7:11; 9:2; 11:2; as an evil, cf. Rom. 10:2; 13:13; 2 Cor. 12:20; Gal. 5:20; Phil. 3:6; James 3:14,16.
29. Josephus, *Life* 156.
30. Cf. the same verb in Luke 2:12,16; 12:19; John 20:5-7.
31. Simons, *Complete Writings*, p.12.
31. E.g. Deut. 4:24; Mal. 3:2; Matt. 3:12; Luke 3:17; 2 Thess. 1:7; Heb. 12:29; Rev. 14:10.
33. Or, in some Greek texts, 'what we have accomplished'.
34. Cf. Matt. 25:14-30; Luke 19:11-27; Rom. 14:10; 2 Cor. 5:10.
35. Cf. Amos 4:11; Zech; 3:2, which refer to partially-burned branches saved from the flames.
36. Matt. 25:21,23; Luke 19:17.
37. The Roman Catholic *Catechism of Christian Doctrine*, p.19, mentions this verse specifically in order to justify the doctrine.
38. Cf. 15:25; Matt. 28:18; Eph. 1:22; Col. 1:17.
39. Cf. what Peter says about such matters (1 Peter 4:10; 5:1-4).
40. Hillerbrand, *The Reformation in its own Words*, p.91.
41. Cf. Acts 10:42; 17:31.
42. That he should have received adequate pay: 9:6,11-12,17-18; Phil. 4:15; that he did work hard: Acts 18:3; 20:34; 1 Thess. 2:9; 2 Thess. 3:8.
43. Josephus, *Life* 429.
44. E.g. 11:1; Eph. 5:1; Phil. 4:9; 1 Thess. 1:6; 2:14; cf. Heb. 6:12.
45. Cf. 2 Cor. 1:17-20; Gal. 5:11; Phil. 1:17.

3. Immorality in the church
1. Cicero, *Speech in defence of Aulus Cluentius Habitus* 5.6; Gen. 35:22; Lev. 18:8; Deut. 22:30; 27:20; 2 Sam. 16:22.
2. Cf. 7:2,12,29; Matt. 14:4; Mark 6:18.
3. Hughes, *Second Epistle to the Corinthians*, p.277.
4. 2 Thess 3:6. Cf. the instruction of Paul to the evil spirit who possessed the girl at Philippi: 'I command you in the name of Jesus Christ to come out of her' (Acts 16:18).
5. Lenski, *Interpretation of I and II Corinthians*, p.209; Hodge, *1 & 2 Corinthians*, p.83.
6. Josh. 7:1-26, particularly 7:25-26.

Notes 389

7. Job 1:12; 2:6; Luke 13:16; 2 Cor. 12:7.
8. Exod. 12:15,20; 13:6-7.
9. Cf. Matt. 26:17-29; Mark 14:17-25; Luke 22:14-23; 1 Peter 1:19.
10. Cf. 2 Cor. 7:8-9, where 'the letter' was a previous communication, and Rom.16:22; Col. 4:16 and 1 Thess. 5:27, where in each case 'the letter' means the epistle which Paul was in the process of writing.
11. Cf. Judg. 11:12; Matt. 8:29; Mark 1:24; 5:7; Luke 4:34; 8:28; John 2:4.
12. Josephus, *Against Apion* 2.177.
13. See 'Background', p.17.
14. Suetonius, *The Twelve Caesars*,' 'Nero' 34,49; Tacitus, *Annals* 15.
15. In this chapter, verses 2,3,9,15,16,19; cf. 3:16; 5:6; 9:13,24; Rom. 6:16; 11:2.
16. Cf. Ps. 49:14; Dan. 7:22; Matt. 12:41-42; 19:27-28; Luke 11:30-32; 22:30; Rev. 2:26-27; 3:21; 20:4.
17. Cf. James 2:6, where the same Greek word, *kriterion*, is translated by the NASB as 'court'.
18. For 'matters of life', cf. Luke 21:34.
19. 'Voluptuous' occurs also in Matt. 11:8 and Luke 7:25. The Greek behind 'homosexuals' is *arsenokoites*, as in 1 Tim. 1:10. Scripture tends to evaluate idolatry as common immorality with a religious veneer (e.g. Num. 25:1; 31:16; Jer. 3:9; Ezek. 16; 23; Hosea 2:1-17; Rev. 2:14,20).
20. 'You have had yourselves washed', 6:11, reflects the Greek *apelousasthe* (aorist indicative middle). A literal English translation might seem cumbersome, hence the NASB's simple 'You were washed'.

In 10:2 the Greek verb behind 'baptized' is in the middle voice, implying personal initiative and self-interest. So, too, with 'wash away' and 'be baptized' in Ananias' charge to Saul (Acts 22:16).
21. Cf. 1 Peter 2:16; 2 Peter 2:19.
22. Cf. Mark 7:15,19; Acts 10:15; Rom. 14:17.
23. Cf. Rom. 8:11; 2 Cor. 4:14; Phil. 3:21; 1 Thess. 4:14.
24. Cf. Eph. 1:19-20.
25. Cf. ch. 12; Rom. 12:1,4-5; Eph. 4:16,25; 5:30.
26. Matt. 19:5; cf. Eph. 5:31.
27. Cf. 11:24; Matt. 20:28; Mark 10:45; Rom. 3:24; Eph. 1:7; 1 Peter 1:18-19.

4. Marriage

1. That 'good' means 'better', cf. 7:8,26; 9:15; Matt. 18:8-9; 26:24; Rom. 14:21. That 'touch' stands for marriage, cf. Prov. 6:29 and the predicament in which Abimelech found himself (Gen. 20:6).
2. Hodge, *Commentary on 1 & 2 Corinthians,* p.112; Lenski, *Interpretation of I and II Corinthians,* p.273.
3. 9:5; 16:19; Matt. 8:14; Mark 1:30; Luke 4:38.
4. For 'defraud', cf. 6:7-8; Mark 10:19.
5. In this letter *charisma* occurs also in 1:7; 12:4,9,28,30-31.
6. Loeb, *Select Papyri,* vol. 1, p.16; cf. Liddell & Scott, *Greek-English Lexicon,* pp.290, 2016.
7. Josephus, *Life* 426-7.
8. Murray, *Christian Baptism,* p.68, expresses this view in a masterly fashion. See also Bromiley, *The Case for Baptizing Infants,* p.8.
9. *Mishnah:* Nashim, Kiddushim.

10. Lenski, *Interpretation of I and II Corinthians*, pp.292-3. Although his writings are difficult to track down now, Abraham Booth, an eminent eighteenth-century British Calvinistic Baptist, presents a valuable discussion of the issue (*Paedobaptism examined*, vol. 3, pp.189-231).
11. Cf. 2 Sam. 12:22; Joel 2:14; Jonah 3:9.
12. For sedition, see John 19:12; Acts 17:7-8; 19:26; 1 Peter 2:16-20; wealth, 1 Tim. 6:9-10,17-19.
13. Cf. 9:14; 11:34; 16:1; Gal. 3:19; Titus 1:5.
14. Josephus, *Antiquities* 12.241.
15. Cf. Acts 15:1,5; Gal. 5:3; 6:12.
16. Cf. Rom. 6:6,17-22.
17. Cf. Eph. 6:6; 1 Peter 2:16; Rev. 1:1; 22:3.
18. The Greek *para* + *theô* ('God' in the dative case), which occurs here, means 'near' or 'beside' God.
19. Lenski, *Interpretation of I and II Corinthians*, p.313. Arndt & Gingrich, (*Greek-English Lexicon*, p.483,) dispute the point being made here. Nevertheless, they give only two inaccessible, non-biblical examples. Liddell & Scott (*Greek-English Lexicon*, pp.1068-9), remain silent on the matter, as also Hodge (*1 & 2 Corinthians*, p.128).
20. Cf. Matt. 24:22; Mark 13:20.
21. Greek, *memeristai*, perfect indicative passive, from *merizô*, 'I divide', suggesting a past action with an ongoing effect.
22. Cf. the Greek text of Prov. 6:5; 7:21; 22:25.
23. Loeb, *Select Papyri*, vol. 2, p.258; cf. Isa. 47:1; Jer. 14:17.
24. Again, Matt. 5:32; 19:3-9; Mark 10:11-12; Luke 16:18.
25. Cf. 11:30; 15:6,18,20,51; Matt. 27:52; John 11:11-12; Acts 7:60; 13:36; 1 Thess. 4:13-15; 2 Peter 3:4. But note Dan. 12:2.

5. Food offered to idols
1. Cf. Acts 21:25; Rev. 2:14,20.
2. When the Bible says that God 'knows' his people, the meaning is that they are chosen (e.g. Exod. 33:12,17; Amos 3:2; Matt. 7:23; Rom. 8:29).
3. Cf. Deut. 4:35,39; 6:4; Ps. 115:4-8; Isa. 41:24; 44:9-20; 46:1-2; Jer. 10:14.
4. Cf. 10:20; Deut. 32:17.
5. Cf. 15:25; Matt. 28:18; Eph. 1:22; Col. 1:16-17.
6. Cf. John 1:3; Col. 1:16; Heb. 1:2.
7. From the anonymous but undoubtedly genuine contemporary *Martyrdom of Polycarp* 8-9.
8. Hodge, *1 & 2 Corinthians*, p.149. Lenski is silent on the matter.
9. Contrary to Fee, *The First Epistle to the Corinthians*, p.387; cf. 1:8; John 6:39-40.
10. Cf. Matt. 25:45.
11. For the essential qualifications for apostolic office, see Acts 1:22 and 2 Cor. 12:12; cf. Acts 9:3; 22:6; 26:16.
12. Hodge, *1 & 2 Corinthians*, p.154.
13. For 'defence', cf. Acts 22:1; 24:10; 25:8,16; 26:1,2,24; 2 Cor. 12:19; Phil.1:7,16; 2 Tim. 4:16.

14. For the families of Jesus and of Peter, and Paul's contacts with some of them and with some apostles, see Matt. 8:14; 12:46-47; 13:55-56; John 2:2; 7:3; Acts 1:14; Gal. 1:17-19; 2:9-14.
15. For 'after the manner of men', cf. Rom. 3:5; Gal. 3:15.
16. Cf. Lev. 6:16,26; 7:6; Num.18:8,31; Deut. 18:1-8.
17. Cf. Matt. 23:15; Acts 15:1; Gal. 5:12; Phil. 3:2.
18. Cf. Rom. 6:14; 10:4.
19. Cf. Rom. 7:7,12; Gal. 3:24 and context.
20. Cf. the accusation levelled at Jesus on numerous occasions (Matt. 11:19; Luke 5:30; 15:1-2; 19:7). For 'lawless', cf. Acts 2:23; 2 Thess. 2:8; 1 Tim. 1:9.
21. Ridderbos, *Paul: An Outline of his Theology*, p.285. Some library shelves have nearly been filled with books and articles on the subject. Two interpretations of 9:21 which have helped me are those by Longenecker, (*Paul, Apostle of Liberty*, pp.182-96), and Wintle, ('The Law of Moses and the Law of Christ', p.321).
22. Pindar, *Olympian Odes* 8.52; 9.86; pp.10,14.
23. Papahatzis, pp.30-36.
24. For the metaphor of the race, cf. Phil. 3:12; Heb. 12:1.
25. According to Pindar, *Nemean Odes* 4.88; Broneer, p.16.
26. The Greek is *pukteuô*, from which, via the Latin *pugil*, may derive the English 'pugilist'.
27. 12:1; Rom. 1:13; 11:25; 2 Cor. 1:8; 1 Thess. 4:13.
28. Num. 9:15-23; 14:14; Deut. 1:33; Ps. 78:14; 105:39.
29. E.g. 2 Sam. 22:2; Ps.18:2; 31:3; 42:9; 71:3; 95:1.
30. Josephus, *Antiquities* 4.155, gives 14,000.
31. Cf. Matt. 4:7; Deut. 6:16.
32. 'Were happening' is a Greek imperfect tense, signifying duration.
33. 'To attain' or 'reach', cf. Acts 16:1; 18:19,24; Eph. 4:13; Phil. 3:11. For 'ages', cf. 1:20; 2:6-8; 3:18; 8:13; elsewhere, some twenty-four times.
34. E.g. Rom. 5:13-14; 2 Cor. 3:1-11; Gal. 4:4.
35. Hodge (*1 & 2 Corinthians*, p.183) agrees; Lenski, (*Interpretation of I and II Corinthians*, p.405) does not.
36. Luke 4:1-2; 2 Chron. 32:31; 2 Cor. 12:7.
37. Cf. 11:24; Matt. 26:26-27; Mark 14:22-23; Luke 22:17,19.
38. E.g. Acts 21:26; 22:17.
39. Cf. 9:13; Lev. 7:6,15; Mal. 1:7,12; Matt. 23:18-21.
40. For Josephus, 'demon' means God (cf. Acts 17:18), while 'demons' are evil spirits (so, *Wars* 1.69; *Antiquities* 6.211).
41. Greek, *dia* + the accusative.
42. *Charis* is a rich word with a range of nuances; Arndt & Gingrich, *Greek-English Lexicon*, p.877.

6. The covered head

1. For Paul's practice of handing down authoritative traditions, cf. 11:23; 15:3; Acts 16:4; 2 Thess. 2:15.
2. In Paul's letters, 'head of all things': Eph. 1:22; Col. 2:10; 'head of the church': Eph. 4:15-16; 5:23; Col. 1:18; 2:19.
3. Cynthia L. Thompson, 'Hairstyles, Head-coverings and St Paul,' *Biblical Archaeologist*, 51, 2, p.112; Lenski, *Interpretation of I and II Corinthians*, p.439.

4. Num. 6:1-8; Deut. 21:12; *Mishnah,* Nazir 9.1; cf. Paul, Acts 18:18; 21:24.
5. Thompson, 'Hairstyles, Head-coverings and St Paul,' pp.104,112. Lenski (*Interpretation of I and II Corinthians,* p.434) thinks that Paul addresses the local situation only.
6. Rom.10:12; Gal. 3:28; 1 Peter 3:7.
7. Cf. Ps. 104:4; Heb. 1:14; 1 Peter 1:12.
8. Cf. in Paul's letters: Rom. 12:17; Eph. 5:31; 1 Thess. 5:15; 2 Thess. 2:10.

7. The Lord's Table

1. Acts 5:17; 15:5; 24:5,14; 26:5; 28:22; cf. Gal. 5:20; 2 Peter 2:1.
2. Calvin, *Institutes,* vol. 1, p.5.
3. E.g. Matt. 23:6; John 12:2; Rev. 19:9.
4. So, the Roman Catholic *A Catechism of Christian Doctrine,* p.46.
5. From the preface to the original edition of Cranmer's *Defence of the True and Catholick Doctrine of the Sacrament,* published in 1550.
6. For any who would query the immediacy of Paul's revelation, Lenski, *Interpretation of I and II Corinthians,* p.462, is quite excellent.
7. See Matt. 26:26-29; Mark 14:22-25; Luke 22:14-23; cf. John 13:1-30; Acts 2:46; 20:7.
8. Cf. the resemblances between 11:24-25 and Luke 22:19-20.
9. Cf. the apocryphal Wisdom of Solomon 16:6-7. Here, the bronze snake of Numbers 21:8-9 is featured as a 'symbol of salvation', a salvation that came to every man who looked at it. Salvation was 'because' of God and not because of the serpent. The unknown Jewish rabbi was right: symbols inform and remind; they do not save.
10. Cf. Zech. 9:11; Heb. 8:8; 9:20.
11. Heb. 9:13; 10:4.
12. Greek, *ouk an ekrinometha,* an aorist passive.
13. Cf. 7:17; 9:14; 16:1; Matt. 11:1.

8. Spiritual gifts

1. E.g. Matt. 7:13-14; Acts 12:19; 23:17. Lenski (*Interpretation of I and II Corinthians,* p.492) queries this conclusion, while Hodge (*1 & 2 Corinthians,* p.240) is ambivalent.
2. 15:1; 2 Cor. 8:1; Eph. 1:9; 3:3,5,10; 6:19; Col. 1:27; 2 Peter 1:16.
3. Cf. Matt. 22:43; Mark 12:36.
4. Septuagint: Lev. 27:28-29; New Testament: 16:22; Rom. 9:3; Gal. 1:8-9.
5. Cf. John 13:12-17; Phil. 2:7.
6. This classification is followed, broadly speaking, by Hodge, *1 & 2 Corinthians,* p.244; Lenski, *Interpretation of I and II Corinthians,* p.499; and Teignmouth Shore, *First Epistle to the Corinthians,* p.335.
7. Guthrie's comments are helpful (*New Testament Theology,* p.595).
8. Published by the Martyn Lloyd-Jones Recordings Trust.
9. Cf. 14:29; 1 Thess. 5:20-21; 1 John 4:1.
10. Chrysostum, *The Fifty-Third Discourse* 6.8.
11. E.g. Gen. 1:11,12,21,24,25; 6:20; 7:14; 8:19; cf. Lev. 11.
12. A. Dumas, *The Three Musketeers,* Pan Books, 1974, p.108.
13. Hippocrates, *Nutriment* 23.

14. Cf. Eph. 4:4-6; 1 Tim. 3:16.
15. Lloyd-Jones, *Romans: An Exposition of Chapter 6*, pp.35-6.
16. Arndt & Gingrich comment about the Greek *en*: 'The uses of this preposition are so many-sided, and often so easily confused, that a strictly systematic treatment is impossible' (*Greek-English Lexicon*, p.258).
17. Lenski, *Interpretation of I and II Corinthians*, pp.514ff., and Hodge, *1 & 2 Corinthians*, p.253 should be consulted; Calvin, *1 Corinthians*, p.264.
18. Consider, for example, the *Book of Common Prayer*, which requires an officiating priest to declare that a baptized infant is 'regenerate, and grafted into the body of Christ's Church' (p.329). Whatever evangelical Anglicans make of this, there is no doubt about the popular interpretation of these words.
19. Matt. 3:11; Mark 1:8; Luke 3:16; John 1:25,33; Acts 1:5; cf. Acts 11:16-17; 19:3-5. Note that the water-baptism of John seems to anticipate that given by Christ through the disciples and, after Pentecost, that given in the church. It is not possible to perceive any fundamental contrast.
20. Beasley-Murray, *Baptism in the New Testament*, p.277.
21. Baptism in the Spirit and/or fire: Matt. 3:11; Mark 1:8; Luke 3:16; John 1:33; Acts 1:5; 11:16; baptism into death: Mark 10:38-39; Luke 12:50; baptism in the sea and the cloud: 10:2. Conant comments that in Greek literature 'The immersing substance is usually *water*' (*The Meaning and Use of BAPTIZEIN*, p.106).
22. 1:13-17; 10:2; 12:13; 15:29; Acts 13:24; 19:3-5; Rom. 6:3-4; Gal. 3:27; Eph. 4:5; Col. 2:12; cf. Acts 9:18; 16:15,33; 18:8; 22:16.
23. *Pace* Martin, who argues that here Paul refers to the greatest love of all, that from God through Christ ('A Suggested Exegesis of 1 Corinthians 13:13', p.120), and others. Attempts to redefine *agape* have, not surprisingly, been many and varied and unconvincing.
24. Lund ('The Literary Structure of Paul's Hymn to Love', 50), Nygren (*Agape and Eros*, pp.133-43) and Guthrie (*New Testament Theology*, p.881), among others, assess chapter 13 as a 'hymn'. That it is not is shown well by Sanders, 'First Corinthians 13', pp.159-60. Nevertheless, as Montgomery Hitchcock pointed out years ago, it is a lovely thing, written by a man who must have felt the fascination of Greek lyric poetry. It is no surprise that 1 Corinthians 13 is often read on occasions when hearts can be moved.
25. Matt. 1:20; 2:13,19; Luke 1:13,19,28-37; 2:14.
26. Dio Chrysostum, *The Corinthian Oration* 10; Josephus, *Wars* 5.201,204.
27. Matt. 17:20; 21:21; Mark 11:23; Luke 17:6.
28. Some Greek texts and English versions give 'that I might rejoice' instead of 'that I might be burned'. Evidence suggests that the latter is more likely to be the original reading. The arguments are balanced well by J. K. Elliot ('In favour of *kauthesomai*').
29. Cf. Rom. 1:18; 2 Thess. 2:10-12.
30. Cf. 2 Peter 2:1; 1 John 4:1.
31. The Greek for 'in part' is *ek merous*. In the Greek Old Testament the expression is adjectival, describing a part of something (e.g. Num. 8:2-3; 20:16; Josh. 15:8; 18:16; 1 Sam. 23:26; 2 Sam. 13:34). So, too, in the New Testament (e.g. 12:27; cf. *apo merous*, also 'in part', Rom. 11:25; 15:15,24; 2 Cor. 1:14; 2:5). This sense is entirely consistent with the extra-biblical Greek of the time.

32. Apostles and prophets: 1:23; 2:6,7,12,13,16; 3:9; 4:8,9,10,11,12,13; 9:4,5,6,11,12; 11:16; 13:12; 15:11,15,19,30,(32?);
All Christians: 5:8; 6:3; 8:1,4,8; 10:6,8,9,(10?),16,17,22; 11:31,32; 12:13,23; 15:49,51,52.
33. Aristotle, *Metaphysics* 5.16.1-5; Cicero, *Of the nature of the gods* 2.38.
34. The Greek is *hotan elthe*, 'when [the perfect thing] ... comes' (3rd person singular, aorist subjunctive of *erchomai*, 'I come').
As a check on both observations, cf. 16:2; Matt. 12:43; 21:40; 25:31; Mark 8:38; Luke 9:26; 14:10; 23:42; John 4:25; 15:26; 16:4,13; Acts 23:35; 2 Thess. 1:10; Heb. 1:6; Rev. 17:10. See Arndt & Gingrich, *Greek-English Lexicon*, p.48.
35. Cf. 2:6; 3:1; 14:20; Phil. 3:15; Col. 4:12.
36. Contrary to the thesis of an important article by Miguens.
37. Cf. 4:11; Matt. 9:18; John 2:10.
38. E.g. Fee, *First Epistle to the Corinthians*,p.647, n.42; Barrett, *A Commentary on the First Epistle to the Corinthians*,p.307; Hodge, *1 & 2 Corinthians*, p.274; Lenski, *Interpretation of I and II Corinthians*, p.569; Fishbane, 'Through the Looking Glass,' p.73. Nevertheless, many commentators (e.g. Dautzenberg, *Urchristliche Prophetie*, p.172) remain uncertain as to how or why Paul alludes to the passage.
39. For this type of Hebrew construction, cf. Ps. 45:7; 109:4. The translation adopted here is that suggested by Young, *My Servants the Prophets*, pp.47-8.
40. Grudem, *The Gift of Prophecy in 1 Corinthians*, p.145, n.53; Bassett, '1 Cor. 13:12,' 47; Gill., 'Through a Glass Darkly,' p.25. Elsewhere the word usually suggests hard questions (so, Judg. 14:12-19; 1 Kings 10:1; 2 Chron. 9:1).
41. See ch. 1, n.1; Ellis, *Paul's Use of the Old Testament*, pp.143,146; Hanson, *Studies in Paul's Technique and Theology*, pp.147,199.
42. Josephus, *Antiquities* 12.81; cf. James 1:23.
43. Grudem, *The Gift of Prophecy in 1 Corinthians*, pp.146-7; p.147, n.55.
44. Vos (*Biblical Theology*, p.105) is excellent. See also Salvoni, 'Quand sara' venuto cio' che e' Perfetto,' pp.27-8.
45. E.g. Behm, 'Das Bildwort vom Spiegel', vol. 1, pp. 315-42; Dupont, *Gnosis*, p. 148; Wischmeyer, *Der höchste Weg*, 1981, pp. 132-5.
46. Plutarch, *Isis and Osiris* 382, A,C; *The E at Delphi* 393, D-E; *To an Uneducated Ruler* 781.
Nor it is necessary to accept the suggestion of some that Paul recalls the hazy oracles allegedly received by the Greeks from the Olympian pantheon (Hugedé, *La métaphore du miroir*, p.149; Barrett, *First Epistle to the Corinthians*, pp.307-8). The latter notes that the prophetess Cassandra was believed to have spoken in riddles because she was inspired by Apollo, whose custom it was to speak obscurely. This is no more than a vague coincidence in terminology.
47. Arndt & Gingrich, *Greek-English Lexicon*, p.391; Blass & Debrunner, *Greek Grammar*, p.236; cf. 1:5-6; 5:7.
48. Picirelli, 'The Meaning of "Epignosis"', pp.85-93.
49. Rom. 5:1-5; Gal. 5:5-6; Eph. 4:2-5; Col. 1:4-5; 1 Thess. 1:3; 5:8; 2 Thess. 1:3; Heb. 6:10-12; 10:22-24; 1 Peter 1:3-8,21-22; Barnabas 1:4; 11:8; Polycarp to the Philippians 3:2-3; cf. the apocryphal Ecclesiasticus, ch. 2.
50. In early times, Irenaeus, Origen, Tertullian, Cyprian, Athanasius, Augustine, Jerome, Ambrose and Chrysostum, among others (see the *Ante-Nicene Library* and

Notes 395

Nicene & Post-Nicene Fathers); Lenski, *Interpretation of I and II Corinthians*, p.566; Calvin, *First Epistle of Paul the Apostle to the Corinthians*, pp.281-2; Hodge, *1 & 2 Corinthians*, p.275; very recently, Kistemaker, *Exposition of the First Epistle to the Corinthians*, Baker, p.467. R. L. Thomas ('Tongues ... will cease,' p.82) writes that 13:12 concerns 'the condition which so obviously will be realized only at the *parousia*'. But is it so obvious?

51. See Andersen, 'We speak ... in the words ... which the Holy Ghost teacheth,' *Westminster Theological Journal*, 22, pp.123,125; Chantry, *Signs of the Apostles*, p.34.

52. In an interesting article Jean Carmignac suggested that 'servants of a new covenant, not of the letter, but of the Spirit' (2 Cor. 3:6) means that 'God ... has made us adequate as ministers of a new covenant which is not *only* in writing but in the Spirit.' This is not unreasonable. If 'the ministry of death' appeared in writing, why not 'the ministry of the Spirit'?

53. Fee, *First Epistle to the Corinthians*, p.644, n.23.

54. Ignatius, Philadelphians 8:2; Liddell & Scott, *Greek-English Lexicon*, p.251; Warfield, *The Inspiration and Authority of the Bible*, Presbyterian and Reformed, 1970, p.413. Loeb, *Apostolic Fathers*, vol. 1, p.247, n.1, opts on balance for the approach taken in this commentary.

55. See O'Callaghan, 'New Testament Papyri in Qumran Cave 7?' *Supplement to Journal of Biblical Literature*, 91, No. 2, and Estrada & White, *The First New Testament*, Thomas Nelson, 1988.

56. Hope: e.g. Rom. 5:2; 8:20,24; 2 Cor. 3:12; Gal. 5:5; Eph. 4:4; Col. 1:5,27; 1 Thess. 1:3,10; 2:19; Titus 1:2; 2:13; 3:7.

So, too, for faith: e.g. 2 Cor. 5:6-7; Gal. 5:5; Phil. 1:27-8; 3:9-11; 2 Thess. 1:8-10; 1 Tim. 6:11-14.

For the record, because her thesis is relatively modern and should not be ignored, it is to be noted that Wischmeyer tries to solve the problem by detaching 13:13 from the flow of thought presented by 13:8-12. This idea does not make sense because it interprets Paul as claiming that faith, hope and love *plus* the whole range of gifts remain until the second advent. Clearly, the gifts are said to flee the field at an earlier time, leaving the graces in possession.

That 13:13 is a problem for many is acknowledged by Sanders, who thought that 'the perfect thing' is the coming of Christ: 'It is most perplexing that Paul brings in here faith and hope, when verses 2 and 7 have implied that these two characteristics would not survive the Parousia'('First Corinthians 13,' p.186).

57. Ridderbos, *Paul*, p.250. Vernon Moss ('1 Corinthians xiii. 13,' p.3) is most helpful.

58. Judisch, *Evaluation of Claims to the Charismatic Gifts*, p.47.

59. 15:23; 1 Thess. 2:19; 3:13; 4:15; 5:23; 2 Thess. 2:1,8; cf. James 5:7-8; 2 Peter 1:16; 3:4,12; 1 John 2:28.

60. This assertion can be checked out with the help of a good Greek New Testament concordance.

61. The evidence of 1 Clement cannot easily be ignored. Obviously alluding to this verse, 1 Clement 36:2 states that 'Through him [Christ] we see the reflection [*enoptrizometha*] of his [God's] faultless and lofty countenance.' It might seem that the writer also had in mind 2 Corinthians 3:18, the verse's near neighbour.

62. So, Hugedé, *La métaphore du miroir*, p.150.

63. Cf. 15:9; Acts 9:4; Phil. 3:14.
64. Luke 19:40; 2 Peter 2:16, referring to Num. 22:21-30. In Paul's letters Scripture is mentioned as that which 'speaks': Rom. 4:3; 9:17; 10:11; 11:2; Gal. 4:30; 1 Tim. 5:18.
65. 14:2,4,5,6,9,13,18,19,21,23,27,28,39.
66. In this letter, 2:7; 4:1; 15:51.
67. Cf. 1:5; 12:8; 13:2,8.
68. Lenski, *Interpretation of I and II Corinthians*, p.591; Hodge (*1 & 2 Corinthians*, p.288) disagrees.
69. For the 'spirit' of a man, cf. 4:21; 16:18; Matt. 26:41; Mark 2:8; Luke 23:46; Acts 7:59; 17:16; Gal. 6:1; Eph. 4:23; 1 Peter 3:4.
70. See, too, Matt. 13:22; Eph. 5:11; Titus 3:14; 2 Peter 1:8; Jude 12.
71. Arndt & Gingrich, *Greek-English Lexicon*, p.310.
72. Budgen (*The Charismatics and the Word of God*, p.53) expounds well.
73. 'Ordinary person' translates the Greek *idiōtēs*; cf. 14:23,24; Acts 4:13; 2 Cor. 11:6.
74. Cf. the Septuagint readings of Gen. 25:21 and Ezra 8:23.
75. Marcus Aurelius, *Meditations* 1.16.4.
76. Cf. John 10:34; 15:25; Rom. 3:20.
77. See Hoekema, *What about Tongue Speaking?*, p.51.
78. Walvoord ('Spiritual Gifts Today') is helpful.
79. Lenski, *Interpretation of I and II Corinthians*, p.608, disputes this.
80. Plato, *Phaedrus* 244,A-B; *Timaeus* 71,E; Cicero, *Concerning Divinations* 1.2.4; Plutarch, *Obsolescence of Oracles* 432,D; *The Oracles at Delphi* 397,C. See Callan, 'Prophecy and Ecstasy in Greco-Roman Religion and in 1 Corinthians,' pp.128-31.
81. Lenski, *Interpretation of I and II Corinthians*, p.613; Hodge, *1 & 2 Corinthians*, p.303.
82. Hodge, *1 & 2 Corinthians*, pp.209,305.
83. Old Testament: Miriam, Exod. 15:20; Deborah, Judg. 4:4; Hannah, 1 Sam. 2:1-10; Huldah, 2 Kings 22:14; Isaiah's wife, Isa. 8:3; New Testament: Elizabeth, Luke 1:41-45; Mary, Luke 1:46-55; Anna, Luke 2:36-38; Philip's daughters, Acts 21:9; cf. Joel 2:28-32; Acts 2:17.
84. The notion is set out by Griffith Thomas, *The Catholic Faith*, pp.142,192,248-56, as well, perhaps, as it could be.
85. Samarin, *Tongues of Men and of Angels*, pp.127-8,225-31.

9. The resurrection of the body
1. Plato, *Republic* 523, has a similar expression with a similar meaning.
2. Based upon the Greek *huper* + a genitive, the formula 'for our sins' is common in the New Testament, the contexts frequently implying substitution. See, for example, 1:13; 11:24; Mark 14:24; Luke 22:19-20; John 6:51; 10:11,15; 11:50-51; 15:13; 18:14; Rom. 5:6,8; 8:32; 14:15; 2 Cor. 5:14,15,21; Gal. 1:4; 2:20; 3:13; Eph. 5:2,25; 1 Thess. 5:10; 1 Tim. 2:6; Titus 2:14; Heb. 2:9; 5:1; 10:12; 1 Peter 2:21; 3:18; 1 John 3:16.
3. Cf. Luke 24:24-27,46; Acts 26:22-23; Rom. 3:21; 2 Peter 1:19.
4. Jonah 1:17; Matt. 12:39-40; Luke 11:29; cf. Hosea 6:2.
5. Cf. Matt. 28:16; Mark 16:7; Luke 24:33-36; John 20:19,26; 21:1-22.

Notes 397

6. Acts 12:17; 15:13; 21:18; Gal. 1:19; 2:9; James 1:1; Jude 1. Lenski (*Interpretation of I and II Corinthians*, p.637) claims surprisingly that this James was a cousin of Jesus, as also the other 'brothers' (9:5). This is unnecessary speculation.
7. Cf. 11:30; 15:18,20.
8. Cf. Luke 16:31; Acts 1:22; 2:32.
9. Num. 12:12; Job 3:16; Eccles. 6:3; see Arndt & Gingrich, *Greek-English Lexicon*, p.246.
10. 1:1; 4:8-9; 9:1; cf. Rom. 2:16; 2 Cor. 11:5; 12:11-12; Gal. 1:1; 1 Tim. 2:7.
11. In Paul's writings alone: 15:12,13,20,42; Rom. 1:4; 4:24; 6:4,9,13; 7:4; 8:11,34(?); 10:7,9; 11:15; Gal. 1:1; Eph. 1:20; 5:14; Phil. 3:11; Col. 1:18; 2:12; 1 Thess. 1:10; 2 Tim. 2:8; see also John 12:1, the raising of Lazarus 'from the dead'; cf. Heb. 11:19.
12. Cf. Matt. 26:59; Acts 21:28.
13. Owen, *The Death of Death in the Death of Christ*, p.69; Rom. 8:34; Heb.9:24; 1 John 2:1.
14. Cf. 2 Peter 2:9.
15. 1:18; Rom. 2:12; 2 Cor. 2:15; 4:3; 2 Thess. 2:10; cf. Matt. 10:28; 18:8; 25:41,46; Mark 3:29; 2 Thess. 1:9; Heb. 6:2; Jude 7.
16. Cf. John 5:28-29.
17. For the concept of a pledge, see Exod. 23:16; 34:22; Lev. 23:10-11,15-21; Deut. 26:1-11; Prov. 3:9-10; for Paul's handling of 'firstfruits', see 16:15; Rom. 8:23; 11:16; 16:5; 2 Thess. 2:13.
18. The gift of the Spirit: Eph. 1:13-14; 2:17-18; Titus 3:6; our bodies like his body: Rom. 8:29; Phil. 3:21.
19. Greek, *hemarton*, 3rd person aorist, 'they sinned' (not 'they were sinning').
20. In Paul's letters: 16:17; 2 Cor. 7:6-7; 10:10; 1 Thess. 2:19; 3:13; 4:15; 5:23; 2 Thess. 2:1,8-9.
21. Alford, *Acts, Romans & 1 & 2 Corinthians*, vol. 2, p.577.
22. Seiss, *The Apocalypse*, 1957, p.476.
23. This would seem to be the thrust of 'then' in, say, Mark 8:25; Luke 8:12; John 13:5; 19:27; 20:27; 1 Tim. 2:13; 3:10; James 1:15; cf., in the Septuagint, Job 5:24; 11:6; 13:22; 14:15; 22:26; 23:6; 33:27; Prov. 6:11; 7:13.
24. The NASB 'then' translates a different Greek word (*hotan*). But the sense is similar.
25. Matt. 26:63-64; Mark 14:61-62; Luke 22:67-70. See Young, *The Prophecy of Daniel*, p.156.
26. Cf. 4:20; 6:9-10; 15:50; Matt. 8:11; 13:43; 16:28; 25:34; Rom. 14:17; Gal. 5:21; Eph. 5:5; Col. 1:13; 4:11; 1 Thess. 2:12; 2 Thess. 1:5; 1 Tim. 1:17; 2 Tim. 4:1,18; Heb. 12:28.
27. Matt. 22:43-45; Mark 12:35-37; Luke 20:41-44; Acts 2:33-35; 5:31; 7:55-56; Rom. 8:34; Eph. 1:20-22; Col. 3:1; Heb. 1:3,13; 8:1; 10:12-13; 12:2; 1 Peter 3:22.
28. See Blass & Debrunner, *Greek Grammar*, p.168.
29. Lenski, *Interpretation of I and II Corinthians*, p.687, deserves to be read.
30. The Greek particle *ne* introduces the oath.
31. Ignatius, *To the Romans* 5:1.
32. Taken from *The Oxford Dictionary of Quotations*, p.218.
33. Cf. Gen. 1:21,24-25.
34. Josephus, *Antiquities* 17.170,177.

35. Cf. James 3:15; Jude 19.
36. Cf. Ps. 40:6-8; Heb. 10:5-7.
37. Menno, *Complete Writings*, p.432.
38. Quoted from Bettenson, ed., *Documents of the Christian Church*, Oxford University Press, 1959, p.35.
39. Cf. 1 Thess. 4:16; Exod. 19:16; 20:18; Josh. 6; Isa. 27:13; Joel 2:1; Zech. 9:14; Rev. 1:10; 4:1; 8:2,6,13; 9:14.
40. Cf. Acts 26:22-23.
41. Cf. 3:22; Luke 23:43; Acts 7:59; Rom. 8:38; 14:7-9; Phil. 1:21-23.

10. The conclusion
1. 1:3; Rom. 1:7; 2 Cor. 1:2; 13:14; Gal. 1:3; 6:18; Eph. 1:2; 6:24; Phil. 1:2; 4:23; Col. 1:2; 1 Thess. 1:1; 5:28; 2 Thess. 1:2; 3:18; 1 Tim. 1:2 (6:21); 2 Tim.1:2 (4:22); Titus 1:4 (3:15); Philem. 3,25.

Appendix II — Visions and mirrors
1. Harrison, *Introduction to the Old Testament*, p.213
2. As noted by Warfield, *Inspiration and Authority of the Bible*, p.98.
3. It should be noted that in the Old Testament there are two other words for 'mirror' (to be found in Job 37:18 ; Isa. 3:23). This does not affect the present argument.
4. Gordon, ed. *Ugaritic Manual*, p.257.
5. Kim, *The Origin of Paul's Gospel*, p.205. Cf. Dan. 10:6-8.
6. Charles, *The Apocrypha and Pseudepigrapha of the Old Testament*, p.433.
7. Aristotle, *On Prophecy in Sleep* 2.464b.9-10; Philo, *On the Migration of Abraham* 190. There are many similar references in Philo's works.
8. Vermes, trans., *The Dead Sea Scrolls in English*, p.228; Strugnell, ed., 'Angelic Liturgy at Qumran', p.336.
9. Gruenwald, *Apocalyptic and Merkavah Mysticism*, pp.134-5; Chernus, 'Visions of God in Merkabah Mysticism',p.131.
10. Jastrow (*Dictionary of the Targumin*.... vol. 2, p.835) insists upon the semantic shift.
11. Young, *My Servants the Prophets*, p.47.
12. Baillet, ed., *Discoveries in the Judaean Desert*, VII, p.199.
13. As Dupont points out, *Gnosis*, p.116.
14. D'Angelo, *Moses in the Letter to the 'Hebrews'*, p.115.
15. Courtenay-James, *Language of Palestine and Ancient Regions*, p.252.
16. Macho, 'The recently discovered Palestinian Targum', p.236.
17. *Babylonian Talmud:* Seder Nashim, Yebamoth, p.324.
18. E.g. Hugedé (*La métaphore du miroir*, p.149); Behm ('Das Bildwort vom Spiegel', p.339); D'Angelo (*Moses in the Letter to the 'Hebrews'*, p.99); and Grudem (*The Gift of Prophecy in 1 Corinthians*, pp.145-6) suggest *mar'ah* as the provenance for 'mirror' without following it up. Unfortunately, many have failed altogether to consider the possibility (e.g. Dautzenberg, *Urchristliche Prophetie*, pp.172-225).

Bibliography

Biblical texts and other sources

A Catechism of Christian Doctrine, revised edition, Catholic Truth Society, 1971.
Aland, Kurt and others, eds, *The Greek New Testament*, 3rd corrected edition, United Bible Societies, 1983.
Ante-Nicene Library, T. & T. Clarke, 1868.
Baillet, M., ed., *Discoveries in the Judaean Desert —VII : Qumran Grotte 4*, Oxford University Press, 1982.
Barthélemy, D. and J.T. Milik, eds, *Discoveries in the Judaean Desert — I : Qumran Cave I*, Oxford University Press, 1956.
Bettenson, Henry, editor, *Documents of the Christian Church*, Oxford University Press (The World's Classics), 1959.
Charles, R. H., *The Apocrypha and Pseudepigrapha of the Old Testament in English*, vol. 1, Oxford University Press, 1913.
Dyson, H. V. D., ed., *Pope: Poetry and Prose*, Clarendon Press, 1966 (first published 1933).
Freedman, H. and M. Simon, eds, *Midrash Rabbah*, English translation, 10 vols, 3rd edition, Soncino Press, 1961.
Gordon, C. H., ed., *Ugaritic Manual*, Rome, 1955.
Hebrew New Testament, Trinitarian Bible Society, 1939.
Hebrew New Testament, trans. Franz Delitzsch, British & Foreign Bible Society, 1953.
Kittel, R., ed., *Biblia Hebraica*, 12th edition, Württembergische Bibelanstalt Stuttgart, 1961.
Levertoff, P. P., trans., *Midrash Sifre on Numbers*, London, 1926.
Loeb Classical Library, Cambridge, Mass.; various dates, for the Apostolic Fathers, Josephus, Philo, etc.
Macho, A. D., ed., *Neophyti 1: Targum Palestinense MS de la Biblioteca Vaticana*, vol. 4, Madrid, 1974.

Mebartenorah, O., editor, *The Mishnah*, 3 vols, J. Weinfeld & Co., Jerusalem, no date.
New American Standard Bible, Thomas Nelson, 1977 (first published 1960).
Nicene and Post-Nicene Fathers, James Parker, 1899.
Rahlfs, Alfred and others, eds, *Septuaginta*, 2 vols, Deutsche Bibelgesellschaft Stuttgart, 1982 (first published 1935).
Sperber, A., ed., Targum Onkelos, *The Bible in Aramaic based on Old Manuscripts and Printed Texts*, 4 vols (Leiden, 1959-73), vol.1 (1959).
Strugnell, J., ed., 'Angelic Liturgy at Qumran', *Supplements to Vetus Testamentum*, 7 (1960), 318-45.
The Babylonian Talmud, English translation compiled by J. J. Slotki, 18 vols, Soncino Press, 1935-52.
The Book of Common Prayer, Oxford University Press, no date.
The Koran, translated into English by N. J. Dawood, 5th edition, Penguin, 1990 (first published 1956).
The New Testament: The Greek Text Underlying the English Authorized Version of 1611, Trinitarian Bible Society, no date.
Vermes, G., trans., *The Dead Sea Scrolls in English*, 3rd edition, Penguin, 1987 (first published 1962).

Reference works

Arndt, William F., and F. Wilbur Gingrich, *A Greek-English Lexicon of the New Testament and Other Christian Literature*, University of Chicago Press, 1979 (first published 1957).
Blass, F., and Debrunner, A., *A Greek Grammar of the New Testament and Other Early Christian Literature*, translated into English by R. W. Funk, University of Chicago Press, 1961.
Courtenay-James, J., *The Language of Palestine and Ancient Regions*, Edinburgh, 1920.
Jastrow, M., *A Dictionary of the Targumim, the Talmud Babli and Jerushalmi, and the Midrashic Literature*, 2 vols, New York, 1950 (reprint of the New York, 1903, edition).
Liddell, H. G., and R. Scott, *A Greek-English Lexicon*, 9th edition, Clarendon Press, 1968 (first published 1843).
The Oxford Dictionary of Quotations, 3rd edition, Oxford University Press, 1979.

Articles and books

Alford, Henry, *The Greek Testament: Acts, Romans & 1 & 2 Corinthians*, Rivingtons & Deighton, Bell, 1857.
Andersen, Francis I., 'We speak ... in the words ... which the Holy Ghost teacheth', *Westminster Theological Journal*, 22 (1960), 113-22.

Barrett, C.K., *A Commentary on the First Epistle to the Corinthians*, A. & C. Black, 2nd edition, 1971 (reprinted 1987).
Bassett, Samuel E., '1 Cor. 13:12', *Journal of Biblical Literature*, 47 (1928), 232-6.
Beasley-Murray, G.R., *Baptism in the New Testament*, 2nd edition, Paternoster, 1976.
Behm, J., 'Das Bildwort vom Spiegel 1. Korinther 13,12' in *Reinhold-Seeberg Fs*, edited by W. Koepp, 2 vols., Leipzig, 1929.
Booth, Abraham, *Paedobaptism Examined*, London, 1829.
Bromiley, Geoffrey W., *The Case for Baptizing Infants*, T. & T. Clark, 1979.
Broneer, Oscar, 'The Apostle Paul and the Isthmian Games', *Biblical Archaeologist*, 25,1 (1962), 2-31.
Brown, Raymond E., 'The Semitic Background of the New Testament *Mysterion*' (I), *Biblica*, 39 (1958) 426-48.
Budgen, Victor, *The Charismatics and the Word of God*, Evangelical Press, 1985.
Callan, Terrance, 'Prophecy and Ecstasy in Greco-Roman Religion and in 1 Corinthians, *Novum Testamentum*, 27 (1985), 125-40.
Calvin, John, *Institutes of the Christian Religion*, translated into English by Henry Beveridge, 2 vols, James Clarke, 1957.
The First Epistle of Paul the Apostle to the Corinthians, translated into English by John W. Fraser, Eerdmans, 1989 (reprint of the 1960 edition).
Carmignac, Jean, 'II Corinthiens III.6,14 et le début de la formation du Nouveau Testament', *New Testament Studies*, 24 (1978), 384-6.
Chantry, Walter, *Signs of the Apostles: An Examination of the New Pentecostalism*, Banner of Truth, 1973.
Chernus, I., 'Visions of God in Merkabah Mysticism', *Journal for the Study of Judaism in the Persian, Hellenistic and Roman Periods*, 13 (1982), 123-46.
Childs, Brevard S., *The New Testament as Canon: An Introduction*, SCM, 1984.
Conant, Thomas Jefferson, *The Meaning and Use of BAPTIZEIN*, Kregel Publications, 1977 (first published 1864).
Cranmer, Thomas, *The Sacrament of the Lord's Supper*, Parker Society, 1844.
D'Angelo, M. R., *Moses in the Letter to the 'Hebrews'*, Scholars Press, 1979.
D. Martyn Lloyd-Jones: Apostle and Prophet of the 20th Century, The Martyn Lloyd Jones Recordings Trust, no date.
Dautzenberg, Gerhard, *Urchristliche Prophetie*, Kohlhammer, 1975.
Dumas, Alexandre, *The Three Musketeers*, Pan Books, 1974 (second printing of the 1968 edition of the original English translation by William Barrow, 1844).
Dupont, J., *Gnosis. La connaissance religieuse dans les épîtres de saint Paul*, Catholic University of Louvain, 1949.

Elliot, J. K., 'In Favour of *kauthesomai* at I Corinthians 13,3', *Zeitschrift für die neutestamentliche Wissenschaft*, Band 62 (1971), 297-8.
Ellis, E.E., *Paul's Use of the Old Testament*, Oliver & Boyd, 1957.
Estrada, David and William White, junior, *The First New Testament*, Thomas Nelson, 1978.
Fee, Gordon D., *The First Epistle to the Corinthians*, Eerdmans (NICNT), 1988.
Fishbane, Michael, 'Through the Looking Glass: Reflections on Ezek 43:3, Num 12:8 and 1 Cor 13:12', *Hebrew Annual Review*, 10 (1986), 63-75.
Gill, David H., 'Through a Glass Darkly: A Note on 1 Corinthians 13,12', *Catholic Biblical Quarterly*, 25 (1963), 427-9.
Griffith Thomas, W. H., *The Catholic Faith: A Manual of Instruction for Members of the Church of England*, Church Book Room Press, 1955 (first published 1904).
Grudem, W. A., *The Gift of Prophecy in 1 Corinthians*, University Press of America Inc., 1982.
Gruenwald, I., *Apocalyptic and Merkavah Mysticism*, E.J. Brill, 1980.
Guthrie, Donald, *New Testament Theology*, IVP, 1981.
Hanson, A. T., *Studies in Paul's Technique and Theology*, Eerdmans, 1974.
The New Testament Interpretation of Scripture, SPCK, 1980.
Harrison, R. K., *Introduction to the Old Testament*, Tyndale Press, 1970 (first published 1969).
Hillerbrand, Hans J.,*The Reformation in Its Own Words*, SCM Press, 1964.
Hodge, Charles, *A Commentary on 1 & 2 Corinthians*, Banner of Truth, 1974 (first published 1857).
Hoekema, Anthony A., *What about Tongue Speaking?*, Paternoster, 1972.
Hugedé, N., *La métaphore du miroir dans les épîtres de saint Paul aux Corinthiens* (Neuchâtel/Paris, 1957).
Hughes, Philip E., *The Second Epistle to the Corinthians*, Eerdmans (NICNT), 1988 (first published 1962).
Judisch, Douglas, *An Evaluation of Claims to the Charismatic Gifts*, Baker Book House, 1978.
Kaiser, W. C., Jr, 'A Neglected Text in Bibliology Discussions: I Corinthians 2:6-16', *Westminster Theological Journal*, 43 (1981), 301-19.
Kim, S., *The Origin of Paul's Gospel*, Tübingen, 1981.
Kistemaker, Simon J., *New Testament Commentary: Exposition of the First Epistle to the Corinthians*, Baker Books, 1993.
Lenski, R. C. H., *The Interpretation of I and II Corinthians*, Augsburg Publishing House, 1963 (first published 1937).
Ling, Trevor, 'A Note on 1 Corinthians ii.8', *Expository Times*, 68,1 (1956), 26.
Lloyd-Jones, D. M., *Romans: An Exposition of Chapter 6, The New Man*, Banner of Truth, 1975 (first published 1972).
Longenecker, R. N., *Paul, Apostle of Liberty*, Baker Book House, 1976 (first published 1964).

Lund, Nils W., 'The Literary Structure of Paul's Hymn to Love', *Journal of Biblical Literature*, 50 (1931), 266-76.
Macho, A. D., 'The recently discovered Palestinian Targum: Its antiquity and relationship with the other Targums', *Supplements to Vetus Testamentum*, 7 (1960), 222-45.
Martin, Ralph P., 'A Suggested Exegesis of 1 Corinthians 13:13', *Expository Times*, 82 (1971), 119-20.
Miguens, E., '1 Cor. 13:8-13 Reconsidered', *Catholic Biblical Quarterly*, 37 (1975), 76-97.
Montgomery Hitchcock, F. R., 'St. Paul's Hymn of Love (1 Cor. xiii)', *Theology* (1933), 65-75.
Morris, Leon, *The Epistles of Paul to the Thessalonians: An Introduction and Commentary*, Tyndale Press, 1966 (first published 1956).
Murphy-O'Connor, Jerome, 'The Corinth that Saint Paul saw', *Biblical Archaeologist*, 47,3 (1984), 147-59.
Murray, John, *Christian Baptism*, Presbyterian & Reformed Publishing Company, 1974.
Nygren, Anders, *Agape and Eros*, SPCK, 1953.
O'Callaghan, José, 'New Testament Papyri in Qumran Cave 7?', *Supplement to Journal of Biblical Literature*, 91 (1972), No. 2, 1-14.
Owen, John, *The Death of Death in the Death of Christ*, Banner of Truth, 1989.
Papahatzis, Nicos, *Ancient Corinth: The Museums of Corinth, Isthmia and Sicyon*, Ekdotike Athenon S.A., 1991 (first published 1977).
Picirelli, R. E., 'The Meaning of "Epignosis"', *Evangelical Quarterly*, 47 (1975), 85-93.
Ridderbos, H. N., *Paul: An Outline of His Theology*, Eerdmans, 1975.
Salvoni, Fausto, 'Quando sara' venuto cio' che e' Perfetto l'Imperfetto scomparira' (1 Cor 13,10)', *Ricerche Bibliche e Religiose*, (1977), 1, 7-30.
Samarin, William J., *Tongues of Men and of Angels: The Religious Language of Pentecostalism*, Macmillan, 1972.
Sanders, Jack T., 'First Corinthians 13: Its Interpretation Since the First World War', *Interpretation*, 20 (1966), 159-87.
Seiss, J. A., *The Apocalypse: Lectures on the Book of Revelation*, 3rd edition, Zondervan Publishing House, 1957.
Simons, Menno, *Complete Writings*, translated into English by Leonard Verduin, Herald Press, 1956.
Teignmouth Shore, T., *The First Epistle to the Corinthians*, Cassell & A.B. Nelson (Ellicott Series), no date.
Themelis, Petros G., *Ancient Corinth: The Site and the Museum*, Editions Hannibal, no date.
Thomas, Robert L., 'Tongues ... will cease', *Journal of the Evangelical Theological Society*, 2 (1974), 81-9.
Thompson, Cynthia L., 'Hairstyles, Head-coverings, and St Paul: portraits from Roman Corinth', *Biblical Archaeologist*, 51,2 (1988), 99-115.
Vernon Moss, F., '1 Corinthians xiii.13', *Expository Times*, 73,3, (1961), 93.

Vos, Geerhardus, *Biblical Theology*, Banner of Truth, 1975 (first published, 1948)

Walvoord, J.F., 'Spiritual Gifts Today', *Bibliotheca Sacra*, 130 (1973), 315-28.

Warfield, Benjamin B., *The Inspiration and Authority of the Bible*, Presbyterian & Reformed, 1970.

Wintle, B. C., 'The Law of Moses and the Law of Christ: An Exegetical Study of Pauline Teaching on the Authority of the Law over the Christian Believer' (unpublished Ph.D. dissertation, University of Manchester, 1977).

Wischmeyer, O., *Der höchste Weg: Das 13. Kapitel des 1. Korintherbriefes*, Gerd Mohn, 1981.

Young, E. J., *My Servants the Prophets*, Eerdmans, 1952.

The Book of Isaiah, 3 vols, Eerdmans, 1976-7 (first published 1965-72).

The Prophecy of Daniel, Eerdmans, 1957 (first published 1949).

Subject index

Administrators, 248, 249
Agape (love), 227, 252, 253, 257-8, 259, 260, 272, 277, 278, 283, 284, 286, 393
Anabaptists, 71, 239, 350
Angels, 85, 109, 133, 204, 209, 255, 282, 337, 343
Annihilation, 325, 329, 338
Apostle, definition of, 22
Apostolic tradition, 203, 217
Arrogance, 89, 97, 167, 245, 257
Ascension of Christ, 130, 317, 318, 324, 327
Assessment of spirits, 232, 233, 235, 303

Baptism, 33-4, 113-14, 185, 186, 240-42, 393
Baptism for the dead, 337-9
Baptism of the Spirit, 239-43, 247, 393
Body of Christ, 9, 237-50, 330

Canon, New Testament, 272-6
Charisma/Charismatic gifts, 25, 227-311
Childhood/Children, 131-6, 263-4, 280, 296-7
Christian prophecy/prophets — see Prophets/Prophecy in the churches
Christian teachers — see Teachers
Church, definition of, 23

Communion — see Lord's Table
Conscience (see also Paul, good conscience), 163, 164, 201
Contentment, 121, 139-43
Corinthian church,
  divisions in, 28-91
  epistle to, relevance to all, 9, 216-17
Council of Jerusalem, 158-9
Court action, 92-4, 105-14, 137
Covering the head — see Head covering
Creation, 162, 207, 208, 336, 345, 348
Cross, the, 18, 33, 34-5, 36, 38, 39, 46, 55, 56, 316

'Dead Sea' scrolls, 276, 379
Death and the Christian, 22, 29-30, 154, 318, 327-9, 330, 354, 357
Death of Jesus, 11, 18, 29, 49, 55, 56, 57
Demons — see Evil spirits
Dietary restrictions (see also Food offered to idols), 116
Discernment of spirits — see Assessment of spirits
Discipline, 95-105
Divorce, 121, 127-9, 135, 136-8, 143, 145, 149

Elders, 79, 104, 150, 302, 308
'End' (*telos*), 26, 279, 330-32
Eternal security, 21, 26, 55, 193

Eternal state — see Heavenly state
Evil spirits, 157, 161, 184, 195-9
Excommunication, 104-5

Faith, 232, 233, 234, 239, 256, 272, 276-7, 278, 283, 284, 286, 395
Faithfulness of God, 26-7, 194
False prophecy/false prophets, 259
Fathers and daughters, 121, 150-53
Fellowship, 27
Financial giving — see Money
First fruits, 327
Food offered to idols, 155-202

Gift of faith — see Faith
Gifts of the Spirit — see Charisma
Giving — see Money
Glossolalia — see Tongues
Greek Old Testament — see Septuagint

Head covering, 203-11, 306
Healing, 232, 233, 234, 237, 247
Heathen prophecy/prophets — see Prophecy
Heavenly state, 73, 282, 343-51, 354
Heresies/heretics, 312-13
Homosexuality, 105, 112, 389
Hope, 272, 276-7, 278, 283, 284, 286, 395

Idolatry, 103, 104, 110, 112, 155-63, 166, 184-202, 208, 228-9, 338, 389
Immorality, 92-120
Immortality, 354-5
Inability of natural man, 61-2
Inerrancy, 60, 144, 274, 293
Infallibility, 45, 59, 234, 274, 310
Infant baptism, 131, 393
Inspiration, 44-5, 59, 60, 128, 144, 146, 221, 234, 275, 310, 352
Interpretation of tongues — see Tongues
Israel, old and new, 18-19, 23-4, 82, 96, 101, 104-5, 184-95, 196, 198, 219, 220, 228, 241, 270, 271, 298, 299, 301, 355, 360, 373

'Kingdom', the, 330, 331, 332-5
Kingdom of God, 84, 90, 103, 111-12, 334-5, 351-2, 363
Knowledge, 159, 163, 164, 166, 256, 262, 278, 280, 282, 283, 286, 287, 288
word of, 232, 233, 260
Koran, 316

Last day — see Return of Christ
Last Supper, 218-21
Law of Christ, 177, 179-80, 199
Law of Moses, 88, 104, 168, 171-2, 177, 178-9, 192, 356
'Legal holiness', 133, 135
Liberal theology, 274
Lord's day, 65, 362, 364
Lord's Supper — see Lord's Table
Lord's Table, 186-7, 195-6, 197, 198, 212-26, 243, 338, 351, 372
Love — see Agape

Mar'ah (Hebrew for 'mirror'/ 'vision'), 269, 376-7, 378, 379-80, 381, 384, 385
Mar'eh (Hebrew for 'form'), 381, 382
Marriage, 121-54, 351
Massoretes, 376
Maturity, 50-52, 66, 264-5, 297
Mediation of Christ, 324, 335-6,
Millennium, 330-35
Ministerial pay, 171-4
Miracles, 251, 274
Mirrors, 265-70, 273, 280-82, 376-85, 398
Mishnah — see Rabbinic literature
'Mixed marriages', 129-39
Money, 171-4, 359, 360-66
Mysteries, 53-5, 78, 175, 256, 260, 280, 285, 286, 292, 352

'Offer' of the gospel, 176
Old Testament,
  allusions and quotations, 20, 190-91, 266-7, 269-71, 273, 297, 301, 310, 335, 341, 345, 348-50, 355, 373-5

precedents, 37-8, 39, 56-7, 74, 75, 79, 80, 82, 100-101, 104, 118, 134-5, 172, 173, 184-94, 195, 196, 219-20, 227, 229, 234-5, 268, 271, 336, 339, 340
prophets — see Prophets
Original sin, 132, 352

Papacy — see Roman Catholic Church
Parousia — see Return of Christ
'Partial thing', the, 261, 262, 263, 278-9, 280
Passover, 100-101, 218, 220, 225, 327
Paul,
  and oratory, 18, 44, 45-9
  apologia, 91, 170-71
  apostolic rights, 147, 168-76
  authority, 21, 71, 98, 128, 129-30, 140, 144, 154, 169, 226, 309-10, 320
  background, 11, 135
  conversion, 78, 217, 301, 319, 321, 356
  example, 88, 115, 117, 158, 168, 169, 170, 177, 181, 183, 202
  good conscience, 47, 77, 80-81, 97, 175
  irony, 51, 83, 84, 85, 144, 154, 172, 269, 308, 315
  journeys, 11, 12, 362, 365-6
  missionary strategy, 12-14, 18
  sufferings, 18, 339-40
  'thorn in the flesh', 195
Pay of ministers — see Ministerial pay
Peace, 24, 138, 305
Pentecost, 235-6, 260, 299
Pentecostalism, 283, 310-11
'Perfect thing', the, 261-2, 263, 265, 267, 271, 272-83, 395
Persecution, 18, 81, 145, 320, 361
Person of Christ, 82, 162, 350, 351
Pharisees, 59, 119, 140, 319
Predestination, 54
Premillennialism, 193, 332-3
Prophecy/prophets, 227, 247-8, 284-311
  heathen, 304-5
  in the churches, 232, 233, 234-5, 237, 259-60, 262, 270, 278, 283, 284-311

  in the Old Testament, 234-5, 269, 296-301, 316-17, 377-8, 380-85
Rabbinic literature,
  Babylonian Talmud, 383
  Leviticus Rabbah, 384
  Mishnah, 135, 379-80
  Visions of Ezekiel, 380
  Siphre Bemidbar, 382-3
  Targum Neophyti, 383
  Targum Onkelos, 383
Rabbinic traditions, 135, 380-84
Redemption, 43, 235, 315, 331
Remarriage, 138, 143-50
Resurrection, 84, 116, 117, 280, 282, 312-59
Return of Christ, 26, 116, 276-83, 330-35, 351, 352-3
Righteousness, 43
Roman Catholic Church, 71, 73, 198, 214, 217, 239, 309
'Rulers of this age', the, 52-3, 55

Sadducees, 313, 342
Sanctification, 21, 23, 43, 113, 130-36
Sayings of Christ, 128, 143-4, 146, 172, 221, 256
Second advent of Christ — see Return of Christ
Second marriage — see Remarriage
'Secondary judgement', 73
Sectarianism, 309
Septuagint, 20, 23, 44, 86, 267, 370, 381, 387, 388, 392, 393, 396, 397
Sexual misconduct, 93, 94-5, 102-5, 114-20, 190
Singles, 121, 125-7, 143-50
Slavery, 77, 141-3
Sodomy — see Homosexuality
Spiritual gifts — see Charisma
Stewards, 77-91, 175
Subordination, 204-10, 336

Teachers, 234, 248
Teaching of Christ — see Sayings of Christ
Teleioi ('perfect'; 'mature'), 50, 297
Teleion (to) ('the perfect thing'), 261
Telos — see 'End'

Tithing, 363, 365
Tongues, 284-311
   in the New Testament, 227-8, 232, 233, 235-7, 248, 255-6, 260, 278, 283, 284-301, 302, 303, 310
   interpretation of, 232, 233, 235-7, 286, 290, 292-3, 302, 303
   modern version, 292, 310-11
Transubstantiation, 187, 217, 220-21
Trinity, 113, 119, 161, 231, 237, 242-3, 290, 330, 337

Visions, 266, 267, 269-70, 376-85

Widows, 121, 126, 149, 153-4
Wilderness journey, 184-95
Wisdom, 29, 39-40, 43, 53-5, 56, 57, 75
   word of, 34-5, 232, 233
Women in the churches, 203-11, 228, 306-8, 309
Word of knowledge — see Knowledge
Word of wisdom — see Wisdom
Working of powers, 232, 233, 234

Index of persons

Aaron, 189, 191, 266, 267, 270, 287, 309
Abed-nego, 158
Abimelech, 389
Abraham, 24, 42, 51, 79, 101, 134-5, 141, 196, 299
Absalom, 96
Achaicus, 19, 369
Achan, 98
Adam, 132, 204, 206, 207, 209, 210, 246, 306, 327-9, 336, 348-50
Agabus, 235
Agrippina, 106
Ahab, 189, 259
Ahithophel, 75
Alexander, 99, 313
Alexander, Cecil, 26
Alford, Henry, 332
Amos, 188
Ananias (baptizer of Saul), 242, 389
Ananias (husband of Sapphira), 146, 234
Anna (the prophetess), 396
Anna (wife of Tobit), 86
Aphrodite, 15, 157, 190
Apollo, 157, 304, 394
Apollos, 19, 28-30, 31, 63, 66-8, 74, 76, 78, 79, 82, 366, 367-8, 370
Aquila (husband of Priscilla), 19, 123, 234, 370
Aquila (Onkelos), 383

Aratus, 341
Aristotle, 261, 378
Athena, 157

Balaam, 190
Barnabas, 22, 170-71, 257
Bathsheba, 132
Beasley-Murray, G. R., 241
Bezalel, 377
Booth, Abraham, 390
Brown, Raymond E., 387

Calvin, John, 214, 240, 273
Carmignac, Jean, 395
Cassandra, 394
Cassius, Dio, 16
Cephas — see Peter
Charles, R. H., 378
Charles V, Emperor, 81
Chaeremon, 128
Chloe (household of), 19, 31, 213
Chrysostum, Dio, 15, 236, 256
Cicero, 96, 261, 262, 305
Claudius Caesar, 16, 17
Cornelius, 33, 274
Cranmer, Thomas, 217
Crispus, 33
Cyrus, 331

Daniel, 158, 266, 335
David, 41, 132, 335

Deborah, 396
Diotrephes, 88
Dumas, Alexandre, 237

Ebed-melech, 87
Eldad, 287, 310
Eli, 192, 377
Eliphaz, 75
Elisha, 293
Elizabeth, 396
Elymas, 234
Epaenetus, 387
Epaphroditus, 22, 358
Epimenides, 341
Erastus, 79, 88, 366, 367
Eve, 204, 206, 207, 208, 210, 246, 306
Ezekiel, 145, 266, 378, 379, 380, 384

Fee, Gordon D., 275
Fortunatus, 19, 368
Francis I, 214
Franklin, Benjamin, 344

Gabriel, 335
Gaius, 33
Gallio, 16-17, 106
Gamaliel, 323
Goliath, 41
Grudem, Wayne, 268

Hagar, 135
Hannah, 396
Herod the Great, 347
Herod Agrippa II, 106
Herod Antipas, 53
Hezekiah, 195
Hippocrates, 238
Hodge, Charles, 98, 122-3, 166, 167, 170, 305, 307
Huldah, 396
Hymenaeus, 99, 313

Ignatius, 275-6, 340
Isaac, 134, 187
Isaiah, 37, 56, 57, 62, 266, 298, 301, 341
  his wife, 396
Ishmael, 134-5, 187

James, 318, 397
Jehoshaphat, 259
Jeremiah, 43-4, 57, 146, 219, 220
Jeroboam I, 189
Jesse, 132
Jezebel (at Thyatira), 190
Jezebel (wife of Ahab) 189
Job, 51, 75, 80, 99, 194, 224
John (apostle), 11, 182, 220, 319, 332
John the Baptist, 171, 241
John Mark, 257
Jonah, 316
Joseph (husband of Mary), 170, 255
Joseph (son of Jacob), 118, 331, 336, 339
Josephus, 14, 60, 69, 88, 106, 129, 140, 267, 347
Joshua, 98, 270, 287, 310
Judas Iscariot, 75, 218
Judisch, Douglas, 278,
Judith, 62
Julius Caesar, 16

Korah, 191

Lazarus (beggar), 42,
Lazarus (brother of Martha), 220, 316, 397
Lenski, R. C. H., 98, 122-3, 135, 145, 272
Leo X, Pope, 81
Lloyd-Jones, D. Martyn, 234, 240
Lot, 101
Luke, 39, 236, 289, 348
Luther, Martin, 81
Lyte, Henry, 147

Macho, A. D., 383
Malachi, 134-5
Marcus Aurelius, 297
Martha, 150, 316
Mary (mother of Jesus), 162, 170, 255, 291, 335, 350, 396
Mary (sister of Martha), 220
Matthias, 318, 319
Medad, 287, 310
Menander, 341
Meshach, 158

Index of persons

Miriam, 266, 267, 270, 287, 309, 396
Moses, 96, 100, 113, 118, 158, 172, 179, 185, 186, 188, 189, 191, 219-20, 241, 254, 266, 267, 268, 270, 271, 287, 298, 309, 370, 377, 378, 380-84
Mummius, 16

Nabal, 341
Nebuchadnezzar, 192, 331
Nero Caesar, 12, 17, 106
Noah, 51, 341

Onesimus, 142
Onkelos, 383
Orsenouphis, 151
Owen, John, 324

Paul — see topics listed in subject index
Peter, 28, 31, 32, 33, 123, 158, 170, 182, 218, 220, 273, 274, 318
Pharaoh, 186, 225, 331, 336, 339, 377
Philip's daughters, 262, 396
Philo, 16, 378
Phoebe, 12, 308
Pindar, 181
Plato, 304
Plutarch, 269, 305
Polycarp, 166
Pontius Pilate, 11, 16, 53, 55, 57
Pope, Alexander, 14
Poseidon, 46, 157
Priscilla, 19, 123, 234, 370
Ptolemy, 267

Reuben, 96
Ridderbos, H.N., 180, 277

Samarin, William, 310-11
Samson, 210
Samuel, 377
Sanders, Jack T., 395
Sapphira, 234
Sarah, 135
Satan, 99, 103, 104, 224, 357, 379
Saul (king of Israel), 293
Saul of Tarsus — see Paul
Sceva (sons of), 230
Seneca, 16
Serapion, 151
Shadrach, 158
Simon Peter — see Peter
Simons, Menno, 71, 350
Sirach, 378
Sosthenes, 18, 21
Stephanas, 18, 19, 34, 368
Stephen, 188, 317, 338
Suetonius, 106

Tacitus, 106
Tertullus, 36
Thomas, 258
Timothy, 87, 88-9, 133, 308, 358, 366-7
Titus, 367
Tobias, 86
Tobit, 86

Xenophon, 15

Young, E. J., 381

Zachariah, 255
Zechariah, 266, 301
Zedekiah, 259

Index of places

Achaia, 18, 19, 87, 186, 284, 367, 387
Acrocorinth, 15, 17, 181
Adriatic Sea, 11
Aegean Sea, 92
Alexandria, 11, 16, 19
Antioch in Pisidia, 55
Antioch in Syria, 15, 19, 22, 361
Asia, 19, 366, 369
Assyria, 37, 62
Athens, 18, 24, 39, 72, 162, 257

Babel, Tower of, 236
Babylon, 43-4, 53, 158, 192, 220, 331
'Babylon' (i.e. Rome), 12
Berea, 18
Bethlehem, 55, 162, 188, 350, 351
Beautiful Gate, 256
Bithynia, 15

Calvary, 33, 50, 56, 197, 222, 223, 331
Canaan, 188, 191, 219
Cenchrea, 12, 15, 19
Chebar, 380
Corinth,
    background and history, 14-17
Corinthian Isthmus, 14, 181
Crete, 340

Damascus, 54
Dardanelles, 366
Dead Sea, 276
Delphi, 304, 387

Eden, 328-9, 349
Edom, 37
Egypt, 16, 19, 20, 37, 100, 128, 185, 188, 301, 336
Ephesus, 12, 19, 23, 31, 88, 92, 98, 286, 328, 340, 362, 365, 366, 367, 369, 370
Ethiopia, 301

Galatia, 19, 361
Greece, 14, 15, 16, 47, 198
    map of, 13

Horeb, 23

India, 198, 236
Isthmia, 181, 182, 208

Jerusalem, 12, 14, 16, 37, 44, 55, 56, 196, 197, 218, 222, 256, 266, 267, 273, 308, 318, 331, 341, 360, 361, 362, 365

Index of places

Joppa, 158, 274
Judah, 43, 266, 298
Judea, 11, 121, 364, 365

Lechaeum, 15

Macedonia, 88, 362, 365, 366
Mars' Hill, 18
Mediterranean Sea, 11, 12, 14
Miletus, 128

Nazareth, 162, 324
Nicaea, 351

Olympus, 158

Parthenon, 72
Patmos, 332
Peirene Fountain, 14
Peloponnese, 14, 15
Philippi, 18
Philistines, land of, 37
Phoenicia, 377
Phrygia, 19

Qumran, 276, 379, 381

Ramoth-gilead, 259
Ras Shamra, 377
Red Sea, 331
Rome, 11, 12, 14, 19, 106, 275, 370

Sabeans, 301
Sinai, 40, 56, 104, 118, 180, 185, 192, 219, 220, 268, 356, 381
Smyrna, 166
Sodom, 101
Spain, 11
Syria, 11, 19, 37

Tarsus, 11, 17
Temple (in Jerusalem), 173, 196, 256, 267, 331
Thessalonica, 18
Tiber, 17
Tiberias, 69
Troas, 366
Turkey, 273
Tyre, 53

Ugarit, 377

Zoan, 37

Scripture index

Old Testament		9:6	207, 374	13:7	373
		9:24	341	13:21-22	185, 373
Genesis		11:6	236	14:19	186, 188
1:11	345, 374, 392	16	135	14:20-22	185, 373
1:12	392	17:1	387	14:22	186
1:21	374, 392, 397	19:26	101	14:28	186
1:24	392	20:6	389	15:1-21	331
1:24-25	374, 397	21:2	135	15:20	396
1:25	392	21:10-12	135	16:4	185, 374
1:27	207, 374	25:21	396	16:35	185, 374
2:7	348, 349, 354, 374, 375	35:22	388	17:6	188, 374
		39:15	118	18:7	370
2:17	348-9, 374	40:8-22	388	19:16	398
2:18	122, 208, 374	41:7	377	20:1-17	179
2:19-20	207	41:12	388	20:4-5	189
2:21-23	208, 210, 374	41:13	388	20:5	249
2:23-24	118	41:15	388	20:14	118
2:24	118, 375	41:40	336	20:18	398
3	328	41:41-42	331	23:15-16	327
3:7	246	42:15	339	23:16	397
3:16	204, 306, 374	46:2	376	23:20	188
3:17-19	374			23:23	188
3:19	349	*Exodus*		24:8	219-20, 374
3:20	210	5:12	72	32	271
5:1	207, 374	9:16	225	32:4	189
5:3	374	12:14	101, 373	32:6	189, 190, 375
5:5	349	12:15	389	32:19	189
6:9	387	12:20	389	32:34	188
6:20	392	12:21	373	33	271
7:14	392	12:39	100	33:2	188
8:19	392	13:6-7	389	33:11	268

Scripture index

33:12	390	14:14	391	18:1-8	391
33:12-13	271	14:16	188, 374	18:18	185
33:17	390	14:23	374	18:20-22	303
33:17-23	268	14:29-30	374	18:21-22	235
33:20	271, 381, 383	14:36	191, 374	19:19	104, 373
34	271	15:34	388	20:6	171, 373
34:22	374, 397	16:11	191	21:12	392
34:28-29	271	16:41-49	191, 374	22:21	104, 373
38:8	376, 377, 383	18:8	373, 391	22:24	104, 373
		18:31	373, 391	22:30	388
Leviticus		19:20	74	24:7	104, 373
6:16	373, 391	20:11	188, 374	25:4	172, 375
6:26	373, 391	20:16	393	26:1-11	397
7:6	374, 391	21:5-6	190, 374	27:20	388
7:15	374, 391	21:8-9	392	28	297-8
11	392	22:21-30	396	28:49	297-8, 375
15:31	74	25	190	32:4	27, 188
18:8	388	25:1	190, 374, 389	32:15	188
23:2	101	25:1-9	190	32:15-21	198
23:5-10	327	25:4-5	190	32:17	198, 374, 390
23:10-11	397	25:9	190, 374	32:18	188
23:15-21	374, 397	31:15-16	190	32:21	198, 374
27:28-29	392	31:16	389	32:30	188
				32:31	188
Numbers		*Deuteronomy*		34:10	268, 270
6:1-8	392	1:33	391		
8:2-3	393	4:2	304	*Joshua*	
9:15-23	391	4:10	23	5:15	321
11	286-7	4:12	268	6	398
11:4	189, 374	4:24	388	7:1-26	388
11:14-30	270	4:35	373, 390	15:8	393
11:28	310, 374	4:39	373, 390	18:16	393
11:28-29	287	5:4	268		
11:29	374	5:6-21	179	*Judges*	
11:34	189, 374	5:8-9	189	4:4	396
12	270, 271, 286-7, 310	5:18	118	6:22	268
		6:4	373, 390	11:12	389
12:1-2	270	6:16	391	13:21-22	268
12:6	267, 269, 270, 376, 377, 380, 381, 383, 384	7:9	27, 194, 373, 374	14:12-19	394
				16:13	210
		8:3	185, 374		
12:6-8	266-7, 269-70, 271, 273, 309, 374, 380-84	10:20	118, 373	*1 Samuel*	
		12:32	304	2:1-10	396
		13:3	214, 374	3:13	192
12:8	267, 381, 382, 383	16:3	100	3:15	376, 377
		16:9-11	374	9:9	266
12:12	397	17:7	104, 373	16:23	293
14:2	191, 374	18:1-3	373	17:39	41

1 Samuel		*Job*		94:11	75-6, 375
17:50	41	1:1	387	95:1	391
23:26	393	1:12	389	103:7	271
25:37	341	2:3	387	104:4	392
		2:4-5	224	105:39	391
2 Samuel		2:6	389	106:19-21	189
12:22	390	3:16	397	106:37	374
13:34	393	5:13	75, 375	109:4	394
15:12	75	5:24	397	110	335
16:22	388	11:6	397	110:1	335, 374
17:23	75	12:17-18	37, 373	115:4-8	390
22:2	391	13:22	397	119:141	367
22:26-27	387	14:15	397	136:15	331
23:2	388	22:26	397		
		23:6	397	*Proverbs*	
1 Kings		27:6	80, 373	3:9-10	397
5:3	335	33:27	397	3:12	225
8:61	387	37:18	398	6:5	390
10:1	394	42:7	75	6:11	397
11:4	387			6:29	389
12:26-33	189	*Psalms*		6:32	297
15:3	387	2:2	52, 373	7:7	297
15:14	387	2:7	317	7:13	397
16:29-33	189	2:10	52, 373	7:21	390
22:11	259	8:6	336, 375	9:4	297
22:28	235	16:10	317, 374	15:13	247
		16:11	317	15:30	247
2 Kings		18:2	391	21:18	86
3:15	293	18:25	387	22:25	390
16:7-20	387	19:1	57		
22:14	396	22	340	*Ecclesiastes*	
		24:1	199, 374	6:3	397
2 Chronicles		24:8-10	388		
9:1	394	31:3	391	*Isaiah*	
28:16-25	387	40:6-8	398	2:1	266
32:31	391	42:9	391	3:23	398
36:22-23	331	45:7	394	7:1-25	387
		49:14	389	8:3	396
Ezra		50:12	374	8:14-15	39, 373
1:1-4	331	51:5	132	14:3-23	53
8:23	396	55:6	108	19:11-12	37, 373
		71:3	391	22:1	341
Nehemiah		78:14	391	22:13	341, 374
9:8	79	78:18	374	24:1 - 27:13	355
9:15	187	78:24	186	25:7	355
		78:31	374	25:8	333, 355, 375
Esther		89:11	374	27:13	398
1:6	72	89:27	317	28	297-8

Scripture index

28:7-10	298	1:4-28	378	3:8	60
28:11	298	7:12	373	4:11	388
28:11-12	297, 298, 375	8:1-2	378	5:25-27	188
28:12	298, 300	8:3	376, 378		
28:15	298	10	379	*Jonah*	
28:16	373	10:1-22	378	1:17	396
29:14	37, 374	16	389	3:9	390
33:18	373	23	389		
33:18-19	37-8	24:16-18	145	*Zechariah*	
40:7	347	28:1-19	53	3:2	388
40:13	62, 373, 388	40-48	379	8:17	374
41:24	390	40:2	376, 378	8:23	301, 374
42:2	31	43:3	376, 378	9:11	374, 392
44:9-20	390			9:14	398
44:25-26	37, 373	*Daniel*			
44:28	331	1:8	158	*Malachi*	
45:1	331	1:16	158	1:7	374, 391
45:14	301, 374	2:18-47	387	1:12	374, 391
46:1-2	189, 390	4:9	387	2:15	134
47:1	390	4:28-33	192	3:1	185
53:7	289	5:12	388	3:2	388
53:8-9	374	5:16	388		
53:11	336	7:7	11	**New Testament**	
53:12	179	7:14	334		
54:13	60	7:19	11	*Matthew*	
64:1-3	56	7:22	373, 389	1:20	393
64:4	56, 375	9:24	274	2:13	393
		10:6-8	398	2:16	347
Jeremiah		10:7	376	2:18	254
3:9	389	10:8	376	2:19	393
3:16	56	10:16	376	3:11	393
9:11-12	43	12:2	390	3:12	388
9:24	43, 44, 374			4:7	391
10:14	390	*Hosea*		4:21	31
14:17	390	1:9	219	5-7	180
16:1-4	147	2:1-17	389	5:13-14	109
17:9	194	6:2	396	5:17	356
25:9	331	13:14	333, 355, 375	5:32	128, 138, 390
27:6	331	14:9	39, 373	6:7	291
28:9	235			7:13-14	392
31:31	219, 220, 374	*Joel*		7:16	112
31:33	179	2:1	398	7:20	112
38:1-13	87	2:14	390	7:23	390
39:16-18	87	2:28	377	8:11	397
		2:28-32	396	8:14	389, 391
Ezekiel				8:29	387, 389
1	379	*Amos*		9:4	258
1:1	376, 378	3:2	390		

Matthew		23:6	392	6:18	388
9:18	394	23:10	177	6:52-53	276
10:10	174	23:15	391	7:15	389
10:28	397	23:18-21	391	7:19	389
11:1	392	24:13	387	8:11-12	387
11:8	350, 389	24:22	390	8:15	100
11:11	317	24:31	354	8:25	397
11:19	391	24:38	147	8:38	394
12:19	31	24:45 - 25:30	332	10:11-12	128, 390
12:33	112	25:14-30	388	10:15	296
12:38	387	25:15	32, 289	10:19	389
12:39-40	396	25:21	388	10:38-39	393
12:41-42	389	25:23	388	10:45	389
12:43	394	25:31	394	11:2	145
12:44	125	25:31-46	87	11:23	128, 393
12:46-47	391	25:34	397	12:18	313
13:11	54	25:41	397	12:24	342
13:22	396	25:45	390	12:25	343
13:43	397	25:46	397	12:35-37	397
13:52	66	26:12	220	12:36	392
13:55-56	391	26:17-29	389	12:41-44	363
14:4	388	26:24	389	13:13	387
16:1	387	26:26-27	391	13:20	390
16:4	387	26:26-29	392	14:8	220
16:6-12	100	26:41	396	14:17-25	389
16:17	351	26:49	370	14:22-23	391
16:18	187	26:59	397	14:22-25	392
16:28	397	26:63-64	397	14:24	396
17:20	128, 393	26:67	86	14:45	370
18:3	296	27:24	386	14:55	323
18:8	397	27:52	390	14:61-62	397
18:8-9	389	28:5-7	317	15:15	386
18:10	282	28:16	396	16:7	396
19:3-9	128, 390	28:18	388, 390	16:9	317
19:5	389			16:17	236
19:9	138	Mark			
19:11	125	1:8	393	Luke	
19:27-28	389	1:19	31	1:13	393
19:28	109, 279	1:24	387, 389	1:19	393
20:28	389	1:30	389	1:28-37	393
21:2	145	2:8	396	1:32-33	335
21:21	128, 393	3:29	397	1:35	162
21:40	394	4:19	291	1:41-45	396
22:23	313	4:24	341	1:46-47	291
22:29	342	4:33	64	1:46-55	396
22:30	343	5:7	389	2:12	388
22:43	392	5:38	256	2:14	393
22:43-45	397	6:14	317	2:16	388

Scripture index 419

2:36-38	396	21:1-4	363	6:39-40	332, 390
3:14	171	21:34	389	6:45	60
3:16	393	22:8-9	220	6:51	396
3:17	388	22:14-23	389, 392	6:63	329
4:34	387, 389	22:17	391	7:3	391
4:1-2	391	22:19	391	7:5	318
4:38	389	22:19-20	392, 396	7:37-40	243
5:30	391	22:30	389	7:38	349
6:43-44	112	22:37	179	8:7	119
7:25	389	22:47	370	8:21	324
7:36-50	119	22:67-70	397	9:7	292
8:12	397	23:25	386	10:11	396
8:28	389	23:34	55	10:15	396
9:16	196	23:42	394	10:34	396
9:26	394	23:43	154, 398	11:5	371
10:7	174, 273	23:46	396	11:11-12	390
10:20	304	24:15-51	348	11:16	258
10:40	150	24:24-27	396	11:24	332
11:25	125	24:27	292	11:39	316
11:29	396	24:33-36	396	11:50-51	396
11:30-32	389	24:37	348	12:1	220, 397
12:1	100	24:39	348, 350	12:2	392
12:13-15	103	24:46	396	12:7	220
12:19	388	24:49	327	12:24	344
12:20	344			13:1-30	392
12:50	393	*John*		13:5	397
13:16	389	1:3	390	13:10	101
14:10	394	1:25	393	13:12-17	392
15:1-2	391	1:33	393	14:3	56
15:2	239	1:38	292	14:6	55, 258
15:11-32	99	1:42	292	14:27	24
16:1-9	363	2:2	391	15:13	396
16:18	128, 390	2:4	389	15:25	396
16:19-31	42, 329	2:10	394	15:26	394
16:31	340, 397	2:17	249, 388	16:2	81
17:6	393	3:5	242	16:4	394
17:7-10	175	3:13	350	16:8	301
17:27	147	3:14-15	191	16:8-11	48
17:32	101	3:21	258	16:13	130, 235, 394
18:17	296	4:13-14	243	17:24	282
19:7	391	4:25	394	18:14	396
19:11-27	388	4:36	172	18:38	388
19:17	388	5:21	329	19:12	390
19:30	145	5:26	349	19:12-16	386
19:40	396	5:28-29	397	19:27	397
20:27	313	5:29	349	19:36	219
20:36	343	6:30	387	20:5-7	388
20:41-44	397	6:35-40	193	20:14-18	317

John		5:31	397	15:13	397
20:17	77	5:39	323	15:17	387
20:19	348, 364, 396	7:2	388	15:20	158
20:25	258	7:10	336	15:23-29	308
20:26	348, 364, 396	7:39-43	188	15:28-29	158
20:27	348, 397	7:52	388	15:39	171, 257
21:1-22	396	7:55-56	397	16:1	89, 133, 391
21:22	182	7:56	317	16:3	178
		7:59	387, 396, 398	16:4	391
Acts		7:60	168, 390	16:6-8	90
1:1	130	8:1	361	16:6-10	366
1:2-10	318	8:32	289	16:15	393
1:3	319	9:1-20	319	16:16	304
1:4	327	9:3	390	16:17	230, 387
1:4-6	40	9:4	168, 301, 396	16:18	388
1:5	393	9:18	393	16:19 - 17:34	47
1:14	318, 391	9:21	387	16:22 - 17:15	18
1:18-20	75	9:36	292	16:25	293
1:21-26	318, 319	10:14	158	16:28	47, 250
1:22	390, 397	10:15	389	16:29-30	108
2:1-13	299	10:36	274	16:33	393
2:4	236	10:41	348	16:37	386
2:4-11	235	10:42	191, 387, 388	17:7-8	390
2:6	236	10:46	236, 299	17:16	257, 396
2:8	236	10:48	33	17:18	391
2:11	236, 260	11:16	393	17:21	24, 39
2:17	377, 396	11:16-17	393	17:22	47
2:21	387	11:19-20	361	17:23-29	387
2:23	388, 391	11:26	15	17:26-27	139
2:26-27	317	11:28	235	17:28	341
2:27	317	11:29	361	17:30	162
2:31	317	12:17	397	17:31	191, 351, 387, 388
2:32	397	12:19	392	17:32	387
2:33-35	397	13:2-3	22	17:33	211
2:40	299	13:11	234	17:33-34	18
2:46	392	13:24	393	18:1	18, 45, 367
3:2	256	13:27	388	18:1-18	63
3:10	256	13:27-28	55	18:2-3	19, 370
3:13	386	13:28	388	18:3	171, 388
3:14-18	388	13:33	317	18:8	135, 387, 393
3:17	223, 388	13:34-35	317	18:10	12, 47, 69
4:10	388	13:36	390	18:11	365
4:13	396	13:41	387	18:14-15	106
4:26	52	14:15-17	387	18:15	17
5:1-11	234	14:23	302	18:17	18
5:6	146	15	158	18:18	178, 392
5:17	392	15:1	387, 390, 391	18:18-19	19, 370
5:30-31	388	15:5	387, 390, 392		

Scripture index

18:19	391	23:8	313	2:12	397
18:19 - 19:1	19	23:11	12	2:16	70, 397
18:24	391	23:17	392	2:17-24	141
18:24-28	19	23:35	394	2:22	97
18:26	234, 370	24:2-8	36	3:5	391
18:27-28	367	24:5	392	3:9-19	329
19:3-5	393	24:10	390	3:20	396
19:6	236, 299	24:14	214, 392	3:21	396
19:9	366	24:15	327	3:24	389
19:13-16	366	25:8	390	4:3	396
19:14	230	25:11	106	4:12	101
19:15	387	25:11-12	387	4:15	357
19:21	362, 365	25:16	390	4:23	273
19:22	88, 366	25:27	305	4:24	397
19:23-28	366	26:1	390	4:25	166, 324
19:26	390	26:2	390	5:1-5	394
19:32	23	26:3	106	5:2	395
19:41	23	26:5	392	5:3-4	194
20:1	365	26:10	338, 361	5:6	396
20:3	365	26:11	168, 230	5:8	396
20:7	364, 392	26:14	168, 301, 356	5:9	315
20:20	64	26:16	78, 319, 390	5:10	315
20:27	64	26:22-23	396, 398	5:12	328
20:28	55	26:24	390	5:12-19	328
20:29-30	366	26:29	126	5:13	357
20:30	88	27:21	47	5:13-14	391
20:31	19	27:24	12, 387	5:17	84
20:32	286	28:2	289	5:17-19	328
20:34	388	28:3	47	5:19	329
20:35	128	28:22	392	5:20	357
21:9	262, 396			6	240
21:11	235	*Romans*		6:1	343
21:18	397	1:3	163	6:1-11	240
21:24	178, 392	1:4	397	6:3	186
21:25	390	1:7	387, 398	6:3-4	393
21:26	391	1:10	90	6:4	397
21:28	397	1:13	391	6:6	390
21:37	295	1:14	289	6:7	101
21:40	295	1:15-16	12	6:9	397
22:1	390	1:18	393	6:13	397
22:3	323, 386	1:18-32	15, 141	6:14	193, 391
22:6	390	1:20	269	6:15	343
22:7	168, 301	1:20-28	387	6:16	329, 389
22:16	113, 387, 389, 393	1:21	106	6:17	48
		1:28	291	6:17-22	390
22:17	391	1:32	329, 357	6:21-22	279
22:20	338	2:2	329	6:23	347, 352
22:25	386	2:6-8	329	7:2	153

Romans		12:1	389	1:6	25, 26
7:4	397	12:2	180, 291	1:7	25, 51, 57,
7:5	357	12:4-5	389		72, 84, 251,
7:7	343, 391	12:4-8	232, 248		352, 389
7:8	357	12:17	392	1:8	21, 26, 99, 390
7:11	357	13:4	350	1:9	26, 30, 194, 373
7:12	391	13:13	388	1:10	30, 31, 291
7:13	251, 343	14:5	291	1:10-11	30-31, 213
7:24	193	14:7-9	398	1:10-13	30-33
7:24-25	80	14:8	22	1:10-17	28, 30-35, 63
8:1	357	14:10	388	1:10 - 4:21	28-91
8:9-10	118	14:13	165	1:11	19, 25, 31,
8:11	84, 389, 397	14:15	396		66, 369
8:13	183	14:16	201	1:12	31-2, 170
8:14	229	14:17	389, 397	1:13	32-3, 396
8:15	91	14:21	389	1:13-17	393
8:20	395	14:23	164	1:14	33
8:21-25	278	15:4	273	1:14-17	33-5
8:23	327, 387, 397	15:15	393	1:15	33
8:24	315, 395	15:16	175	1:16	19, 34
8:26-27	290	15:24	386, 393	1:17	34, 35
8:27	388	15:26	361	1:18	34, 36-7,
8:28	76, 387	15:27	361		314, 397
8:29	390, 397	15:28	386	1:18-20	45
8:29-30	54	16:1	12, 308	1:18-21	36-8
8:32	396	16:3	370	1:18-31	28, 35-44
8:34	397	16:5	370, 387, 397	1:18 - 2:5	50
8:38	398	16:16	370	1:19	374
9:3	392	16:17	80	1:19-20	34
9:5	56	16:22	371, 389	1:19-21	37-8
9:17	396	16:23	79, 387	1:20	20, 37, 52,
9:17-18	225	16:25	70, 387		373, 391
9:19	343			1:21	34, 38, 39
10:2	388	*1 Corinthians*		1:22-23	39
10:4	391	1-3	214	1:22-25	39-40
10:7	397	1-14	314	1:23	46, 202,
10:9	313, 397	1:1	18, 22, 78, 397		228, 373, 394
10:11	396	1:1-3	21-4	1:24	39
10:12	392	1:1-9	9, 21-7	1:25	40
10:12-14	387	1:2	9, 22, 23, 95,	1:26	41, 75
10:18	57		124, 132, 140,	1:26-28	44
11:2	389, 396		141, 216, 230,	1:26-29	41-2
11:11-12	331		353, 387	1:26-31	40-44,
11:12	111	1:3	24, 398		45, 85
11:15	397	1:4	24, 163	1:27	41-2
11:16	397	1:4-9	21, 24-7	1:27-28	41, 143
11:25	387, 391, 393	1:5	25, 396	1:28	41, 110,
11:34	388	1:5-6	394		259, 357

Scripture index 423

1:30	42	3:3	66	4:6	82, 257
1:30-31	42-3	3:4	66, 368	4:6-7	77, 82-3
1:31	43-4, 374	3:4-6	82	4:6-13	30
2:1	45-6, 63, 221, 387	3:5	78	4:7	82, 223
2:1-5	18, 29, 44, 45-9	3:5-9	66-8	4:8	51, 83-4,
2:1-16	29, 44-62	3:6	67		90, 394
2:2	18, 46	3:7	67	4:8-9	397
2:3	47	3:8	67, 82, 358	4:8-10	372
2:4	47, 48, 49	3:9	68, 394	4:8-13	78, 83-7
2:4-5	47-9	3:10	69, 78	4:9	84, 85,109,
2:5	49, 233	3:10-11	29, 69-71		339, 394
2:6	50-53, 55, 62, 64,	3:10-12	387	4:9-13	84-7
	233, 259, 331,	3:10-17	63, 69-74	4:10	85, 112, 394
	357, 373, 394	3:11	70, 71, 74, 373	4:11	86, 394
2:6-7	59	3:12	72	4:11-13	85
2:6-8	391	3:12-15	71-4	4:12	86, 320,
2:6-9	29, 50-57	3:12-17	29		358, 394
2:6-12	44	3:12-18	73	4:13	86, 394
2:6-16	49-62	3:13	72, 73	4:14	87, 110, 342
2:7	53-5, 56, 78,	3:14	73, 84	4:14-21	30, 78, 87-91
	352, 394, 396	3:14-15	82	4:14-16	87-8
2:7-8	52	3:15	73, 99, 183	4:15	88, 169, 369
2:8	53, 55-6,	3:16	74, 117,	4:16	88, 115, 202
	223, 373, 387		119, 389	4:17	88-9, 366
2:9	56-7, 58, 59, 375	3:16-17	74	4:18	257
2:10	57, 287	3:17	74	4:18-21	89-91
2:10-12	57-9	3:18	52, 75, 391	4:19	90, 257, 366
2:10-13	29	3:18-20	75-6	4:20	90, 112, 397
2:11	58, 290	3:18-23	29, 63, 75-7	4:21	90, 91, 396
2:12	58, 60, 394	3:19	20, 375	5	100, 105
2:12-13	234	3:19-20	75	5:1	95-7, 228
2:13	45, 58, 59-61,	3:20	375	5:1-8	95-102
	233, 273,	3:21	76, 247	5:1-13	93, 95-105
	292, 394	3:21-23	76-7	5:1 - 6:20	92-120
2:14	61, 66,	3:22	84, 170, 259,	5:2	97, 257
	110, 348		321, 398	5:3	98, 99
2:14-15	62, 80	3:22-23	76	5:3-5	97-100
2:14-16	29, 45, 61-2	4:1	78, 352, 367, 396	5:5	99
2:15	61, 62, 301	4:1-2	175	5:6	100, 389
2:16	62, 144, 291,	4:1-3	78-9	5:6-8	100-102
	373, 394	4:1-5	30, 77, 78-82	5:7	100, 225,327,
3	61	4:1-21	30, 77-91		373, 394
3:1	35, 51, 64, 394	4:2	79	5:8	101, 102,
3:1-3	51, 61	4:3	79, 80		373, 394
3:1-9	29, 63-8	4:3-4	169	5:9	102, 121
3:1-23	29, 63-77	4:4	80, 81, 373	5:9-11	19, 102-3, 120
3:2	64	4:4-5	80-82	5:9-13	102-5
3:2-3	64-6	4:5	81, 84	5:10	102, 108, 131

1 Corinthians

Ref	Pages
5:11	103, 272
5:12	103, 104
5:12-13	103-5
5:13	103, 373
6	100, 115
6:1	105, 107, 112
6:1-4	105-10
6:1-8	137
6:1-11	93, 105-14
6:2	104, 107, 109, 301, 373, 389
6:2-3	107-9
6:3	109, 389, 394
6:4	109-10
6:5	110, 223, 342
6:5-7	110-11
6:6	110
6:7	111
6:7-8	389
6:8	111
6:8-10	111-12
6:9	105, 112, 120, 389
6:9-10	111, 397
6:11	58, 108, 112-14, 389
6:12	115, 124, 199
6:12-14	114-17
6:12-20	114-20
6:13	116, 259, 357
6:14	114, 116-17
6:15	114, 117, 238, 353, 389
6:15-16	120
6:15-17	117-18
6:15-20	117-19, 179
6:16	114, 117, 120, 375, 389
6:17	118, 373
6:18	118-19, 195
6:19	114, 117, 119, 389
6:19-20	119
6:20	119, 142
7	120, 130
7:1	19, 121, 122-3, 124, 125, 126, 360, 369
7:1-5	125
7:1-7	121, 122-6
7:1-40	121-54
7:2	124, 126, 388
7:3	124
7:3-6	124-5
7:3-7	124-6
7:4	124
7:5	124, 139
7:6	125, 127
7:7	124, 125-6, 148
7:8	122, 126, 144, 153, 389
7:8-9	121, 126-7, 143
7:8-16	143
7:9	95, 126
7:10	127, 128, 144
7:10-11	121, 127-9, 143
7:10-15	138
7:11	122, 129, 137
7:12	129, 134, 144, 388
7:12-13	129-30
7:12-16	121, 129-39, 143
7:14	130-36, 149
7:15	136-8, 305
7:16	108, 129, 139
7:17	139, 392
7:17-18	139-40
7:17-24	121, 139-43
7:18	140
7:19	140-41
7:20	41, 140, 141
7:20-24	141-3
7:21	141-2
7:22	142
7:23	77, 119, 142-3
7:24	143
7:25	143-4, 154, 360
7:25-35	121, 143-50
7:26	123, 144-5, 147, 148, 389
7:27	145
7:27-28	138, 145-6
7:28	143, 148
7:29	146, 147, 351, 388
7:29-31	146-8
7:30	147
7:30-31	373
7:31	147, 148
7:32	122, 148, 149
7:32-34	148-9, 150
7:32-35	124, 148-50
7:33	148
7:33-34	148
7:34	122, 148, 149
7:35	149-50
7:36	143, 150-51
7:36-38	121, 150-53
7:37	152, 358
7:37-38	151
7:38	153
7:39	153-4
7:39-40	121, 153-4
7:40	126, 144, 154
8	156, 157, 184, 199
8:1	121, 155, 159, 164, 177, 360, 394
8:1-6	159-63
8:1-13	159-68
8:1 - 11:1	155-202
8:2	160
8:3	160
8:4	139, 160-61, 197, 373, 394
8:5	161, 184, 229, 259
8:6	161-3
8:7	163, 164
8:7-9	180
8:7-13	159, 163-8
8:8	164, 165, 394
8:8-9	164-5
8:9	165, 199
8:10	165, 200, 338
8:10-12	165-8
8:11	166
8:12	168
8:13	52, 168, 391
9	156, 157, 199
9:1	169, 170, 346, 397
9:1-2	169, 170
9:1-18	168-76
9:2	87, 169

Scripture index

9:3	169, 170	10:1	185, 186	10:25	199
9:3-6	170-71	10:1-2	373	10:26	199, 374
9:3-11	169-72	10:1-4	185-8	10:27	200
9:3-18	169-76	10:1-13	184-95	10:28-29	200-201
9:4	170, 394	10:1 - 11:1	184-202	10:30	201
9:5	170, 389, 394, 397	10:2	113, 186, 241, 242, 389, 393	10:30 - 11:1	201-2
9:6	170, 171, 388, 394	10:3	374	10:31	201, 259
9:7	171, 174, 373	10:3-4	186, 187	10:32	202
9:7-11	171-2	10:4	187, 188, 374	10:33	257
9:8	171	10:5	188, 374	10:33 - 11:1	202
9:9	375	10:5-10	188-91	11-14	301, 309
9:10	172	10:6	188, 270, 273, 374, 394	11:1	388
9:11	172, 394			11:2	203, 212, 216
9:11-12	388	10:6-10	189	11:2-3	203-5
9:12	171, 174, 258, 394	10:7	189, 375	11:2-16	203-11
		10:8	190, 374, 394	11:2 - 14:40	307
9:12-18	169, 172-6	10:9	190-91, 194, 374, 394	11:2-34	307
9:13	173, 373, 389, 391	10:10	191, 374, 394	11:3	124, 203, 204, 374
9:13-14	173-4	10:11	52, 189, 192, 270, 273	11:3-16	306
9:14	174, 221, 390, 392			11:4	205, 207
		10:11-13	192-5	11:4-6	203, 205-7
9:15	174, 389	10:12	193-4	11:5	204, 205-6, 307
9:15-16	174-5	10:13	194-5, 374	11:6	206-7
9:16	174	10:14	195	11:7	207, 374
9:17	175	10:14-15	195	11:7-12	203, 207-10
9:17-18	175-6, 388	10:14-22	103, 184, 195-9	11:8	374
9:18	147, 175, 182			11:8-9	208-9
9:19	178	10:15	195, 210, 351	11:9	374
9:19-22	387	10:16	195-6, 394	11:10	209
9:19-23	177-81	10:16-17	187, 216	11:11	209
9:19-27	176-83	10:17	196, 394	11:11-12	209-10
9:20	179	10:18	196, 374	11:12	210
9:20-23	178-81	10:18-20	196-7	11:13	210
9:21	177, 178, 199, 356	10:19	197, 351	11:13-16	203, 210-11
		10:19-20	161	11:14-15	210
9:22	180	10:20	197, 228, 229, 374, 390	11:16	211, 306, 308, 394
9:23	180			11:17	213, 216
9:24	181, 389	10:20-22	338	11:17-18	213
9:24-25	181-2	10:21	187, 198, 374	11:17-19	213-15
9:24-27	181-3	10:21-22	198-9	11:17-22	212-16
9:25	182	10:22	198, 353, 374, 394	11:17-34	212-26, 338
9:26	182, 288			11:18	215
9:26-27	182-3	10:23	115, 199	11:19	214-15, 312, 374
9:27	183	10:23-27	199-200		
10	156, 157, 193, 199, 270	10:23 - 11:1	184, 199-202	11:20	213, 215
				11:20-21	222
		10:24	199	11:20-22	215-16

1 Corinthians

11:21	215	12:9-10	233	13:2	54, 128, 234, 256, 352, 396
11:22	216	12:10	232, 233, 236, 251, 285, 289, 303	13:3	256-7
11:23	217, 218, 249, 316, 391			13:4	249, 257
11:23-26	212, 216-21	12:11	237	13:4-7	227, 253, 257-8
11:23-34	128	12:12	238-9, 247		
11:24	389, 391, 396	12:12-31	227, 237-50	13:5	213, 257, 258, 374
11:24-25	392	12:13	58, 239-43, 247, 393, 394		
11:25	219-21, 374			13:6	258
11:26	219, 221, 222	12:14	243	13:7	113, 258
11:27	222	12:14-26	243-7	13:8	259-60, 262, 263, 282, 321, 396
11:27-29	222-4	12:15	244		
11:27-34	212, 222-6	12:15-16	243-4	13:8-12	395
11:28	223	12:16	244	13:8-13	227, 253, 259-83, 384
11:29	223-4, 224	12:17	244		
11:30	99, 212, 216, 224, 325, 390, 397	12:18	244, 272	13:9	260-61, 271, 278, 280
		12:18-20	244-5		
		12:19	245	13:10	260, 261-3, 264, 272, 275, 276, 277, 279, 330
11:31	223, 224, 394	12:20	244, 245		
11:31-32	224-5	12:21	245		
11:32	224, 394	12:21-24	245-6		
11:33	213, 225	12:22	245	13:10-12	281
11:33-34	225-6	12:23	246, 394	13:11	263-5, 274, 278-9, 280
11:34	213, 225, 226, 390	12:24	246		
		12:24-26	246-7	13:12	20, 260, 262, 263, 265-71, 273, 278, 280, 281-2, 286, 374, 377,380, 384, 385, 394
12	264, 389	12:25	246		
12-14	227, 254, 278	12:26	246		
12:1	121, 228, 391	12:27	247, 393		
12:1-3	227, 228-30, 303	12:27-30	250		
		12:27-31	247-50		
12:1 - 14:40	227-311, 360	12:28	232, 247, 260, 289, 389	13:13	244, 259, 272, 277-8, 287
		12:28-29	233, 247, 251	14	227, 237, 302, 306, 310
12:2	228-9, 235, 289	12:28-30	247-50		
12:3	229-30, 294, 314, 371	12:29-30	249	14:1	234, 248, 249, 284, 310
		12:30-31	389		
12:4	389	12:31	248, 249, 251, 272, 310	14:1-5	285-6
12:4-6	230-31, 243			14:1-11	227
12:4-11	227, 230-37, 238	12:31 - 13:13	227, 251-83	14:1-12	284-9
		13	251, 252-5, 261, 264, 268, 281, 282, 296, 309, 310, 382, 393	14:1-19	284-96
12:6	237			14:1-25	227
12:7	231-2, 290			14:1-40	284-311
12:7-10	248			14:2	260, 285, 286, 292, 352, 396
12:7-11	231-7				
12:8	34, 232, 233, 256, 396	13:1	255-6	14:3	286, 292
		13:1-3	227, 252, 253, 255-7	14:4	286, 396
12:8-10	232-7			14:5	126, 248, 272, 287, 310,374, 396
12:9	232, 389	13:1-13	252, 280		

Scripture index

14:6	233, 256, 287, 290, 292	14:33-40	228	15:17	317, 323, 324
14:6-12	287-9	14:34	306, 308, 374	15:18	324-5, 329, 338, 390, 397
14:7	288	14:34-36	306	15:19	325-6, 394
14:8	288	14:35	307	15:20	244, 272, 317, 326, 327, 346, 390, 397
14:9	288, 289, 396	14:36	9, 308, 309		
14:10	288	14:36-38	211		
14:11	288, 289	14:37	61, 128, 144, 273, 309	15:20-28	193, 322, 326-37
14:12	289, 290	14:37-40	309-10		
14:12-14	289-93	14:38	310	15:21	327, 374
14:12-19	227, 284	14:39	234, 249, 310, 374, 396	15:21-22	327-9
14:13	290, 396			15:22	328, 349
14:14	285, 290, 291, 292	14:40	310	15:23	330, 331, 332, 351, 395
		15	116, 309, 313, 322, 325, 343, 355		
14:15	293, 302, 305			15:23-24	330, 334
14:15-17	293-4	15:1	314, 392	15:24	26, 90, 259, 279, 330, 331, 332, 333, 334, 335, 336, 357
14:16	294	15:1-2	314-15		
14:16-17	292	15:1-4	314-17		
14:17	294	15:1-11	313, 314-21		
14:18	264, 294, 295, 396	15:1-58	312-59	15:25	335, 374, 388, 390
		15:2	315		
14:18-19	294-6	15:3	217, 249, 374, 391	15:25-26	335-6
14:19	88, 295, 371, 396			15:26	259, 334, 357
		15:3-4	128, 315	15:27	375
14:20	296-7	15:4	374	15:27-28	336-7
14:20-25	227, 248, 296-301, 394	15:5	318, 321	15:29	337-9, 340, 393
		15:5-7	317-18	15:29-32	337
14:21	20, 297-9, 300, 375, 396	15:5-8	326	15:29-34	322, 337-42
		15:5-11	317-22	15:30	339, 394
14:22	300, 301	15:6	318, 390	15:30-34	339-42
14:22-25	300	15:7	318, 321	15:31	339-40
14:23	213, 300, 396	15:8	319, 346	15:32	124, 340-41, 374, 394
14:24	301, 396	15:8-10	319-21		
14:25	301, 374	15:9	320, 396	15:33	100, 341
14:26	213, 302	15:10	320, 358	15:33-34	313
14:26-27	302	15:11	28, 321, 394	15:34	341-2
14:26-33	302-5, 306	15:12	312, 313, 317, 322, 327, 346, 397	15:35	343
14:26-40	227, 301-10			15:35-41	343-6
14:27	302, 396	15:12-13	322	15:35-49	343-51
14:28	303, 396	15:12-19	322-6, 337	15:35-58	313, 342-59
14:28-32	303-4	15:12-34	313, 322-42	15:36	344
14:29	302, 303, 392	15:13	317, 323, 327, 397	15:36-37	344-5
14:30	303			15:36-38	353
14:31	304	15:14	315, 317, 322-3, 324	15:37	344
14:31-32	302			15:38	345, 374
14:32	304, 305	15:15	323, 394	15:38-39	346
14:33	211, 305, 306	15:15-16	323	15:38-41	345-6
14:33-36	306-9	15:16	317	15:39	345, 374

1 Corinthians		16:6	365, 367	4:14	389
15:40	345	16:7	366	4:17	251, 278
15:40-41	346	16:8	366, 374	5:1	353
15:41	346	16:9	366	5:6-7	395
15:42	327, 346, 347, 397	16:10	358, 366, 367	5:7	350
		16:10-12	366-8	5:10	388
15:42-44	347-8, 353	16:10-24	360, 366-72	5:14	396
15:42-49	343, 346-51	16:11	367	5:15	396
15:42-55	278	16:12	367	5:16	387
15:43	347	16:13	368	5:20	371
15:44	348	16:13-14	368	5:21	396
15:44-5	375, 388	16:14	368	6:14-16	138
15:45	329, 336, 348-9, 375	16:15	18, 34, 397	6:15	198
		16:15-16	368	7:6-7	397
15:46	349, 388	16:15-18	368-9	7:7	249
15:46-49	349-51	16:17	19, 367, 368, 397	7:8-9	389
15:47	336, 349, 374			7:11	388
15:48	350	16:18	369, 396	7:12	96
15:48-49	346	16:19	369, 370, 389	8-9	361
15:49	350, 374, 394	16:19-24	9, 369-72	8:1	392
15:50	112, 351-2, 354, 397	16:20	370-71	8:10	154
		16:21	371	8:12	363
15:50-57	343, 351	16:21-24	371	8:19-21	362
15:51	352-3, 390, 394, 396	16:22	371, 392	9:2	361, 388
		16:22-24	371	9:6-11	364
15:51-52	352-4	16:23	372	10:7	32
15:52	280, 353-4, 394	16:24	372	10:10	397
15:53	354			10:12	388
15:53-54	354	2 Corinthians		10:17	43
15:54	333	1:2	398	11:1 - 12:10	85
15:54-55	20, 355	1:8	251, 391	11:2	388
15:55-56	355-7	1:14	393	11:2-3	116
15:56	356	1:15-17	365	11:5	397
15:57	357	1:17-20	388	11:6	396
15:58	343, 358-9, 367	1:23	387	11:23	358
16	309, 359	2:5	393	11:23-33	340
16:1	121, 360, 361, 390, 392	2:12	366	12:4	54
		2:14	231	12:7	389, 391
16:1-4	361-5	2:15	397	12:11-12	397
16:1-9	360-66	2:17	25	12:12	387, 390
16:1-24	360-72	3:1-11	391	12:18	367
16:2	361, 363, 364, 394	3:6	395	12:19	390
		3:12	395	12:20	388
16:3	360, 362, 365	3:18	281-2, 395	13:5	112, 371
16:4	362	4:3	397	13:5-7	183
16:5	365	4:6	281	13:12	370
16:5-9	365-6	4:9	85	13:14	398

Scripture index

Galatians		1:7	389	5:27	116
1:1	22, 397	1:9	387, 392	5:30	389
1:3	398	1:11	54	5:31	389, 392
1:4	334, 396	1:13-14	397	6:1-3	133
1:8-9	387, 392	1:14	387	6:6	390
1:12	217, 316	1:17	388	6:10-17	194
1:13	251, 320	1:18	141	6:12	161, 351
1:15	22	1:19-20	389	6:19	387, 392
1:16	351	1:20	397	6:24	347, 398
1:17-19	390	1:20-22	397		
1:18	218	1:22	388, 390, 391	Philippians	
1:19	397	2:4	387	1:1	302
2:7	22	2:5	315	1:2	398
2:9	397	2:8	234, 315, 387	1:7	390
2:9-14	390	2:11-22	40	1:16	390
2:11-14	32	2:12	387	1:17	388
2:20	396	2:17	22	1:21	325
3:13	396	2:17-18	397	1:21-23	398
3:15	219, 391	2:19	387	1:23	278
3:19	390	2:20	70, 260, 387	1:27-28	395
3:24	391	3:3	392	2:7	147, 350, 392
3:24-25	88	3:3-4	387	2:22	367
3:27	186, 393	3:4-5	54	2:25	22
3:28	392	3:5	57, 260, 392	2:30	358
3:29	24, 141	3:9	387	3:2	391
4:4	163, 391	3:10	392	3:6	320, 388
4:29	187	4:1	141	3:9-11	395
4:30	135, 396	4:2-5	394	3:11	391, 397
5:1-15	141	4:4	141, 395	3:12	391
5:3	390	4:4-6	393	3:14	396
5:5	395	4:5	393	3:15	52, 394
5:5-6	394	4:11	260	3:21	278, 350, 389, 397
5:9	100	4:11-12	248		
5:11	388	4:13	391	4:9	388
5:12	391	4:15-16	391	4:15	388
5:20	388, 392	4:16	389	4:23	398
5:21	397	4:23	291, 396		
6:1	31, 159, 396	4:25	389	Colossians	
6:6	363	4:30	387	1:2	398
6:11	371	5:1	388	1:4-5	394
6:12	390	5:2	396	1:5	395
6:16	387	5:5	397	1:13	397
6:18	398	5:11	396	1:16	390
		5:14	397	1:16-17	390
Ephesians		5:23	391	1:17	388
1:2	398	5:25	396	1:18	391, 397
1:5	54	5:26	113	1:26-27	387

Colossians
1:27	392, 395
2:2	387
2:10	52, 66, 391
2:12	393, 397
2:19	391
3:1	397
3:1-2	358
3:20	133
4:3	387
4:11	397
4:12	394
4:16	389
4:18	371

1 Thessalonians
1:1	398
1:3	394, 395
1:6	388
1:10	395
2:9	388
2:12	397
2:14	388
2:19	395, 397
3:1	258
3:5	258
3:13	395, 397
4:3-7	134
4:9	60
4:13	391
4:13-15	390
4:14	389
4:15	352, 395, 397
4:15-17	353
4:16	398
5:8	394
5:10	396
5:15	392
5:20-21	392
5:23	395, 397
5:24	27
5:26	370
5:27	389
5:28	398

2 Thessalonians
1:2	398
1:3	394
1:5	397
1:7	388
1:8-10	395
1:9	397
1:10	394, 397
2:1	395, 397
2:1-12	26
2:8	391, 395
2:8-9	397
2:10	392, 397
2:10-12	393
2:13	397
2:15	391
3:6	388
3:8	388
3:17	371
3:18	398

1 Timothy
1:2	89, 398
1:5	279
1:9	391
1:10	389
1:13	81, 320
1:16	320
1:17	397
1:20	99
2:5	239, 350
2:6	396
2:7	386, 397
2:11-15	307
2:12	307
2:13	397
3:10	397
3:1	308
3:16	393
3:16 - 4:3	276
4:1	197
4:3	122
4:4	200
4:4-5	133
4:12	367
5:18	174, 273, 396
5:23	367
6:9-10	390
6:11-14	395
6:16	354
6:17-19	359, 390
6:18	363
6:20	387
6:21	398

2 Timothy
1:2	398
1:5	133
1:6-8	367
1:8	46
1:9	141
2:1-7	367
2:8	70, 317, 397
2:10-12	258
2:17-18	313
2:22	387
3:7	38
3:8	183
3:15	133, 185
3:16	273
4:1	397
4:3	387
4:6	175
4:7	12
4:16	390
4:17	340
4:18	397
4:19	370
4:22	398

Titus
1:2	395
1:4	398
1:5	302, 390
1:12	340, 341
1:16	193
2:5	307
2:13	351, 395
2:14	396
3:6	397
3:7	395
3:14	396
3:15	398

Philemon
3	398
12	142
25	398

Scripture index

Hebrews		13:17	249	1:10	141
1:2	390			1:16	392, 395
1:3	397	*James*		1:19	396
1:6	394	1:1	397	1:21	388
1:12	210	1:3-4	194	2	193
1:13	397	1:9	44	2:1	392, 393
1:14	392	1:9-10	142	2:9	356, 397
2:1-4	274	1:13	195	2:12	305
2:2	255	1:15	397	2:16	396
2:3-4	338	1:17	388	2:19	347, 389
2:9	396	1:23	394	3:4	390, 395
2:14	350, 351	2:6	389	3:12	395
2:17	350	2:7	387	3:16	273
3:6	389	3:14	388		
3:14	389	3:15	398	*1 John*	
5:1	396	3:16	388	1:6	258
5:12	65	4:13-16	366	1:8	193
6:2	397	5:7-8	395	1:10	193
6:9	113	5:10	194	2:1	397
6:10-12	394			2:8	147
6:12	388	*1 Peter*		2:17	147
7:2	292	1:3-8	394	2:28	395
8:1	397	1:5	193	3:2	268, 350
8:8	392	1:7	194	3:4	357
8:9	179	1:9	277	3:16	396
9:12	387	1:12	85, 392	4:1	303, 392, 393
9:13	392	1:17	387	4:6	91
9:20	392	1:18-19	389		
9:24	397	1:19	389	*2 John*	
9:27	356	1:20	166	1	371
9:28	26	1:21-22	394	8	73
10:4	392	1:24	347		
10:5-7	398	2:16	389, 390	*3 John*	
10:12	396	2:16-20	390	9	88
10:12-13	397	2:20	258		
10:22-24	394	2:21	396	*Jude*	
10:24	258	3:1-2	108	1	387, 397
11:4	338	3:4	396	4	193
11:16	387	3:7	392	7	397
11:19	397	3:18	396	10	305
12:1	391	3:22	397	12	396
12:2	397	4:10	388	15	356
12:3	80, 258	5:1-4	388	19	396, 398
12:6	225	5:14	370	24	193
12:28	397				
12:29	388	*2 Peter*		*Revelation*	
13:3	87	1:4	347	1:1	390
13:7	249, 339	1:8	396	1:4	290, 370

Revelation					
1:5	387	4:5	290	17:14	387
1:10	364, 398	5:6	290	19:9	392
1:11	370	6:10	276	20	333
1:17	319	7:9	353	20:1-10	332
1:19	235	8:2	398	20:4	389
1:20	387	8:6	398	21:2	116
2:14	190, 389, 390	8:13	398	21:4	277, 279
2:20	190, 389, 390	9:14	398	21:9	116
2:23	388	10:7	387	21:27	354
2:26-27	389	13:1-2	11	22:3	390
3:1	290	14:10	388	22:4	268, 282
3:21	389	17-21	12	22:18-19	273
4:1	398	17:7	387	22:19	304
		17:10	394	22:20	371